LEGAL FOUNDATIONS OF CAPITALISM

LEGAL FOUNDATIONS
OF CAPITALISM

BY

JOHN R. COMMONS

[1924]

WITH A PREFATORY NOTE BY
JOSEPH DORFMAN

AUGUSTUS M. KELLEY • PUBLISHERS
CLIFTON 1974

First Edition 1924

(*New York*: The Macmillan Company, 1924)

Reprinted 1974 by

Augustus M. Kelley Publishers

Clifton New Jersey 07012

Library of Congress Cataloging in Publication Data

Commons, John Rogers, 1862-1945.
    Legal foundations of capitalism.

    (Reprints of economic classics)
    Reprints of the ed. published by Macmillan, New
York, with a new pref.
    Includes bibliographical references.
    1. Value. 2. Property--United States. I. Title
LAW   346.04   75-184663
ISBN 0-678-00897-3

PRINTED IN THE UNITED STATES OF AMERICA
by SENTRY PRESS, NEW YORK, N. Y. 10013
Bound by A. HOROWITZ & SON, CLIFTON, N. J.

Prefatory Note

John R. Commons's *Legal Foundations of Capitalism* (1924) has acquired the status of a classic not only in the discipline of economics but also in the fruitful interdisciplinary field that in recent years has risen to great prominence—the area which its pioneers described as legal economics and now generally bears the name "law and economics." So much has been written about Commons and his work which is easily available that there is little need here for a general account.[1] There are, however, some little known but significant episodes in the history of the development of *Legal Foundations of Capitalism* that may facilitate the reader's grasp of this fertile book.

Commons's deep interest in the relations between law and economics was clearly revealed at least as early as 1893 in his first major treatise in economic theory, *The Distribution of Wealth.* Three years later he reported to his old Johns Hopkins mentor, Professor Richard T. Ely, that in preparing a rather comprehensive treatise on the principles of sociology, "I am planning my work to center around the legal aspects of sociology—expanding the doctrines in my *Distribution of Wealth.* I am moved to it especially by the curious productions of [Simon N.] Patten and [Franklin H.] Giddings, neither of whom in their treatises on sociology gives more than passing notice to the two great features of society, law and education."[2]

[1] For a brief sketch of Commons with a bibliography, see Joseph Dorfman, "Commons, John R.," in *The International Encyclopedia of the Social Sciences,* volume 3 (New York: Macmillan, 1968) pp. 22-24.

[2] Commons to Ely, March 3, 1896, Ely Papers, State Historical Society of Wisconsin, published in Joseph Dorfman, *The Economic Mind in American Civilization,* 5 volumes (1946-1959; New York: Augustus M. Kelley Publishers, 1967-1969) III, 285.

As the years passed, Commons began narrowing somewhat the scope of his inquiry to the formulation of an evolutionary theory of progressive economic policy and legislation, which he tentatively titled "Reasonable Value." He hoped that it would serve as a guide to policy makers.

While preparing it, he wrote on January 4, 1922, to his friend, Professor Wesley C. Mitchell of Columbia University, "Referring to our conversation on theory of value in Pittsburgh [at the annual meeting of the American Economic Association], I am sending herewith an article on Correlation of Law and Economics, which I have in course of preparation for a law magazine. I am also sending the first chapter of my latest revision of my valuation theories."[3]

On October 23, Commons sent Mitchell the remainder of the revised version and the following note: "I am taking the liberty of sending you by express the manuscript of my latest revision of my chapters on value-theories, based on court decisions. This year I am working on Veblen's theories and on wage theories which will about complete the circuit of applications, so that I probably have a couple of years ahead of me before the manuscript can be ready for publication. . . . I think that some of the chapters throw light on the chapter on Transactions which I sent you some time ago. The difficulty about this whole thing is that the point of approach is so different from anything else and the problem of the reconciliation of legal and economic theories has been so little attended to that it requires a great deal of revision and correction in order to reduce it to its simple elements. I shall greatly appreciate whatever comments and criticisms of the chapters you may have."

On March 24, 1923, Mitchell having read carefully the whole enormous manuscript informed Commons: "After long delay I have at last gotten time to read your manuscript book on 'Reasonable Value.' . . . As a critic I am going to fail you most shamefully on this

---

[3] Commons to Mitchell, January 4, 1922, in W. C. Mitchell Papers, Special Collections, Columbia University Libraries. All correspondence between Mitchell and Commons subsequently referred to is also in this collection. On the relations between Mitchell and Commons, see Joseph Dorfman, "The Mutual Influence of Mitchell and Commons," *The American Economic Review*, June 1958, pp. 405-408.

occasion. . . . The truth is that 'Reasonable Value' is a most remarkable book in its combination of constructive theorizing, legal analysis, economic history and history of economic theory. It is so original that it will bewilder many of its readers, and I am numbered among its early victims. I think that your work will have a profound influence on economic theory and perhaps on jurisprudence but that the development of the influence is likely to be rather slow. Think, for instance, how hard economists will find it to readjust their ideas so as really to make use of your illuminating suggestion that the value problem requires five persons. That seems to me really a great idea, as sound as it is important, but one that will take a good deal of digesting before it can be fully assimilated. And the economists will find a great deal of difficulty in learning to think, as you do so easily by this time, of judicial decisions, historical developments and economic distinctions at one and the same time. No, the book is too original to have a rapid success.

"It is also too large a volume to be read by many people. Have you considered the possibility of publishing chapters 1-9 first, giving people a little time to digest that volume, and then coming out with chapters 10-12, perhaps under an independent title? The manuscript as you prepared it of course is a logical unit. But psychologically there may be wisdom in giving your public two moderate doses instead of one big one."

Mitchell then singled out what is today considered a most important contribution of *Legal Foundations of Capitalism;* namely, those chapters on legal and economic development in which Commons described what he called the evolution of capitalism from feudalism. Mitchell declared: "What I have found most helpful personally is your contribution to the history of the money economy. From time to time for ten years, I have been taking every opportunity that offered to pick up information about the gradual stages through which our pecuniary institutions have grown out of the barter economy in the early Middle Ages. Particularly I have talked with my legal friends, here and elsewhere, about the development of the juridical concepts involved in modern pecuniary transactions. I have found no other contribution toward this subject so coherent and enlightening as what you have to say."

Mitchell then said that he had only two critical suggestions to make. "The first is a small detail. [Hermann Heinrich] Gossen ought not to be credited with bringing the notion of diminishing utility into the discussion of economic problems. Jeremy Bentham did that, and [Daniel] Bernouilli before him. I shall send you under separate cover an article I prepared some time ago on 'Bentham's Felicific Calculus,' which may be of some interest along this line.[4] My second suggestion is that chapters 10-12 be followed by a summary chapter that serves the same purpose for the second half of the book that chapter 9 serves for the first half."

Commons quickly replied (April 9) that in accordance with Mitchell's suggestion he would be "issuing it as two volumes, making a division as you suggest. I am starting in at once to get the first volume ready and hope to have it completed by next fall. That will give me two or three years to work on the review of different cycles of economic theory." The first volume appeared the following year as *Legal Foundations of Capitalism*.

We now also have some light on a source of one of Commons's most explosive and controversial concepts in the book; namely, that individual labor contracts could not in equity be assimilated to other contracts. Commons used this doctrine to argue for the right of a union to persuade workers to join the union in spite of the fact that employees individually had signed a ("yellow dog") contract with their employer not to do so. In an introduction in 1921 to a book on industrial conflict in the West Virginia coal mining industry, he not only gave a lucid presentation of his view, but also pointed out that it accorded with a recent editorial in the *Yale Law Journal*. He wrote: "It is . . . a proper legal question whether these anti-union contracts are really contracts at all. They assume the guise of contracts, but a labor contract is at most only a contract at will, or from day to day, or from week to week. The

---

[4] The essay in question was originally published in the *Political Science Quarterly* in 1918; it is reprinted in Mitchell, *The Backward Art of Spending Money and other Essays*, compiled and edited by Joseph Dorfman (1937; New York: Augustus M. Kelley Publishers, 1950) pp. 177-202.

employer can discharge without notice and, as pointed out recently by the editor of the *Yale Law Journal* (April 1921), neither of the parties to such a contract 'is under a contractual duty as to succeeding days and consequently no third person can induce a breach thereof.' . . . In this case there is no contractual duty of employment on the part of the Mining Company. Yet, although there is no contractual duty to continue employment, the court treats the matter as though there were. This is doubtless due to the origin of this action in the ancient law of master and servant. Originally the master had a right of action against a third party, for seducing his servant to leave and thus causing a loss of the services due to the master. 'Even though this seduction theory is properly exploded,' says the editor of the *Yale Law Journal*, 'there seems to be a vestige of it still remaining in the minds of the courts.' That vestige is visible in West Virginia. Persuasion to join a union is as unlawful as violence."[5]

Mitchell has succinctly summarized Commons's point and its bearing. "[O]ne important type of bargain still lacks a satisfactory set of working rules [acceptable to the courts]. Labor is not a commodity or a promise [to stay on the job]; the laborer is free to quit at will and the employer to lay him off at any time. The courts could not maintain the personal liberty of the worker if they assimilated the wage contract with other contracts. The legally anomalous position in which that contract stands has been made more anomalous still by the intervention of trade-unions, which have thrust themselves as third parties between employer and employee." Mitchell then quoted from *Legal Foundations:*

"Apparently a 'new equity' is needed—an equity that will pro-

---

[5] Commons, "Introduction," to Winthrop D. Lane, *Civil War in West Virginia: A Story of the Industrial Conflict in the Coal Mines* (New York: Huebsch, 1921) pp. 9-10; Editorial, "Present Day Labor Situation," *Yale Law Journal*, April 1921, pp. 619, 620. This discussion appeared in the opening section of the *Journal* headed "Comments." Walter Mendelson was Case and Comment Editor. Charles P. Taft 2nd was Editor-in-Chief.

tect the job as the older equity protected the business."[6]

In a review article Mitchell saluted *Legal Foundations of Capitalism*[7] as a major contribution to economic theory "That contribution belongs to the institutional type of economics, the type represented in Germany by Sombart, in England by Mr. and Mrs. Webb, in America by Veblen and many of the younger men."

Legal Foundations of Capitalism, however, was generally not received well when it appeared. Economists for the most part ignored it as outside the province of economics. Law professors and jurists, with the notable exception of the path-breaking Judge Learned Hand, held it up as a warning to economists to stop messing with the realm of law. But gradually it gained influence among economists and students of the law. As I have said elsewhere, "Its concepts of 'going concern' and 'transaction' as well as 'bargaining power' were accepted as realistic descriptions of the behavior of the modern economy. Intangible values were increasingly recognized as real, and modern economic activity was viewed as an endeavor to acquire intangible rights rather than physical goods. Markets began to be conceived not so much as concrete things, but as modes of action, and the objects changing hands in market transactions were viewed not so much as physical goods but as legal claims or property rights. The concept of 'limiting or strategic factors' became a part of the language of public policy and even of enlightened business executives. Philosophers and psychologists took over the concept of 'transaction' as preferable to such terms as 'interaction' and 'experience.' Commons especially helped to clarify the role of authority.

"Commons was among those economists who attempted to give concrete meaning to the doctrine that the alleviation of the ills of

---

[6] Mitchell, "Commons on Institutional Economics," 1935; reprinted in *The Backward Art of Spending Money,* p. 324. The quotation is from *Legal Foundations of Capitalism,* p. 307.

[7] "Commons on the *Legal Foundations of Capitalism,*" *The American Economic Review,* June 1924, p. 253.

Mitchell gave as recent examples of contributions of younger men to institutional economics, "John Maurice Clark's *The Economics of Overhead Costs* (1923) and the papers by Morris A. Copeland, Robert L. Hale, Sumner H. Slichter and Reyford G. Tugwell in *The Trend of Economics* (1924)."

the nation lay not through one single, simple remedy, but through a variety of instruments generally taking the form of group action."[8]

Not least of the contributions of *Legal Foundations of Capitalism* was its portrayal of the creative and adaptive role of ever-evolving American jurisprudence to the needs of the modern progressive industrial economy.

---

[8] *The Economic Mind in American Civilization*, IV, 393.

Mitchell continued to serve as a constructive critic for the sequel volume, which appeared a decade later as *Institutional Economics: Its Place in Political Economy*. After reading what might be called a preliminary draft chapter, he replied April 18, 1923: "I read over your discussion of 'Principles of Price Determination' with a very lively interest." He thought that it was too abstract and this obscured "its inherent merit[s] . . . its power as a scheme for interpreting genuine experience."

In his last comment on the book in the correspondence Mitchell wrote (May 7, 1937): "I am winding up my year's course on Types of Economic Theory by discussing with the class your *Institutional Economics*. I think a large proportion of them at least feel more drawn toward your kind of work than toward any of the other masters whom they have studied." For Mitchell's class lectures on Commons, see *Types of Economic Theory: From Mercantilism to Institutionalism*, 2 volumes, edited by Joseph Dorfman (New York: Augustus M. Kelley Publishers, 1967, 1969) I, chapter 21.

LEGAL FOUNDATIONS
OF CAPITALISM

BY

JOHN R. COMMONS

PROFESSOR OF ECONOMICS IN THE UNIVERSITY OF WISCONSIN

New York
THE MACMILLAN COMPANY
1924

PREFACE

The aim of this volume is to work out an evolutionary and behavioristic, or rather volitional, theory of value. It was commenced thirty-five years ago at Johns Hopkins University under my stimulating teacher, Richard T. Ely.

Thirty years ago I published a book under the name of *Distribution of Wealth* in which I tried to mix things that will not mix—the hedonic psychology of Böhm-Bawerk, and the legal rights and social relations which he had himself analyzed and then excluded from his great work on the psychological theory of value. Afterwards I had various opportunities for the investigation of labor problems and problems connected with the regulation and valuation of public utilities. This led to a testing of economic and legal theories in the drafting of bills as an assistant to legislative committees in Wisconsin.

It was this experience, shared by my students, that led directly to the theoretical problems of this book. We had to study the decisions of the courts, if the new laws were to be made constitutional, and that study ran into the central question, What do the courts mean by reasonable value? Somehow the answer was tied up with reasonable conduct. None of us could find much in the writings of economists except those of Professor Ely that threw light on the subject. From the court decisions it seemed that anything "reasonable" would be sustained, and so we had to use the words reasonable value, reasonable safety, reasonable wage, and fix up reasonable conduct for public officials and private citizens, whether we knew what it meant or not.

I had read Veblen's brilliant criticisms, beginning in 1895, on the theories of the classical, socialistic, and psychological economists, and his suggestion that an evolutionary theory of value must be constructed out of the habits and customs of social life. But he had not studied the decisions of the courts which are based on these customs, and I went to work with my students digging directly out of the court decisions stretching over several hundred years the behavioristic theory of value on which they were working. We were puzzled, for we tried to reconcile the economists from Quesnay to Cassel with the lawyers from Coke to Taft. We found eventually that what we were really working upon was not merely a theory of Reasonable Value but the Legal Foundations of Capitalism itself.

This work is essentially theoretical, dealing only with concepts derived from the decisions of the English and American courts, but with an eye on the concepts of leading economists from the Physiocrats to modern times. Another volume is in contemplation reviewing these theories of the economists and leading up to practical applications of a theory of Reasonable Value to current problems.

In these researches, I have had important assistance and criticism from Wesley C. Mitchell of Columbia University, Arthur L. Corbin of the Yale Law Faculty, and William H. Page of the Wisconsin University School of Law.

JOHN R. COMMONS.

UNIVERSITY OF WISCONSIN,
    July, 1923.

TABLE OF CONTENTS

LEGAL FOUNDATIONS OF CAPITALISM

LEGAL FOUNDATIONS OF CAPITALISM

CHAPTER I

MECHANISM, SCARCITY, WORKING RULES

Economic theory deals with two concepts, Value and Economy. Abstract reasoning regarding these concepts rests ultimately on mathematical concepts of quantity, time and energy. The three are inseparable, for quantity and time are dimensions of energy. The quantity relationships of energy, usually termed "statics," turn on the problem of the relation of the parts to the whole, while the time relationships, usually termed "dynamics," are the relations of a process that connects past, present and future.

Value and Economy are distinguishable as two quantitative relationships of the parts to the whole. The whole is always a function of its parts, but the whole may be the *sum* of its parts or the whole may be a *multiple* of its parts. The former is the quantitative concept of Value, the latter of Economy. A "fund of value" is the sum of the values of all the parts that constitute the whole. A certain quality which we call Value is abstracted from other qualities of commodities, is measured in money as prices, and these are then added together, so that the sum of the parts is the sum of a *similar* quality of all the parts.

But Economy is the proportioning of parts that have *different* qualities yet are complementary to each other, such that one kind of energy acts upon another kind, and the resultant is larger or even smaller than the sum, according to the good or bad proportions in which the limiting and complementary parts are combined. Value is a sum of similar values, but economy is a proportioning of dissimilar values.

These two quantitative relationships of the parts to the whole run everywhere in economic theory. A sum of individuals is the total population, but a proportioning of different kinds of activity of different individuals is a society. A sum of prices is the total business assets of a firm, but a proportioning of land, labor, capital and management is a going concern. Wages are a sum of money paid for periods or pieces of work, but a proportioning of different kinds of activity in acquiring the wages is a job. A sum of all the prices of all kinds of commodities is the total nominal wealth of a nation, but the proportion existing between one commodity and all the others is supply and demand.

The concept of good or bad economy is so self-evident, and its psychological equivalent, the sense of fitness or unfitness, which is "common sense," or "good sense," or merely habit and approved custom, is so continually present in every act that, in the history of economic thought, good economy, which is merely a good proportioning of the parts, has often been either taken for granted or erected into an entity existing outside or above the parts. For, is it not an astonishing and blessed thing that the whole should be greater than the sum of its parts? And, how can the parts be greater than their sum unless a benevolent deity or "law of nature" organize them harmoniously? But a mark of the progress that has occurred in economic theory, from the time of Quesnay and Adam Smith, has been the emergence of the concept of good or bad political economy out of mythical entities such as nature's harmony, natural law, natural order, natural rights, divine providence, over-soul, invisible hand, social will, social-labor power, social value, tendency towards equilibrium of forces, and the like, into its proper place as the good or bad, right or wrong, wise or unwise proportioning by man himself of those human faculties and natural resources which are limited in supply and complementary to each other.

An accompanying mark of progress in economic theory is indicated by changing views as to the Time dimensions of value and economy. Early economists found the "cause" and "substance" of value in the stored-up energy of the past, either Quesnay's vital forces of nature, or Ricardo's and Marx's stored-up labor power. Then followed the hedonic economists who found value in the pains and pleasures of the present, aided perhaps by a calculating mechanism of the future, while the later theories find value in the hopes, fears, probabilities and lapse of time of the future, depending on the will of persons existing in the present. The progress has been from "efficient causes" flowing from the past into the present, to "final causes" originating in the purposes and plans for the future and guiding the behavior of the present. While the earlier theories were quantity theories of value and economy, the later are expectancy theories.

These changes in concepts of quantity and time have accompanied changes in the concept of the energy itself which is the "substance" of value and the "cause" of economy. Early theories attempted to get away from the human will, since that was conceived to be internal, capricious, not subject to law, and therefore economics should be reduced to one of the nature sciences, analogous to chemistry, physics, or physiology. It should be a theory of commodities or mechanisms, not a theory of the will. But a larger knowledge of the human will, derived from the human-nature sciences of psychology, ethics, law and politics, begins to find the will, not in an unknowable caprice, but merely in human behavior, and this behavior begins to be formulated into natural laws of its own.

These many sciences of human nature furnish increasingly a foundation for economic theory, which is concerned with both physical nature and human nature. In one direction economy is a relation of man to nature, in another it is a relation of man to man. The first is Engineering Economy; the second is Business Economy and Political Economy. The first has given us theories of Production, Exchange and Consumption of Wealth, while Business Economy and Political Economy give us a variety of theories specialized in different branches of learning. Theories of Psychology deal with the relations both of man to nature and man to man—his feelings, intellect and will, his persuasions and coercions, his commands and obedience. These are inseparable from Morals, or Ethics, which deals with the good or bad, virtuous or vicious, right or wrong, uses that man makes either of nature or of other persons. This leads to Jurisprudence which concerns itself with both the rights, duties and liberties of Property and the powers and responsibilities of Sovereignty, which, again, are relations of man to man. And, finally, Politics deals with the mass movements and mass psychologies which define, enact and enforce private rights and official responsibilities according to notions pertaining to ethics, politics and economics.

Thus economic theory runs into other theories of man and nature, or else assumes certain common-sense notions regarding them. Early economists, whose outstanding theorists were Quesnay, Smith, Ricardo, Karl Marx and Proudhon, started with man's relation to nature, or engineering economy, in the form of commodities which are produced, exchanged and consumed. But these commodities involved certain notions, express or implied, of human nature, of use-value, utility, scarcity, exchange-value, labor, saving, expectation, private property, liberty, government and economy, which split these physical or technological economists into the several schools of Physiocrats, Classical Economists, Socialists and Anarchists.

They were followed or accompanied by a school of Hedonists, or Hedonic Economists, whose outstanding names are Bentham, Senior, Gossen, Jevons, Menger, Walras, Böhm-Bawerk, Clark, and these concerned themselves with the subjective side of economic theory. Instead of a commodity their starting point was a feeling of pleasure or pain, of satisfaction or sacrifice, but these feelings turned out to be commodities after all. And while the later hedonists, by the device of diminishing and marginal utility, were able to interpret the concept of value as a function of economy, yet their individualistic point of approach required certain notions, express or implied, of ethics, law, private property, liberty, society, government, which the hedonists either took for granted without investigation, or avoided as being "non-economic" or "anti-economic," or erected into an entity such as "social value" or "fund of value."

These two classes of theories we designate mechanistic theories of value and cost, since they look to the physical sciences for their models of economic theory, and they work out their solutions on what may be designated the Principle of Mechanism. Finally, another class of theories, which we designate Volitional Theories, whose initial thinkers are Hume, Malthus, Carey, Bastiat, Cassel, Anderson, but especially the Supreme Court of the United States, start, not with a commodity or with a feeling, but with the purposes of the future, revealing themselves in rules of conduct governing transactions which give rise to rights, duties, liberties, private property, governments and associations. These are the reciprocal promises and threats, express or implied, of man to man which determine the limits of human behavior in its social and economic transactions. Instead of a commodity or a feeling, their unit of observation becomes a Transaction between two or more persons looking towards the future. Theirs becomes a theory of the human will-in-action, and of value and economy as a relation, partly of man to nature but mainly of man to man; partly of quantities and partly of expectancies depending on future quantities.

Meanwhile, ethical, philosophical and psychological, as well as economic theories, have been approaching a volitional theory. Psychology is becoming "behavioristic," philosophy and ethics "realistic" or " pragmatic," and economics has become historical, experimental and idealistic in that it deals with past, present and hoped-for or dreaded transactions as well as commodities and feelings. In fact, transactions have become the meeting place of economics, physics, psychology, ethics, jurisprudence and politics. A single transaction is a unit of observation which involves explicitly all of them, for it is several human wills, choosing alternatives, overcoming resistance, proportioning natural and human resources, led on by promises or warnings of utility, sympathy, duty or their opposites, enlarged, restrained or exposed by officials of government or of business concerns or labor unions, who interpret and enforce the citizen's rights, duties and liberties, such that individual behavior is fitted or misfitted to the collective behavior of nations, politics, business, labor, the family and other collective movements, in a world of limited resources and mechanical forces.

Thus economic theory began with a Commodity as its ultimate scientific unit, then shifted to a Feeling, in order to explain a Transaction which is its practical problem.

Underlying all of these concepts of commodities, feelings and transactions have been certain principles of explanation, which the theorists either avowedly assumed or took for granted out of the prevailing habits of mind or ways of thinking of the time when they wrote. These may be distinguished as the Principle of Mechanism, the Principle of Scarcity and the Principle of Working Rules of Going Concerns. The principle of mechanism, established by Sir Isaac Newton, became the principle of explanation not only for all physical sciences, but also for biology, physiology and the human sciences of psychology, ethics, law, economics and politics. Gradually, however, the principle of scarcity, always taken for granted but not always definitely incorporated, began to be pointed out along with the principle of mechanism, first by David Hume and Robert Malthus, then was generalized by Darwin for biology and by Gossen, Jevons and the hedonic economists for psychology and economics.

The principle of scarcity did not materially change the habit of mind that relied on principles of mechanism, but rather gave to the latter a more precise formulation in the theories of marginal utility.

This was because commodities and feelings were concepts related to the wants and efforts of individuals rather than groups or associations of individuals, and the theories could be worked out on Adam Smith's mechanical principles of individualism, selfishness, division of labor, exchange of commodities, equality, fluidity, liberty and that divine providence which led individuals to benefit each other without intending to do so.

But later theories have had to account for the incoming of corporations, trade unions, voluntary associations of all kinds, said to number 25,000 in America in the field of business alone, as well as the interference of government through taxes, the police power, and the legal tender power. Consequently later theories have concerned themselves with what may broadly be named the Working Rules of Going Concerns, taking many forms and names, such as the common law, statute law, shop rules, business ethics, business methods, norms of conduct, and so on, which these governing or regulating groups of associated individuals have laid down for the guidance of transactions.

Consequently, it is not only principles of mechanism and scarcity conceived as working themselves out automatically and beneficently, through commodities, feelings and individual selfishness, but also principles of the collective control of transactions through associations and governments, placing limits on selfishness, that are more recently included in economic theory. For a working rule lays down four verbs for the guidance and restraint of individuals in their transactions. It tells what the individuals *must* or *must not* do (compulsion or duty), what they *may* do without interference from other individuals (permission or liberty), what they *can* do with the aid of the collective power (capacity or right), and what they *cannot* expect the collective power to do in their behalf (incapacity or exposure). In short, the working rules of associations and governments, when looked at from the private standpoint of the individual, are the source of his rights, duties and liberties, as well as his exposures to the protected liberties of other individuals.

These changes from mechanism to scarcity and thence to working rules as the underlying principles of economics have had a profound effect upon the concept of property, changing that concept from a principle of exclusive holding of physical objects for the owner's private use, into a principle of control of limited resources needed by others for their use and thus into a concept of intangible and incorporeal property arising solely out of rules of law controlling transactions. The change was gradually accomplished in American jurisprudence between the years 1872 and 1897, and consisted in changing the definitions, by the Supreme Court, of the terms "property," "liberty" and "due process of law," as found in the Fourteenth Amendment to the Constitution.

Thus both legal theory and economic theory, in modern times, have based their explanations first on Newton's principle of mechanism, then on Malthus' principle of scarcity, then on juristic principles of common rules that both limit and enlarge the field for individual wills in a world of mechanical forces and scarcity of resources. Since transactions are the economic units, and working rules are the principles on which the Supreme Court of the United States has been working over its theories of property, sovereignty and value, and since that court occupies the unique position of the first authoritative faculty of political economy in the world's history, we shall begin with the court's theory of property, liberty and value. For it is mainly upon that theory that modern business is conducted and that American legislatures, executives and inferior courts are held in conformity to the Constitution of the United States, which, as latterly interpreted by the Supreme Court, prohibits the taking of property, liberty *or value* without due process of law or equal protection of the laws.[1]

While the economists start with a commodity or an individual's feelings towards it, the court starts with a transaction. Its ultimate unit of investigation is not an individual but two or more individuals —plaintiff and defendant—at two ends of one or more transactions. Commodities and feelings are, indeed, implied in all transactions, yet they are but the preliminaries, the accompaniments, or the effects of transactions. The transaction is two or more wills giving, taking, persuading, coercing, defrauding, commanding, obeying, competing, governing, in a world of scarcity, mechanism and rules of conduct. The court deals with the will-in-action. Like the modern

---

[1] Fifth Amendment (1791) applicable to the Federal Government:—No person shall be "deprived of life. liberty, or property, without due process of law; nor shall private property be taken for public use without just compensation." Fourteenth Amendment (1868) applicable to State Governments:—"Nor shall any state deprive any person of life, liberty, or property, without due process of law; nor deny to any person within its jurisdiction the equal protection of the laws."

physicist or chemist, its ultimate unit is not an atom but an electron, always in motion—not an individual but two or more individuals in action. It never catches them except in motion. Their motion is a transaction.

A transaction occurs at a point of time. But transactions flow one into another over a period of time, and this flow is a process. The courts have fully developed the notion of this process in the concept of a "going concern," which they have taken over from the customs of business, and which is none other than a technological process of production and consumption of physical things and a business process of buying and selling, borrowing and lending, commanding and obeying, according to shop rules or working rules or laws of the land. The physical process may be named a "going plant," the business process a "going business," and the two constitute a "going concern" made up of action and reaction with nature's forces and transactions between human beings according to accepted rules.

Thus economic theory has passed from commodities to feelings, and finally to a process, and from principles of mechanism to principles of scarcity, and then of working rules that apportion the conduct of individuals. Value and economy become verbs instead of nouns. Value becomes *valuing;* economy becomes *economizing.* Economizing becomes the operation of rules of conduct in the nation or the business concern. A transaction is a unit picked out of the process for minute examination. Value and economy become millions of people valuing and economizing through billions of transactions in conformity to numberless working rules over a stretch of time that has no beginning and no ending. The mathematical concepts of deductive reasoning become statistical concepts of quantity and time, of correlations, probabilities, lags and forecasts, respecting billions of valuations in billions of transactions, moving forward on that energy which we call the will, within limits set by the accepted rules of conduct.

This process has three attributes which give us three meanings of value, each of which was separately emphasized by different schools of economists. Value has that subjective or volitional meaning of *anticipation* which may be named *psychological value* and which is the moving force. It has next that objective meaning of *commodities* produced, exchanged and consumed, which may be named *real value.* It has lastly that behavioristic meaning of *prices* which emerge in the transactions of buying, borrowing and hiring, in terms of standards of weights and measures prescribed by the working rules, which may be named *nominal value*.

The system of prices is like the system of words or the system of numbers. Words, prices and numbers are nominal and not real. They are signs and symbols needed for the operation of working rules. Yet each is the only effective means by which human beings can deal with each other securely and accurately with regard to the things that are real. But each may be insecure and inaccurate. Words are deceptive if they do not convey the meaning intended; numbers are liars if they do not indicate the actual quantities; prices are inflated or deflated if they do not reflect the course of real value. Every transaction has these three aspects of valuing. It is a meeting of wills, a transfer of commodities, a determination of their prices. A transaction is thus a compendium of psychological value, real value and nominal value. The courts, in their decisions, endeavor, by means of common rules, to make the nominal value or prices, represent, as nearly as practicable, the psychological value, or anticipation, and the real value, or quantity, of commodities and services. Their goal is a scheme of "reasonable value."

But the court does not cover the whole of the will-in-action. Individuals deal with the forces of nature as well as with other persons. This dealing with nature may be distinguished as action and reaction, so that the behavior of individuals consists in two kinds of acts, action and reaction with nature's forces and transactions with other persons. The one is production and consumption of wealth, the other is buying and selling, borrowing and lending, leasing, renting, "hiring and firing," exchanging, competing and governing.

Now, a transaction may be looked upon from several points of view, each of which is related to the others, though with widely different implications. It may be looked upon as the activity of one of the forces of nature, say, will-power, operating like other forces, in which case we have a physical or mechanical equivalent of the will-in-action. It may be looked upon as accompanied by anticipation and memories which are its psychological equivalent. These expectations may be looked upon as induced by and inducing others to act or avoid action, giving us an equivalent in social psychology. This social psychology of two or more individuals is influenced, in turn, by a mass psychology, or collective psychology, giving us ethical, juristic or political grounds for the working rules. Finally, both the individual and the mass psychology are an adaptation of the will to the principle of scarcity, and this point of view gives us an economic equivalent of the transactions and the working rules. The words which express one order of phenomena are tinged with meanings projected from the others. We simply look upon the same process from different angles, always seeing the same outline, but with different shapes, colors and shades.

We thus have two concepts with which economic theory deals, the concepts of Value and Economy. These are inseparable from the subject-matter which various schools have picked out for investigation, namely, Commodities, Feelings and Transactions. And three ultimate principles have been relied upon, the principles of Mechanism, of Scarcity and of the Working Rules of associations, concerns and governments. Hence, while we begin with the working rules that underlie the decisions of the Supreme Court of the United States, we shall find the economic and juristic dimensions derived from those rules shading off into mechanical, psychological, ethical and political dimensions.

CHAPTER II

PROPERTY, LIBERTY AND VALUE

I. Use-Value and Exchange-Value

In the year 1872 the Supreme Court of the United States was called upon, in the Slaughter House Cases,[1] to interpret the meanings of the words Property and Liberty as used in the Constitution of the United States. The Thirteenth Amendment to the Federal Constitution, adopted in 1865, prohibited slavery and involuntary servitude except as punishment for crime, and the Fourteenth Amendment, adopted three years later, prohibited a state from depriving any person of "life, liberty, or property" without "due process of law," and gave to the federal courts jurisdiction. The legislature of Louisiana had granted to a corporation a monopoly to maintain slaughtering places for stock in the city of New Orleans, and had regulated the charges to be made to other butchers who used these facilities. The latter, through their attorneys, contended that the statute deprived them of both their property and their liberty without due process of law. The Supreme Court divided. If the court should hold that property meant exchange-value, then the federal court would take jurisdiction under the Amendments. But if property meant only the use-value of physical things, then the court would not interfere with the legislature of Louisiana. Justice Miller, for the majority, declared that the act was not a deprivation of property or liberty as the terms were used in the Thirteenth and Fourteenth Amendments. The term "liberty," he said, should be construed with reference to the well-known purpose of those Amendments, namely, to establish freedom from slavery or personal servitude. Even conceding that the term "liberty," as popularly used, might mean "civil liberty" or the right to buy and sell, yet that aspect of liberty was not included in the meaning of the term as used in the Amendments. Prior to the adoption of these amendments the liberty of citizens, whether personal, civil or economic, was, for the

[1] 16 Wall. 36 (1872).

most part, in the keeping of the states. The Thirteenth and Fourteenth Amendments only transferred from the states to the federal government the protection of such fraction of the total concept of liberty as was comprehended in freedom from personal slavery. All other aspects of liberty were left, as they had been, to the keeping of the states.[1] And as to the meaning of the term "property," as used in the Fourteenth Amendment, he held that the term retained its common-law meaning of physical things held exclusively for one's own use. Property, according to the Fourteenth Amendment meant use-value, not exchange-value. "Under no construction of that provision that we have ever seen," he said, "can the restraint imposed by the state of Louisiana upon the exercise of their trade by the butchers of New Orleans be held to be a deprivation of property within the meaning of that provision." [2] The state of Louisiana had not deprived the butchers of the use-value of their property—it had deprived them of its exchange-value.

The minority of the court, however, contended that the police power (which they admitted, of course, might justly deprive a person of liberty or property for public purposes without compensation), could have been exercised in this case without resorting to a monopoly, by merely regulating all of the butchers alike in the interest of public health, but that the monopoly feature of the law deprived the other butchers of their liberty and property and turned it over to the monopolist.   They then went on to define the property and liberty which was thus unjustly taken away, not by a proper exercise of the police power, but by a special privilege granted to the slaughter-house monopolist.   A man's "calling," his "occupation," his "trade," his "labor," was property, as well as the physical things which he might own; and "liberty" included his "right of choice," his right to choose a calling, to choose an occupation or trade, to choose the direction in which he would exercise his labor. Justice Bradley, of the minority, for example, declared that the "right to choose one's calling is an essential part of that liberty which it is the object of government to protect; and a calling, when chosen, is a man's property and right. . . . Their right of choice is a portion of their liberty; their occupation is their property." (116, 122.) Justice Field, also of the minority, desired to change the meaning of "slavery" from physical coercion to economic coercion. He said, "A person

---

[1] 16 Wall. 69-73.   [2] 16 Wall. 81.

allowed to pursue only one trade or calling, and only in one locality
of the country, would not be, in the strict sense of the term, in a
condition of slavery, but probably none would deny that he would
be in a condition of servitude. . . . The compulsion which would
force him to labor even for his own benefit only in one direction,
or in one place, would be almost as oppressive and nearly as great
an invasion of his liberty as the compulsion which would force him
to labor for the benefit or pleasure of another, and would equally
constitute an element of servitude." (90.) Thus Justice Field described slavery as physical coercion and servitude as economic coercion.
And Justice Swayne declared, "Property is everything which has
exchangeable value, and the right of property includes the power
to dispose of it according to the will of the owner. Labor is property,
and as such merits protection. The right to make it available is
next in importance to the rights of life and liberty." (127.) Thus
Justice Swayne defined property as the exchange-value of one's
ability to work, and liberty as the right to realize that exchange-
value on the labor market.

These minority definitions of liberty and property as exchange-
value were unavailing in the Slaughter House Cases. The majority
held to the older meaning of use-value. Twelve years later the
municipal authorities of New Orleans, acting under a new constitution for the state, granted to another company privileges in conflict with those of the original monopolist, thus infringing upon their
exclusive right. This time, therefore, the Slaughter House company
was plaintiff against the municipality. The majority of the court
now retained its original definition of property and liberty, but now
held that not only the original act, as they had contended before,
but also this annulling act were a proper exercise of the police power.[1]
But Justices Bradley and Field, while concurring in the court's
decision, placed it on the grounds of their dissenting opinions in the
original Slaughter House Cases, and repeated their earlier views
that the original act was itself an unlawful deprivation of liberty
and property. In their earlier dissent the minority had not cited
any cases where the term property had been used in the sense of a
trade, occupation, calling, or one's labor, whose value to the owner
is in its exchange-value, though they asserted that it *ought* to have
that meaning. Thus, in the constitutional sense of the term, they

[1] Butchers' Union Co. *v.* Crescent City Co., 111 U. S. 746, 751 (1884).

had not been able to controvert Justice Miller's denial that that meaning had ever been given to it.   In the later case, however, they suggested the origin of their new definition.   Justice Field now stated that this meaning of property was derived from Adam Smith who had said: "The property which every man has in his own labor, as it is the original foundation of all other property, so it is the most sacred and inviolable." [1]   And Justice Bradley contented himself with saying, "If a man's right to his calling is property, *as many maintain*, then those who had already adopted the prohibited pursuits in New Orleans, were deprived, by the law in question, of their property, as well as their liberty, without due process of law." [2]   Thus the new meanings of property and liberty were found in Adam Smith and the customs of business, and not in the Constitution of the United States.

After the Slaughter House Cases the minority definitions of property and liberty began to creep into the constitutional definitions given by state and federal courts,[3] as indeed was inevitable and proper if the thing itself was thus changing.   Finally, in the first Minnesota Rate Case, in 1890 [4] the Supreme Court itself made the transition and changed the definition of property from physical things having only use-value to the exchange-value of anything.

This decision was a partial reversal of the decision of the court in the case of Munn *v.* Illinois in 1876.[5]   In the Munn case the Supreme Court had held, agreeably to its holding in the Slaughter House Cases, that when a state legislature reduced the prices which a warehouse company charged for the use of its services the resulting reduction in exchange-value of the business was not a deprivation of property in the sense in which the word was used in the Fourteenth Amendment and therefore was not an act which the federal courts might restrain.   It was only a regulation of the "use and enjoyment" of property under the police power of the state.   The court went so far as to declare that, if the legislature abused its power, "the people must resort to the polls, not to the courts." [6]

That the state legislatures might possibly abuse their power had

---

[1] III U. S. 746, 757; SMITH, *Wealth of Nations*, 1:123 (Cannan ed., 1904).

[2] III U. S. 765 (my italics).

[3] Powell *v.* Penn., 127 U. S. 678, 684 (1887); Matter of Jacobs, 98 N. Y. 98 (1885); People *v.* Marx, 99 N. Y. 377 (1885); People *v.* Gillson, 109 N. Y. 399 (1888).

[4] Chicago, M. & St. P. Ry. Co. *v.* Minnesota, 134 U. S. 418 (1890).

[5] 94 U. S. 113 (1876).

[6] 94 U. S. 113, 134,

been clearly suggested in the decision of the Supreme Court of Illinois in sustaining the act of the Illinois legislature, when the Munn Case was before that court. The Illinois court had held [1] that the authority was not abused in that case by the Illinois legislature, since the property of the owner was not "taken" from him, in that he was not deprived of the "title and possession" of the property. In this respect the Illinois court adhered to the primitive definition of property as the mere holding of physical objects for one's own use and enjoyment. The legislature, under the police power of the state, might reduce the charges which a warehouse company had established for its services, but that was not "taking" their property. The owners continued to hold their physical property even though deprived of the power to fix the prices for its use. To this Justice Field had rightly answered, "There is indeed no protection of any value under the constitutional provision which does not extend to the use and income of the property, as well as to its title and possession." [2] For, of course, the title of ownership or the possession of physical property is empty as a business asset if the owner is deprived of his liberty to fix a price on the sale of the product of that property.

But Justice Field in the Munn Case had gone too far. He denied the authority of *both* the legislature *and* the courts to fix the compensation. The majority had only denied the authority of the court to fix it. Fourteen years after Munn *v.* Illinois this further issue came up in the Minnesota Rate Case,[3] and the petitioners for the railroads asked the court to review the decision in the Munn and similar cases and to restrain the state legislature from fixing finally the prices charged for the use of property. (445.) The court now acceded, and Justice Blatchford, for the majority, wrote, "This power to regulate [police power] is not a power to destroy, and limitation is not the equivalent of confiscation." (456.) And confiscation, or the reasonableness of a rate, "is eminently a question for judicial investigation, requiring due process of law for its determination." (458.) Thus Justice Field's definition of property as the exchange-value of property was approved and, therefore, the protection of that property was brought under the jurisdiction of the federal courts conformably to the Fourteenth Amendment.

---

[1] As interpreted by Justice Field, 94 U. S. 139; Munn *v.* People, 69 Ill. 80 (1873).
[2] 94 U. S. 143.
[3] Chicago, M. & St. P. Ry. Co. *v.* Minnesota, 134 U. S. 418 (1890).

But Justice Bradley, who in the Slaughter House Cases had agreed with Justice Field, now again dissented (supported by two other justices) and held that the majority opinion asserted an "assumption of authority on the part of the judiciary which. . . it has no right to make." (418, 463.) "If not in terms, yet in effect," he said, "the present cases are treated as if the constitutional prohibition was, that no state shall take private property for public use without just compensation—and as if it was our duty to judge of the compensation. But there is no such clause in the Constitution of the United States." (465.) "There was," he said, "in truth, no deprivation of property in these cases at all. There was merely a regulation as to the enjoyment of property, made by a strictly competent authority, in a matter entirely within its jurisdiction." (466.) In this respect he, like the Illinois court in the Munn Case, continued to adhere to the primitive definition of property as the mere exclusive holding of objects for one's own use, a kind of property that is not taken from the owner unless he is deprived of its title and possession, for which he is entitled to just compensation.

The majority, however, now held, as they had not held in the Munn Case, that not merely physical things are objects of property, but the *expected earning power* of those things is property; and property is taken from the owner, not merely under the power of *eminent domain* which takes *title* and *possession*, but also under the police power which takes its *exchange-value*. To deprive the owners of the *exchange-value* of their property is equivalent to depriving them of their property. Hence, differently from the Munn Case decision, they now held that, under the Fourteenth Amendment, it is the province of the court and not the legislature, to determine the extent to which that "taking" of the value of property might go and yet not pass beyond the point of confiscation. They thus extended to the exercise of the police power the judicial authority to ascertain just compensation which the judiciary had exercised over the power of eminent domain.[1]

Thus the transition in the definition of property from physical objects to exchange-value was completed. "Title and possession" of physical property could be taken from its owner for public purposes under the power of eminent domain, but only on condition

---

[1] Under the original constitutional provision that no state should take private property for public use without just compensation.

that equivalent value should be paid, such that the owners' assets should not be reduced; and this equivalent value, or just compensation, is a judicial question. Now it is enlarged to read: The exchange-value of property may be taken from its owners under the police power, but only to the extent that they retain sufficient bargaining power to maintain the same exchange-value that they had, and this also is a judicial question. The definition of property is changed from physical things to the exchange-value of anything, and the federal courts now take jurisdiction.

Evidently, however, the exchange-value of property has no existence if either the owner or expected purchasers are forbidden access to markets where they can sell and buy the property. Hence liberty of access to markets is essential to the definition of exchange-value. This attribute was finally added seven years after the Minnesota Rate Case, in the Allgeyer Case, and the minority definition of liberty in 1872 became the unanimous definition of liberty in 1897.[1] The court now said: "The liberty mentioned in that Amendment [Fourteenth] means not only the right of the citizen to be free from physical restraint of his person, but the term is deemed to embrace the right of the citizen to be free in the enjoyment of all his faculties; to be free to use them in all lawful ways; to live and work where he will; to earn his livelihood by any lawful calling; to pursue any livelihood or avocation, and for that purpose to enter into all contracts which may be proper, necessary, and essential to his carrying out to a successful conclusion the purposes above mentioned. . . . His enjoyment upon terms of equality with all others in similar circumstances of the privilege of pursuing an ordinary calling or trade, and of acquiring, holding, and selling property is an essential part of liberty and property as guaranteed by the Fourteenth Amendment."[2]

Furthermore, while liberty of access to markets on the part of an owner is essential to the exchange-value of property, too much liberty of access on the part of would-be competitors is destructive of that exchange-value. During the past three hundred years this

---

[1] Allgeyer v. Louisiana, 165 U. S. 578, 589 (1897).

[2] *Ibid.*, at 580, 589. This latter sentence was quoted in part from earlier decisions cited above, Powell v. Pennsylvania, 127 U. S. 678, 684 (1888); quoted in 165 U. S. 578, 590. For a discussion of the change in meaning of these terms while the process was going on, in 1891, see Shattuck, C. E., "The True Meaning of the Term 'Liberty' in those clauses in the Federal and State constitutions which protect life, liberty and property." 4 *Harv. Law Rev.* 365 (1891).

excessive liberty has been restrained by the courts in the long line of cases going under the name of "goodwill" or "unfair competition." Evidently, these decisions of the courts had been designed to protect the exchange-value of property, and now that the definition of property itself had been changed from physical things to the exchange-value of anything, it was an easy step to change the definition of goodwill from "fair competition" to "property." The long-recognized goodwill of a business which had always possessed exchange-value, but which was merely the expected beneficial behavior of other people, now became simply a special case of property. Other courts followed, and the transition from the meaning of property as physical things to that of the most ethereal invisibility was reached in 1902 in a case involving the right to exclusive telephonic communication of news to the daily press by mere word of mouth. The lower court then said, "Property . . . is not, in its modern sense, confined to that which may be touched by the hand, or seen by the eye. What is called tangible property has come to be, in most great enterprises, but the embodiment, physically, of an underlying life— a life that, in its contribution to success, is immeasurably more effective than the mere physical embodiment." [1] And, in 1911, by another lower court, Justice Swayne's definition in 1872 of labor as property became "the right to labor in any calling or profession in the future." [2]

The foregoing cases, it will be noted, have turned on a double meaning of property, and the transition is from one of the meanings to both of the meanings. Property, in the popular ordinary usage, the usage of the old common law and the one adhered to in the Slaughter House Cases and the Munn Case, meant any tangible thing owned. Property, in the later decisions, means any of the expected activities implied with regard to the thing owned, comprehended in the activities of acquiring, using and disposing of the thing. One is Property, the other is Business. The one is property in the sense of Things owned, the other is property in the sense of exchange-value of things. One is physical objects, the other is marketable assets.

Thus it is that "corporeal property," in the original meaning of the term, has disappeared, or, rather, has been relegated to what may be described as the internal "economy" of a going concern or

---

[1] National Telephone News Co. v. Western Union Tel. Co., 119 Fed. 294, 299 (1902), by Justice Grosscup.
[2] Gleason v. Thaw, 185 Fed. 345, 347 (1911).

a household in the various processes of producing and consuming physical objects, according to what the economists call their "use-value." And, instead of the use-value of corporeal property, the courts are concerned with its exchange-value. This exchange-value is not corporeal—it is behavioristic. It is the market-value expected to be obtained in exchange for the thing in any of the markets where the thing can or might be sold. In the course of time this exchange-value has come to be known as "intangible property," that is, the kind of property whose value depends upon right of access to a commodity market, a labor market, a money market, and so on.[1] Consequently, in conformity with the customs and usages of business, there are only two kinds of property, both of them invisible and behavioristic, since their value depends on expected activities on the commodity and money markets. One of these may technically be distinguished as "incorporeal property," consisting of debts, credits, bonds, mortgages, in short, of promises to pay; the other may be distinguished as "intangible property" consisting of the exchange-value of anything whether corporeal property or incorporeal property or even intangible property. The short name for intangible property is *assets*. Assets is the expected exchange-value of anything, whether it be one's reputation, one's horse, house or land, one's ability to work, one's goodwill, patent right, good credit, stocks, bonds or bank deposit, in short, intangible property is anything that enables one to obtain from others an income in the process of buying and selling, borrowing and lending, hiring and hiring out, renting and leasing, in any of the transactions of modern business. We shall identify these two classes of property as "encumbrances" and "opportunities." Encumbrances are incorporeal property, that is, promises to pay, enforced by government; opportunities are intangible property, that is, accessibility to markets, also enforced by government.

Going back, therefore, to the common-law meaning of property as physical things held for the owner's use, we find that what property really signified, even in that original sense, was not the physical thing itself but the expected "uses" of the thing, that is, various activities regarding the thing. These uses, or activities, arose from the producing and consuming power of a person in control of, or working with, the thing. The legal terms carry this futuristic, behavioristic meaning. The legal term "use," is said to have been

[1] Below, Chap. VII, Sec. III.

derived from the Latin *opus*, meaning work or working, through the Anglo-French *oeps* and the Old French *oes*.[1] It means the work a person can do with a thing, his behavior respecting the thing. Thus it differs from the economic term, "utility," which is derived from the Latin *usus*, through the French *utilité*, and means the satisfaction a person gets in using a thing. Use is behavior. Utility is feeling. The early feudal grants of land to tenants were granted *ad opus*—that is, "to the use" of the tenant in production and consumption. Then when property began to yield exchange-value as well as use-value, the term "uses" was simply enlarged by the courts to include it. It now means both the expected use-values of production and consumption and the expected exchange-values of selling and buying.

The difference is unimportant in the law of private property. In fact, the term "uses" has a social meaning and a business meaning. Socially it means what we understand by producing and consuming things; that is, increasing the supply and enjoyment of things. But in the business sense it means also acquiring and disposing of the thing in transactions with other people. This explains the easy transition from the common-law meaning of property as physical things, valuable to owners on account of the expected physical uses of production and consumption, to the business-law meaning of property as *assets*, valuable to owners on account of their expected bargaining uses as purchasing power in buying and selling.

The common-law and popular notion of property as physical things is, therefore, but an elliptical statement of what common-sense can take for granted without the pedantry of explaining every time that what is meant by property is the *uses* and not the thing. The trouble is that, by using this common-sense notion of uses, not only the courts and business men, but also theoretical economists, pass over from the significance of "uses" in the sense of producing an increase in the supply of goods, to its exact opposite meaning in the business sense of an increase in the power of owners to command goods from other persons in exchange. The one is *producing power* which *increases* the supply of goods in order to increase the quantity of use-values; the other is *bargaining power* which *restricts* the supply of goods in proportion to demand, in order to increase or maintain their exchange-value. Bargaining power is the willful *restriction*

---

[1] Pollock, F., *Principles of Contract*, 5 (9th ed., 1921); 3 Law. *Quar. Rev.*, 115 (1887); Bouvier's *Law Dictionary*, title "Use."

of supply in proportion to demand in order to maintain or enlarge the value of business assets; but producing power is the willing *increase* of supply in order to enlarge the wealth of nations.

Hence the transition in the meaning of property from the use-value to the exchange-value of things, and therefore from the producing power that increases use-values to the bargaining power that increases exchange-values, is more than a transition—it is a reversal. The reversal was not at first important when business was small and weak—it becomes important when Capitalism rules the world.

The transition in meanings of property and liberty applies to agriculture as well as manufactures, commerce and transportation, and to individuals, partnerships and associations as well as corporations. Farming has become a going-business, or a bankrupt business, like other businesses. The isolated, colonial, or frontier farmer might produce and consume things, attentive only to their use-value, but the modern farmer lives by producing "social-use-values" and buying other social-use-values produced and sold by other business men. In this way he also "produces" exchange-value, that is, assets. He farms for sale, not for use, and while he has the doubtful alternative of falling back on his own natural resources if he cannot sell his products, yet his farm and crops are valuable because they are business assets, that is, exchange-values, while his liabilities are his debts and his taxes, all of them measured by his expectations and realizations on the commodity markets and money markets, in terms of exchange-value or price.

This, we take it, is the substance of Capitalism distinguished from the Feudalism or Colonialism which it displaced—production for the use of others and acquisition for the use of self, such that the meaning of property and liberty spreads out from the expected uses of production and consumption to expected transactions on the markets where one's assets and liabilities are determined by the ups and downs of prices. And this is, in substance, the change in the meanings of Property and Liberty, from the Slaughter House Cases in 1872 to the Allgeyer Case in 1897, a change from the use-value of physical things to the exchange-values of anything.

II. Opportunity and Encumbrance

If the meaning of property (as distinguished from rights of property), is not merely that of a thing, but is the liberty of expected activity in acquiring, using and disposing of things, then the significance of property is in the behavior expected with regard to the thing, and the value of the thing is in the expected desirable behavior regarding it. In other words, value resides in the expected will-in-action, and the expected will-in-action is its expected actions and transactions. We shall name this a going concern,[1] consisting of two inseparable components, a Producing Organization turning out use-values, and a Going Business bringing in exchange-values.

The transition from rights of property in the use-values of things, to rights of property in their exchange-value is a change from physical things to a going business and, first in point of significance is the fact that it unites property and liberty in an identical concept. Property means anything that can be bought and sold, and since one's liberty can be bought and sold, liberty is assets, and therefore liberty is property. A person may sell a portion of his liberty in two ways. You agree to pay me a thousand dollars a year from now. Originally such a promise was a matter of conscience and the confessional. Now the state will physically compel you to pay, if your conscience and the priest do not morally do so. You have sold a part of your liberty, and I, in turn, can sell it to a third party.

Or you sell to me the goodwill and trade-name of your business by agreeing to refrain from competing with me or using your name in your business. Originally one or both of us might have been imprisoned or fined for making such a contract in restraint of trade.[2] Now the court will punish you if you do not keep your promise and it will punish others who make use of that trade-name in competing with me. Again you have sold to me a part of your liberty and I, in turn, can sell it to a third party.

What is it that I have bought and now own in each of these cases? It is not a physical thing. It is a promise of future behavior on your part and a permission to me to get the officers of the law to compel you to behave as you promised if you do not do so willingly. You have sold to me a part of your liberty. Let us call it an Encumbrance on your Liberty. An encumbrance has two ends exactly equal in size. One end of it is my right, my asset, the other end is your duty, your liability.

I now may own two kinds of encumbrances on your liberty, both

---

[1] Below, Chap. V.
[2] BOUVIER'S *Law Dictionary*, under title "Restraint of Trade."

of which constitute my assets, or the exchange-value of my property. One is positive, the other is negative. One is your promise to do something, the other your promise to not-do something—your promise to pay and your promise not to compete. One is a debt, the other is a goodwill. Each is an encumbrance on the field of your expected behavior. One restricts your liberty of action by requiring a performance, usually described as compulsion; the other restricts your liberty by compelling an avoidance, usually described as restraint. Each has a present value to me. Each is my property, which I have acquired, am holding and can sell. The exchange-value of each is my asset.

But the two objects which I buy, hold and sell are different. When I buy or sell your indebtedness I am buying or selling your positive duty to do something at a future date measured by, say, one thousand dollars. When I buy your promise *not* to do something I am apparently buying nothing at all. I am evidently not buying your customers. I do not own my customers, you did not own yours. I do not own any duty or encumbrance imposed upon them requiring them to do anything positive for me. They are not my assets. My customers still have their liberty to buy elsewhere. They are not compelled to buy of me. What I own is not an encumbrance on them. Let us call it an Opportunity to deal with them if I can. I simply own the opportunity to sell my goods or services to them if I can. And I do not own it against all the world—I own it only against you, to the extent that you have promised not to try to sell to them, and against competitors only to the extent that they are prohibited from using my trade-name, or otherwise unfairly competing with me. Outside these rights I am exposed to competitors.

Thus the meaning of property has spread over from visible things to invisible things. The invisible things are encumbrances and opportunities. Encumbrances are the duties that other people owe to me, and opportunities are their liberties, their absence of duties to me. Yet both are valuable to me and valuable to third parties who buy them of me, and are therefore property in the sense of exchange-values, or assets.

These two kinds of property are rightly described as intangible, incorporeal, invisible. They cannot be seen by the naked eye like physical things, and they are not always even symbolized by words written out on paper as evidences of ownership. They may be created by word of mouth. They may even be implied from the conduct of the parties. Their intangibility is the invisibility of the promised and expected behavior of people, which is felt, not seen, by the inner eye of confidence.

These intangible and incorporeal properties are more valuable than all physical things, in a land whose government and people are stable, for upon them are built both the credit system and the business initiative that have displaced feudalism by capitalism. They have arisen in manifold varieties. Encumbrances range from merely implied promises inferred only from simple acts, to elaborate bonds that bind a business or a nation for a century to come. Opportunities range from the simple choices between alternatives made daily in every transaction, to that expanse of enduring market opportunities known variously as goodwill, patent rights, the right to continue in business or to continue business connections, the right to a labor market, the right to liberty of contract, and the many kinds of public franchises, corporation charters, and public utility franchises.

Generally, as we noted above, the encumbrances are coming to be known as "incorporeal" property, or debts; the opportunities as "intangible" property, or exchange-value. Each is invisible, for each exists only in the unseen future. One is the invisibility of future behavior of creditors and debtors, the other the invisibility of future behavior of buyers and sellers, whether they be borrowers and lenders, merchants and customers, landlords and tenants, principals and agents, employers and employees. In the one case they are the expected beneficial performance of duty; in the other they are the expected beneficial exercise of liberty; in both cases they are expected beneficial actions or transactions. In both cases they are assets, since they are the exchange-values of things.

Though invisible and in the future, they are more substantial than even the physical property which we see in the present, for it is they that have produced all physical capital, that reproduce it when it wears out, and that enlarge it faster than the growth of population. Though physical capital may disappear through war or other catastrophy, yet if these invisible expectations of beneficial behavior remain intact, then the physical capital will be shortly reproduced.

The invisible capital of many a going concern is more valuable than all of its machinery, lands, buildings, stock on hand, and, indeed, if that invisible capital loses its value all of the visible capital is likely to sink at once to the value of old iron and scrap. It would not be incorrect to say that all capital is invisible value, in that it is the present value, not of physical things, but of the hopes of the future aroused through confidence in the now invisible but expected transactions of the future.

For, what is the value of lands, buildings, machinery, commodities, but the value of their expected "uses"? And what are their uses but the uses not yet made but yet to be made of them, either in using them directly or in selling their products for money or other products? One is use-value, the relation of man to nature. The other is exchange-value, the relation of man to man. Both of them lie in the future but have a value in the present. We may call them Expectancies. All value is expectancy. Use-value is the expected behavior of things in man's activity of production and consumption. Exchange-value is the expected behavior of people in buying and selling, lending, hiring, borrowing and paying debts.

The meaning of property has thus expanded so that it includes expectancies of two kinds of future behavior of other people, one of which is the expected restraint or compulsion placed on others in my behalf; the other is opportunities afforded by them and open to me. Both of these are measured off and determined by that power superior to both of us, the state, and therefore one of them, the encumbrances, is recognized as their legal duties; the other, the opportunities, as their legal liberties. Expected restraints and compulsions by the state, that is, encumbrances, are legal duties; expected absence of restraint or compulsion, that is, opportunities, are legal liberty.

If liberty is the *absence* of duty, that is, of compulsion or restraint, then this *absence* of something, paradoxical though it seem, must *contain* something in order to be valuable. What it "contains" is an economic equivalent. My liberty is valuable to me to the extent of the different economic objects which may happen to be its equivalent. What it contains is not things but expected transactions. Liberty is the legal equivalent of expected transactions. If I sell the goodwill of my business to you, I am selling a part of my liberty. Here my liberty is valuable *in exchange*. Its value consists in what I can get for it when I part with it. I am at liberty to sell my liberty to a limited extent. I am not at liberty to sell *all* of my liberty. The value of liberty is its exchange-value in terms of money—realized assets. Here I capitalize my expected liberty and sell it.

Another way in which my liberty is valuable is in using it or leasing it for the sake of increasing my income. When I own the goodwill of a business what I own is my absence of restraint, compulsion, or duty in selling things that I own. The valuable equivalent of this absence of duty is the more profitable bargains I can make by using my liberty than I could make if I did not have that liberty. That profit is the difference between the prices I could get for my products, if I did not own and keep the goodwill, and the prices I can get by keeping and owning it. Likewise with others. If I am a laborer and my present employer pays me $3.00 a day, but another employer offers me $3.50 a day, the daily income from my liberty to leave one employer and to work for another is 50 cents a day. The valuable content of this part of my liberty is therefore exchange-value measured by money. But in this case it is a surplus that gives greater value to the thing sold. What I sell is the use of my labor power. The exchange-value of my labor power is my assets. Yet I am not permitted to sell all of it permanently. I cannot capitalize it. I can only hire it out for a daily income. It is of greater value to me at $3.50 a day than at $3.00. The liberty to choose between opportunities is worth the difference between the higher and lower value received in exchange. Thus the value of liberty in this case is the surplus exchange-value one can get by choice of opportunities.

Yet in either case I give up a part of my liberty. The practice of selling or leasing a part of one's liberty goes along with all transactions. The sale of liberty is a necessary part of every sale. Liberty is thrown in with every valuation in making an exchange. The owner who sells his horse, or the investor who lends his purchasing power, or the laborer who sells the use of his labor power, sells with it a part or the whole of his liberty to use his horse, or his purchasing power, or his labor power. The landlord leases to the tenant his liberty to use the farm and impliedly agrees to obey the commands of the tenant to keep off. The lender sells to the borrower his liberty to use his right to draw checks on a bank. The agent or employee who sells the use of his labor power sells a part of his liberty by accepting obedience to the commands of the other. Each sale is the acceptance of a duty either of avoidance or performance, and each duty is a deduction from liberty, and therefore a sale of a part of one's liberty.

In these cases the value of the liberty when sold seems to be wholly absorbed by the value of the thing sold. The sale of liberty is not distinguished from the sale or lease, or loan, of the horse, of the bank deposit, or of the labor power. Value received seems to have a positive basis for exchange only in the positive thing that is sold and not in such a negative thing as the absence of restraint or compulsion. But in the sale of goodwill the value of liberty often visibly separates itself out from the value of the plant and merchandise, and is computed as a separate or additional value. The physical plant of a certain newspaper, for example, is worth $100,000. Its goodwill is separately worth $900,000. The goodwill is not in the plant but in the customers.

Yet is it so very different? When a person sells his "business" the courts usually infer that he sells his goodwill with the physical plant, for goodwill is nothing more or less than the profitable or beneficial exercise of the will over the thing sold. So when I sell my horse I sell the liberty to exercise my will over my horse, which is something that would have been profitable or beneficial to me and therefore good, but is henceforth to be the beneficial exercise of the buyer's will over the horse, and therefore a goodwill for him.

So it is with the sale of my bank deposit or labor power. When I sell either of these peculiar objects I sell the beneficial or profitable exercise of my will over it, and the borrower or employer buys the expectation of a profitable exercise of *his* will over it. My goodwill—not sentimentally good but economically good, not good-will but goods-will, because good for my benefit or profit—becomes his goodwill, good for him.

Hence the sale of that part of one's liberty that goes along with every transaction is not such a paradoxical sale of the *absence* of something as it seemed at first, but is the transfer of something very positive, substantial and good, namely, an economic equivalent in the expected free exercise of one's will in acquiring things from the world and people about us.

This is the economic equivalent of liberty and property, and it is this that has come to be known as "intangible" property, distinguished from "incorporeal" property. Intangible property is opportunity. Incorporeal property is debt. Here is where value lies—not in the visible things or persons, but in the will to acquire, to use, to control, to enjoy and so to get an expected benefit or profit out of things or persons. What we buy and sell is not things, but our goodwill over things. And when we say that liberty is valuable and liberty is therefore property, what we mean is that the free and beneficial exercise of the will in dealings with nature and other people is economically valuable and therefore is property.

Thus it is that the terms Property, Value, Capital, Assets, Liberty, and The Will have come to mean the same thing from different points of view. Property is none other than the beneficial exercise of the will in dealing with nature or other persons. But dealings with nature are "corporeal property" and "corporeal property" has dropped out of sight. The business man is not interested in his corporeal property except as a means to an end and that end is its exchange-value. The right to have this exchange-value is simply the right of access to markets. And it is these rights of access to markets that were named "liberty" in the Slaughter House Cases but are now known as "intangible property." But intangible property is merely the expected beneficial behavior of other people to be obtained by way of expected transactions with them, while incorporeal property is their expected fulfillment of promises which they have made to us. And this is Capital. Capital is the present value of expected beneficial behavior of other people. Property has become intangible and incorporeal; liberty has become intangible property; duties are incorporeal property; each is the expected beneficial behavior of others in dealings with self, and the present value to self of that expected behavior is capital or assets.

III. Power

We have seen that liberty is valuable, and liberty is property, in two directions. It is valuable because it will bring in something in exchange for something. The two are equivalent. The value of the liberty is the exchange-value of the thing given in exchange. The other direction in which liberty is valuable is by bringing in a surplus equivalent to the difference. The first of these directions is power in exchange, purchasing power, or bargaining power, that is, economic power, or briefly *power*. The other direction is choice of opportunities, that is choice of alternatives, or, briefly, *opportunity*.

Thus, liberty is absence of restraint, or compulsion, or duty, and is equivalent to the exercise of power and the choice of opportunities which it permits. But choice of opportunities is, in fact, but *a choice between two degrees of power*. If I can sell the use of my labor for $3.00 a day, that is one degree of power over my employer. If I can sell it for $3.50 a day that is another degree of power. If a railway corporation charges 3 cents a mile, that is one degree of power over passengers; if it charges 2 cents that is a lesser degree of power. The economic equivalent of liberty, therefore, is freedom to choose between two degrees of power over other persons.

In some cases this power dimension of property attracts more attention than the opportunity dimension. Public-utility laws, usury laws, labor laws, are designed sometimes to curb the bargaining-power of property where it seems to be excessive. The courts have declared certain of these laws unconstitutional or void, on the ground that they restricted liberty. They do indeed restrict liberty, for liberty is *absence* of restraint, compulsion or duty, and these laws are the *presence* of restraint, compulsion or duty. But these decisions of the courts failed to distinguish "liberty" from the economic equivalent which is the "content" of liberty. Liberty itself is empty and meaningless. Its meaning is in its content. Its content is freedom to choose. But even this is empty, and the will does not exist in vacuum. It exists in its choice of opportunities. But its opportunities are degrees of power over nature or man. The economic equivalent of liberty is liberty to choose between degrees of economic power. Liberty is inseparable from power. Courts, in more recent decisions, have discovered that liberty is economic power, as well as economic opportunity.[1]

We may designate opportunity and power as the *external* dimensions of the will in action, to be distinguished from "economy," the internal dimension of property. They are external in that they are the dimensions that come into contact with other persons. They are the dimensions which tell us whether property, including its liberty to exercise the will, is enlarged or diminished in dealings with other people. For this reason they may be named the *expansion* side of the will and property. Property, then, the free exercise of the will, is expanded by one and the same act, which, however, has the two dimensions of opportunity and power.

But opportunity and power differ greatly in their method of expan-

[1] Below, Chap. III.

sion. Opportunity is expansion *without cost* to self. It is the costless enlargement of power by merely choosing between two degrees of power, both of which are accessible at the moment. It is the passive aspect of choosing. But power itself costs something. It is effort, outgo, as well as income. It means that something is given up, that something is given in exchange. It may be a day's labor that is given up; it may be a horse or a bushel of wheat that has been owned; it may be a part of one's liberty that is sold. One school of economists reduces all costs to commodity costs, including the commodity money paid out; another reduces them to pain-costs, the pain endured. But all costs are property-costs. The laborer does not sell his pain—he sells his labor power; it is the same when he sells his horse or a part of his liberty. In all cases he gives up property and throws in liberty.

But the sale has a purpose. It is something given up in order to induce something else to come back. It is outgo of property, in exchange for income of property. It is power-in-exchange. It is realization of assets. We measure the degree of power by a ratio of exchange. I sell a day's labor for $3.00. The ratio is one day's work = $3.00. I sell it for $3.50. The ratio is $1 = 3.50. I sell a bushel of wheat for two bushels of oats. The ratio is 1 bu. = 2 bu. I sell it for 3 bushels—the ratio is 1 : 3. I sell my goodwill for $1000. The ratio is 1 : 1000. I sell it for $2000. The ratio is 1 : 2000. The *ratio of exchange* measures the degree of power because it measures the ratio between what I give up and what I get back in the exercise of power.

But when I merely choose between two ratios of exchange, both of which are accessible at the moment, I give up *nothing in addition*. I choose between the power ratio of 1 : 3 and 1 : 3.50, between 1 : 2 and 1 : 3, between 1 : 1000 and 1 : 2000. I give up, in either case, only the identical day's labor, or bushel of wheat, or part of my liberty. But I gain a pure surplus, a costless addition to my property. We may designate this costless increment a *ratio of surplus*, or *ratio of opportunity*. My ratio of opportunity is the ratio which the surplus bears to what I would have had were it not for the costless choice. When I gain 50 cents by merely choosing to sell my labor for $3.50 instead of $3.00, my ratio of opportunity is 50 : 300, that is 1 : 6 or $16^2/_3$ per cent pure costless gain.

Thus, while the ratio of exchange is a measure of power, the ratio of opportunity is a measure of the difference between two degrees of power. The two ratios are merely the measurement of two dimensions of the same transaction, like two dimensions of a box. The ratio of exchange measures the *cost* side of a transaction, the ratio of opportunity the *costless* side. The one measures the sacrifice, the other the "velvet." But in measuring sacrifice the ratio of exchange also measures power, and in measuring velvet the ratio of opportunity measures the costless choice of opportunities that goes along with the exercise of power.

But power may be increased directly without choice of opportunities. Suppose the laborer has his employer at a disadvantage where the employer has no alternative opportunity. The laborer demands and receives $3.50 instead of $3.00; or the corporation demands and receives 3 cents a mile instead of 2 cents, if the passenger has no alternative. In either case one has increased his power, not by choosing between two persons, but by a direct increase of power over the same person. The same service is given to the same person, but at a higher ratio of exchange, a greater degree of power.

Thus liberty and property have two meanings, either of which signifies *expansion* of power. One is choice of opportunities, a passive, indirect, *costless* increase of power. The other is choice of greater or less degree of power. Liberty applies to both. Liberty is the absence of restraint, compulsion, or duty, but in one case liberty is expansion through choice of two degrees of power over two others: in the other it is expansion through choice of two degrees of power over *one* other.

In either case, likewise, the increase of power is, in modern business, expressed in terms of price, and prices are referred to a standard of money. We say that money is a measure of value and a medium of exchange. But it is a peculiar medium. Money is a kind of universal container of everything within reach at the option of its owner and the prices of commodities. It is a medium and a measure because it is a universal power of acquisition at certain prices. As such it becomes the measure of one's assets and liabilities, as well as the medium through which one's assets are usually realized on the markets in the form of other things to be acquired in exchange. We may, therefore, speak of assets as the quantity of other things expected from the prices to be obtained by sale of the things owned, and money as the medium by which those things are obtained. The things owned are simply Things. The quantity of other things *expected* in exchange for them is the expected prices to be obtained for things owned; and expected prices are book assets, that is, assets hoped for. Money is the medium and measure for changing hopeful assets into realized assets. So that an increase of power over others in terms of price is an increase in one's assets or diminution of one's liabilities, and this is the expansion equivalent of property and liberty through opportunity and power. Inversely, the diminution of power or absence of opportunity is the contraction-equivalent of property and liberty, or rather exposure,[1] which reduces one's assets or enlarges one's liabilities.

Thus we see that the legal term "liberty" has a two-fold economic content, namely, opportunity and power. Yet these two are really but two aspects of one act of the will, namely, choice between two degrees of economic power. This concept of the economic power of property and liberty was first admitted to the decisions of the Supreme Court in the case already cited, of Munn v. Illinois, in 1876. Prior to that decision the term power had meant only the physical power of the sovereign in enforcing the laws, out of which power came the grants of special privileges or monopolies which were not property, but were arbitrary infringements upon the rights of property. The concept of property itself had come up out of the common law and carried with it the idea of a natural, or common-law right of liberty to acquire, use and dispose of physical things. Hence property was not power— property was liberty, and there was a world of difference between the power of the sovereign and the liberty of the subject. But, in the Munn Case, for the first time, it came to be seen that this liberty of private property meant also the economic power of private property. The power of sovereignty was the physical power to compel obedience; the power of property was the economic power to withhold from others what belongs to self but is needed by others. The legislature of Illinois had fixed the maximum charges permitted to be made by grain elevator and warehouse companies for the handling and storage of grain. This business of a warehouse had always been a private business, and had never been granted any special privilege or franchise by the sovereign either in England or America. The majority and the minority in the Supreme Court agreed that in the case of a special grant of sovereign power, the power of the sovereign to regulate the charges went along with the grant. The charges must be reasonable and this was the common-law rule applying to all special grants or licenses, whether express, implied, or claimed by prescription through long usage and consent, such as public ferries, bridges, turnpikes,

[1] Below, Chap. IV.

wharfingers, or hackmen and draymen who made use of the King's highways.[1] The judges disagreed as to whether this sovereign power could lawfully be extended to a grain elevator and warehouse which did not need and did not have a special grant of sovereign power to carry on its business.

The majority introduced a new principle of law, as charged by the minority, in order to sustain the power of the Illinois legislature to fix the prices for handling and storage of grain, and to compel the owners to furnish service at those prices. This was, in effect, the principle that it was *economic conditions* and *not a special grant of sovereignty* that determined the right of the sovereign to regulate prices. The Munn Case was not the case of a railway depending on a public franchise, but of a private business. These warehouses, without a special grant of sovereign power, had become strategic centers for control of the prices of grain shipped from the Northwest, by the mere fact of location, character of the business, and power to withhold service. The majority, recognizing this economic fact, held that property lost its strictly private character and became "clothed with a public interest when used in a manner to make it of public consequence and affect the community at large." Thus the *fact* of economic power over the public in withholding service and thus fixing prices need not proceed from a sovereign grant of a privilege, but proceeds, in this case, from the circumstance that the public had come to depend on the use of the owner's private property, and that therefore the owner had employed his property, not merely to his own use and enjoyment, but had devoted it to use by the public. To that extent he must submit to be controlled by the public. (113, 126.)

Justice Field, who, in the Slaughter House Cases, had denied the right of the state to restrain liberty, now denied its right to restrain the power to withhold services. He distinguished both between a sovereign privilege and private property, and between the use and enjoyment of the property by the owner and the *price* that the owner could charge for its use and enjoyment by others. A sovereign privilege, he agreed, might be regulated as to the compensation, or prices, derived from its exercise, and indeed such regulation was implied in such a grant. "When," however, "the privilege ends, the power of regulation ceases." (147.) And the owner of the private property might be restrained, under the police power, as to its *use and enjoyment*

[1] 94 U. S. 113, 149 (1876).

if that became dangerous to the life and health of others, but *not as to the compensation* or price charged for its use by others. The police power, he thus held, extended only to the *use* and *enjoyment*, that is to the use-value of things, and *not* to the *compensation* for the use, that is, the prices of things, except in cases where some right or privilege is conferred by the government which gives the beneficiary special advantage over others. "In the case of the warehousemen of Chicago no right or privilege is conferred by the government upon them." (113, 149.) "Their buildings are not nuisances." (148.) "The business of a warehouseman was, at common law, a private business, and is so in its nature." (154.)

Notwithstanding these cogent and accurate historical objections of Justice Field, supported by two other justices, the majority of the court recognized that the coercive power of property emerges with changes in economic conditions, even when not supported by a special grant of sovereignty. For it was evidently not the health of the public that was menaced by the warehouses but the *prices* that the public as producers and consumers should receive and pay for food. And so, in sustaining the authority to restrain that economic power, they reduced the scope of property by enlarging the police power of the state legislatures. But the property which they reduced in scope was not the ownership of physical property—it was the ownership of the exchange-value of that property.

The decision in Munn *v.* Illinois recognized for the first time the economic power of property, or power to withhold, growing out of economic conditions, as distinguished from the physical power of sovereignty, or power to compel, exercised on behalf of citizens as their privilege or "liberty." Thenceforth, it would require, not a special, personal favor of the sovereign in order to justify the legislature in regulating the prices to be derived from that favor, but a mere showing that the citizen had engaged in business upon which other citizens depended for their liberty and property. The grant of power over citizens in fixing prices now comes, not from the sovereign directly, but indirectly from the citizen's ownership of a kind of property to which that economic power attaches. The transition is made from a legal monopoly, the ancient "liberty" of the subject to exercise sovereign power, to a "natural" monopoly, the modern liberty to exercise economic power, since it proceeds automatically from economic conditions rather than designedly from an act of the sovereign.

Previously it was only the grant of a special privilege that gave to the sovereign the right to prevent extortion by regulating the prices charged, and *private property* was *not* such a grant from the sovereign but was a natural right derived from the common law, which expressed the common usages of the people without privilege, and therefore carried the natural right of liberty in fixing prices. Now, when the grant of special privilege no longer avails, another source of authority, the "police power," which had been used only to prevent excessive nuisance, is enlarged to prevent excessive economic power.

Where the decisions that followed the minority in the Slaughter House Cases enlarged property at the expense of sovereignty, the police power enlarges sovereignty at the expense of property. The citizen himself, since the Munn decision, now takes the initiative without waiting for the sovereign to act, and of his own free will grants to the sovereign the authority to regulate his prices, because he no longer uses his property only for his own use and enjoyment, but he devotes it to the use of other citizens who necessarily depend upon it for the prices that give value to *their* liberty and property. Liberty is no longer defined merely by the dimensions of choice of opportunity, as was done by the minority in the Slaughter House Cases. It is now defined also by the dimension of economic power.

This dimension was not conceded by the minority in the Munn Case. Had that case been one of a railroad with a franchise to operate a highway, the minority would doubtless not have dissented, for such a franchise is a special grant of sovereign power. But the case was that of a warehouse without a public franchise, and the minority could not see that mere property as such, when not aided by a franchise, could possess a similar kind of power. If, however, property, as perceived by the majority, did possess this similar kind of power, it followed, by a stretch of the implied powers of sovereignty, that the sovereign should have power to restrain the owner of that property. This the majority affirmed, and in doing so, enlarged the definition of the "police power" beyond the mere control of the use and enjoyment of property where prejudicial to health or comfort, to the control of the bargaining power of property where prejudicial to the bargaining power of others. The police power was thus extended from use-value to exchange-value, from physical things to business assets.[1]

---

[1] See Justice Field's criticism that the police power had never before been extended to the *compensation* for the use of property except where "some right or privilege" was con-

Yet the decision in the Munn Case left the authority to exercise this enlargement of the police power solely in the hands of the legislature. This was because, as we noted above, the court had not yet changed the definition of property from physical things to the prices of things. Not until the first Minnesota Rate Case,[1] already referred to, fourteen years after the Munn Case, was this change made. The result was, after 1890, that the judicial branch of government, rather than the legislative branch, took jurisdiction of the police power in determining how far the legislature might go in exercising it. The Munn Case recognized the economic power of property, distinguished from the economic power of a monopoly; the Minnesota Rate Case defined this economic power, or exchange-value, as the essence of property, which therefore could not be taken from its owner except by judicial process instead of legislative process. The rate case reversed the Munn Case as to the limits of the police power, but not as to the definition of economic power.

IV. Economy

We have considered two economic or volitional dimensions of the legal concepts, liberty and property, the one being choice of opportunities, the other choice of greater or less degrees of economic power. When these two dimensions are joined together, they constitute what may be named the principle of Expansion, since they signify an enlargement of economic power through dealings with other persons. A person may expand the field of his will or resources in the threefold dimensions of (1) a *costless* choice between alternative degrees of power over opposite persons, a dimension measured by a ratio of opportunity; (2), the degree of power chosen, however, is a *costful* expansion measured by a ratio of exchange; but this ratio of exchange may be reduced by, (3), a forbearance [2] which is a choice of a less instead of a greater degree of power over a single person. Liberty therefore means absence of constraint or compulsion in the Expansion of one's will or resources. But liberty also signifies the absence of

ferred by government, 94 U. S. 146. At a later date the Supreme Court of Oregon, in the minimum wage case, referring to this concept of the police power, said, "when new conditions arise which injuriously affect the health or morals or welfare of the public, we no longer say that we will expand the police power to reach and remedy the evil. Instead we say that a new evil has arisen which an old principle of government—the police power—will correct." Stettler *v.* O'Hara, 69 Ore. 519, 532 (1914).

[1] Chicago, M. & St. P. Ry. Co. *v.* Minn., 134 U. S. 418 (1890).

[2] Below Chap. IV, Sec. II.

constraint or compulsion in a fourth dimension of the will-in-action, which is the obverse of Expansion, namely, Economy.

A worker receives a salary of $1000 a year. This marks the limit of his economic expansion through choice of opportunities and economic power. If he received $1200 his economic power would be expanded; if he received $900 his power would be contracted. Supposing his power of expansion is measured by $1000 per year, he distributes this $1000 among food, clothing, shelter, amusement, tobacco, whiskey, religion, books, education, etc. He spends 40 per cent for food, 20 per cent for clothing, 25 per cent for shelter, 15 per cent miscellaneous. Another man spends 40 per cent for whiskey, 10 per cent for tobacco, and the rest on his family for food, clothing, shelter.

We infer from this scheme of proportioning his purchasing power something as to the character of the man. One person spends 40 per cent for food, the other 40 per cent for whiskey. Their power and opportunity are equal, but their *proportioning* of that power and opportunity is different. Each presumably proportions his expenditures so as to get what for himself he judges to be the maximum satisfaction. His personality reveals itself in his scheme of proportioning his powers and opportunities. His scheme of proportioning resources is his plan of life. It is his scheme both of economy and of ethics. Ethically it is his moral character, his personality, his individuality, his selfishness, sympathy or sense of duty towards other people. Economically, it is the proportioning of resources so as to obtain the maximum expansion of that personality.

It is remarkable how much both nature and man accomplish by mere economy without expansion. It is believed that nature does not enlarge the total quantity of the elements in the universe, but she accomplishes all of her work by merely re-proportioning them. Her economy, in one respect, is precise and effective. The several chemical elements unite or repel in fixed proportions. Water is always H_2O. Protoplasm is always a certain CHNO. An explosion of TNT gives off a definite amount of gas. Heat, electricity, motion, life, are the kinds of work these elements perform when uniting and repelling in predetermined proportions.

Each element or part in a group is, not an item added to a lot of others, but each element is in turn a limiting factor and a complementary factor. Each is complementary to the work of all the others and each places a limit on the work of the others. A surplus of one factor does no work of that kind. It is wasted. The limiting factor limits the total amount of work of the complementary factors. For this reason nature is wasteful. She does not hunt around for methods to increase the supply of the limiting factors in order to produce the kind of result desired. She lets them come along as they happen. The sun turns out more heat than anybody can use. But when they do come along, the elements combine and repel in definite, powerful proportions. Nature's economy, from man's standpoint, is exact and powerful, but wasteful.

Animal and vegetable life is different, or rather, additional. Unconsciously the primitive protoplasm exerts itself to supply the limiting factors. The rootlet pushes itself downward where it finds food, and the leaves and blossoms bend toward the sun. The internal constitution of a living creature is a proportioning of chemical elements, and the creature must obtain a similar proportion from the world about. It seeks out the limiting factors, avoids the useless factors, acquires without effort the complementary factors, and thus unconsciously enlarges life both by expansion and economy.

Conscious life advances a step. More highly organized, peculiarly guided or warned by pleasure or pain, it maximizes the pleasure and minimizes the pain by proportioning the limiting and complementary factors in its endeavor to get the best proportioning under the circumstances. Each separate pain or pleasure is a part of the whole, and the best proportioning of the parts is the maximum contentment of the animal.

Self-conscious life is a further step upwards. It is the life of man in society, the life of *expansion* of the individual through opportunities and power available mainly through transactions with others, and the life of *economy* through proportioning these opportunities and powers. It is this scheme of proportioning, as already suggested, that reveals character, individuality, personality, and coördinates ethics with economics. For, morally and *ethically*, this proportioning of opportunities and powers is the means of self-expression, self-development, "self-realization." Economically it is economizing one's power over the services of others in order to obtain the maximum result as determined by the character of the man who is thus realizing himself. The ethical aspect is the scheme of *human* values that centers about his personality. The economic aspect is the proportioning of all the external factors according to their *instrumental* value in realizing this scheme of human values.

In all of this ascending scale of economy from the lowest to the highest, a proper proportioning may be said to multiply all of the complementary factors by the limiting factor. For economy is not the mere addition of separate units whose result is an arithmetic sum, but economy is similar to a multiplication of one factor into the complementary factors. Five and six are arithmetically eleven, but five times six are geometrically thirty. Hydrogen and oxygen may be a numerical sum of atoms, but hydrogen and oxygen rightly proportioned are thunder, lightning, and rain. Salt is but a small item in the economy of life, but a deprivation of salt means decay and corruption of all parts of the body. Potash is a small item in agricultural economy, but without potash the yield may be five bushels per acre, with it twenty bushels. Coal and oil are relatively small quantities of material in a manufacturing plant, but the total product is limited by the amount of coal under the boilers and the oil on the bearings. Managerial ability is but one of several kinds of ability and it costs relatively little in terms of money, compared with the total cost, but without it a thousand men are a mob—with it they are a going concern. Physical capital is often a small item in a business compared with labor, but without the willingness of investors and capitalists the concern goes bankrupt. The business man proportions his product to his market. If he furnishes too many potatoes and not enough cabbages, he loses on the one and misses on the other. He proportions also his factors within the concern. If he pays too much for capital and not enough for labor, or hires too many laborers and not enough capital, his concern winds up in the courts.

It is said that nature takes no leaps. She does not jump from one species to another entirely different. No, she does not, but when she reproportions her existing factors she jumps from gases to liquids, from liquids to solids, from physics to biology, biology to psychology, psychology to sociology. Pantaleoni has well said: [1]

"The law of definite proportions is one of the most generally applicable of natural laws, and economic science only recognizes a particular aspect of it. It is well known that bodies combine chemically only in definite proportions, and that any quantity of an element in excess of that required for

[1] PANTALEONI, MAFFEO, *Pure Economics*, 83, 85 (1898).

combination with other elements present in definite quantities, remains *free*. If the quantity of one element is deficient with respect to that of other elements present, the combination only takes place to the extent the former element admits of. Just in the same way, any quantity of a commodity, in excess of the proportion in which nature, or any technical art, can combine it with a determinate quantity of other complementary commodities present, is *useless* or *noxious* as regards the economic result; and if all the complementary commodities requisite for the production of a direct commodity are present in various quantities, then the quantity of the complementary commodity that is *present in a lesser quantity than any other*, is that which determines the quantity that can be produced of the direct commodity in question; the superfluous quantities of the other complementary commodities being, for this purpose, destitute of utility. This law of definite proportions is of capital importance in explaining a very frequent form of economic crisis, consisting in the disproportionate production of complementary commodities. It must, however, not be understood as if there were only *one* definite proportion in which complementary commodities can be combined. There are generally a *great many*, but only one gives a maximum hedonic result. This *maximum* combination is the one towards which every economic effect *tends*. . . . If an instrumental commodity cannot be transformed forthwith into a direct commodity, but requires the concurrence of other instrumental commodities, as is generally the case, we cannot discuss its utility, as such, *singly*, because it is subject to the law of complementary commodities. Here, too, recurs the phenomenon, that the single element that is lacking may come to possess the total utility [value] due to the complex of instrumental commodities required for the production of a direct commodity. Instrumental commodities are also subject to the law of *definite proportions*." [1]

Here we must distinguish between a part-opportunity and a whole opportunity. Each transaction of buying or selling is a part of the total opportunity. To sell a bushel of potatoes to one customer is a single transaction. To sell a thousand bushels to a thousand buyers is a total of which each sale is a part. Yet the total is not a mere addition of a thousand bushels. The total is the exchange-value of a thousand bushels, that is, their purchasing power, that is, the assets of their owner. Ten bushels may sell for fifty dollars, but a thousand bushels may overstock the market and sell for less than ten dollars. The diminishing value of the added bushel is *not added* to the *preceding* value of the ten bushels, but it actually *changes* their value and brings it down, and it does this even before they are

---

[1] Pantaleoni ascribes the original statement of this law to Ortes, 1774, but not made current until 1871, by Menger, who, however, "added nothing to it." It was explained, in 1854, "in the most masterly fashion by Gossen."

sold. The one is a *multiple* of the *other*, not a mere addition to it. Each added increment affects the value of all the other increments. Its own diminished value diminishes the value of the entire stock on hand. Here the limiting factor is the demand of other persons. But the demand of other persons is not their mere psychic wish, it is the supply of other things they offer in exchange. Hence the limiting factor is the supply of other commodities. The complementary factor is the supply of one's own commodity. Proportioning supply to supply is business economy by which assets are enlarged in value, and the total opportunity of a business is not a physical problem of adding separate items to obtain a total, but is a psychological and social problem of proportioning factors, each one of which changes the dimensions of all the others and thus changes, not things, but assets and liabilities, which are the exchange-values of things.

So it is with happiness and virtue. A single glove on the one hand may yield a certain pleasure, but if there is no glove for the other hand the total happiness is grievously impaired. The whole is not the sum of the parts but an amazing multiple of them. Throughout the entire scheme of proportioning food, clothing, shelter, whiskey, and miscellaneous, the pleasure derived from all is *not* a *sum* of pleasures or virtues but a *multiple*, in which one little mistake or vice, though it be but one act in ten thousand, vitiates the pleasure or virtue of all the others and transforms happiness into misery, morality into scandal.

Thus it is that in the economy of nature and man the mere proportioning of resources, without enlarging or expanding them, or even in spite of their contraction and repression, creates of itself new and astonishing products of a higher, or at least different order in the scale of values. Chemical activity is a reproportioning of chemical elements; business assets, personal happiness and moral character are a proportioning of the opportunities and powers that constitute resources.

In each distinct field of human life is the similar practice of economy; home economy is the proportioning of resources within the family; business economy the proportioning of lands, machinery, man-power, within the going concern; political economy the proportioning of human factors within the nation. And with each distinct field of economy are the outside limits set by opportunities and powers, which we name expansion of resources, so that home economy and business economy are limited by the bargaining powers of its members with outsiders, and Political Economy by the Political Expansion and Contraction of conquest, defense, treaties, and so-called "penetration" into other lands and peoples.

Throughout this ascending scale of economy from nature to man and society the peculiar operation of the principle of economy seems to be that of a central but unknown focus, a force, a unity, a nucleus, of a higher order which collects and proportions the units of lower orders and thereby lifts them up to a higher unity of its own. The lowest order of all, supposed to be the electron, is lifted into a higher unity by the unknown nucleus of the atom; the atoms by a still higher unity or chemical "force" are proportioned into chemical compounds or molecules; the biological nucleus, whatever it may be, call it Life, proportions these lower orders, already themselves a proportioning of still lower ones, and thus lifts them up to the higher unity of a living organism. The self-conscious focus, the human will, again lifts the lower orders into a higher unity of personality, and finally, the principle of association, or management, or collective will, or society, the working rules of concerns, or whatever we describe it, is the proportioning of human activities into a higher, or at least different and larger unity. Throughout it is an ascending scale of economy, each within its own rather distinct level, but in all cases it is a proportioning of parts which are themselves wholes in their own lower domains, and each proportioning focuses about an unknown force which both subordinates the lower orders to itself and coördinates them into a larger whole.

Yet economy is not separable from expansion; or rather economy is the internal, expansion the external, aspect of the identical behavior. One is the outside, the other the inside, one is the obverse of the other. On the internal side some unifying principle or force, the principle of life or of human personality, or of national existence, coördinates, subordinates, and thereby proportions the parts into a new and larger unity. On the external side it is the same unifying force or principle, but it is now in contact or conflict, in action and reaction, in power or weakness, dealing with and controlling others like or unlike itself.

It is this principle of economy that makes it impossible to say that any one factor in a business concern or a nation produces any definite part of the total wealth. Capital is productive, labor is productive, managers are productive, investors are productive, not because they physically do any particular thing, but because they are limiting and complementary factors. Each is productive simply because it is a necessary part of the whole. But if it is badly proportioned to the others, the excess is unproductive. Each is productive in *limited quantities*, and production of wealth is not the mere production of things—it is a good proportioning of all limiting and complementary factors.

It is this good proportioning that gives rise to the phenomena of value. None of the factors of production produce *value* unless they produce things in limited quantities. Restriction of physical production is as necessary as expansion of physical production. The important purpose of each of the economic factors is, not the production of things, but the production of values. And this is accomplished by the principle of Economy. Hence the two concepts, Value and Economy, are the basic concepts of economic theory.

It will thus be seen that, in passing from the economy to the expansion of the individual we are moving upward to a still higher economy in that ascending scale which we have previously noted. Economy is the inward, self-centered, aspect of behavior; expansion is the outward aspect that comes into contact with the world and other persons. Yet this outward aspect may itself be a correlation of opposing individuals within a higher unity which we distinguish as a greater or less degree of Reciprocity.[1] This lower, self-centered economy we may name Private Economy; the higher is Political Economy. The lower 'is the proportioning of opportunities and powers by the individual, the family, or the business concern, for their private purposes. The higher is the proportioning of that same behavior of individuals, families, or other concerns, by the State for public purposes. And, just as there may be a good or a poor, an economical or wasteful, a virtuous or vicious, private economy and private expansion, so there may be a good or a poor, an economical or wasteful, a just or unjust, political economy and political expansion.

Liberty, then, has this fourth meaning or content, the absence of restraint, compulsion, or duty, in proportioning one's opportunities, powers and forbearances, according to one's own scheme of

[1] Below, Chap. IV, Sec. IV.

life and one's own ideas of the way to get a maximum benefit and endure a minimum burden in dealings with other people. And the fourfold economic content of liberty is opportunity, power, forbearance and economy. Opportunity, power and forbearance [1] are the outward aspects of the content of liberty, which therefore we name, from the economic standpoint, expansion or contraction, and from the ethical standpoint, justice or injustice; while the inward aspects of the content of liberty are, economically, a good or poor economy, and, morally, a virtuous or vicious economy.

We have said that the obverse of expansion is economy. We may now say that the inverse of economy is waste. Here there are three different meanings of the term "opposition" or "opposite" which should be distinguished. A thing is wasted if it is furnished in excess of the best proportioning with other factors. It is then to be looked upon as a complementary factor. If it is not provided adequately in order to combine with the other factors in the best proportion, its deficiency is the cause of their waste, since it is then a limiting factor. In any changing economy from day to day each factor is in turn a limiting factor up to a certain point, and the waste of complementary factors, is reduced and the work of all the factors, therefore, increases at *an increasing rate*. By increasing it beyond that point the aggregate product may continue to increase but at a *diminishing rate of increase*. At that point another complementary factor begins to be the limiting factor. It now must be increased, if the total result is to increase.[2] Thus all of the limiting factors yield, in turn, increasing returns and diminishing returns. The optimum is perhaps a mean of the maximum and minimum returns of all the available factors, ascertained by approximating that point where "marginal utilities" of all factors are equal. If this optimum is not maintained, it is because certain factors are in excess and therefore wasted, because certain other factors are deficient and therefore limiting the work of the others. The term "opposite" here is used in the sense of two conditions that vary inversely with each other, of which the positive is a *good* economy and the negative is a *poor* economy. The opposition of economy and waste is not the opposition between something that *is* economy and something that *is not* economy, but between an economy that is *good* and an economy that is *poor*. One is the inverse of the other.

When, however, we speak of "expansion," as above, we refer to something that is the opposite of economy in a different sense of the word "opposite," in that it is something that is not economy at all but is the *obverse* of economy.

---

[1] The equivalent physical terms, avoidance, performance, forbearance, are explained below, Chap. IV, Sec. II.

[2] Cp. CLARK, J. B., *Distribution of Wealth*, 403 ff. (1899).

Again, a person may enlarge his powers and have access to large opportunities and yet make a wasteful use of them. Here the opposite of expansion is contraction, in the sense that one is the *reverse* of the other. Expansion is enlargement, but its opposite, that is its reverse, is contraction or recession.

Thus a person's powers and opportunities may diminish through causes external to himself but he may still make an economical use of them. A good or poor economy may go along with either one's enlarging or one's diminishing opportunities and powers. While expanding, one is also economizing, and even while contracting one is also economizing, and whether enlarging or contracting, his economizing may range from the good to the poor, the best to the worst. Economy and expansion are the *obverse* sides of the same transactions, one the internal, the other the external. But poor economy is the *inverse* of good economy, and contraction is the *reverse* of expansion.

A fourth meaning of "opposition" comes to the surface when we speak of two *opposing persons* and their two *opposing economies*, in the same transaction. Here the expansion of one may be the contraction of the other. If the seller can force up a price from ten cents to twenty cents, then, for him, it is a process of expansion, but for the buyer it is a process of contraction. The economy of one is enlarged by the very transaction which contracts the economy of the other. The latter may find compensation elsewhere, but, so far as that single transaction is concerned, it is expansion for one and contraction for the other. Here the opposition between two economies of two persons signifies that one is the *adverse* of the other. The compensation, or offset, which the other gets, arises from his choice of opportunities. If the buyer's best alternative was, say, 25 cents, then he gains a surplus of five cents even though he is forced to pay 20 cents. Always this happens. A person always gains by choosing, and the harder the alternative avoided the more he gains, even though the opportunity actually chosen is a hard one in itself.

Here the term "opposition" refers to *opposite persons*, and we shall employ the terms "correlative" and "correlation" to indicate this relation of two opposite persons. The two correlated persons in any transaction are expanding and contracting their powers and opportunities at that particular point. The one is the adversary of the other. Yet each is also an opportunity for the other to escape from a worse alternative, and each gives to, and takes from, the other. It is this opportunity to escape from worse alternatives by exchanging their services that correlates them into a larger unity of interest, and which, according to the accompanying degree of power exerted by each and the hardship of the alternative avoided, we may distinguish as a greater or less degree of *reciprocity* of adversary interests. Here we may speak of a high or low degree of reciprocity of opposing persons, the higher being the reverse of the lower; the higher constituting a social unity, the lower a social conflict.

Thus the relation between economy, expansion and reciprocity is fourfold, implying a fourfold meaning of the term "opposite" or "opposition." (1) For the identical person economy is the obverse of expansion in that it is the internal, the self-centered, the introspective, the subjective, aspect of all transactions, which unifies all the separate transactions by proportioning them into a different and larger unity around the individual's central purpose. Expansion, then, is the *obverse* of economy, the external, the other-than-self, the objective, aspect of all transactions, the opportunities, powers and forbearances by which the person adapts himself to conditions and enlarges or recedes in his control of resources which, at the same time are economized.

But, again, (2) for the identical person, economy is the *inverse* of waste in that the one is a poor economy, the other a good economy. Or (3) contraction is the *reverse* of expansion, in that the one is a subjection to, the other a control over, the forces and powers of the environment.

Lastly, (4) for *opposing persons*, one economy is the *adverse* of another, and one person the correlative of another person, in the sense that the two are related, each as an opportunity for the other to escape from worse alternatives and thereby to enlarge his powers without cost, yet each as exerting power over the other, to the extent that each takes and yields. Out of this correlation arises that still larger *unity of opposing persons* which we distinguish as a high degree of reciprocity, the inverse, or low degree of reciprocity, being the source of conflict.

Consequently, the term "opposite" or "opposition" of interests, will necessarily be used in four meanings depending on the context. (1) Waste and economy are opposite in the sense of the *inverse* fortunes of the *same* person, in that one is poor or bad, the other is good. (2) Economy and expansion are opposite in the sense that they are the *obverse* relations of the *same* person in the same transaction, in that one is inward, the other outward. (3) Contraction and expansion, conflict and reciprocity are the *reverse* relations of the *same* person, in that contraction or conflict is a reduction of his opportunities and powers, expansion and reciprocity is an enlargement. (4) Contraction and expansion are opposite in the sense that they are the *adverse* experiences of *opposing* persons in the same transaction, such that the contraction of one is the expansion of the other. Yet each may be better off than without the society of the other, depending on the degree of reciprocity.

CHAPTER III

PHYSICAL, ECONOMIC, AND MORAL POWER

Modern economic theory started with the Industrial Revolution of the 18th and 19th centuries. The steam engine was invented by John Watt in the same year that his friend, Adam Smith, published the *Wealth of Nations*. This coincidence of wealth and machinery explains, in part, the prominence of physical things in the form of commodities, rather than legal relations in the form of transactions, which dominated economic theory for a hundred years.

But the economic theories of the Supreme Court go back to the business revolution of the 17th century. It was that revolution, which, from the close of Elizabeth's reign to the Act of Settlement of 1700, displaced Feudalism by Capitalism. The dissenting opinions in the Slaughter House Cases went back to the time of Elizabeth, James and Charles, where they discovered the precedents for their definitions of economic liberty. Justice Field cited the Case of Monopolies, decided in 1602,[1] where a grant by the Crown to a private citizen of the sole right to import, manufacture and sell playing cards within the realm was declared void as against the common law and acts of Parliament. Also, he cited the case of Davenant *v.* Hurdis, decided three years earlier,[2] in which a gild of merchant tailors operating under a charter granted by the Crown, had attempted to restrict the trade of cloth-worker to members of the gild, but the by-law was declared void by the court. Likewise, the Statute of Monopolies, enacted in 1624, which declared void all grants of the Crown for "the sole buying, selling, making, working, or using of anything" within the realm, except patents for new inventions, for printing, and for the manufacture of certain implements of war.

Justice Bradley went back still further, to the year 1215, and claimed that the right to economic liberty was asserted in Magna Carta where it was declared, "No freeman shall be taken, or impris-

---

[1] 161 Wall. 102; Trin. 44 Eliz. (1602), 11 Coke's Repts. 84, 86.
[2] Trin. 41 Eliz., Moore (K. B.) 576 (1599); 72 Eng. Rep. 769.

oned, or be disseized of his freehold, or liberties, or free customs, or be outlawed or exiled, or any otherwise destroyed, nor will we pass upon him nor condemn him, but by lawful judgment of his peers or by the law of the land." [1]

Historically, this reference to Magna Carta is now known to be incorrect.[2] The term "liberties," as used in that document, did not mean personal liberty nor economic liberty. Personal liberty was provided for under the other clause, "No freeman shall be taken or imprisoned." But the term "liberties" meant, in general, the feudal or other special privileges, immunities, jurisdictions, charters, or franchises, either granted directly by the crown to the subject or claimed by prescription, which presupposed a grant. They were not different, so far as validity was concerned, from the grants of lands by the sovereign to his subjects. The King could sell privileges and franchises, just as he could sell or give away the land belonging to the Crown.[3] Each, when granted, became a recognized exercise of the King's prerogative in the hands of grantees. The grant of even monopolies of trade was one of these privileges or franchises, so that when the barons of 1215 claimed their "liberties," or a gild of 1599 claimed the right to make by-laws under its charter, or a grantee of the King in 1602 claimed the right to his monopoly, or when feudal lords claimed their lands, they were claiming their "liberties."

"Franchise and liberty," said Blackstone, "are used as synonymous terms and their definition is a royal privilege, or branch of the King's prerogative, subsisting in the hand of a subject. Being therefore derived from the crown, they must arise from the King's grant; or in some cases may be held by prescription, which presupposes a grant." Blackstone mentions franchises to hold criminal (leet) or civil court; to have a manor or lordship; to have waifs, wrecks, estrays, treasure-trove, royal fish, or things that had caused the death of a man (deodand); to have a fair, or a market, or right of taking toll; to have a forest, chase, park, warren or fishery, carrying the King's exclusive right to kill the game. "It is likewise a franchise, for a number of persons to be incorporated, and subsist as a body politic; with a power to maintain perpetual succession, and do other corporate acts." [4]

---

[1] *Magna Carta*, Chap. 29, cited in 16 Wall. 114.
[2] McKechnie, W. S., *Magna Carta*, 394 (1914). Also Shattuck above cited.
[3] Holdsworth, W. S., *A History of English Law*, 1:169, 476 (3d ed., 1923).
[4] Bla. Com. 37.

Thus "liberties" were royal privileges and powers, all of them monopolistic in character, subsisting in the hands of subjects, and the very different meaning of liberty as absence of monopoly came not from the prerogative, but from the common law.

The common law originated in the customs of "freemen," or rather privileged men, in that they enjoyed the privilege of bringing suit in the King's court and of appearing as witnesses and jurors in assisting the King's justices to decide suits between each other. This privilege attended them on account of their military services to the King and their holding of lands as tenants directly or indirectly of the King. The "freeman" was a "freeholder," while the "unfree" were the serfs or copyholders and even the merchants and manufacturers of the villages and towns, who afterwards obtained their "freedom" by way of charters granted to their gilds or corporations.

It was out of these customs of freeholders, sanctioned and enforced by the King's justices, that the institutions of property and liberty were fashioned. The process consisted simply in prohibiting private vengeance on account of murder, robbery or theft, and requiring the plaintiffs and defendants to appear in court and to submit to the processes of court. It was the invention of writs requiring parties to attend the sessions of the court which "was really the making of the English Common Law." [1]

The King's object was originally only that of obtaining revenue and keeping his subjects peaceful, and it was out of this public purpose that his justices, with the help of freeholders, developed the procedure of trials and the remedies on behalf of suitors that henceforth became the legal rights of persons, property, and liberty.

From the earliest times these justices and landlords established the common-law rule against restraint of trade on the part of the petty merchants and manufacturers who were "unfree" in the sense that they might not participate in the King's courts. As early as the year 1300, it is asserted, an unlearned local court imposed a fine on several candle-makers who "made a covenant among themselves that none should sell a pound of candles cheaper than another." [2] Thus liberty of trade among business men became the common-law rule of the landlords until modified, in the 17th century, by the business-law rule of "fair trade."

[1] JENKS, EDW., *A Short History of English Law*, 45 (1912).
[2] POLLOCK, F., *The Genius of the Common Law*, 13 Col. Law Rev. 2-3 (1913).

It was these common-law concepts of personal rights, of property rights and liberty that came into conflict, in the reigns of Elizabeth and the Stuart Kings, with the prerogative of the monarch. The way was prepared for a double meaning of the word liberty. It might mean the "libertates" of Magna Carta, which were the privileges of land-lords granted by the monarch, or it might mean the liberty to buy and sell, to be free from violence, theft and trespass, derived from the approved customs which constituted the common law. The two were inconsistent. One was a contradiction of the other. Freedom, or liberty, in the sense of a grant out of the royal prerogative, stood for a relation of superior to inferior; freedom or liberty in the sense of the common law stood for a relation of equality between members of the same class. The first is more properly to be distinguished as "free-dom," the second as "liberty." [1] Freedom was a grant of power to participate in the privileges of those who were specially favored by a superior. Liberty was a common-law right to equality of treatment among individuals who belonged to the same class whether privileged or unprivileged. Equal liberty was consistent with unequal freedom.

It was this contradiction and double meaning of liberty that char-acterized the long struggle of the 17th century until it was finally closed by the Act of Settlement in the year 1700. When, during the reign of Elizabeth, industry expanded into national markets, one out of the several prerogatives of the King, the exclusive privilege to a market, likewise expanded. At first it was used by Elizabeth to foster the development of mineral resources, new industries, new processes and new materials or products, whether newly imported or newly invented. In this way it came to be extended to innumerable articles of merchandise and to sheer abuse by privileged favorites.[2] The political uprising on this account, which ended in the Common-wealth, is well known. On the legal side it was reflected in new defini-tions of monopoly and liberty, based on errors in interpreting the original meanings. These errors found their way into the cases of Davenant v. Hurdis and the Case of Monopolies at the close of Eliza-beth's reign, as well as other cases in the reign of James I.[3] The histor-ical error is attributed by McKechnie mainly to Coke, who, "following his vicious method of assuming the existence, in Magna Carta, of a

[1] Below, Chap. IV, Secs. IV, V.

[2] CUNNINGHAM, W., *The Growth of English Industry and Commerce*, 1:58, 75, 286 (1903). Justice Field's reference is at 16 Wall. 47.

[3] Tailors of Ipswich, 11 Coke, 53 (1615).

warrant for every legal principle of his own day, misled generations of commentators." [1]   Specifically, Coke, commenting on the term "liberties" (de libertatibus) as used in Magna Carta, declared that all monopolies were against the Great Charter, because "they are against the liberty and freedom of the subjects and against the law of the land." In this error, says McKechnie, Coke "has been assiduously followed." [2] The error, however, was made in a good cause, for, says McKechnie (133) "if the vague and inaccurate words of Coke have obscured the bearing of many chapters of Magna Carta and diffused false notions of the development of English law, the service these very errors have done to the cause of constitutional progress is measureless."

Thus the so-called "liberties" of Magna Carta on which the dissenting justices in the Slaughter House Cases relied in order to attach the notion of liberty of choice to the definition of property were exactly the opposite of liberty and property, for they were not only *not* property-rights but were a denial of rights of property and liberty in the hands of subjects other than those who held the original "liberties." The monopolies which came to the front with the expansion of industry in the time of Elizabeth were but what had been the unquestioned exercise of prerogative in granting to subjects the enjoyment of sovereign powers over other subjects. When, in Magna Carta, the barons claimed their "liberties" they were claiming personal privileges, or the right to exercise the powers of sovereignty. They were claiming, not liberty or property, but an advantageous position in government based on the personal relations of superior and inferior, of dominion and submission, which characterize the relation of sovereign power to privileged persons, and what Magna Carta asserted was that the barons should not be deprived by the King of these personal sovereign privileges. They were claims to the privileges of monopoly supported by the personal favor and superior power of the sovereign, and not claims to the equal liberty of all subjects to own and buy and sell property. In short, "liberty" meant, not liberty nor property, but political privilege.

The historical error of Coke in the definition of liberty was repeated by the minority justices in the Slaughter House Cases, in interpreting the Fourteenth Amendment, and afterwards by all of the justices in the Allgeyer Case. Meanwhile the court, in the Munn Case and the

---

[1] *Op. cit.*, McKechnie, 385.
[2] *Ibid.*, at 384; Coke, Second Institute, 47.

Minnesota Rate Case, as we have noted,[1] had been changing also the definition of power from physical power to economic power. The Constitution of the United States as well as the Fourteenth Amendment, as contended by the majority in the Slaughter House Cases, had been framed on the principles of the common law, in which the term property signifies physical objects, whether chattels or lands, held by one citizen for his own use against other citizens, and the term liberty signified freedom from slavery, as against other persons.

At the same time, under American conditions, the ancient prerogative of the King had become the police power of the legislature. Afterwards, in the Munn case the majority changed the definition of power. The prerogative, that is, the police power, is the physical power of the sovereign over subjects; whereas the kind of power recognized in the Munn Case was the economic power of citizen over citizen. Here, again, the two meanings of power coalesce, just as the two meanings of liberty had coalesced, for a legal monopoly or franchise, based, as it is, on direct participation in the physical power of the sovereign preventing competition, is economically similar to the power of such private property as a grain elevator in Chicago, whose owners have power to charge for their services more than they cost, owing to superior location but without legally preventing competition. In the one case competition is physically prevented; in the other case competition is economically prevented. In the one case the monopolist is favored by the sovereign as against the equal competitive liberty of others; in the other case the owner is favored by his economic situation while the sovereign treats his property and liberty equally with all others. Ultimately each, of course, rests upon the physical power of sovereignty to protect the holder of either the monopoly or the situation. But in the case of a legal monopoly the protection is the direct prohibition of competition, while in the case of a favorable situation the sovereign protects only the ownership of the situation. In either case, economic power emerges, since economic power is simply power to withhold from others what they need. In short, the change in the concept of property from physical things to the exchange-value of things is a change from a concept of *holding* things for one's own use to *withholding* things from others' use, protected, in either case by the physical power of the sovereign.

The transition from the notion of holding things for one's own use

[1] Above, Chap. II.

and enjoyment to the notion of economic power over others evidently accompanies the historical evolution of property from slavery, feudalism, colonialism and a sparse population, to marketing, business and the pressure of population on limited resources. Where production was isolated, or the owner held under his control all of the material things as well as the laborers necessary to the support of himself and dependents, the concept of exclusive holding for self was a workable definition of property. But when markets expanded, when laborers were emancipated, when people began to live by bargain and sale, when population increased and all resources became private property, then the power to *withhold* from others emerged gradually from that of exclusive *holding* for self as an economic attribute of property. The one is implied in the other, but is not unfolded until new conditions draw it out. Just as the scales of the reptile become the feathers of the bird when the environment moves from land to air, so exclusive *holding for self* becomes *withholding from others* when the environment moves from production to marketing. The transition was hardly noticeable as long as the merchant, the master, the laborer, were combined under small units of ownership, but becomes distinct when all opportunities are occupied and business is conducted by corporations on a credit system which consolidates property under the control of absentee owners. Then the power of property *per se*, distinguished from the power residing in personal faculties or special grants of sovereignty, comes into prominence. In the case of a sparse and isolated agricultural population and its accompanying handicraft stage of industry, represented by the butchers in the Slaughter House Cases, the owner's manual, mental and managerial faculties are inseparable from the operation of the physical plant. But in the corporations involved in the railroad and warehouse cases the managers and the laborers are agents and employees of owners at a distance, and the property of the latter exerts its silent power of command and obedience by the mere resolutions of unseen boards of directors. When to this is added the pressure of population and the increasing demand for limited supplies of mineral and metal resources, of water-powers, of lands situated at centers of population, then the mere holding of property becomes a power to withhold, far beyond that which either the laborer has over his labor or the investor has over his savings, and beyond anything known when this power was being perfected by the early common law or early business law. It becomes a power to extract things in exchange from other persons, in the absence of and wholly separate from individual human faculties—a power of property *per se*, silently operating but clearly seen and distinguishable from the manual, mental and managerial abilities of its owners.

This power of property in itself, the power to withhold, seen in these extreme cases, is but an enlargement of that power which exists in all property as the source of value-in-exchange and which may be distinguished as *waiting-power*, the power to hold back until the opposite party consents to the bargain. While, *as investors*, they perform the indispensable service of waiting for compensation, yet *as bargainers* they determine through their power to wait what shall be the terms on which that compensation shall be made. Waiting-power emerges out of waiting-service when both the natural opportunities are occupied and the individual services of hundreds and thousands of investors are brought together in the collective power of corporations holding access to market opportunities.

The concept of the functioning of property correspondingly enlarges. The concept of exclusive holding for use and enjoyment of self is identical with that aspect of property which we have distinguished as "economy." It is the activity merely of proportioning, without expanding, one's possessions and powers so as to obtain the maximum net income from all. The legal concept of *holding* is the economic concept of *economy*. But this proportioning consists solely in determining the various directions in which actual power shall be exerted. Hence, when the expansion side of property emerges in an environment of buying and selling, then the legal concept of exclusive holding becomes also the economic concept of power through withholding from others. Holding is economy, withholding is economic power.

It is the slow unfolding of property from *holding* to *withholding* that prevents its significance from being observed at first. The minority justices in the Slaughter House Cases added the notion of choice to the notion of holding physical things, but their idea of choice was evidently not that of choice between two degrees of power over other people but a *choice between physical things*. This kind of choosing is, however, in fact, a choice between degrees of power, but the object over which power is exercised is the forces of nature, not the will of other persons. Such a concept of power belongs properly enough to the physical sciences in their engineering aspects. Man conquers nature by overcoming her resistance, which as Adam Smith suggested, is a kind of exchange with nature. And in doing so he chooses what appears to be the line of least resistance, which is also the line of greatest power. This is true of physics, chemistry, biology or even psychology, all of which are aids in overcoming resistance of things, of animals and of human beings.

But in these cases the resistance is set up by objects which have no right to resist and no right to withhold their services in exchange. It is different with citizens as distinguished from human beings. They have an ethical or legal *right* to withhold, a right protected, or believed to be protected, by a superior power, and the degree of power therefore is believed to be of consequence to that superior authority in determining what should be done in the matter. This feature was overlooked, or perhaps not called in question, at first, and therefore the definition of liberty of choice, or "liberty of contract," given by the minority in the Slaughter House Cases and adopted afterwards by the majority, was left in the position of a kind of "natural right" to choose between different degrees of power over the forces of nature, or else of a merely passive choice between social opportunities offered, but without any exercise of power over the offerer. In this respect their idea of choosing belongs rather to the notion of "economy" instead of "expansion." It is choice in the sense of a preference that concerns nobody else, not choice in the sense of power over others. The definition still lingers in the stage of engineering economy, or business economy, and has not advanced to that of political economy which was afterwards reached in the Munn Case. In the latter case the power to withhold from others is deemed to be a coercive power to be restrained by the physical power of the sovereign.

This enlargement of property from economy to economic power also separates, or at least distinguishes, management from ownership. For the activity of management is mainly that of proportioning the factors so as to get the largest net result from all; but the function of ownership is that of determining the conditions, terms, prices or values, at which the factors shall be obtained from others or the product sold to others.

It is the slow and often scarcely perceptible unfolding of property from holding to withholding, from economy to power, from ownership to management, that serves to explain in part the adherence of the courts to the primitive ideas of property, while the thing itself has been moving unnoticed into a larger environment. It is this that leads us to distinguish not merely economic power from physical power, but also to distinguish these from that power of personality which we shall name Moral Power.

Under the primitive common-law notions of property as exclusive holding of physical objects for one's own use, it scarcely was visible that the functioning of property is the power which it adds to the owner's commands, persuasions or coercions. These relationships were personal relationships depending on the relative strength of the manual, mental and managerial faculties of persons. If there came before the court inequalities to be corrected, the inequalities did not spring from the power of property but from the inequalities in the personal faculties, or from personal privileges granted by a personal sovereign. These inequalities of personal faculties arose through some advantageous position which one person held, compared with another, not so much through ownership as through personal relations of superior and inferior, dominion and submission, essential to human intercourse. The principal relation of this kind, the relation of sovereign to subject, we have just now considered in the grants of "liberties" or special privileges to favored subjects. This is historically a personal relation of dominion and submission, and not a property relation of equal rights of ownership. Similar power of superior over inferior persons, distinct from the economic power of property, are the relation of parent and child, man and wife, guardian and ward, physician and patient, attorney and client, confessor and penitent, principal and agent, master and servant, and so on. It is out of these personal relations of superior to inferior, and not out of the property relations of economic power, that the courts, previously to the Munn Case, had developed the doctrine of the possibility of an undue exercise of personal power under the various names of "undue influence," "duress," "coercion" and "inadequacy of compensation."

As we have already observed, the monopolies which came to the front with the expansion of industry in the time of Elizabeth were but what had been the unquestioned exercise of the personal physical power of the sovereign in granting to subjects the enjoyment of his sovereign powers over other subjects. They were personal privileges, not property ownership. That which permitted the ownership of property itself to emerge was both the abolition of some of these special privileges and the extension of others of these privileges to citizens on terms of equality. This signified the reduction of the personal influence of the sovereign or of his favorites, in using the sovereign power of physical coercion over persons, and, along with the abolition of violence, fraud and similar unequal personal relations, permitted the mere holding of private property to start on its own line of strictly economic power.

In those fields where absentee ownership did not offer an evident distinction between management and ownership the evolution of legal doctrine adhered closely to personal inequalities and did not recognize nor concede inequalities springing from the mere economic power of property. In the early common law "duress," for example, arose from personal inequality. The standard of coercion required to be proven in order to avoid a contract on the plea of duress was at first that of physical violence, and consisted in such imminent danger to life, limb or property as might overcome the will of a courageous and steadfast man. This was gradually modified so that the standard became, for a time, that of a person of only ordinary firmness. These objective standards applied only to acts or threats of physical violence, such as loss of life, or limb, disablement or imprisonment, and did not even apply to threats or actual detention of property. Finally, in recent times, another modification has been made, and duress has come to mean, not these external standards but the actual condition of mind produced in a person by threats of almost any kind rendering him incapable of exercising free will.[1] At no point, however, is duress or coercion conceived to reside in the mere unequal economic power of withholding objects that others need. It is always inequality of physical, mental or managerial faculties, not inequality of economic power springing from ownership.

A similar distinction between unequal faculties and unequal ownership appears in the doctrine of "undue influence," a doctrine growing out of confidential or special relations of superiority, such as those suggested above, of parent and child, guardian and ward, husband and wife, lawyer and client, broker and customer, and so on. Here the undue, or unequal, influence is considered to be a variety of fraud [2] or breach of confidential or other personal relations of trust, advice, or influence. Even in these cases the fact that the consideration, or the compensation, received by the weaker party to a contract is inadequate

---

[1] Galusha v. Sherman, 105 Wis. 263, 274, 278 (1900).
[2] Pollock on Contract, 648 ff., 667 (9th ed., 1921).

will not, of itself, afford ground for cancelling the contract between them, although there may arise a presumption that it is voidable.[1] It is a personal relationship of confidence that is taken advantage of, not a property relationship of economic power.

But if there is no personal relation between the parties recognized as confidential or special—relations which are not supposed to exist in the usual contracts of merchant and customer, employer and employee—then inadequacy of compensation not only does not furnish, of itself, a presumption of undue influence, but the presumption is against it and in favor of letting the parties alone. The courts will not weigh the relative skill of parties to a contract and, merely from a disparity between them, avoid a contract obtained from the less skillful party. This obtains even if one of the parties is an individual and the other a skillful lawyer or manager acting as the agent of a corporation.[2] According to these views it is not unlawful to impose upon another person a pecuniary sacrifice if the prevailing party or his agent is otherwise within his legal rights.[3] Even at the extreme limit of the "unconscionable contract" it is not mere inequality of ownership but inequality of personal relations that is looked for if the contract is to be annulled. Such a contract is one in which the inequality is "so strong, gross and manifest that it must be impossible to state it to a man of common sense without producing an exclamation at the inequality of it." In such a case "where the inadequacy of price is so great that the mind revolts at it, the court will lay hold on the slightest circumstances of oppression or advantage to rescind the contract." But the inadequacy of consideration is itself "merely a circumstance among others to be used in determining whether fraud or undue in-

---

[1] Page on Contracts, par. 225 (1905).

[2] Dundee v. Connor, 46 N. J. Eq. 576, 581 (1890), where a widow was induced by the company's attorney to accept less than the amount due on account of the death of her husband.

[3] Coppage v. Kansas, 236 U. S. 1, 9 (1915), where an employee was required to resign his union membership carrying life insurance if he retained his job. Cases cited in support are: Hackley v. Headley, 45 Mich. 569 (1881), where a creditor in immediate danger of bankruptcy was coerced by his debtor in scaling down a debt although it was already overdue, in order to get immediately the means of avoiding bankruptcy. Emery v. City of Lowell, 127 Mass. 139, 141 (1879), where the principle was stated, "it would be unsafe to leave the question of recovering money paid to depend on the urgency of the need of the party when paying it." Silliman v. U. S., 101 U. S. 465, 471 (1879), where certain claimants yielded to a "plain violation" of their right and accepted reduced compensation "solely because they required, or supposed they required, money for the conduct of their business or to meet their pecuniary obligations to others." Custin v. Viroqua, 67 Wis. 314 (1886), where the claimant was not allowed to recover an illegal license fee which he had paid under business necessity.

fluence exist," though it may be so "gross as of itself to prove fraud or imposition." [1]

There is, however, to be noted an important distinction between "duress" and economic coercion. The courts distinguish "duress of person" and "duress of goods." Duress of person is threats of physical violence, duress of goods is the retention by one person of goods belonging to another in order to force the latter to do something against his will. Hence duress of goods is *unlawful* withholding from others, but economic coercion is *lawful* withholding from others. Duress of goods is withholding from a person what rightfully belongs to him and is needed by him, but economic coercion is withholding from a person what does not belong to him, yet is needed by him. Duress of goods is unlawful economic coercion; economic coercion is lawful coercion.

Thus it is perfectly lawful, as follows from Justice Pitney's conclusion in the Coppage Case, in 1915, to exercise either superior economic power or superior mental and managerial faculties, over others, provided advantage is not taken of recognized special personal relations of confidence, trust, dependence, or the like, which are deemed peculiarly liable to abuse. And if there is revolting abuse of economic power, that of itself is not a legal abuse, though the court may be stirred by it to "lay hold on the slightest circumstance of oppression or advantage to rescind the contract." It would be a "most dangerous" and "unequal doctrine," said Justice Cooley in the case mentioned in the footnote,[2] that "the same contract which would be valid if made with a man easy in his circumstances becomes invalid when the contracting party is pressed with the necessity of immediately meeting his bank paper."

It is proper enough that the courts should hesitate to rescind contracts even in these extreme "hold-up" cases, for a judicial decision is usually retroactive legislation. It is different, however, when the court declares unconstitutional the acts of a legislature designed to prevent in advance the making of coercive contracts. Having established by judicial precedents the right of the stronger party to take advantage of his strength, the courts have declared unconstitutional, as in the Coppage and other cases,[3] various statutes attempting to prevent the coercion which the courts hesitate to correct *ex post facto*.

---

[1] See cases cited in preceding note.

[2] Hackley v. Headley, 45 Mich. 569, 577, (1881). See also Pollock, Anson, Page, on the general subject of duress, undue influence, inadequacy, and unconscionable contracts.

[3] See below, Chap. IV. Sec. II.

These statutes were usually annulled on the ground that they deprived owners of liberty or property without due process of law. The opinions seem often to be survivals of the primitive definition of "property" as mere holding things for one's own use, or of "liberty" as the mere passive choosing of opportunities, after the thing itself had expanded into power to withhold and after the court itself, in other cases, as in the Munn Case and the railroad cases, had recognized this expansion. It could hardly be expected that the legal ideas should keep pace with all the facts, and the lag might not have been important had it not been that under the American constitutions the courts exercise a veto on the legislatures and executives when the latter endeavor to keep up with the changes in economic conditions. It is quite proper that the courts should not change their definitions too suddenly, for people and legislatures act on the expectation that the courts will adhere to the old definitions, and a change in definition amounts to *ex post facto* legislation, for a dispute is not usually acted upon by the court until after somebody has acted or threatened to act, and a change in definition changes the terms of all contracts and all expectations upon which the people, the legislatures and the congress had previously acted. This was evidently what happened when the court changed the definition of liberty and property in the 14th Amendment from liberty of the slave to liberty of the owner of property. It is different with the legislatures which are expressly prohibited by the Constitution from enacting *ex post facto* laws, and consequently the acts of that branch of government apply only to future contracts and future acts of the people. When, then, in such cases, the court adheres to the old definition and vetoes the statute, it prevents the legislature from advancing the definition of property to fit the new facts of power, although the court itself, in other cases, had advanced the definition to fit the new facts of liberty.

It is not, of course, intended that there is a clear-cut, predetermined, division between personal power and property power. The two are always associated, for property is but the instrument through which persons operate. Property is opportunities for the exercise of faculties. The line of division between persons and property is rather a zone of uncertain width, the one or the other clearly predominating only as they emerge on either side of the zone, according to the observed facts in each case. It is only intended to assert that the power of property emerges with the progress of economic conditions after the progress of democracy has leveled the political privileges of superior persons.

The economic conditions advance at different rates of speed in different fields, or are called to the attention of the court with different degrees of popular or influential support, as was the situation in the case of Munn v. Illinois, and the Minnesota Rate Case. In other fields they advance more slowly or are not so vigorously protested. There is one respect, however, that of the usury laws, in which the acts of the legislature restraining economic power have not been questioned. These laws appear to be a deprivation of property and liberty in the same sense as various labor laws which have been declared unconstitutional. A reason for this distinction was given by Justice Field, in the Munn Case, where he contended that the loaning of money at interest was a special privilege. Referring probably to the statute of 1545, which, although as a concession to prevailing prejudice it condemned exactions for the mere "use" of money, yet permitted payment of "interest" at a limited rate,[1] Justice Field had said in the Munn Case, "The practice of regulating by legislation the interest receivable, for the use of money, when considered with reference to its origin, is only the assertion of a right of the government to control the extent to which a privilege granted by it may be exercised and enjoyed. By the ancient common law it was unlawful to take any money for the use of money. . . . Parliament interfered and made it lawful to take a limited amount of interest. It was not upon the theory that the legislature could arbitrarily fix the compensation which one could receive for the use of property which, by the general law, was the subject of hire for compensation, that Parliament acted, but in order to confer a privilege which the common law denied." [2]

Thus even the legal justification of restraints on the rate of interest taken for money, where mere economic power stands out distinct from personal inequalities, is based, not on the sovereign's authority to restrain the power of property but on his authority to regulate a privilege granted out of the royal prerogative. To the medieval mind and the common law, property as such, the mere holding of lands and chattels, did not endow one with economic power. Such property was for use and enjoyment, and the power which owners possessed proceeded not from ownership but from superior personal station or the

---

[1] CUNNINGHAM, W., The Growth of English Industry and Commerce, 153 (1903).
[2] 94 U. S. 113, 153, (1876).

enjoyment of special privileges bestowed personally by rulers. The ownership of money, on the other hand, was the ownership of mere power, for money produced nothing, could not be consumed, and was used only to take advantage of the necessities of others. When, therefore, the privilege of charging interest on money was granted, it was a grant out of the physical power of the sovereign, overriding the common law from which the rights of property had been derived, and carried with it the sovereign's reservation of authority to determine the limit beyond which that grant of power should not be exercised. And Justice Field was historically correct in his contention that restraints on the rates of interest, based on a sovereign grant of power, afforded no precedent for restraints on the economic power of property.[1]

The Munn Case was an innovation in that it recognized a source of power unknown to the common law and unrevealed until property assumed its modern dimensions. The Munn Case decided that the power of property might be restrained in dealings with customers. It was not until the year 1898 that the highest court decided that the similar power of property in the transactions of employer and employee might also be restrained. In that year an act of the legislature of Utah came before the court limiting the hours of labor in underground mines to eight per day. Justice Brown, after reviewing the cases and disavowing any intention of criticising those courts which had declared similar laws unconstitutional, went on to show that modern economic conditions had increased the power of property over employees, and that the courts had begun to notice it. They "had not failed to recognize the fact," he said, "that the law is a progressive science," that the right of contract, only recently asserted in the Allgeyer Case was nevertheless subject to certain limitations which the state might impose under the police power; that this power had greatly expanded during the past century; that in its exercise a large discretion is necessarily vested in the legislature, and that "the legislature has also recognized the fact which the experience of legislators in many states has corroborated, that the proprietors of these establishments and their

---

[1] But see Hand, Learned, "Due Process of Law and the Eight Hour Day," 21 *Harv. Law Rev.* 495, 505 note (1908); Pound, "Liberty of Contract," 18 *Yale Law Jour.* 454, 483 (1909), says the "obvious answer" to this contention of Justice Field is that, "enforcing a promise not under seal is also a late, law-granted privilege." I have not been able to locate the statute here referred to, and Jenks (*History of English Law*, 136) seems to trace the appearance of the law enforcing an unsealed promise to the common law without the aid of statute, except the mere procedural provision in Westminster the Second, 1285, which permitted enlargement of the common-law writs "in similar cases."

operatives do not stand upon an equality and that their interests are, to a certain extent, conflicting. The former naturally desire to obtain as much labor as possible from their employees, while the latter are often induced by the fear of discharge to conform to regulations which their judgment, fairly exercised, would pronounce to be detrimental to their health or strength. In other words, the proprietors lay down the rules and the laborers are practically constrained to obey them. In such cases self-interest is often an unsafe guide, and the legislature may properly interpose its authority. . . . The fact that both parties are of full age and competent to contract does not necessarily deprive the state of the power to interfere where the parties do not stand upon an equality, or where the public health demands that one party to the contract shall be protected against himself." [1]

This principle, limited in 1898 to the industries of mining and smelting, was extended in 1916 to apply to all manufacturing industries.[2] In 1917 the principle was still further extended to cover wages as well as hours of labor. This occurred, however, through the deadlock of an equally divided court, which therefore sustained a statute fixing the minimum wages for women. Since no opinion was given in the case it may be inferred that the court supported the Oregon court wherein it had declared "Every argument put forward to sustain the maximum hours law, or upon which it was established, applies equally in favor of the constitutionality of the minimum wage law as also within the police power of the state and as a regulation tending to guard the public morals and the public health." [3]

The foregoing enables us to distinguish the three kinds of power above referred to which are inseparable in fact but emerge with different degrees of prominence in different transactions. One is physical power, the power of violence, upon which the grants of special privilege by a sovereign to subjects are based and protected. This was the main type of power recognized during the period of feudalism.

Second, is economic power, a kind of power which could not emerge until physical power had been regulated by "due process or law," and thus the rights of property had been established by the business revolu-

---

[1] Holden v. Hardy, 169 U. S. 366, 381, 392, 397 (1898). A different state of facts afterwards determined the veto of a ten-hour law for bakers. Lochner v. New York, 198 U. S. 45 (1905).

[2] Bunting v. Oregon, 243 U. S. 426 (1916).

[3] Stettler v. O'Hara, 69 Or. 519, 535 (1914); 243 U. S. 629 (1917). This opinion apparently has been reversed in 1923 in Adkins v. Children's Hospital, 43 Sup. Ct. 394 (1923).

tion that ended with the Act of Settlement, in 1700; and even then not until modern economic conditions had revealed the power which property has by mere withholding from others what they need but which does not belong to them.

Third, is moral power, which, however, may be "immorally" used; the power of personal influence unaided by violence or economic power, a kind of power which emerges only when unequal physical and economic power are eliminated.

It is the relative predominance of these three types of power that distinguishes the three great types of going concerns which we shall later examine,[1] namely, the state, based on the fear of physical power, or violence; the business, based on the fear of economic power, or poverty; and the great variety of modern cultural, religious, or moral concerns, based only on the fear of opinion unsupported by fear of violence or poverty.

[1] Below, Chap. V.

CHAPTER IV

TRANSACTIONS

I. The Parties

When economists and courts speak of an "exchange" they usually think of two persons exchanging products or services, but when they speak of a "market" they think of two or more sellers and two or more buyers of similar commodities at a common place and time. Thus the distinction may be made between actual transactions and potential, possible and impossible transactions. The *actual* transactions occur, of course, between those who actually exchange products. The *potential* transactions are those which *may* or *may not* occur, since the parties are on the market and ready to exchange but do not. The *possible* transactions are those which *might* occur if conditions were different, such that parties not now upon the market should decide to come upon the market. To which may be added the *impossible* transactions which, owing to remoteness in time or place and the consequent inaccessibility of the parties to the market, cannot, under any circumstances, take place.[1]

These four degrees of probability are taken into account, more or less consciously, by every person who comes upon, or contemplates coming upon, the given market. But the actual choice made by any person who actually exchanges upon the market is a choice, not between the actual exchange and the possible or impossible exchanges, nor even all of the potential exchanges, but is a choice between only the actual and the next best of the potential exchanges which he has an option of making at the moment of exchange. He gains a surplus by choosing, but the actual surplus obtainable is measured by the choice between the *two best accessible* options. Failure to observe this limitation on the act of choice has led to palpable fallacies of both optimistic and pessimistic schools of economists, which may be designated in general as the fallacy of inaccessible or non-concomitant options, inaccessible in space, or non-concomitant in time.[2]

[1] Below, Sec. III.
[2] Cp. BASTIAT, F., *Harmonies of Political Economy*, 104 (tr. 1860); below, Sec. III.

At the same time, each person coming upon the market has in mind, or is faced by, these several degrees of probability. Choice of opportunities is always choice between the two best accessible options at the moment of choice, and if there is no possible alternative, then the exchange may be of that "hold-up" character which we have noted,[1] in which there is no real freedom of choice; or the next best alternative may be possible but not potential, and even if potential may not be the next best potential. Thus there is a gradation of alternatives taken into account by each party to a transaction, and consequently, *from the standpoint of the motives affecting the parties*, the minimum number of persons necessary to constitute a transaction is four parties, two buyers and two sellers, namely, the actual buyer and seller, and the next best alternative for each. Other potential, possible or impossible exchanges are in the background. This may be illustrated as follows:

A TRANSACTION

ACTUAL	POTENTIAL	POSSIBLE	IMPOSSIBLE
$100 B	B' $ 90	$ 80	o
$110 S	S' $120	$130	o

The actual buyer, B, of, say, a horse or cow, comes upon the market hoping to buy at, say, $100, the actual seller, S, hoping to sell at $110. The potential buyer hopes to buy at $90, the potential seller hopes to sell at $120. The other potential, or possible buyers and sellers will not ordinarily become actual buyers and sellers until those who are nearest together have first gotten off the market. They are possible exchangers. Hence the two best opportunities for the actual seller, S, are the offers of $100 and $90. Evidently the actual seller cannot be forced to sell for less than $90. On the other hand, the best two opportunities for the actual buyer are the offers to sell at $110 and $120. Evidently the actual buyer cannot be forced to pay more than $120. Consequently the actual price agreed upon by B and S will lie somewhere between $90 and $120. Between these two points may be said to be the field of persuasion and coercion, and at these points are the limits of coercion, because at these points the opposite party has a costless alternative. Beyond these two points only persuasion can induce the exchange to be made.

It will be seen that the transaction, involving four persons, indicates

[1] Above, Chap. III.

the two dimensions of opportunity and power present in every transaction. For the seller, S, the opportunities offered are the $100 offered by B and the $90 offered by B'. For the buyer, B, the opportunities are the $110 asked by S and the $120 asked by S', and the actual power in exchange lies somewhere between $90 and $120.

This typical transaction describes the minimum of all economic and social relations whatever, whether it be that of the family, of business or politics. Each person is considering the alternatives open to himself, the existence of actual, potential, possible or impossible rivals, and the degree of power which he can exert within the limits of these alternatives. One is his choice of opportunities, the other is his exercise of power, but they are inseparable, and choice of opportunities is choice between two degrees of power. Out of this ultimate and universal nature of a transaction, *from the standpoint of the motives affecting the will*, economics derives its concepts of cost and value, of "opportunity-cost" and "dis-opportunity value," that is, its concepts of exercise of power and choice of opportunities.[1]

But there are an indefinite number of possible disputes between the parties to the transaction that may arise before or after the completion of the transaction. These disputes do arise and always have arisen in the history of the race from the most primitive times, simply because man has always been subject to the principle of scarcity which limits his choice of opportunities and exercise of power. Consequently, if transactions are to go on peaceably without resort to violence between the parties there must always have been a fifth party to the transaction, namely, a judge, priest, chieftain, paterfamilias, arbitrator, foreman, superintendent, general manager, who would be able to decide and settle the dispute, with the aid of the combined power of the group to which the five parties belonged. This fifth party might, indeed, be a lawless and arbitrary ruler, in which case each of the four parties would be victims of conquest or slavery and not recognized members of the group to which the ruler belonged. But if he and they are members of the same family, tribe, nation, business concern, club or what not—in short, members of the same going concern— then his arbitrary and lawless power has always been found to be itself limited by common rules, or working rules, the "laws" of the concern.

These working rules of going concerns, have, in point of their his-

[1] Cp. DAVENPORT, H. J., *Value and Distribution* (1908); *Economics of Enterprise* (1913).

torical origin, been ascribed to many different sources, such as gods, ancestors, conquerors, "nature," "will of the people," etc., the general idea being to clothe them with a certain sanctity or authority above that of the particular priest, chieftain, judge, et al., who may, for the time being, be in position of power to give effect to his interpretation of them. At any rate, they appear, in the history of the race, as the essential and ultimate means by which the members of a going concern are able to work together for a common purpose and to exert their united power against other concerns.

The way in which these working rules operate is by placing certain limits or by opening up certain enlargements for the choices and powers of the individuals, who are parties to the transactions, and these limits and enlargements of the individual wills may be condensed into the four volitional verbs, (1) may, (2) must, (3) can and (4) cannot. These verbs express the limits of behavior for any individual who is subject to any common rule or working rule of any concern. The rule merely tells him what he may, must, can or cannot do.

But when these permissions, compulsions, capacities, and incapacities suggested by these four verbs have been organized into a system of thought by later generations of theologians, philosophers or jurists, they take certain ethical or juristic names which may be distinguished, in the order in which we have named them, as (1) liberty or immunity (2) duty or liability, (3) right or power, (4) disability or exposure. These we shall consider later.[1] It is needful here only to note that in consequence of the need of common rules applying to the wills of the individual members of families tribes, nations or the modern business concerns, there is a fifth party to every transaction, namely, the governor, or rather, the judge who lays down the working rules of the concern under the name of rights, duties, liberties, etc., involving the further social relation of command by a superior representing the power of the group, and obedience by inferiors, who are members of the group.

A transaction, then, involving a minimum of five persons, and not an isolated individual, nor even only two individuals, is the ultimate unit of economics, ethics and law. It is the ultimate but complex relationship, the social electrolysis, that makes possible the choice of opportunities, the exercise of power and the association of men into families, clans, nations, business, unions and other going concerns.

[1] Below, Sec. VI.

The social unit is not an individual seeking his own pleasure: it is five individuals doing something to each other within the limits of working rules laid down by those who determine how disputes shall be decided.

II. Performance, Avoidance, Forbearance

There hangs over from early theories a notion of the individual will which may be described as the *will-in-vacuo*, instead of the *will-in-action*. According to John Locke, who formulated this concept, the will is conceived, not as the will-in-action overcoming resistance and choosing between different degrees of resistance, in actual space and time, but the will is a "power," in the sense of a faculty, a capacity, an ability, to act or not-act.[1] It conforms to that notion of "power" characteristic of all branches of knowledge at the mythological stage prior to their passing over into the quantitative or scientific stage, where "power" was a kind of potency, a potentiality, a hidden essence of things, a "ding an sich," a kind of spirit, entity or inner substance, dwelling in things, like the phlogiston of chemistry, or the vortexes of astronomy. These notions of power have disappeared more or less from the other sciences, and power has become power-in-action, known only by its behavior, not power in its essence or substance, known by magic, intuition, or introspection.

The notion of the will as a potency still remains, however, in legal and ethical doctrine, as John Locke formulated it, just as it is, in fact, the most intimate and personal of all the notions which one can have of himself. We naturally consider our will as something different from ourselves in action. We will to do one thing and actually do something else.

Yet is our actual will anything but what we actually do? The concept of the will-in-vacuo arises from a process of introspection. But introspection can give us only that small part of our will which rises above the threshhold of the unconscious or physiological. John Locke's concept of power was the equivalent of this unconscious or physiological part of the will, undiscoverable in the attempt to explain the will in terms of introspection. The great unconscious part, with its potential feelings, emotions and ideas, coming from heredity, habit, custom and past willings, rises up and takes its part in shaping the act at the moment of action. We do not even know ourselves fully until

[1] Locke, John, *An Essay concerning Human Understanding*, Chapter on "Power," (1696).

we act. For our act is our adaptation of our faculties to and our control over our opportunities, and our real will is our will adapting itself to and controlling the environment.

Hence we have two concepts of the will and its faculties, one of which is that of the potential, possible, idealistic, or imaginary, springing from the puzzle of the unconscious, and the other is that of the actual behavior. The actual is always acting. The imaginary is what it might have done, or ought to have done, or what we hope it would be able to do, or consciously would like to do, if it did not have to choose between actual alternatives.

It is this introspective potency, this will separated from its behavior, that dominates the concept of choices formulated by John Locke and repeated in the law-books. This appears in the definition of an "act" and an "omission." An "act" is a "voluntary movement of the muscles," an "omission" is a not-act. Back of the act is the will; the will is volition, that is, choice; the will chooses between an "act" and an "omission"—between an acting and a not-acting. As far as quantitative dimensions are concerned there is none. An omission to act is a zero act. Not-acting is nothing. The will chooses between something and nothing.

Neither is there any dimension to the something. As far as the definition goes, the act may be an infinite act—an act of God. If the will merely chooses between acting and not-acting, its choice may just as well be between infinity and zero, which, for finite beings, is the same as between nothing and nothing.

The reason why this empty concept of the will has been a workable concept in ethics and law proceeds from the two-fold fact that the moralist or the trial court already has a particular act in mind,[1] and he is concerned with the *quality* of that act, whether it be virtuous or vicious, right or wrong, or with the *responsibility* of the actor for doing or not doing it. The act is already there, in its quantitative dimensions as shown in the testimony, and the question remaining is, Did he do it intentionally or unintentionally? Was he compelled to do it? Was he prevented from doing it? Was it voluntary or involuntary? Was the act virtuous or vicious, right or wrong? These are questions relating to the *kind* of an act and the kind of will that acted. Was that will just or unjust when it performed that act or omitted to perform it? An act is properly defined as "a voluntary movement

[1] Below, Sec. IV.

of the muscles." But the attention of the court is directed, not to the muscles, but to the intentions that moved the muscles.

With this limited purpose in view, and the quantitative dimensions of the act and its consequences already in evidence, the legal classification of acts as merely "acts and omissions" is perhaps adequate in a trial court. The fallacy emerges when, from such a limited purpose, the larger purpose is not distinguished. The larger purpose is the definition of the will itself. If that definition is restricted to the idea of a choice between acting and not-acting, then the will is merely a separate faculty or power, a potency to act or not-act, a will in a vacuum. Freedom of the will becomes freedom to act or not-act. Liberty becomes simply the absence of restraint or compulsion and therefore becomes liberty to act or not-act.

This larger purpose of defining the will in all its diminsions does not come before a trial court which takes the law as it finds it, but it sometimes does come before a Supreme Court which decides upon the validity of the law itself under the due-process clause of the Constitution. Here the court is dealing with the will as an economic quantity and is passing upon the economic or quantitative question of public policy. This becomes a practical question when the court is considering that quantitative problem which turns on the meaning of "equality" and "inequality" as used or implied in the Constitution of the United States. Is the will of an individual equal to the collective will of a corporation? A majority of the Supreme Court of the United States holds that it is, and overruled the Legislature and the Supreme Court of Kansas which held that it was not.[1] The Kansas Legislature attempted to protect the will of the individual against the will of the corporation. The higher federal court said that the attempt was not due process of law because the *rights* of the two were exactly equal. The workingman had the right to choose between working for the corporation and not working for it. The corporation had the equal right to choose between employing the man and not employing him. The two *rights* on the two sides of the transaction were exactly equal. There was "equality of right," because each had the equal right to choose between acting and not-acting, between an "act" and an "omission."

This abstract conclusion flows from the concept of the will as a mere potency, a mere faculty of acting and not-acting. But, as such,

[1] Above, Chap. III.

it is empty, and in the quantitative concept of the will, which, whether it be economic, physical, ethical, or legal, is a concept of choosing between two degrees of power in acting, it is not true. If the corporation has 10,000 employees it loses only one ten thousandth part of its working force if it chooses to not-employ the man, and cannot find an alternative man. But the man loses 100 per cent of his job if he chooses to not-work and cannot find an alternative employer. From the standpoint of an abstract concept of the will as a mere faculty of acting or not-acting, the two *rights* may be equal, just because nothing is equal to nothing. But, from the quantitative concept of the will as a choosing between actual alternatives in a world of limited opportunities, the right of the one is infinitely greater —or perhaps 10,000 times greater—than the right of the other.

Likewise, from this *qualitative* standpoint, the duty of one is doubtless equal to the duty of the other. It is the duty of the man not to force that corporation to hire and pay him against its will. It is the duty of the corporation not to force the man to work for it against his will. The two duties of *omission* may be said to be equal, simply because they have no quantitative content, just as infinity may be said to be equal to zero, or nothing equal to nothing.

But, from the quantitative standpoint, the duty of each is the necessity of each to choose something else; and that something else is not a "thing," it is a degree of power over persons or things. The behavioristic concept of the will is that of a will continuously in action through all the waking and conscious hours of life. Some of its choices are instinctive, habitual, unconscious. But its crucial choices are conscious, perhaps deliberative. Such a will never chooses between acting and not-acting—it always chooses between two degrees of power in acting. It cannot help choosing, consciously or unconsciously. If not pulled on by unconscious wish it is pushed on by conscious want or necessity, and its choices, quantitatively considered, differ only in the different degrees or durations of power opened up by the actual opportunities offered at the time. If the will does not do one thing, it is doing and *must* do something else where its power is less.

The question is not a mathematical question of imaginary points and lines, of equality or inequality, of an empty right or duty, but is a question of relative degrees of economic or physical power in the process of choosing between alternative opportunities. This is a question of valuation and the proper proportioning of relative degrees of power of persons over persons. Such a question is one of public policy, not one of mathematics. We are not here concerned as to whether the attempt of the Kansas Legislature was *wise* as a matter of public policy. Perhaps it was not. We are concerned with the difference between logic and value. Logic is an after-thought— valuation comes first, then logic comes in to justify the valuation. The majority of the Supreme Court did not of course place their veto of the Kansas Legislature and the Kansas Supreme Court on the grounds of public policy—they placed it on John Locke's definition of the will. Questions of public policy involve a weighing, a valuing, of the alternatives actually present. Locke's definition of the will admits of no valuation of alternatives in an actual world of limited resources which resist the will. It is as empty, logical, and non-quantitative as the imaginary lines and points of mathematics. The logic of the majority in the Coppage Case suggests an earlier remark of Justice Holmes, when he said, "Perhaps one of the reasons why judges do not like to discuss questions of policy, or to put a decision in terms upon their views as law-makers, is that the moment you leave the path of merely logical deduction you lose the illusion of certainty which makes legal reasoning seem like mathematics. But the certainty is only an illusion, nevertheless. Views of policy are taught by experience of the interests of life. Those interests are the field of battle. Whatever decisions are made must be against the wishes and opinion of one party, and the distinctions on which they go will be distinctions of degree." [1]

These distinctions of degree require us to note the difference between a transaction and a process. A transaction occurs at a point of time, a process is a flow of transactions over a period of time. We are concerned here with the point of time.

But we are concerned with the two kinds of transactions previously considered, physical and economic, each of which is a relation of power. The same terminology will apply to each, though with the different meanings of physical power and economic power.

The physical or mechanical equivalent of the will corresponds to a concept of the will employing its faculties in the actual mechanical process of action and reaction with nature's forces, or in transactions with other wills, also employing their faculties. With such a concept

---

[1] HOLMES, O. W., "Privilege, Malice, and Intent," 8 *Harv. Law Rev.* 1, 7 (1894).

of the will the idea sought to be expressed by the term "omission" is better expressed by the term *avoidance*. The duty to omit a certain act is the duty to avoid that act, with the implied command to choose any other potential, possible, or impossible act not prohibited. So that, instead of speaking of a person's "negative" right, that is, his right to have another person "omit" a certain act, which is the first person's right to be let alone—his right of *laissez faire*—and instead of speaking of the correlative duty of that second person as his duty to "omit" that act and let the first person in-so-far alone, we shall speak of the right of avoidance of one person corresponding to the duty of avoidance of another person, with its accompanying compulsion on the latter to choose any different alternative open to him.

On the other hand, a "positive" right signifies the correlative duty of a second person actually to perform an act—the "positive" duty to pay a debt or render a service. Here there is little risk that the quantitative dimensions of the act will be overlooked, for, if the duty is once established by the testimony, then the question is immediately the quantity of performance required of the debtor or servant. Since, however, the duty, from the economic or ethical standpoint, is not usually a single transaction, but is a duty to perform a series of acts or transactions which shall furnish a quantity of commodities or of claims to commodities, all of them necessary to fulfill the duty, we shall substitute the term *performance* for the term "act." The "positive" right of one person is the correlative duty of another person to perform all the necessary acts and transactions that make a complete performance.

Lastly, in addition to "acts" and "omissions," certain legal writers introduce a third class of acts, namely, "forbearances," or rather, they subdivide omissions into "omissions" and "forbearances." This is done, however, as already suggested, not in order to obtain a physical dimension of the omission, but in order to go back of the omission and to distinguish whether it was *intentional* or *unintentional*.

Thus, Salmond, following Austin, distinguishes omission as an "unintentional negative act," and "forebearance" as an "intentional negative act." "If I fail to keep an appointment through forgetfulness, my act is *unintentional* and negative; that is to say, an omission. But if I remember the appointment, and resolve *not* to keep it, my act is *intentional* and negative; that is to say, a forbearance." [1]   Terry,

[1] Salmond, Jur. 324 (6th ed., 1920), following Austin, Lect. XIV, XIX.

however, holds that this distinction between forbearance and omission, is of little legal importance. "When an act is not done it is seldom of any consequence for legal purposes why the person did not do it." [1] Whether Terry is correct or not, legal writers generally use the term "forbearance" as the equivalent of "omission."

This distinction between an omission and a forbearance is what we would name a *qualitative* distinction, since it is made with reference to the *kind* of an act, from the ethical or legal standpoint of responsibility. The "omission" itself being already described, the qualitative question is, was it an intentional or an unintentional omission, and, if intentional, was the intent rightful or wrongful? Evidently the same qualitative distinction applies to a positive act. Was it an intentional or an unintentional performance? Were the intentions lawful or unlawful?

The foregoing does not imply that qualitative distinctions are not also quantitative. All "qualities" are, perhaps, quantities of a different order of phenomena from the one we happen to be considering. White and yellow are two *qualities* of external things in the field of psychology or esthetics, but in the field of physics they are two quantities of motion. Likewise with the qualitative distinctions as to the *kind* of an act from the standpoint of right or wrong, good or bad, intentional or unintentional. They are differences in *quality* from the standpoint of physical or economic behavior, but differences in *quantity* from the standpoint of the intensity of feelings accompanying them or passing judgment upon them. These qualitative distinctions belong to the order of mental processes that place subjective values on transactions, and they should have their separate terminology in the field of psychology or ethics, distinct from the economic or physical terminology.

Psychologically and ethically then, we may speak of both performance and avoidance as either intentional or unintentional, right or wrong, legal or illegal. But we are concerned, at this point, with the mere physical description of the will as a physical force that moves things and persons. From this standpoint we require a term, "forbearance," with a strictly physical, quantitative meaning, as follows:

The term "omission," even from the quantitative standpoint, has a double meaning. A negative right, the right to an "omission," may be not only a right to be let absolutely alone—the right to an avoid-

[1] TERRY, H. T., *Principles of Anglo-American Law*, 67 (1884).

ance—but may also mean the right to be let alone *beyond a certain degree of power* in acting, and this we shall name the right to a forbearance. It is this that constitutes the distinction between economic persuasion and economic coercion. Persuasion and coercion, from the physical standpoint, are exactly the same physical behavior, differing only in the degree of economic power. Each is simply the withholding of things or services from the opposite party to the transaction in order to induce action on his part. Each is a refusal to act until the terms are deemed satisfactory. Each is but economic pressure or notice of intent to use economic pressure, backed up by physical violence, or threat of compulsion, if necessary. Though physically alike they are economically different. To exact a price of ten cents as a condition of no longer withholding a service is not different, so far as physical behavior is concerned, from exacting a price of twenty cents. But the latter may be deemed coercive and the former persuasive, according to the ethical standards in vogue for determining the allowable pressure.

Transactions may, therefore, be defined either qualitatively, that is, psychologically, or quantitatively, that is economically or physically. The former pays regard to the *intentions*, the latter to the *degree of power*, and each varies independently of the other. A hostile blow in the face may be looked upon as a *different kind* of transaction from a joking tap, because the intentions are different; or it may be looked upon as the *same kind* of a transaction but exhibiting a higher degree of power, because the intentions are the same but the exertion is greater. To charge twenty cents may be looked upon as a *different kind* of transaction from charging ten cents for the same service, because the intentions in the one case are condemned, in the other case are approved; or it may be looked upon as the *same kind* of a transaction with a *higher degree* of power, because the intentions are the same but the economic power is greater.

The former seems to be the ethical or legal method of approach, because the moralist or lawyer is looking for the *intent* back of the transaction, which gives to it the psychological *quality* of right or wrong. For this reason we shall use the term "forbearance," not with its qualitative meaning of intentional omission, but with the quantitative, physical or economic meaning of a limit placed on the degree of power put forth in overcoming resistance. Forbearance is a limit placed on performance.

Here an ambiguity must be noticed in speaking of "positive" and "negative" acts, similar to the ambiguity of the term "omission." The term "negative" has the double meaning of *negation* and *limitation*. An act is said to be a "positive" act and an omission of that act is said to be a "negative" act. One is the *negation* of the other. One is *Yes*, the other is *No*. But forbearance is also the "negative" of a performance, but it is not a *negation* of performance, it is a *limitation* of it. Negation is a not-act. Limitation is a restrained act. Both are "negative" distinguished from "positive," but one is nothing; the other is more or less.

And this is a peculiarity of the will, compared with any other force in nature. The will is the only force that can place a limit on its own performance. Other forces always go to the limit of their power in overcoming resistance. What gravitation does, what electricity does, is all that it possibly can do in that direction under the circumstances. This might be found true also of the will if we knew all about its physiological and unconscious sub-structure. But consciously, as we know it in our persuading, coercing and commanding one another, the will alone forbears to go to the limit of its possible power of performance. Except in moments of great crisis the will forbears to make a full use of its powers. Forbearance is the limit which it places on its own performance.

Likewise with legally authorized transactions. A person may be permitted to exert pressure on an opposite party but may be prohibited beyond a certain point by a duty of forbearance. He may be free to administer physical discipline to his child, wife or slave, but forbidden to carry his manual powers beyond a certain degree of power. He may be free to charge ten cents but not twenty cents.

Adopting this three-fold dimension of behavior, which is physical and economic rather than psychological, every transaction is a double-ended performance, avoidance, forbearance. Each party to the transaction acts, at one and the same moment, in three dimensions. His performance is his power put forth in acting. His forbearance is the limit which he or a superior authority places on the degree of power in acting. His avoidance is his choice of that performance instead of any alternative performance. Every act of an individual is, at one and the same point of time, a performance, a forbearance, an avoidance. While the person is not doing an alternative thing (avoidance), he is doing something else (performance), and the thing which he is doing is usually something less (forbearance) than the total degree of power he might exert.

FIGURE I

	A		D		B	
"Act"	:	Performance	:	Forbearance	:	C
	:		:		:	
"Omission"	A:		Avoidance		:	
	:				:	

In the above figure, of two alternative acts the extreme ability, faculty, or potency, in one act is A B, in the other is A C. If the person chooses or is compelled to choose the act A B, he avoids the act A C, and if he restrains himself, or is restrained by command, from going to the limit of his ability in performing the act A B, then the actual limit at the point D is the limit of performance set by forbearance. Performance is A D; forbearance is D B; avoidance is A C. The double meaning of the term "negative" is here illustrated. Performance is a positive act, but a "negative act" may be a forbearance, in which it signifies *limitation* (D B) on the possible performance, A B; or the "negative act" may be an avoidance, in which case it signifies, not a limitation, but a total negation of the alternative performance, A C.

We thus distinguish between *faculties* and *powers*. Faculties are the total *possible* power of which the individual is capable under the circumstances. It is John Locke's will in the sense of "power" as he used the term. It is ability to act but not acting, potency but not power, capacity but not content, the will but not the will-in-action. But power, in the behavioristic sense of the term, is the *actual power* which he employs in acting. Power is actual performance, and the amount of difference between faculty and power is forbearance.

The meaning usually given in ethics and law to the term "power" is this meaning of faculty, ability or capacity, given by John Locke. One's faculty, ability, capacity or potency, to act consists in the total of all his faculties, or abilities. These may be physical, economic or moral faculties. Taken together they constitute potential manpower. In each case they consist only in the power to move things or persons. Physical, economic or moral power is power to move them directly or indirectly. Mental power is power to take a long leverage in moving them. Managerial power is power to induce other persons to move things. Each, when in action, is a performance and a forbearance. Only at the moment of a crisis does performance exhaust the total of all faculties or abilities to act, and at that moment forbearance is reduced to its minimum. At the other extreme, performance reaches its minimum and forbearance is at the maximum only when the person is at the point of not acting at all, that is, when he is nearly unconscious, asleep or dead.

At the same time, each performance of physical, economic or moral power is an avoidance of any and all alternative performance. Persons, of course, differ greatly in their faculties, that is, in their potencies. Faculty is ability, potency is possible or potential power; but power is the actual use made of ability or potency. The two terms, potency and power, are necessary in all economic reasoning as well as all concepts of the will, but in a very different sense from that employed by John Locke, as we shall see.

III. Actual, Potential, Possible, Impossible

Thus it appears that the will is not Locke's will-in-vacuo, nor the hedonists' conscious pleasure and pain, separate from the will and forcing it to act, but is the will-in-action, and the will-in-action is the faculties-in-action. It does not operate in infinite space, does not lay down unconditional laws, does not choose between something and nothing, but the will is always "up against" something. It is always performing, avoiding, forbearing, that is, always moving along lines, not of least resistance like physical forces without purpose, but of overcoming resistance, avoiding and forbearing effort to overcome resistance, with a purpose looking toward the future. Every transaction is a two-ended action. It is two wills acting on each other. Even what we have distinguished as nature-transactions are two-ended. The difference between them and the ethical-juristic transactions is the difference between performance, avoidance and forbearance in dealing with nature's forces, and the same in dealings with persons.

We may distinguish, then, these two-ended actions as the physical dimensions of the will-in-action. They are transactions. But as such, they are only a part of behavior. They are behavior at a point of time, uncorrelated with the past or the future. As mere physical dimensions they have no meaning, no expectation, and hence no value. The *whole* of behavior is the proportioning of these moving acts and transactions according to a purpose that binds them together, that is, according to their relative values in making up the whole.

For this reason we distinguish actual, potential and possible transactions, from the infinite, impossible, or inaccessible. The actual is reality. It is the will actually against something. It is the moving point of performance, avoidance, forbearance. The potential and the possible are in the future—the world of imagination and the world of value—the place where man lives. The actual has no value. It is a moving point, gone as soon as acted. The actual is the future anticipating itself in the present behavior, and passing at once into memory and into further confidence or dread of the future further on, where lie the potential and possible. The potential is near at hand. It may or may not happen. The possible lies beyond in time and space. The potential and the possible lie in the field of the probable or improbable, in the world of expectation and expectancy, of encumbrance and opportunity, of right, wrong and duty. Further on is the infinite—the vacuum, the void, the empty, nothing, zero, the impossible, the inaccessible.

The potential or possible future also has its dimensions—dimensions that expand with the unfolding of life and imagination. Yet these future dimensions are not what science says is probable or improbable. They are what the person *believes* is potential or possible, probable or improbable. They belong to a different order of phenomena—the phenomena of mental processes. The child's world is a very little world; man's world pushes the finite further away into an expanding potential and possible world, and even imagines the infinite possible. To Alexander the potential extended to the Indus River and there were no possible worlds beyond; to the modern business man the potential circles the globe; to the worker it is his job. To each it is the whole of which each act or transaction is a part.

It is in view of the potential and possible that the act or transaction has its value. And, if we say that each actual transaction is the physical dimensions of the will-in-action at a moving point of time, then all of the potential and possible transactions are the economic, ethical and juristic dimensions of the future, the great field of Desire or Purpose, the field of mental anticipation, that gives value to the part which is in the present, and determines how far the act or trans-action shall go in its actual performance, avoidance and forbearance.

Thus the dualism of spirit and matter, the trinity of intellect, feeling and will, the potencies of John Locke and the courts, are resolved into the valuation of one's own behavior. Metaphysically or philosophically, the dualism remains, because there are two orders of phenomena, the psychological and the physical, whose connections we do not understand. But scientifically we deal with each one in its own field, for science is superficial. It deals only with behavior, which is the surface of things. It is not fundamental, for it knows not the essence of things, nor how one order of phenomena gets into another order of phenomena. It may push the unknown back a bit, but it always leaves a field of the unconscious and unknown, a field of hypothesis and guessing, where the conscious goes under-ground into physiology, biology, physics and chemistry. We do not know *what* the soul is, nor what substance is. We do not even know ourselves as we really are until we act. We only know ourselves truly as we analyze ourselves acting.

Each act is an action and a reaction with external nature, or a transaction with persons, and, as such, is a moving point, a flow of performance, avoidance, forbearance, playing its little part towards realizing the whole that lies in the future. It is valued as we go along. For it is, at the moment of valuation, the limiting factor, or what we deem to be the limiting factor, in realizing the potential and possible further on. It is, as we have seen, accompanied by an expec-tation and an expectancy, an emotion, an intuition, a feeling, but it is such only while it is potential. As soon as actual it is gone and no longer is felt and valued. While potential it is valued as a part of the total expected economy, the expected proportioning of potential and possible acts and transactions into a hoped-for world of reality. And, while it is potential, it is opportunity—the option of choosing between different degrees of power in acting. While potential it is also potential power, the valuable power of overcoming the resist-ance of nature and man for larger purposes beyond. Thus each transaction, with its physical dimensions of performance, forbearance and avoidance, slides into its economic dimensions of economy and expansion—of expected economy, opportunity and power, which reflect backward a value upon the present performance, avoidance, forbearance.

For purposes of science, therefore, it does not matter whether we know or do not know what the substance of the will is. Science deals with probabilities and superficialities. Whether we hold to "determinism" or "indeterminism," does not matter for economic purposes. The "determinist" cannot tell what a business man, a workingman or a judge on the bench is going to do the next minute any more than the "indeterminist," notwithstanding his superior confidence that behavior is determined or predetermined. Each, if he is wise, follows the approved procedure of knowing his man by knowing how he has acted in the past, and figuring out the probabilities of how he will act in the present and future. The problems of determinism and indeterminism are too fundamental; or rather, the behavorist defines the will as what the will does and passes over to others the question of whether the will is predetermined by physiology, physics, chemistry, or the cosmos. Schiller,[1] in order to support the freedom of the will, must logically go back to the atom and support a little bit of freedom on the part of the electron in choosing the way in which it will act, undetermined by anything that has gone before. And, indeed, it does not seem possible that, at some unknown point where man emerges, an indeterminate element should get into the universe where it never was found before. But that is another order of phenomena. Be that as it may, economic determinism arises only from the fact that the will acts in a world of limited resources and that these resources are tied up or loosened up by means of working rules that vouchsafe to the individual certain rights, duties, and liberties of performance, avoidance or forbearance. For this reason the doctrine of an indeterminate free will is often as cruel as it is empty. It assumes freedom where there often is none, and substitutes an empty equality of right, where there is actual inequality of abilities or opportunities, or actual inaccessibility of alleged alternatives. Economics and law are concerned with freedom of choice rather than freedom of will, and the progress of society consists in creating freedom of will by creating freedom of choice. Freedom is a social product whereby society opens up for the individual an enlarging world of the potential and possible within which he may construct his own future as he will.

All that we can say, then, is that every transaction may be looked at

[1] SCHILLER, F. C. S., *Studies in Humanism* (1907); *Riddles of the Sphinx*, 439 ff. (1912).

from several points of view, and that each point of view presents a distinct order of phenomena such that we are unable to explain fundamentally how one gets into the other. We content ourselves with measuring quantities of one order of phenomena at one time and letting the others go, for the time, under the name of qualities, to be taken up afterwards in their own field and measured quantitatively, if we can. Thus every transaction has its physical dimensions of performance, avoidance, forbearance; its economic dimensions of opportunity, power, economy and expectation; its psychological dimensions of thinking, feeling, willing, persuading, coercing, commanding, obeying and expectation; its ethical and legal dimensions of rights, duties, liberties, and exposures, and its political or governmental dimensions of authority and authorization in the use of physical power, economic or moral power, according to common rules or working rules that set the limits and directions of conduct. It is the last that we now proceed to examine.

IV. AUTHORIZED TRANSACTIONS

A person's world of potential and possible transactions is not limited to a single going concern, except perhaps in that primitive society where family, state and business were unknown separately. He is a member of several concerns, or has transactions with members of several concerns, each of which is a government that enforces rules of conduct. These concerns have been more or less separated out, in the evolution of society, according to the kind of fear or duty on which they specialize as the sanction of their collective commands or rules. Since, however, the state, which regulates the fear of violence, is supreme, it is the one whose functionaries, the courts, lawyers, and jurists, have analyzed most fully the notions of right, wrong and duty, and it is from their analysis of legal transactions that we may gather the elements of the ethical equivalent of all transactions. What we discover regarding legal transactions guided by rules of law and backed by fear of violence under the jurisdiction of political government, will hold true, in substance, of business transactions guided by the common rules of business and backed by fear of poverty under the jurisdiction of business concerns, and of moral transactions guided by accepted codes of conduct and backed by fear of opinion under the jurisdiction of cultural concerns. As already stated, this separation of concerns is a matter of predominance and not isolation, for the fear of violence, poverty and opinion are interwoven. But once discovering the meaning of legal rights and duties, we shall have the elements of economic and moral rights and duties.

All rights and duties are relative. If we say that a right of one person is absolute, we can only mean that it is unlimited, and corresponds to an unlimited duty of an opposite person. This being so, an absolute right-duty is without quantitative content, and, as such, it matters not whether we say that it is an infinite right or a zero right. It simply does not exist as an actual or potential right and duty. It is at the point of disappearing from the field of ethical or juristic transactions and of sinking into the physical realm of action and reaction between man and nature.

For a right is a compendious term for a complicated set of wishes and fears entertained by human beings toward each other. It is a wish of one party to have a performance, avoidance, or forbearance of an opposite party whose wish is contrary, and to have it, not by means of one's own power, but by aid of the fear of compulsion imposed by a superior third party who also is believed to aid that opposite party by similar fears imposed on the first party; provided, however, that this superior third party is believed to act in conformity with rules or principles and not out of the mere caprice or lunacy of an unreasoning or irresponsible party. If this superior reasonable third party is not believed to exist or to intervene then the relation of right and duty between the two disappears altogether, and the relation sinks back into a different order of phenomena, that of the physical action and reaction between forces of nature. Hence the term "absolute right" and its correlative "absolute duty" can only mean that the superior party either does not exist or does not intend to intervene. If it does not exist, then the relation is a physical relation between two animals which are mere forces of nature unrestrained by a superior will. If it does intervene, or is believed to promise or threaten to intervene, in conformity with predetermined rules, then it does so by restraining or compelling the will of one or of the other, and the restraint is quantitative and therefore relative. Absolute right and duty are figures of speech like the rights and duties of tigers or tornadoes applied to a physical order of phenomena, which have no dimensions or limits applicable to an ethical order, and may be represented as follows, where the proper terms are action and reaction instead of right and duty.

Figure II

"ABSOLUTE" RIGHT AND DUTY

Action			Reaction	
	B			
	S			

The so-called "absolute" right of B is the "absolute" duty of S. There is no limit of restraint or compulsion placed on the behavior of either party by a superior authority. Each, without compunction of conscience or appeal to divine or earthly authority or to binding custom, or to any other accepted rule of conduct, may kill, enslave or rob the other to the extent of his ability. The transaction is a "natural" transaction without ethical or juristic meaning. An absolute right, being unlimited, is an infinite right and therefore a zero-right.

The first step out of this physical relation of misnamed absolute rights and duties is when one or the other party believes that a superior will-power acting according to predictable rules, may be expected to come to his aid or the aid of the other by means of fear. This transition from physics to ethics has usually been formulated under the names of "divine" right or "natural" right. These terms indicate historically the mental processes by which the concepts of right and duty originated. A right seems to have been historically none other than the wished-for act of an external superior power imposing a fear on other persons, while the duty is the fear itself. Tribes, nations, families and individuals have formulated in one way or another their hopes and fears into beliefs respecting guardian spirits or natural laws, with power, will and habit of commanding and enforcing obedience.

There is, however, a difficulty with these ethical mandates. They are mental processes and therefore as divergent as the wishes and fears of individuals. Hence when they emerge into action they are individualistic and anarchistic. They are unrestrained in action by an actual earthly authority to whom each party yields obedience. The wish of one that he had a divine or natural right to a certain behavior of another may not coincide with the fear of the other that he is bound by a divine or natural duty to behave with exactly that amount of performance, avoidance or forbearance. There is thus the chance of a lack of correspondence, a failure to correlate the wish of one with the

fear of the other.   When this lack of subjective correlation expresses
itself in action it may be illustrated as follows:

FIGURE III

UNAUTHORIZED TRANSACTIONS—ETHICAL

——————————UNCORRELATED——————

O			
p	Right	B	Duty
p			
o			
s			
i	——————	S	——————
t			
e	No-right		No-duty
s			

B or S each concedes that his right to performance, avoidance, or
forbearance on the part of the other is limited, but neither of them
agrees exactly on the point where the limit shall be placed. This is
the historical stage of "divine" right or "natural" right, the stage of
appeal to a super-human unearthly authority, and is the stage of
anarchy, dogmatism and metaphysics, where there are as many concepts of divine or natural right proceeding from divine or natural rules
of conduct as there are individuals, and which, behavioristically expressed, is the stage of unauthorized transactions. The ethical concepts of right and duty are there, and it is admitted that the resulting
behavior is limited at points beyond which there is no-right and no-
duty, but where those limits shall be placed is undecided.

It seems that the only procedure that will *correlate* the wishes and
fears of each and prevent anarchy is to resort to a third person of an
earthly quality whom each consents to obey, or each is compelled to
obey. Thus we reach the social necessity of judges, chiefs, kings,
despots, priests, governors, managers, and so on, whose behavioristic
function, guided more or less by ethical beliefs which they share with
some of the others, is that of correlating in practice conflicting asser-
tions and denials of rights and duties. Individuals with opposite
interests or beliefs cannot always agree on the correlation, but the
correlation is necessary in order to hold together the constituents of a
collective will. Ethics is anarchy, law is order, and the correlation of

rights and duties is not a conclusion of logic, as is often inferred, but is a command of government.

For this reason we pass over from the merely ethical transactions depending on individual interests and beliefs, to authorized transactions where the will of a superior party or parties imposes limits on their transactions by imposing or interpreting a rule of conduct applicable to the dispute. This brings about that correlation of right and duty which is the starting point of jurisprudence. It may be shown as follows, where a specified right of one party is identical with the duty of another party, and each is limited by a superior authority enforcing a rule common to both at a determined point where no-right and no-duty begin.

FIGURE IV

AUTHORIZED TRANSACTIONS—LEGAL

————————CORRELATIVES————————

O p p o s i t e s	Right	B	Duty
	No-right	S	No-duty

This indicates that a minimum of three persons is required to constitute the social relation of rights and duties—two inferiors and one superior. But we have seen that a minimum of five persons is required to constitute the concept of a modern business transaction. There is an intermediate historical step before this concept of a transaction—involving a minimum of five persons—is obtained.

A government of some kind sets up its working rules which determine rights of property and liberty on behalf of one class of parties, say those represented by B and B′ (Figure V), but deny rights of property and liberty to another class, say S and S′. This is a condition of authorized slavery, where B and B′ have rights and duties toward each other, but no rights and duties toward S and S′. The right of B is his right to require B′ to keep off and let B do as he pleases with S. Likewise B′ has a similar right against B respecting S′.

Not until a superior authority begins to place a limit on the right of B and B', to the services of S and S', does the question arise of rights and duties between them.   Until that point is reached S and S' are physical things and not persons.   When that point is reached then the modern stage of universal equality and liberty is reached and the typical transaction involving a minimum of five parties is universalized for all classes of persons as follows:—

FIGURE V

AUTHORIZED TRANSACTIONS

————————CORRELATIVES————————

O p p o s i t e s	Right	Opportunity P o w e r	Duty
	No-right	B B' S S'	No-duty

This typical transaction proceeds from the concept of personality, that self-directing unit which we name the will, and it is this extension of rights and duties that actually creates the "free will."   Thus the five parties necessary to the concept of a right are:— the first party who claims the right; the second party with whom the transaction occurs; the "third" parties, of whom one is the rival or competitor of the first party, the other is the rival or competitor of the second party; and the fifth party who lays down the rules of the concern of which each is an authorized member.   It will be seen, too, that the two relations of opportunity and power are here provided for.

The claim of the first party against the third parties is the claim that all others shall let the first party alone in the act of dealing with the second party.   "Third" parties are "all the world" or rather, a right against "all the world," a right *in rem*, is a "multital right,"[1] in that it is one of innumerable similar rights possessed against all or nearly all other members of organized society, each one of whom is under a similar correlative duty.   These innumerable third parties,

[1]Hohfeld's term. See below, p. 92ff.

however, as we have seen, are narrowed down, in any particular transaction at a point of time, into the two next third parties whom the
first party must have in mind when actually deciding upon his choice
of alternatives. Concretely, his right is therefore a limited right,
imposed by the superior person, that the immediate rivals shall,
up to a certain point, let him alone, and correspondingly his right
is a specified duty which limits their liberty to interfere regardless
of either their self-interest or their sympathy with the second party.
The working rule tells these third parties what they *must not* do.

Thus the fifth party, superior in power to the four participants,
introduces, by interpreting an accepted rule of conduct, the idea
of a right. If the first party has no hope or expectation except that
he alone must enforce his claim to be free to deal with the second
party, we have a situation no different from that of animals under
similar circumstances. But if he believes that a superior person,
a god, spirit, fetish, or tabu, with power to lay down rules of conduct,
can be induced to come to his aid and keep third parties off by fear,
then we begin to have the beginnings of human nature distinguished
from animal nature. If, at later stages of civilization, the first party,
having lost somewhat his faith in personal spirits, yet continues to
believe that a beneficent order of nature, a natural law of harmony,
a government of friendly powers external to man, that is, an ideal
set of working rules, may be expected to come to his aid, then we
have that philosophy of natural rights proceeding out of the natural
order and emerging out of divine rights which had proceeded out of
the divine order of the universe, which, however, is eminently "natural" in another sense, in that it springs from the deepest hopes
and fears of human nature. It was at this stage of faith in a beneficent "nature," in the eighteenth century, that both our modern
legal theories and economic theories of natural law and natural order
took their rise, before Malthus and Darwin showed us the niggard-
liness and cruelty of nature, and before science taught us to frame
our definitions, not in terms that imply theories of cause and effect
or opinions of right and wrong or hopes and fears of goodness and
badness, but in colorless terms of behavior.

But ethical ideals still remain, nevertheless, for they spring not
from abstract reason, intellect, or external nature, but from the
hopes and fears that are fundamental to the helplessness of man
and the concept of enduring personality; and they guide the behavior

of business men, laborers, judges and philosophers. It remains, therefore, to give to them their proper place.

The concept of rights with their correlative duties has a relation to human beings similar to that which expectation has with reference to commodities. Use-values and exchange-values are the wished-for activities—the expectations which give value in the present to that bundle of physical qualities which we name expectancies. So with the relationship of right-duty. It is the wished and dreaded activities of persons, the expectation of hope and fear respecting the relations of man to man, which are objectified and given present reality in the persons who are expected to act. The persons themselves are bundles of qualities which we name expectancies—their hoped-for or dreaded behavior is the expectations attributed to them. When these expectations are predictable they take the form of a law, a principle or guide of human conduct, which is none other than an anticipation of how individuals or classes will act upon the occurrence of certain facts. Economically they act under the impulse of utility; ethically they act under the impulse of sympathy and duty. Or, more specifically stated in volitional terms, the economists' "utility" is the will to subordinate the physical world and other persons to self—the one being use-values, the other exchange-values. But the moralists' "sympathy" is willing subordination of self to others, while "duty" is unwilling subordination of self to others. Sympathy and duty are each a behavioristic outcome of human values, giving rise to rights, while utility is the outcome of commodity values. Since a duty imposed creates a corresponding equivalent right, the creation of rights is the creation of duties. And the legal relation of right and duty existing between two persons is therefore none other than an expectation of a dependable rule of conduct, a "prediction," in the words of Corbin, "as to what society, acting through its courts or executive agents, will do or not do for one and against the other."[1]

Courts and executives are human beings, acting like others under the feelings of utility, sympathy and duty, and consequently legal relations differ from non-legal relations only in the fact that legal relations are the expected activities of officials in directing the use of the physical powers of society, while non-legal relations are the expected actions of private persons. Each is economic and each is

[1] Corbin, A. L., "Legal Analysis and Terminology," 29 *Yale Law Jour.* 163, 164 (1919).

ethical, but the one is official ethics and political economy, the other is private ethics and business economy or cultural economy.

These considerations lead us into the metaphysical and scientific problem of the fundamental nature of legal concepts, a problem whose discussion was started in America by the late W. N. Hohfeld, of the Yale Law Faculty, and which may be stated as that of three different points of view respecting the analysis, terminology and classification of legal relations. References to this discussion are given in the footnote.[1] Since these three points of view will appear frequently hereafter they may be briefly stated at this point in a preliminary way:

The first point of view is that of the legal practitioner advising his client before a trial court, when the facts respecting a given transaction are assumed to be already in evidence and the court is construing a specified right and duty as applicable or not to the case. Here the practical question is, Does this previously accepted right-duty relation apply to this transaction? Will or will not the court affirm the said right of one of the parties and its correlative duty of the opposite party? Will the working rules of society grant or not grant a right in this case? The answer is positive or negative,

[1] HOHFELD, W. N., "Some Fundamental Legal Conceptions as applied in Judicial Reasoning," 23 *Yale Law Jour.* 16 (1913); 26 *Yale Law Jour.* 710 (1917); CORBIN, KOCOUREK, PAGE, "Terminology and Classification in Fundamental Jural Relations: a symposium," 4 *Amer. Law School Rev.* 607 (1921); KOCOUREK, ALBERT, "The Hohfeld System of Fundamental Legal Concepts," 15 *Ill. Law Quar.* 23 (1920); "Various definitions of Jural Relations," 20 *Col. Law Rev.* 394 (1920); "Rights in Rem," 68 *Pa. Law Rev.* 322 (1920); "Plurality of Advantage and Disadvantage in Jural Relation," 19 *Mich. Law Rev.* 47 (1920); "Tabulæ Minores Jurisprudentiæ," 30 *Yale Law Jour.* 215 (1921); "Polarized and Unpolarized Legal Relations," 9 *Ky. Law Jour.* 131 (1921); CORBIN, A. L., "Legal Analysis and Terminology," 29 *Yale Law Jour.* 163 (1919); "Contracts for the benefit of third Persons," 27 *Yale Law Jour.* 1008 (1918); "Does a Pre-existing duty defeat Consideration?" 27 *Yale Law Jour.* 362 (1917); "Offer and Acceptance and some of the Resulting Legal Relations," 26 *Yale Law. Jour.* 169 (1917); "Jural Relations and their Classification," 30 *Yale Law Jour.* 226 (1921); COOK, W. W., "Hohfeld's Contribution to the Science of Law," 28 *Yale Law Jour.* 721 (1919); "The Powers of Courts of Equity," 15 *Col. Law Rev.* 37, 106, 228 (1915); "Privileges of Labor Unions in the Struggle for Life," 27 *Yale Law Jour.* 779 (1918); "The Alienability of Choses in Action," 29 *Harv. Law Rev.* 816 (1916); 30 id., 449 (1917); POUND, ROSCOE, "Legal Rights," 26 *Int. Jour. Ethics,* 92 (1915); GOBLE, GEO. W., "Affirmative and Negative Legal Relations," 4 *Ill. Law Quar.* 94 (1922); SUMMERS, W. L. "Legal Intents in Oil and Gas," 4 *Ill. Law Quar.* 12 (1921); POWELL, T. R., "Collective Bargaining Before the Supreme Court," 33 *Pol. Sci. Quar.* 396 (1918); HALE, ROBERT L., "Rate Making and the Revision of the Property Concept," 22 *Col. Law Rev.* 209 (1922); "Law Making by Unofficial Minorities," 20 *Col. Law Rev.* 451 (1920); SALMOND, J., Jurisprudence, 6th ed. (1920), Chapts. X to XV, pp. 179–298; TERRY, H. T., *Anglo-American Law* (1884), Chapts. III, IV, V, VI, pp. 50–155. The best simplified statements of Hohfeld's analysis are in the above articles by COOK on "Hohfeld's Contributions," and by CORBIN on "Legal Analysis and Terminology." HOHFELD's articles, with COOK's Introduction are published in pamphlet form by the Yale University Press.

affirmation or denial, Yes or No. This was Hohfeld's point of approach and may be designated the *individualistic concrete*, or *pragmatic* point of view of a trial court.

The second point of view is that of the logical, mathematical, or syllogistic relations existing between legal concepts, as to whether they are contradictory, contrary, reciprocal, when once the major premise, the law or working rule of society, and the minor premise, the transaction, are ascertained; and What are the advantages and disadvantages in general which these working rules provide for an individual, without reference to any particular concrete case? This is mainly the point of view of Hohfeld's leading critic, Kocourek, and may be designated as the *individualistic abstract*, or *dialectical* point of view of a logician.

The third is the point of view of a supreme court, a legislature, or an economist inquiring, What are the limits and purposes of society's working rules themselves, and what are the economic or social consequences of a particular legal relation created by a particular rule of conduct? In short, What is Due Process of Law applied to a class of transactions? This is the standpoint that takes into account questions of value and economy, namely, What is the public purpose underlying the particular working rule or law asserted or denied? What are the quantitative limits of power and resources of the parties and the nation? How important relatively are the contending interests that will be affected by the law or the decisions conforming to the law, and how intense and extensive are the convictions, beliefs, hopes and fears that favor or disfavor one rule of action as against another? This may be designated as the point of view of the *working rules of going concerns*, that is, the *social-economic* point of view of the economist or supreme court.

These three points of view will be found to occasion decided differences in the meanings and use of words. Hohfeld, from the standpoint of a trial court deciding upon the private interests subserved or restrained by society's rules of conduct, reduces the fundamental jural concepts to eight, and these eight concepts have two sets of relations to each other, that of "jural opposites" and that of "jural correlatives." He tabulates them as herewith:

Jural Opposites	right	privilege	power	immunity
	no-right	duty	disability	liability
Jural Correlatives	right	privilege	power	immunity
	duty	no-right	liability	disability

The primary criticism made by Kocourek against Hohfeld's classification turns on a double meaning of the term "opposite" and of the pair of terms "positive and negative." Hohfeld intended them in the pragmatic sense of Yes and No as applied to a concrete case in a trial court. Kocourek switched them into a dialectical sense of contradiction as applied to abstract universals in the mind of a logician, and then correctly demolished them. Hohfeld intended to answer the question, Will the trial court assert a right or no-right for this plaintiff? No-right is the negative, of which right is the positive, and one is the "opposite" of the other. But from the dialectical or universal and abstract standpoint a "no-right" and its correlative "no-duty" might be the rest of the universe, even the stars and angels. The dialectical negative may be infinity or zero—in either case it means nothing to finite beings.

But instead of rejecting Hohfeld's analysis, its logic and accuracy will be retained if we substitute the quantitative term "limits" for the indeterminate "opposites." The terms positive and negative, as well as the term opposite, as we have previously observed,[1] have not only the dialectic meaning of Yes and No, but also the quantitative meaning of more or less, much or little, plus and minus. Hence, by substituting the term "limits" we have the outside limits of a transaction consisting in the powers and opportunities of the parties, and the inside limits where right-duty ends and no-right—no-duty begins. Hence instead of the *contradictory negative* of the preceding diagram (Figure V) we have the *limiting negative*, as follows, where there is both an outside limit of power and opportunity and an inside limit to the degree of power or choice of opportunities permitted or required:

FIGURE VI

AUTHORIZED TRANSACTIONS

————————CORRELATIVES————————

L i m i t s	Right	Opportunity P B B′ o w e r	Duty
	No-right	S S′	No-duty

[1] Above, Chap. II, p. 44 ff.

It happens, that Hohfeld finds a legal term which he can use for the "negative" of duty, namely, "privilege." Substituting this term for the term "no-duty" we have the following scheme:

FIGURE VII

AUTHORIZED TRANSACTIONS

——————————CORRELATIVES——————————

	Right	Opportunity			Duty
L i m i t s		P o w e r	B	B'	
	No-right		S	S'	Privilege

We have to consider the appropriateness of Hohfeld's terms "no-right" and "privilege." The term "privilege" is used by Hohfeld in an enlarged sense derived from that of the privilege of a witness in court to be exempt from compulsion on refusal to testify where the testimony would be self-incriminating or the subject-matter is a confidential, that is, a "privileged" communication recognized in law. It is evident therefore that "privilege" is identical with Hohfeld's other term, "immunity," in that privilege is the authorized limit where duty ends, while "immunity" is the authoritative limit where liability to compulsion ends. This identification will be considered later.

Confining ourselves, for the present, to the authorized behavior indicated by the term privilege, "the closest synonym of 'legal privilege,'" says Hohfeld, "seems to be legal liberty." [1] We have already seen the double meaning of the term "liberty" in the decisions of the courts beginning with the Slaughter House Cases. Legally, the term liberty means absence of duty, or rather the limit of duty, and is therefore identical with Hohfeld's enlarged meaning of "privilege." But, economically, liberty means choice of opportunities, or choice of two degrees of power in acting.

Kocourek, while pointing out that Hohfeld uses the term "privilege" in the sense of "liberty," contends that liberty is a "non-jural" concept, and this apparently for two reasons:

(1) Liberty is a "positive" act of the will indicated by the "act of choosing." This is undoubtedly correct, for "liberty" applies to every

[1] Op. cit. HOHFELD, 23 Yale Law Jour. 41.

act of choosing, even the most coercive or coerced of choices. But if so, it is because "liberty" has the double meaning of "individual" and "social-economic" liberty. Individually a person is not thought to possess "liberty" if he has no uncoerced options. It is on this account that we substitute the colorless term "choice of opportunities" instead of the colorful term "liberty" as indicating the individual's act of choosing, and applicable to all choices whether "free" or coerced. On the other hand, the social meaning of liberty is that meaning derived from the working rules of the state or other concern which tells the individual what he *may* do with the help of society, in that society will prevent others from interfering with his "act of choosing." "Liberty," from the standpoint of these working rules is *permission* to choose, *protected* by keeping other people off, and it applies to any kind of choosing no matter how coerced or coercive, in so far as the working rules prevent interference by third parties who might resist the particular act of choosing.

(2) This is Kocourek's second reason for holding that liberty is a "non-jural" concept. Jural concepts, according to him, are only those that have to do with constraint or compulsion, but "liberty" is the *absence* of constraint or compulsion. "Duty," he holds, is a legal concept, since it indicates positive compulsion, but "liberty" is a non-legal concept since it is negative in the dialectical sense of "no-duty." This evidently overlooks an essential quality of liberty when vouchsafed by a working rule in that liberty exists only by way of "constraint or compulsion" imposed on third parties. It is indeed the *absence* of constraint on the party entitled to liberty, but is the *presence* of constraint on all potential or possible parties who might interfere with that act of choosing. Liberty is as much a matter of compulsion as duty, but where duty says to a person that he *must* or *must not*, liberty says to *other* persons that they *must not* interfere with that person, or that they even *must* help to prevent still other persons from interfering, if necessary. Duty is compulsion of *the parties* to transactions; liberty is permission to those parties by means of compulsion of *other parties* who might interfere with the choices of the parties.

It will be seen that each of these arguments made by Kocourek in holding that "liberty" is a non-jural concept, proceed from his dialectical point of view as against Hohfeld's pragmatic point of view, or the point of view of a going concern with its working rules. If, instead of defining either liberty or privilege as the "negation" of duty, we define it as the "limit" or deduction from the scope of the behavior indicated by the concrete duty in question, and if, at the same time, we take into account the *purpose* of the rule that creates the duty, then liberty is essentially a legal concept, since, within the potential or possible limits of a transaction, duty and liberty vary inversely to each other, the duty increasing as the liberty diminishes, and the duty diminishing as the liberty (or privilege) increases. Liberty is one of the great purposes of society's rules of conduct, and can be granted only by reducing the duties, which is none other than reducing the rights of opposite parties. If these distinctions are made, then choice of opportunity, or simply opportunity, becomes the economic equivalent of liberty, and liberty takes its proper place as an ethical or legal concept implying a limitation of duty.

The foregoing applies to liberty, or privilege, when one is used with the same meaning as the other. There is, however, an historical reason why we should substitute the term liberty for the term privilege. Privilege, historically and popularly employed, signifies a *special privilege* not permitted to others under similar circumstances, and we shall have occasion to use the term privilege in this sense of *unequal liberty*, contrasted with the concept of goodwill which is that of equal and unprivileged liberty. Furthermore, the term "privilege" is used in the Constitution of the United States as identical with the term "power" employed by Hohfeld; while the term liberty, in the Slaughter House and succeeding cases is given specifically the meaning of free choice of opportunities.[1] Making this substitution of liberty for privilege in Hohfeld's scheme we have the following:

FIGURE VIII

AUTHORIZED TRANSACTIONS

------------CORRELATIVES------------

L i m i t s		Opportunity		Duty
	Right	P o w e r	B B′	Duty
	No-right		S S′	Liberty

[1] Fourteenth Amendment: "No state shall make or enforce any law which shall abridge the privileges or immunities of citizens of the United States; nor shall any state deprive any person of life, liberty, or property," etc.

A similar observation applies to Hohfeld's term "no-right," used by him to signify the absence of right. But the absence of right may be either Kocourek's dialectical *denial* of a right *in toto*, or a *limit* placed on the quantity of behavior claimed as a right. The former meaning (denial, negation) is appropriate when we speak of an "absolute" right as no-right at all, a concept of nothing, in that it refers to the relation of man to nature, and, of course, therefore contains no ethical dimensions. The latter meaning (limitation) is intended when we speak of a right which positively does exist in the actual transaction, but which is limited at a certain point. For this reason, we shall substitute the behavioristic term "exposure" for the dialectical term "no-right" employed by Hohfeld, and our correlation of rights and duties, exposures and liberties, will appear as follows:

FIGURE IX

AUTHORIZED TRANSACTIONS

————————CORRELATIVES————————

		Opportunity			
L i m	Right	P o w	B	B′	Duty
i t s	Exposure	e r	S	S′	Liberty

The claimant, any one of the four parties, asserts a right to a certain behavior of performance, forbearance or avoidance on the part of another, and this claim is then limited by the working rules at a certain point, leaving the claimant thereby exposed, that is, potentially damageable without remedy, or protection, by the acts of the others, to the extent that they are at liberty to act as they please towards him, unrestrained and uncompelled by duty. Their liberty means that they can damage him without committing a legal wrong—*damnum absque injuria*. Thus while the authorized right of one is correlative and equal to the required obedience or duty of any other to whom it applies, the authorized liberty of the other is correlative and equal to the permitted exposure of the one whose right is limited.

This "exposure" is equivalent to one sense of the word "liability," employed by Hohfeld. But the term "liability" has a different meaning when correlated with "legal power," where it signifies accountability, responsibility, or subjection to a superior person. For our present purpose the term liability signifies that the person who has "no-right" is exposed, as far as the protection granted by the working rules is concerned, to the unrestrained or uncompelled behavior of him who, to the same extent, is bound by no duty towards him. Salmond mentions the following examples of liabilities correlative to liberties (privileges), or, as we should say, examples of "exposures" correlative to "liberties," namely: the "liability of a trespasser to be forcibly ejected; that of a defaulting tenant to have his goods seized for rent; and that of the owner of a building to have his windows darkened or his foundations weakened by the buildings or excavations of his neighbors."[1] To these we shall add all of the exposures to which any person is liable on account of the liberty of action of other persons. Thus when the duty to pay a debt was formerly unlimited, in the sense that the debtor could be imprisoned for debt, the creditor had a relatively unlimited right enforced by the power of the state. But when imprisonment for debt was abolished, the increase in liberty of the debtor signified just that much additional exposure of the creditor to the chance of not having the debt paid. The same is true of that great field of "free competition" where injury may lawfully be inflicted upon competitors. It is the field of *damnum absque injuria*, the field of possible damage without legal wrong, remedy or protection. Hence our term "exposure" includes all of the possibilities of damage to which one is exposed without remedy through the operations of free competition in buying and selling. The liberty of others to buy or sell is correlative to the exactly equal exposure to damage without remedy of him who wishes to sell or buy.

This itemization of its applications will enable us to point out the exact difference between "liberty" and "exposure." Each is a corollary flowing from the principle of working rules addressed by a going concern to the conduct of its member's transactions. But where "liberty" is a corollary that tells what a person *may* do with the aid of the concern in compelling others to avoid interference, "exposure" tells what a person *cannot* expect the group to do towards protecting him against interference or damage. It follows then, that liberty and exposure are exactly equal and correlative in any given transaction.

[1] *Op. cit.* Salmond, 195.

The "liberty" of one is his permission to act as he pleases, supported against interference by the power of the concern or government of which he is a member. The "exposure" of the opposite person is his corresponding inability or incapacity or disability to call upon the concern to protect him against any damage inflicted by the one who is thus granted permission to do as he pleases. Thus liberty and exposure are together the great field of free competition—the field of privileged damage exactly equal to the field of permitted liberty. It is the field which we shall find to be identical with that which has come to be known as "intangible property."

Thus the two "opposites" in the sense of "limits," namely, rights and exposures, vary inversely to each other, just as their correlatives, duty and liberty, vary inversely to each other. As a person's right (which tells how far he *can* expect the authorities to help him) is enlarged by the act of a superior authority, just so far is his exposure to the correspondingly reduced liberty of others diminished; and as his exposures are increased his rights to the corresponding duty of performance, avoidance and forbearance on the part of others are diminished.

Liberty, then, is simply the limit of duty, not the absence or denial of any duty at all. Liberty and duty are limiting dimensions of the same transaction. At the limit of duty the limit of authorized liberty begins. To diminish one's duty is to increase one's liberty. But this is also to diminish the protection or assistance promised to the opposite person and thus to enlarge that person's exposure to damage without remedy from the behavior of the liberated one. The field of authorized liberty is the field where behavior is unrestrained or uncompelled by authority. One is at liberty to do as he pleases in dealing with the other, and, in doing so, one commits no unauthorized act, that is, *no wrong*, or legal injury. He is not required to avoid, nor to perform a service, nor to forbear exerting excessive power over another. To say that one has "no right" is to say that the opposite person has "liberty," and to that extent the one is exposed to the possibility of any behavior that the other may choose within that dimension of his physical, economic, or moral power. The correlative of liberty is a limitation of the right, and this is exposure to the behavior of others. Liberty and exposure begin where duty and right end. "Liberty" is protected liberty; "exposure" is unprotected liberty. The two are equal and opposite, that is, correlative.

It will be noted that the term "opposite" and the terms "positive and negative" have now revealed an additional meaning not yet adverted to, in the opposition of interests between the person claiming the right and the person disclaiming the duty. The right of one is "positive," the duty of the other is "negative." While the term "opposite" in both the practitioner's sense and the dialectical sense signifies logical affirmation or denial, and in the behavioristic sense of limits it signifies more or less, much or little, plus and minus, yet in the *social* sense it signifies opposite persons, whether buyer and seller, borrower and lender, employer and laborer, competitor and competitor. The same treble meaning holds respecting the terms positive and negative. Positive and negative meant pragmatically and dialectically Yes and No, then behavioristically it meant more of one and less of another, then socially it means I and You. The first is logical inference or dialectics, the second is economics, the third is ethics and law.

V. Authoritative Transactions

1. *Collective Power*

We have seen that unauthorized transactions are likely to fail in the two respects of lack of correlation and insecurity of expectations. For this reason a government or judiciary, with its rules regarding transactions, is needed to intervene with the double purpose of correlating rights, exposures, liberties, duties, and of maintaining the correlation even if the parties prove false or change their minds. Hence, even these authorized transactions must prove to be empty and ineffective if the superior authority is not at hand with power and willingness to make good on its promises and commands. In order to do so it must bring to the assistance or compulsion of the individual the collective power of the concern.

Even the most autocratic government within a concern is not autocratic, if by autocracy is meant government by the will of one person. That one must always govern, even in that diminutive concern, the family, mainly through the wills of a few or many with whom he shares his power. But autocracy has a juristic meaning as well as psychological. Psychologically it is the promises and commands emanating from the autocrat and holding together about his person a sufficient number of effective spirits through whom he imposes his will on all. Juristically, autocracy is just the absence of any restraints or compulsions on the behavior of the autocrat himself, which prevent him from violating his promises or issuing and enforcing unlimited commands. Psychologically, autocracy is personal influence, juristically it is absence of another supreme power able to control the autocrat. Psychologically, it never can be said that any autocrat was or can be absolute. He is always more or less democratic in psychology, though autocratic in law. This is simply because he cannot be cited to appear before a superior earthly authority which has power to restrain or compel him at points where they might think his behavior objectionable. That is, he cannot be compelled to defend himself in court.

This distinction between psychology and jurisprudence was worked out slowly in England through several centuries of experiment, but without any of these theoretical distinctions which now we are able to make in looking back. Anglo-American law began with William the Conqueror. William and his lawyers, as we have seen, did not distinguish between his sovereignty and his property.[1] He was both lord and landlord. The island was his and the people were both tenants and subjects. They held of him at his will, on their promises of good behavior and his promise of protection. There was no recognized earthly power superior to him that could prevent him from violating any promise he had made to them. He governed them in all activities, the chief of which were the political and economic activities which later became differentiated. Their political activities appeared in the crude form of military assemblages where his decrees were formulated, and his franchises, patents, grants of land—the *libertates* of his favored subjects—were dispensed. This signified, too, his government at will—juristically, if not psychologically—of their economic activities—the production and consumption of wealth. Later theories, originating in the 17th and 18th centuries, after politics and economics had been somewhat differentiated, went back, for the data of their theories, to a more primitive time, a golden age when everybody was supposed to be free, and formulated "natural laws" of self-interest and contract to explain political and economic activities, while still later theories of the 19th century revised these assumptions and went back to a barbarous communistic age and then worked out the evolution of economic conditions from hunting and fishing, herding, trade and commerce, to modern industry, omitting this significant volitional evolution of politics and economics which in the Anglo-American case began with William the Conqueror in 1066. The starting point of modern economics and politics begins with conquest and the simple juristic relations resulting therefrom may be displayed as follows:

[1] Above, Chap. III, p. 48.

FIGURE X

ABSOLUTE POWER

William   *Subjects & Tenants*

Power	Military and economic behavior	Liability

The unlimited legal power of William was equal to, rather was identical with, the unlimited liability of any subject to have that power used against him. Psychologically the absolute monarch might not choose to go beyond a certain limit, and, physically, he might not be able to go. He must command through their will to obey. But juristically he might go to any limit, because he could not be cited to appear in court. Psychologically and physically they might be safe; juristically they were exposed. Their exposure was their subjection, which, more accurately, is named their liability, to his exercise of the collective compulsion which he commanded.

It is presumable that, in addition to any feelings of sympathy for his subjects, William and his successors were moved at times to ethical feelings of obligation toward them, under the theory that his power, being derived from God, ought not to be used without limit on those who were also subject to the same divine power. Assuming that such feelings occasionally weighed upon him, the superior prohibition thus placed on his power can be expressed, in the language of lawyers, as a *disability*. His subjects, too, presumably at times entertained the similar feeling, that, being subject to the same divine rule as William, they ought not to be subject to his unlimited control of the collective power. This limit on their subjection to his power would be expressed, in juristic language, as an *immunity*. These are the terms which we have seen employed by Hohfeld.

The difficulty, however, with these ethical and religious notions was the lack of correlation between the autocrat's feelings and their feelings. While both might agree on the principle they might disagree in its application. This lack of correlation might appear as follows:

FIGURE XI

ETHICAL TRANSACTIONS

William		Subjects & Tenants
Power	Political Economic	Liability
Disability		Immunity

UNCORRELATED

The barons at Runnymede, in 1215, as is well known, attempted to place limits on the collective power of William's successor, John, by organizing a collective power of their own and inducing him to sign a document acknowledging these limits. Had they succeeded in limiting his power they would, of course, correlatively, have limited their liability to subjection, and the resulting correlation of juristic relations could have been shown as herewith:

FIGURE XII

LIMITED POWER—CONSTITUTIONAL GOVERNMENT

CORRELATIVES

	John		Barons
L i m i t s	Power	Politics Economics	Liability
	Disability		Immunity

The difficulty with Magna Carta consisted in the fact that it was a scrap of paper, in that there was behind it no enduring physical power greater than that of the King, able to hold him to his promise and the working rules agreed upon. It was, indeed, agreed that the barons might set up a committee to watch him, and this committee was named in the document,[1] but it provided no executives or judges

[1] *Op. cit.* McKechnie, *Magna Carta*, 466–7; below, Chap. VI, p. 217.

continuously in session who could bring him before them and decide any dispute that might arise between him and the subject. The committee was authorized to declare war on him, but no provision was made for compulsory arbitration or judicial determination short of civil war.

This defect was not fully corrected until nearly five hundred years afterwards, in the Act of Settlement in the year 1700, although many expedients were tried meanwhile, including that of killing the King and taking over the operation of the concern by a debating society that worked badly. The Act of Settlement was more ingenious than this expedient, in that it retained the King but separated him into two personalities, one a sovereign, later known as "The Crown," the other a private citizen, somewhat privileged indeed,[1] but with rights and liberties like other citizens over his own person and his private property. Thus property was finally separated from sovereignty; not only for the King, but also for all other citizens. The way was opened for each citizen to become a member of two concerns, the political concern exercising sovereignty and the business concern operating property, each according to its own rules.

The essential features of this arrangement, constituting a compromise set of working rules, were fourfold. *First*, the device of Collective Bargaining by which the collective physical power of the political concern—the Sovereign, or Crown—could not be exercised except by way of that mutual veto on each other of King, Lords and Commons, acting separately. *Second*, the device of Representation, or Parliamentarism, by which scattered citizens need not assemble in arms in order to exercise their veto but might do so by majority vote through representatives of their own choosing. *Third*, the device of Delegation of Power, by which the exercise of collective power in actual transactions with citizens was taken out of the hands of the King and entrusted to various agents whom he could not remove, the executives and judges. By the last device it became possible, without citing the King to appear in person, to cite his agents and to place limits, under the name of disabilities, on their exercise of collective power. *Fourth*, the device of Official Responsibility by means of which executives, judges and representatives were made liable to removal from office by impeachment or periodic election, or were made subject to the decrees of the same

[1] See CHITTY, JOSEPH, *Treatise on the Law of the Prerogatives of the Crown*, 5, 374 ff. (1820).

courts which decided the disputes between private citizens.[1] By this arrangement of working rules ingeniously set forth as a system of checks and balances, one set of officials, or the citizens participating in elections, were entrusted with power limited by disabilities, and other officials were made liable to the exercise of that power, limited by immunities.

These various devices had been worked out through experiment and then consolidated and clinched in the Act of Settlement, so that what was attempted in Magna Carta by way of provision for civil war was now effected by placing limits on the agents of the King in their exercise of the collective power. In America this arrangement was carried still further, and the Justices of the Supreme Court were given authority to limit even the power of legislatures by disabilities, as well as the power of executives, and besides, to determine the disabilities that limited their own powers as judges.

It will thus be noticed, that the device of Official Responsibility introduced an arrangement, not clearly contemplated in Magna Carta, which may be designated Reciprocity. Officials have reciprocal powers, liabilities, disabilities and immunities in their relations to each other, and, most important, the will of the citizen can take advantage of these reciprocal relations in order to assert for himself a share in sovereignty and thus be able to bring the collective power to the support of what he deems to be his own rights and liberties and the corresponding duties and exposures of others.

Thus it will have been noted, in all cases of constitutional law upon which we have based our analysis, that citizens brought suit not against other citizens but against officials. Holden brought suit against Hardy the sheriff; Munn brought suit against the State of Illinois, that is, against all of the pertinent officials of that state. Having obtained a decision as to the powers, immunities, liabilities and disabilities of officials, Holden, Munn and others obtained thereby a decision as to their own rights, liberties, duties and exposures. Thus, by making officials and citizens responsible to the same courts and the same process of law the citizens themselves became participants in sovereignty, and a reciprocal arrangement is set up between citizens and officials through the action of other officials. Citizens obtain not only a negative immunity from the acts of officials, as contemplated in Magna Carta, but also a positive power in their

---

[1] LIEBER, FRANCIS, *Civil Liberty and Self-Government*, 91 (1853).

own hands to require officials to assist in executing their private will. They need that assistance in enforcing contracts, transferring titles to property, executing their wills indefinitely after death, and so on. In order to accomplish this purpose there must be created a certain degree of *positive* power in the hands of citizens to require officials to perform as well as avoid or forbear, and this power can be neither greater nor less than the correlative liability of officials to do as required. This liability, constituting the official responsibility of officials in the use of the collective power, could scarcely be made unlimited, and the limit becomes the immunity of officials from discipline at the point where their responsibility ends. In this way the citizens themselves become sovereigns and lawgivers to a limited extent, and a reciprocal relation is set up between them and officials, partly their own subjection to officials, partly the responsibility of officials to them. This situation, consummated by the Act of Settlement in 1700, is the culmination of the business revolution and the origin of modern capitalism. The correlation, limitation and reciprocity of the resulting transactions by which citizens may hold officials responsible to a limited extent, while their own liability of subjection to governmental power is greatly limited, is represented herewith.

FIGURE XIII

AUTHORITATIVE TRANSACTIONS

——————————CORRELATIVES——————————

		Official			Citizen
	R	Power			Liability
	e		B	B′	
L	c				
i	i	Disability			Immunity
m	p				
i	r				
t	o	Immunity	S	S′	Disability
s	c				
	a				
	l	Liability			Power
	s				

The important difference to be noted between these authoritative transactions and the previously mentioned authorized transactions consists in the fact that here the subject person is not permitted to choose any alternative when once the superior person has decided. There is no bargaining between citizen and official, no power to withhold service or property, the psychological aspect of the transaction being that of command and obedience, whereas in the authorized transactions it was partly command and obedience, partly persuasion or coercion. There may, of course, transpire certain debates between an inferior and a superior, certain negotiations, appeals, or remonstrances. These may even look like bargaining when they take the form known as lobbying, log-rolling, trading votes, or corruption of officials, but when the decision of the competent official, whether executive, legislative or judicial, is once made, the subject or official must, of course, obey. In order that these authoritative transactions may be protected against bargaining, the well-known devices of a public hearing, notice of hearing, and related procedure have grown up in practice and been consolidated under the name, "due process of law." [1]

It will be seen that here we have a measuring off of degrees of power pertaining to the physical dimensions of performance, avoidance and forbearance similar to that in the case of authorized transactions. The collective physical power which the official brings against the citizen is limited by certain deductions, first, negatively by his disability, or absence of official power, and second, positively, by his responsibility, that is, liability to compulsion if he does not bring the power of the concern to the aid of the citizen. But this liability is itself limited by his official immunity, wherein he is not to be held to answer for any discretionary use which he may have made of the collective power exercised by him.

These collective powers, exercised by officials on behalf of citizens, are likely to be called into action upon two different kinds of contingencies, and to them may be given the names of Remedial and Substantive powers. Remedial powers may be employed on occasion of *wrongful* acts of other persons, substantive powers on occasion of *rightful* acts of self. These two types of legal power are neither separable nor unlimited, but are determined in the extent to which they may be exercised by what may, therefore, be distinguished as

[1] Below, Chap. IX.

the Determining Powers in that the latter are the discretionary or legislative limits placed by legislatures, executives and judges on the exercise of remedial and substantive powers.

2. *Remedial Powers—Wrongful Acts*

A debt is owed by one party to another. If the second party fails to pay at the appointed time and place, the first party forthwith is vested with a right to come into court and there to require the executive and the judicial officers to enforce on the second party specific performance or reparation. Or, rights and liberties of avoidance, forbearance and performance of one party are infringed by another party and forthwith the former is clothed, by operation of common rule applicable to similar cases, with a right to have the courts and executive officers assess, collect and deliver to him the pecuniary compensation or penalties authorized in respect of the damage suffered from the wrongful act. The event which calls into action these potential authoritative transactions is the wrongful act of an opposing party, or even the assertion or affidavit that there has been or will be a wrongful act. Wrongful acts, or threats of wrongful acts, the actual or menaced violation of duty, give rise, at once and automatically, by the implied promises of the superior authority embodied in the working rules, to this "right of action," [1] a procedural, or remedial, right on the part of the claimant to have its functionaries, the judges, juries, sheriffs, constables, executives, police, even the army and all the instruments of collective power, to come to his aid, if necessary. Of course, if the official acts *before* the wrong is committed and thus prevents it, the right of action does not perhaps, arise.

Prior to the wrongful act or menace, the right of action existed only as an alternative expectancy, a potential right. On the side of the claimant the expectancy was a juristic "capacity," a "faculty," an "ability," a "power," signifying a promise of the state expressed in one of its working rules that its officials will come to his aid if he appeals to them. On the side of the opposing party it was a juristic liability, an expectation of subjection to collective power, a potential enforcement of duty by officials, in case the plaintiff appealed to them. The two are correlative and equal. The power of one to get officials to act if the right is violated or menaced *is* the liability of the other

---

[1] "Right of Prosecution" in criminal cases.

to be acted upon by responsible officials if he violates or menaces it. Juristic power and juristic liability are the two opposing sides of the identical remedial transaction. One is potential power, that is, legal capacity, to have an authorized transaction enforced; the other is potential subjection, that is, liability, to its enforcement. Furthermore, the remedy is simply the power of one set of officials to hold another set of officials responsible for enforcing the remedy. The situation may be indicated as follows:

FIGURE XIV

REMEDIAL POWER—WRONGFUL ACT

Official	Citizen			Citizen	Official
Power	Right (power)	B	B′	Duty (liability)	(liability) Responsibility
		S	S′		

The remedial power-liability relation between officials is exactly equal to and is, indeed, the equivalent of the right-duty relation between citizens, since it is the official liability of the one that constitutes the private liability of the other to have his duty lawfully enforced. Quantitatively an authorized transaction is no greater and no less, in its several dimensions, than the authoritative transactions sanctifying it. And the legal right of a person is none other than his power to get the right enforced.

This identity of a right and its remedy, while usually recognized, is yet confused, in its application to the analysis of legal concepts, by certain abstractions taken over from the 18th century philosophy which give to the notion of right and duty an eternal, heavenly, natural, or preëxisting "substance," apart from the actual behavior of mundane courts and executives who are depended upon to recognize and enforce it. In one sense the right does exist as a "fact" before either it or its remedy is exercised—but, if so, then the "fact" is only a mental process, a hope, a fear, an expectation that since a certain working rule has been applied in the past, it will be applied again in similar cases. This tendency of the human mind to objectify dogmatically what is only its hopes, fears and memories, leads to an abstraction and segregation of concepts which are, in reality, identical. Thus Hohfeld refrains from identifying right with power, or duty with liability. The abstraction is more explicit in Kocourek's contrast between the two relations "power-liability" and "claim-duty." These two relationships are "contraries," according to him, in that power-liability relates to the advantage of *one* person who acts to the disadvantage of another person, whereas claim-duty relates to the advantage which the *other* person confers on the first. This contrary direction from which the behavior initiates will be seen in Kocourek's examples of "contraries," as follows: [1]

Claim-Duty—"The dominus may have a 'claim' (right) against the servus to have an act performed by the servus; for example, to render services under a contract; here the disadvantage of the servus is the 'duty' to do the act."

Power-Liability—"When the dominus has a 'power,' he can act toward the servus with legal constraint; for example, an unpaid creditor may bring an action against his defaulting debtor; the debtor is under the disadvantage of a 'liability' to be sued."

Evidently, the two situations relate to two alternatives of the same situation. One is the ethical assertion by the dominus of a duty on the part of the servus to perform an act for the advantage of the dominus. The other is the alternative liability to compulsion of the servus if the dominus resorts to *his* alternative appeal to the court. The "power-liability" relation calls attention to the "remedial" procedure but the right-duty relation calls attention to the "substantive," that is, ethical assertion. Yet the two are identical. When there is no remedy there is no right. The ethical remedy is a fight. The legal remedy is lawful compulsion, either with or without a proceeding in court. Even if there is nominally a legal remedy yet the nominally authorized right extends actually no further and is no less than the actual legal remedy. But the remedy is none other than the activity of officials setting the machinery of government in motion, and getting one set of officials to hold another set of officials responsible for enforcing what they define to be the rights in the case. If the officials are corrupt, negligent, incompetent, biased, or revolutionists, the legal right is nevertheless exactly the equivalent of what they do

[1] *Op. cit.* KOCOUREK, 19 *Mich. Law Rev.* 49. KOCOUREK's "claim" is the equivalent of HOHFELD's "right."

or may be expected to do, and practical sophisticated men, without illusions, act accordingly, although ethically they may condemn the situation.

Thus private law is inseparable from public law, which is the procedure designed to enforce responsibility upon officials. The responsibility of officials is the liability of citizens to be required to fulfill their duties. Responsibility of officials is their liability to be acted upon through judicial mandamus or injunction, through legislative impeachment, through executive removal from office, through popular election or recall. A customary but abstract term for this procedure is government, or the State. Windscheid speaks of it still more abstractly as "the legal order."[1] Since, however, government and the legal order are behavioristically none other than the officials-in-action, we speak of it as simply officials. The correlative of the power of officials is the liability of other officials.

Hence every legal right, that is, every authorized transaction, has two opposite parties burdened each by his correlative duty. The legal right of B is the legal duty of B', S or S', and the legal right of B is also the duty of officials to enforce the duty of B', S, or S'. The legal duty of B', S or S', the *servus*, is identical with his liability that the official will perform *his* legal duty in affording a remedy. Likewise the legal right of B, the *dominus*, is equal to his "power" to set the machinery of justice in motion and thus to hold officials to their responsibility. This legal power is his legal "capacity," "capability," or "legal ability," but since this capacity is none other than the extent to which he is clothed with power of participation in government it might be designated simply as "citizenship." Historically it is Freedom as distinguished from Liberty. Liberty is absence of restraint. Freedom is participation in government.[2] Yet conformity to usage will retain the term "power," understanding, however, that its meaning is identical with that of either citizenship, freedom, or legal capacity or ability.

So that an effective legal right is represented, as above (Fig. XIV), by the correlation and equivalence of right and duty with official power and official responsibility. Performance or punishment are the alternatives offered to one party. They exist together as duty and liability, the duty to perform and the liability to punishment. The

---

[1] Cited by POUND, ROSCOE, 26 *Int. Jour. Ethics*, 107 (1915).
[2] Below, p. 118 ff.

identical performance and punishment are also the alternatives of the other party, but they exist together as the right to have performance and the power to have punishment inflicted. The latter is the authoritative remedial transaction; the former is the authorized substantive transaction, while the two are legal equivalents.

We have suggested above what seems to be the proper distinction between ethical and legal rights and duties. Ethical and legal rights were once conceived to be the "substance"; remedial rights were the "form" through which the substance is realized. Rights were substantive, remedies were procedural. But modern realism reverses this notion of substance and form. It is the "form" that *now* is the reality, for it is none other than the actual behavior of officials which is the only legal reality that we really know. And that which was "the substance" is now only the ethical and legal *ideal*, the *wish*, the *hope* of something that *ought* to exist but may or may not exist. It does exist in one sense—it exists in the mind's eye. As an abstract entity, existing infinitely somewhere unknown, or as an ethical right unauthorized and uncorrelated, or as a right that once existed, the right may fondly seem to have an independent existence, as is implied in the term "substantive right" applied to these insubstantial entities. While lawyers insist that the legal and ethical right is there as a "fact," even though the law provides no remedy, the sagacious legislator, lobbyist, or corruptionist, goes to the heart of the right and cuts out the remedy. For as an actual, living reality, the right exists only in the expected behavior of officials, and there is where the prudent lobbyist, business man or workingman locates it and finds its real substance. Idealism gives to these airy nothings a local habitation and a name, but sagacity inquires what will the judge on the bench, the jury in the box, the executive on the highway, *do?*

This idealism survives in many vestiges. The distinction, for example, is usually made between a "perfect" and an "imperfect" right (Salmond, 197; Terry, 140). A "perfect" right is one enforceable as to all of its collateral implied transactions. An "imperfect" right is one that lacks enforcement as to certain transactions, such, for example, as the right against a laborer for damage on account of breaking a contract to work. Yet according to the Thirteenth Amendment and the wage-exemption laws, this right is unenforceable, and, to that extent, does not exist even on paper, and has no value in the actual practices of a going business. It is an exposure and not a right.

So with a laborer's right against an employer or a corporation. If he cannot get officials to enforce his right, it does not exist in this finite world. The "perfect" right is the lawyer's ideal of what *ought* to be the legal right but actually is not.

But these powers and responsibilities of officials are not unlimited. Hohfeld, as noted above, designates the "opposite " of "power" a "disability," and the opposite of liability an immunity. Kocourek criticises these "opposites" as either mere negations or as non-jural or quasi-jural relations. We have indicated above the justification of Hohfeld's terminology. If, as above, we substitute the term "limits" for "opposites" the same reasoning will apply. Official immunity is the *limit* of official liability, and this is correlative and equal to the disability of other officials in the exercise of power to hold this official responsible. This disability of officials is therefore equivalent to a disability of the citizen to require officials to protect his rights, and hence is identical with his exposure, which now we find to be none other than the limit of his legal capacity, or power, where begins his legal inability, incapacity, incapability, in short, his disability. This, in turn, is the exactly equal immunity of officials which now becomes the equivalent immunity of citizens, identical with their liberty, which in turn is the limit of their duties. The correlation, limitation and equivalence of these legal relations is as follows:

FIGURE XV

REMEDIAL POWER—WRONGFUL ACTS

————————CORRELATIVES AND EQUIVALENTS————————

	Official	*Citizen*			*Citizen*	*Official*
L i m	Power	Right (power)	B	B′	Duty (liability)	Liability (responsibility)
i t s	Disability	Exposure (disability)	S	S′	Liberty (immunity)	Immunity

It must be noted that these diagrams of correlatives, equivalents, and limitations apply only to a *single* legal relation in its simplest form abstracted from all other legal relations. For example, as stated by a friendly critic, "while exposure (no-right) in a citizen is perhaps always accompanied by disability to make it the duty of officials to act, it is not always accompanied by a disability to terminate the exposure. Thus I offer to plough your field for $100. You have as yet no-right against me (you are still exposed to the disadvantage of my not ploughing). And you have a disability to set officials in action of enforcement. But you have *power* to extinguish both your exposure (no-right) and your procedural disability by accepting my offer." In this illustration, it will be noted, we have two sets of legal relations, and not one. The first is a disability, and an exposure to damage; the second is a power, that is a right, to terminate the exposure.

It will be observed that the above-noted equivalence of rights and duties with powers and liabilities follows from the social-economic standpoint of the public purpose that justifies the rules governing official and private transactions. Hohfeld, looking at it from the standpoint of the private purpose of an individual inquiring what he can expect in a trial court, does not consider the economic or ethical consequences of the law. His classification expresses only the *fact* of social compulsion upon the individual—Ours involves the *purpose* of social compulsion on any or all individuals.

We distinguish, therefore, between the ultimate purpose and two levels of instrumental purpose. The ultimate purpose is ethical—the public welfare or commonwealth as conceived by the authorities. The instrumental purpose is primarily legal and secondarily economic. Legally, it is the purpose of controlling the behavior of officials who exercise the collective power of physical compulsion. Secondarily and economically, this legal purpose controls the quantities, values and prices of things produced, sold, bought and consumed. Thus the instrumental purposes of civilized man are two-fold, namely, control of the coercive behavior of officials through citizenship, and control of the economic behavior of other citizens through control of power and choice of opportunities. The ultimate purpose, inseparable from the two, is the ethical purpose of inducing and sharing the production of all the services that constitute the limited resources of the commonwealth.

3. *Substantive Powers—Lawful Acts*

The foregoing relates to the "capacity" of a member of the concern to have the collective power enforce an authorized duty on an opposing party, and his even more important capacity to prevent the collective power from enforcing an alleged duty on himself. But there is a still further meaning of collective power. The "right" to make a will carries no correlative duty of the person to whom the property is willed, and hence calls for no remedy against that party. It is not, indeed, a right, but rather a "power," since it is a capacity of the owner to have future officials of the state make his will effective long after he has quit. It is a right against officials—a highly complex bundle of powers and corresponding responsibilities of officials. But even while he is alive he cannot legally make his will effective by his own power. Mr. A sells or gives to B a watch. It is a physical performance. But A cannot transfer to B the power to do as he pleases with that watch if other persons object, except as the state attributes to B all of the authorized and authoritative transactions necessary to keep, use and sell the watch.

A tells B to go to China and buy for him a coal mine. It is a managerial performance. But B cannot obtain the coal mine for A unless A's government has made arrangements with China and the other great powers, and also unless it attributes to B all of the needful powers of an agent executing the will of A, and imposes on B subjection to the will of A. This implies that all the necessary officials of government are burdened with the responsibility of seeing to it that A's will is executed. It is this type of power which may be named substantive powers of citizenship. Substantive powers and remedial powers do not differ at all in the source of power. Each is the same power of the citizen to call upon officials to obey his will. A substantive power is indeed a mere wish unless backed and enforced by a remedial power. The two are inseparable. The substantive power creates legal relations, the remedial power enforces them. For these reasons legal writers do not find it necessary often to distinguish them. Yet the operative facts which bring the two into existence are separate in time, in character and in person. A substantive power arises out of lawful acts of the principal party creating legal relations for the future. A remedial power arises out of an unlawful act of an opposite party infringing on legal relations created in the past. In the latter case, the state holds another party liable to compulsion in the observance of a duty; in the former case the state authorizes the principal party to create new rights and impose new duties on behalf or against self or others. Windscheid distinguished the two when he said, "the legal order ascribes to the person entitled a controlling will, not for the enforcement but for the existence of a command of the legal order." [1]

Remedial power as we have seen, is that "power of obtaining in one's favor the judgment of a court of law which is called a right of action." [2] But substantive powers, besides the three types mentioned above arising out of wills, alienation and agency, include innumerable others, such as powers of appointment, abandonment, contracts, options, the powers of sale vested in a mortgagee, a landlord's right of entry, the right to rescind a contract for fraud, and so on. [3] Terry describes these remedial and substantive powers as a "fourth species of rights," "facultative rights or faculties," which, however, he says are not "rights" since they have no correlative duties corresponding to them. [4] Salmond, too, points out that, while they are "legally recognized interests" they are not legal rights *stricto sensu*, since they are not rights against any person. They are rather "powers," which he defines as the "ability conferred upon a person by the law to determine, by his own will directed to that end, the rights, duties, liabilities, or other legal relations, either of himself or other persons." "Public powers" are distinguished from "private powers." "Public powers" are the powers "vested in a person as an agent or instrument of the functions of the state; they comprise the various forms of legislative, judicial, and executive authority. Private powers, on the other hand, are those which are vested in persons to be exercised for their own purposes, and not as agents of the state." [5] Yet, as we have seen, it is by making officials responsible to private persons that these "private powers" are also "public powers." These substantive powers *are* rights against other persons, but the *other persons are officials*.

Hohfeld, likewise, correctly criticises the use of the term "right," "so frequently and loosely used," where the proper term is "legal ability" or legal power. And, respecting the correlative of legal power, he says, "While, no doubt, the term liability is often loosely used as a synonym for 'duty,' or 'obligation,' yet it is rather a condition of subjection, responsibility, or accountability to a superior power residing in an opposite person." "The person (or persons) whose volitional control is paramount may be said to have the (legal) power to effect

---

[1] Quoted by POUND, 26 *Int. Jour. of Ethics*, 108 (1915).
[2] *Op. cit.* 3 SALMOND, 192.
[3] SALMOND, 192; HOHFELD, 23 *Yale Law Jour.* 44 ff.
[4] TERRY, Sec. 127.
[5] SALMOND, 193, 194.

the particular change of legal relations that is involved in the problem." [1] In other words, he has the power, by means of the correlative official responsibility (duty) imposed on the agents of the state, to subject the wills of other persons to his own will.

The term "subjection" or "liability" does not signify necessarily coercive subjection. It may be, and is sometimes persuasive. "We are apt to think of liability," says Hohfeld, "as exclusively an *onerous* relation of one party to another. But, in its broad technical significance, this is not necessarily so. Thus X, the owner of a watch, has the power to abandon his property . . . and correlatively to X's power of abandonment there is a liability in every other person. But such a liability, instead of being onerous or unwelcome, is quite the opposite." [2] So with other instances of subjection. The beneficiary of a will, in modern law, enjoys a welcome subjection to the will of the testator, though this would be unwelcome, if, as in ancient law or the law of peonage, the law implied in the will of a testator that his heir should succeed to his debts even though they exceeded the value of the assets. Modern law tends, more and more, to place a limit on the substantive and remedial powers of citizens where those powers are used to coerce, embarrass, or impoverish others, since it is, after all, the power of the state that is called upon to keep them in subjection.

The combined scheme of substantive and remedial powers is presented herewith. The substantive power of B is the subjection of B', S, or S', to his will in that it is his power to create rights for himself and duties upon the others. The extent to which he can create them is no greater and no less than the remedial power which he can obtain through responsibility of officials in case of disobedience of his command. This limit of power to impose compulsion on the others is his exposure to their liberty through his legal disability which is the disability of officials to aid him.

---

[1] *Op. cit.*, HOHFELD, 44, 45.
[2] *Op. cit.*, HOHFELD, 54n.

FIGURE XVI

SUBSTANTIVE AND REMEDIAL POWERS

————————CORRELATIVES AND EQUIVALENTS————————

	Power Remedial, Substantive	Right (power)			Duty (liability)	Liability (responsibility) Remedial, Substantive
L i m i t s			B	B′		
	Disability Remedial & Substantive	Exposure (disability)	S	S′	Liability (immunity)	Immunity Remedial, Substantive

We have noted the statements of Salmond and others that substantive and remedial powers differ from rights in the strict sense, in that they have no duties corresponding to them. Yet, as already suggested, if we look at it, not from the practitioner's point of view in a trial court, but from the governmental point of view in questions of public law, there is, as above stated, a significant duty corresponding to power, namely, the responsibility of officials enforced by mandamus, impeachment or otherwise. Defined in terms of behavior, the citizen's power to make a will is his legal power to command officials to execute his will after death; the power of alienation is the power to command officials of the government to recognize and enforce, for the benefit of the alienee, all of the rights, liberties, etc., previously vested in or disposable by the alienor. So with the power of attorney, and similar powers to make one's will effective. And the power extends just as far as the power and will of government to hold officials to their duties in enforcing the will of the citizen. Hohfeld, therefore, is within bounds, when he says that the correlative, even of substantive powers, is a liability of the person for whose benefit the power is exercised. But, it must be noted, this liability extends no further than the corresponding official liability.

We are now in position to summarize the economic and ethical significance of these substantive and remedial powers. It is these that constitute the historic distinction between "freedom" and "liberty." Liberty, as such, is only the negative of duty, the absence of restraint or compulsion. But "freedom" is positive. The "freedom of the city" was not only negatively an immunity from control by surrounding feudal lords and from subjection to other citizens but also positively a participation in the rights, liberties, and powers needed to make one's will effective in dealings with other citizens. The freedom of the ex-slave was not only that empty immunity from legal subjection to his master provided for in the Thirteenth Amendment of Emancipation from slavery, but also the participation in citizenship provided in the Fourteenth and Fifteenth Amendments. It was the latter that endowed him with legal power to buy and sell, to make wills and contracts, in fact, the power to create, in himself, by his own labor, rights against any or all other persons to the product of his labor, and to create in other persons rights to that product by merely transferring it to them.

This is the historic meaning of freedom distinguished from liberty and, as such, it is identical with what we distinguish as substantive and remedial power. Freedom is power. It belongs to the "freeman," but not to the mere "freedman." It is power to call on the officials to make one's will effective, and its correlative is the subjection or liability of an opposite party through the commands of the law.

It is this ambiguity of "freedom" and "liberty" that constitutes the grand confusion in economic, legal and ethical science. Starting out with a definition of liberty as mere absence of restraint or compulsion, the discussion slides over, without seeing what happens, into a "right to liberty," and, if a distinction is made between "liberty," and "freedom" it somehow is indefinitely thought that freedom is a larger and more beneficent liberty. What really happens is, that the meaning has moved over from absence of compulsion by a private citizen into power to compel others to obey by the help of a superior power. If the slave is given his "liberty," as by the Thirteenth Amendment that confirmed emancipation, it signifies merely a negative limit on the former right of the master in so far as the Amendment prohibited him from commanding the unlimited service of the slave. It did not as yet give the freedman positive participation in all the possible transactions necessary to exercise his liberty. He might be prevented from going away to another state or neighborhood, prevented from contracting to work for other employers, prevented from obtaining payment of wages due him, prevented from having access to the courts and due process of law. While he gained his liberty he did not gain the freedom of choice needed to complete his liberty, nor the power of the state to back him up in his exercise of liberty. In place of his former obedience to commands he gains only choiceless alternatives, and may be coerced to return to his master and "willingly" agree to submit again to commands. Hence the Fourteenth Amendment was necessary, making him a citizen of the United States and providing that "no state shall make or enforce any law which shall abridge the privileges or immunities of citizens of the United States; nor—deprive any person of life, liberty or property without due process of law; nor deny to any person within its jurisdiction the equal protection of the laws."

What this was intended to accomplish was to endow the ex-slave positively with the same rights to call upon the courts and officials that other citizens possessed. It added freedom to liberty, for it added the power of the state to make his will effective by binding all other persons in obedience to him in the execution of all contracts which he and they were permitted to make. This freedom, like theirs, was limited, of course, and these limitations were presumed to accomplish that complete equality of treatment, by which not only none could be deprived of liberty by being compelled to obey another without one's consent, but also none could be deprived of freedom by being compelled to consent through lack of power to make his will effective through the aid of the physical power of the nation. Likewise in other fields of collective power. When the capitalist speaks of "freedom" and "liberty" his freedom is but his share in the collective power of the nation, and his liberty is but his absence of duty, but protection against interference in using that collective power as he pleases.

For these reasons we have distinguished between legal power, and the physical, economic and moral power of the individual. The latter, as we have seen, are various aspects of the individual's power over others. But legal power is Freedom, the power to call on the state to authorize, enforce and sanction his use of physical, economic or moral power. Freedom is the power of the state in the hands of individuals; economic, physical or moral power is their own power exercised by themselves. The two coincide, for individual power is exercised through the performance, avoidance, forbearance, which constitute the physical dimensions of transactions; while freedom, or juristic power, in its dimensions of power, disability, liability and immunity, is the assistance, indifference, or resistance of the state in subjecting others to performance, avoidance, forbearance beyond the power of the individual so to do.

Legal power, that is, Freedom, is substantive though inseparable from remedial power, for it is the very substance on which full membership or citizenship in a concern depends. It signifies the extent to which the collective power listens to, authorizes and executes both the will of the individual and the collective will of subordinate concerns. To the extent that the individual is clothed with this sovereign power of the state, does he rise from the nakedness of slave, child, woman, alien, into the armament of a citizen, and his going concern rises from a conspiracy into a corporation. It is to these substantive powers and remedial powers that modern capitalism owes its powers of expansion, for it is they that enable the business man who is citizen of a great enduring nation to extend his sway from the Arctic to the Antarctic, from Occident to Orient; that enable him to build up a credit system by creating obligations that bind him, his successors, and his debtors, for years and decades to come; that endow him with power to breathe into his going business the immortality of a corporation.[1]

4. *Determining Powers*

Probability.—So far we have considered only what may be described as the rational or logical relations existing between legal and economic ideas, but have not considered the behavior to which the reasoning applies. These rational relations are simply abstract concepts emptied of all content and then correlated mathematically in such a way as to be true no matter what happens. Our

---

[1] It will be seen that the comment of Dean Pound to the effect that the common law is a law whose basic concept is that of "relations" between parties and not that of either the "will" or of "contracts" or of "transactions," does not run counter to the concept of the will or of transactions herein developed. The concept of the will which he criticises is that which we have distinguished as the concept of a "free will" rather than that of a "free choice." His concept of a transaction is that of a "legal transaction," namely a "contract," whereas ours is that of an "economic transaction." And his concept of "relations" is substantially identical with our concept of a transaction. A transaction is an active relation between parties having both the economic dimensions of opportunity and power and the legal dimensions of reciprocal rights, duties, etc., which arise from the working rule to which the transaction belongs. The term transaction is preferable to relations, for our purposes, because transactions are the concrete active operations of the will which come before the court and to which the court applies the rules respecting the legal relations deemed appropriate in the case. Our concept of the will as what the will *does* rather than what the will *is*, combines in one behavioristic concept the legal, volitional, economic and social concepts which Pound, in his history of legal interpretations, necessarily separates into the four concepts of the will, the contract, the legal relation and the economic relation. POUND, ROSCOE, *Interpretations of Legal History*, 57 (1923).

rationalizing would be equally correct whether applied to a band of savages, a soviet, England, Germany, or the United States. It has been simply a scheme of words and definitions, a set of mere symbols or "universals" tied together logically, it is believed, yet serving merely as a kind of mental compass by which we may hope to navigate the actual flux of behavior in the world of reality. We need now to know the *differences* that must be introduced in order to distinguish whether we are talking about savages, soviets, or American judges, executives, business men and workingmen. We construct the compass because we wish to know where we are going and what to do. The compass is an illusion if we do not know the behavior of stars, winds, waves and lighthouse keepers.

It is the duty of a policeman to arrest persons found intoxicated in public places. In order to do this he carries with him the potential power of the state. His exercise of that power is limited at the point where his legal disability begins, and to that extent the alleged intoxicant is legally immune. The policeman also is liable to be held responsible for neglect of duty or excess of power, in ensuing transactions with his superior officer or with the court. And this liability is also limited at the point where he can expect immunity. To that extent the intoxicant is legally liable. These are the just mentioned abstract relations which surround that policeman and that intoxicant when they happen to come together. But the actual relations between them, which determine how much immunity, liability or liberty there actually is, depends on what is done; and what is done is determined by that choice of alternatives which we name "discretion." The policeman decides first, whether the alleged intoxicant is really intoxicated. Whether a given person thus found is intoxicated or not is a matter of definition, of facts, of beliefs, wishes and values. One policeman may not see intoxication until the intoxicated is helpless or violent. Another may see it in a slight entanglement. One may place a high value on liberty, another on duty, another on virtue, another on joy. Within the limits of immunity at which the chief of police cautions, disciplines or removes the policeman, or the court or jury sustains or reverses him, lies his field of discretion where his own definitions and valuations determine both the facts and their weight. Within that field his will is the will of the state. He is the state-in-action. He *is* the state. The state is what its officials do. And what they do is to proportion the behavior of citizens by offering inducements in the directions which they consider important and away from the directions which they reprobate.

So it is with other officials. The legislature levies a tax on property. It lays down a common rule within the limits of its own immunity allowed by the court. But it is the assessor who values the property. Between the maximum and minimum limits of discretion, where the assessor is removed or reversed, his estimates of value give weight to the facts and his will determines the direction where taxpayers can make or lose money. Or a public commission places a value on property for compulsory purchase or for regulation of rates and services. Or another sets a minimum wage to be paid by employers, another a maximum price to be paid by consumers. Or a court and jury determine the damages to be paid by one citizen for infringing the rights of another. Or a court of equity creates a valuable property in the goodwill of customers by enjoining certain practices of a would-be competitor. Each of these official acts determines the direction of opportunities and inducements for citizens. Over all is the Supreme Court, enjoying the immunity of determining its own immunity within which it proceeds with its definitions, feelings, valuations, weighing of facts, and then determines the limits beyond which legislatures, executives, minor judges and itself may not go in proportioning the inducements which guide the behavior of citizens. Throughout, it is the officials-in-action who constitute the state-in-action, and the legal relations which we have discussed are formal statements of ideals, wishes and hopes which may or may not be realized when the officials come to act.

These fields of discretion, with their probable interplay of wills, actually determine the limits of the substantive and remedial powers, or rather, the substantive and remedial powers are the determining powers of the human will in its collective activity. They are legislative in character, but are exercised also by courts, executives and administrative officials in so far as they exercise discretion in choosing between alternatives, and their significance consists in that they determine how far the physical powers of the state shall go. In this respect they have to do, as we have noted, with two sets of relationships—those between private citizens and those between private citizens and the state. The two are equivalent for, when the relations between citizens and officials are determined this determines also the relations between citizens themselves. These determining powers are not only the taxing power and the power of eminent domain, but also the police power which determines the limits of property and liberty, including the limits of defining and enforcing contracts and naming the legal tender by means of which individuals may free themselves of liabilities.

It is these determining powers of individual wills within the limits set by other wills, which, when fully portrayed, give a complete scheme of legal correlatives, equivalents, limits and reciprocals accompanying every transaction, as follows:

FIGURE XVII

CORRELATIVES, EQUIVALENTS, LIMITS, RECIPROCALS

————————CORRELATIVES AND EQUIVALENTS————————

	Official	*Citizen*		*Citizen*	*Official*
L i m i t s	Power	Right	Opportunity	Duty	Liability
and	Disability	Exposure	P B B′ o w e r S S′	Liberty	Immunity
R e c i p r o c a l s	Immunity	Liberty		Exposure	Disability
	Liability	Duty		Right	Power

A logical scheme of this kind is valuable as a compass or method of analysis and contrast, but of itself it not only is open to the criticism of Justice Holmes as to the "illusion of certainty," but that very illusion gives rise to metaphysical "entities" and "substances" conceived as existing apart from and independent of the behavior of officials and citizens. Thus the "state," as above suggested, is often conceived to be a vague entity acting as "principal," and the officials are represented as the "agents" of the state who may or may not execute the "will of the state." But the state, from the practical standpoint of politicians, lawyers, business men and workingmen without illusions, is none other than the officials-in-action. Instead of bringing suit against the "state," Holden brought suit against Hardy, the sheriff. It was nominally the state of Illinois, but actually the officials of Illinois, against whom Munn brought his suit. The citizen can disregard the state—he wants to know what the court and the sheriff will do.

These illusions naturally arise from the hopes and fears of mankind which substitute wishes for behavior. We conceive that what we wish is the reality, the real thing. Thus rights and duties also, like the state, are given the illusion of a reality existing apart from the conduct of officials.

The illusion is concealed in double and even treble meanings of words. The word "right" has one meaning when contrasted with "wrong" and another when contrasted with "duty," and the latter has both an ethical and a legal meaning. Yet the several meanings are merged. Right and wrong, right and duty, are each matters of opinion and differ with different persons, different ages, different civilizations. Right and duty are but an assertion of one person's wishes against another person, guided by opinions of right and wrong. Right and wrong are opposite qualities; right and duty are opposite persons, and both are ideals, rather than realities, a compass rather than the ocean. The reality is the probability of human conduct— the ideal is the hoped-for conduct.

Now the distinction between ethical rights and duties and legal rights and duties is the distinction between two classes of probability respecting human conduct. Legal rights and duties are none other than the probability that officials will act in a certain way respecting the claims that citizens make against each other. The statute law prohibits the manufacture and sale of intoxicating liquors. The common law enforces contracts. The "law" is there. It seems to be an entity existing apart from the conduct of courts, juries and sheriffs. Rather is the law a compass pointing to an ideal in the midst of uncertain probabilities. It is an ethical ideal constructed and registered by a majority that has been brought together according to certain rules of constitutional law or by the slow growth of the common law, and it is a probability that officials will or will not act in conformity to that ideal.

But there is also an ethical ideal not relating directly to the state, and an ethical probability. In most of the transactions of modern society respecting the rights of property, liberty, domestic relations, and so on, scarcely one transaction in a billion gets before the courts or in the hands of public officials. These ethical transactions are guided, nevertheless, to an indefinite extent, by the probabilities of official behavior, but the bulk of transactions are on an ethical level guided by ethical ideals considerably above the minimum legal probabilities of what officials will do. The bulk of transactions are ethical in the sense that they occur on a non-authoritative or non-authorized level above that where the legal power of violence is called into play. And the great difference among laws is in the relative predominance of the ethical and the legal probabilities, very little legal activity being necessary where the ethical probabilities are high and much of it being needed where the ethical probabilities are low, compared with the then legal code.

The fact, however, that the legal and ethical probabilities grow up historically together, has its bearing on the fundamental assumptions underlying the thought of Kocourek and others, that liberty, for example, is a "non-jural" concept. If we start with Herbert Spencer's historical or ethical concept of the individual as a free man existing prior to law, then man's liberty has been gradually taken away from him by the common law, by equity and statute law. But if we start with individuals as subjects of conquest, slavery, serfdom, then liberty has gradually been taken away from the masters and bestowed on the subjects. This is evidently the historic process since the time of William the Conqueror, and therefore, instead of saying that liberty is a non-jural concept, we should say that jural relations are the probabilities of official behavior in apportioning the compulsory powers, liabilities, disabilities and immunities of society according to the minimum ethical ideals current at the time. While a logical scheme of correlation abstracts jural relations from economic or ethical content, a behavioristic scheme conforms to the historical development of law, following, as it does, the economic conditions and the ethical ideals which spring from those conditions. So that, instead of being solely a set of logical or syllogistic deductions from assumed premises, as our abstract discussion in preceding sections might indicate, Law, Ethics, and Economics are different aspects of the same science of probabilities of human behavior. Law is a science of the probabilities of official transactions in the exercise of authorized physical coercion; Ethics is the science of the probabilities of both official and private transactions; while Economics is a science of the probabilities of official and private transactions in utilizing both human and natural resources for ethical, economic and public purposes.

Purpose.—Thus it is that a coördination of the fields of law, ethics and economics cannot be accomplished without including the concept of human purpose. Probability is inseparable from purpose, or, rather, purpose is the choice of probabilities. And this is the difference between "behaviorism" and "volitionism." A behavioristic definition of terms is a *classification* of probabilities. A volitional definition is a *choice* of probabilities. Hence the purpose within the definition is the essential part of the definition. If the concept of purpose is omitted then the social scientist falls into either physics or metaphysics. The term "liberty" for example, as above referred to, was said to be a "non-jural" concept. The law, it was said, deals only with "constraints," and liberty is the contrary of constraint, since liberty is conceived to be the negative "no-duty," which is nothing or anything.

Thus "liberty" is non-jural because the *purpose* of the law is eliminated from the definition of law. But certainly a bald restraint, under the name of duty, without a purpose in imposing it, can hardly be affirmed of the human will. The purpose in imposing duties of avoidance on some persons is that of creating liberty in other persons. An economic liberty, which is none other than choice of opportunities guided by probabilities, is also an ethical and a jural relation because it exists only through official behavior designed to permit and authorize it.

Thus a definition of the will-in-action is a description of purpose-in-action. It requires that the peculiar character of the will shall be distinguished from that of other forces in nature. The will is the only force that can choose between alternative degrees of power and can also place a limit on the exercise of its own power. Other forces do all that they can under the circumstances, which signifies that they run along the lines of least resistance. But the will, by reason of purpose, chooses lines of greater and greatest resistance, while placing its own limits on the power it will exert in overcoming resistance.

"As to the nature of the will and of the control exercised by it," says Salmond, "it is not for lawyers to dispute, this being a problem of psychology and physiology, not of jurisprudence."[1] But the "nature of the will" is the problem of the economist and of the Supreme Court in matters of constitutional law. A trial court, with which Salmond was wholly concerned, may take the will for granted since it has before it the evidence of a particular act of will which it may properly define as "positive" or "negative," the one being the act in question, the other being the "omission" of that act. But, from the standpoint of "the nature of the will" itself, there is no such thing as an "omission." An omission is a not-act. But the will cannot help acting. It must act. And it was this very fact of "the nature of the will" that led Justice Field in the Slaughter House Cases, and all the justices in the Allgeyer Case, to change the definition of "liberty" from absence of physical coercion to absence of economic alternatives. It is a "condition of servitude," says Justice Field, if a person is "allowed to pursue only one trade or calling and only in one locality of the country."[2] Thus "servitude" was defined as economic coercion, while "slavery" was physical coercion. What the court did in changing this definition was to enlarge the *purpose* of the law from the prevention of physical coercion to the prevention of economic coercion, in order that citizens might act according to what they deemed to be "the nature of the will."

But the will not only performs while avoiding, it also chooses between exercising a greater or less degree of power in its performance. While the term "forbearance," as we noted, is usually applied to those omissions which are "intentional" as distinguished from unintentional omissions, yet the degree to which a performance is carried may also be intentional. This meaning of "forbearance" is that of a limit placed by the will on its degree of power put forth in a performance, and it was this dimension of the "nature of the will" that decided the cases of Munn v. Illinois and Holden v. Hardy, and led to the court to place a duty of forbearance on capitalists for the sake of the welfare of farmers and laborers.

The economic judgments arise from limited natural resources

[1] SALMOND, 323.   [2] Above, Chap. II, p. 13.

and over-population, and it is exactly this relation of population to resources that gives rise also to those ethical judgments and restraints which create the ethical ideals of duties and liberties, of performance, avoidance, forbearance. Each transaction is economic in that each individual is endeavoring to make the largest possible use, for his own purposes, of his limited resources and faculties; and it is ethical in that his resources consist in the opportunities and powers which constitute the private property of others. These resources controlled by others he can realize for self and for still others, with whom he sympathizes, only through transactions with them, wherein the inducements and resistance employed are persuasive, coercive, deceptive or violent.

Reciprocity.—It is the concept of purpose that introduces into transactions the concept of reciprocity. Opposite parties are clothed each with a similar outfit of rights, exposures, duties and liberties. From the standpoint of a practitioner before a trial court this complementary scheme takes on a mechanical notion of "reciprocals" as when Kocourek contrasts a "power" as the advantage gained by the person in setting the law in motion against another, and its "reciprocal privilege" as the inability of the other to set the law in motion against one's self.[1] But, from the standpoint of purpose, the question is the volitional one, Why does the law provide reciprocal advantages and disadvantages for opposite persons?

This underlying notion of reciprocity is not brought out by Hohfeld since he is not concerned with the whole scheme of jurisprudence, but only with what an individual may expect the trial courts to do under existing law. But supreme courts, in questions of due process of law are inquiring, Why do they do it? The question is indeed, the legislative one of public policy, usually concealed by the court under an intellectual process of changing the definitions of words as used in the Constitution. We have seen the changes made in the meanings of the terms property and liberty and the resulting changes in public policy. Another constitutional term, "equality," is more deeply embedded in precedent and its meaning is being changed more slowly.

Both modern economic theory and legal theory are founded on doctrines of equality as well as liberty. But the meaning of equality is being gradually changed to that of reciprocity. If all individuals

[1] *Op. cit.*, KOCOUREK, 19 *Mich. Law Rev.* 49–56. Above, p. 110.

were exactly equal in physical, economic and persuasive powers, then there would be no reasonable purpose in placing any limits on their liberties, since no one could harm or mislead another anyhow. But, since the real fact is one of astounding inequalities, limits are placed somewhat on the liberties of the more powerful under the name of duties, such that a more reasonable degree of equality may be maintained. These duties create correlative rights on behalf of the inferiors which are equivalent to reducing the exposure of the weaker parties by reducing the liberty of the stronger. Conversely, a reduction of duties on the part of inferiors increases their liberty while reducing the rights and enlarging the exposures of the stronger. According to the degree to which these determinations are carried is there constructed a reciprocal exposure of each to the liberty of the other and a reciprocity of rights and duties.

We have seen this process in the Thirteenth and Fourteenth Amendments and in the Munn Case and the Holden-Hardy Case. A strict interpretation of the doctrine of equality would have held the laws and even the Amendments in question unconstitutional as depriving the parties of equal liberty, and such interpretations have frequently been made, but a classification of the parties according to differences in their economic strength changed the meaning of liberty into that unequal liberty which is reciprocity. Equality of treatment was retained, but it was equality between those of similar economic power in the same class, and not equal liberty between those of unequal power in opposite classes.

This change from equality to reciprocity depends for its validity on the purpose believed to be effected by the law in question. The physical power of the nation is called upon to limit the economic power of one class and thus to enlarge the economic power of an opposing class, as respects that particular class of transactions. But this could be done in no other way than by giving to the private purposes of a weaker class a public preference over the private purposes of the stronger class; their private purposes became public purposes to that extent.

How far this preference shall go is a matter, not of equality or logic, but of opinion and valuations. The weaker class, for some reason, is valued more highly than the stronger class, at that particular juncture or class of transactions. Those who exercise the determining powers of the nation make a choice between classes of human beings and resolve to employ the sovereign powers in behalf of one class by placing disabilities and responsibilities on the other class. Thus reciprocity is the official valuation of the virtues and vices of human beings.

This point where human value comes into the decisions of courts is clouded, not only by this dubious meaning of equality, but also by dubious meanings of the term "correlation." The opposite of this term, "a lack of correlation," sometimes refers to a lack of reciprocity, sometimes to a lack of correlation between a right and its corresponding duty, sometimes a lack of consistency. These it will be seen from Figure XVII are three entirely different relations. The reciprocal duty differs from the correlative (corresponding) duty in that it is a *subtracting duty* deducted fron one's liberty, whereas the correlative duty is a *supporting duty* imposed upon the opposite party. A correlative duty supports, even creates, one's rights, but the reciprocal duty deducts from one's rights. There is no equality of one's own rights and duties, but there is an equality, that is, correspondence, of one's rights and other's duties.

The same is true of liberty and exposure. One's exposures are exactly equal to the correlative liberties of others, but one's exposure is the reciprocal of one's own liberty, and is always unequal, since no person is ever exactly equal to any other person to whose liberty he is exposed.

If, now, the term "correlation of rights and duties" means "correspondence of rights and duties" it is meaningless in arriving at decisions regarding equality. An authorized right cannot be defined without going in the circle of defining its correlative (corresponding) and exactly equivalent duty of others. One is the "I" side, the other is the "you" side, one the beneficial, the other the burdensome side of the identical transaction.

But, at the same time, a right cannot exist without some deduction, however great or small, by virtue of a reciprocal duty clinging to it and diminishing its possible benefits. The legal maxim, *sic utere tuo ut alienum non lædas*, testifies to this reciprocal duty deducting from the orbit of the right. For, however useless this maxim may be as a measure of the amount of the deduction,[1] it testifies to a minimum deduction accompanying every right, to the effect that one's right or liberty shall not be exercised in such a way as to infringe upon the rights or liberties of others. The very reason why this maxim is useless as a help to decisions, in that it "begs the question," is because it has the double meaning of correlative (correspondence) and reciprocity. In the sense of correspondence it is meaningless, for, as in Figure XVII, the reciprocal duty of one is always exactly equal to the reciprocal right of the other, no matter now

<hr>

[1] BOUVIER, 2163 and cases cited.

big or little it may be, like the two sides of a board. And in the sense of reciprocity the maxim begs the question for it requires a choice between degrees of reciprocity—like two different boards, one of which may be made bigger or smaller than the other to any feasible extent desired. A correlative right and its duty are always identical and equal. One is the shiney, the other the seamy side of the same transaction. A reciprocal right and duty are never identical nor equal, for one is a deduction from the other. A correlative duty, in the sense of "correspondence," cannot by any device be made quantitatively different from the right to which it is correlated. The right is always equal to the duty, no matter how coercive the transaction may be. To speak of equality in this sense is meaningless. But whether the reciprocal duty approaches quantitatively the right to which it is attached is always a matter of discretion as to the degree of power that should be permitted or supported for either party in view of the relative human values attributed to them. This is a matter of belief, feelings, emotions, values, that is, of opinion, and opinions differ.

A third meaning of "correlation" is that of the *logical consistency*, or mechanical coördination, existing between the several parts of a statute or a judicial opinion deciding the case. Here the term correlation signifies as nearly a mathematical process of pure reasoning as the human intellect is capable of attaining, without mixture of values, feelings, opinions, or the weighing of divergent interests. It is a judgment of mechanical perfection, of the workability of the several parts when combined into a mechanism for reaching the ends desired and valued. Professor Freund, who more than other legal writers has brought forward the notion of reciprocity as distinguished from equality in its modern industrial applications, employs this term "correlation" in the double sense of reciprocity and consistency.[1] Yet the two are distinct. Consistency is logic, reciprocity is feelings or opinion.

The threefold distinction gains significance on account of the three different meanings of "lack of correlation." In the sense of "correspondence" there can be no lack of correlation. The correlation cannot be violated in any authorized transaction, although it may be, and is, in what we have distinguished as ethical transactions. For, the resort to authorized transactions is made for the express purpose of correlating rights with duties where there is a lack of correlation if left to private opinion. On the other hand, correlation in the sense of "reciprocity" is a matter of *degree* and may be changed to fit the opinion of what is "reasonable" or "fair" or "equitable" between the parties, under the circumstances. But in the sense of "consistency," correlation is a matter of logic, intellect, mathematics, mechanical perfection or imperfection.

---

[1] FREUND, ERNST, *Standards of American Legislation*, 225 (1917).

To violate the principles of correlation in the sense of correspondence is impossible; to violate them in the sense of reciprocity is injustice; in the sense of consistency is illogical. To remedy the lack of correlation, in the sense of correspondence is meaningless; in the sense of reciprocity is to establish what is felt to be a more reasonable degree of mutual benefits and burdens; in the sense of consistency is to rearrange the parts in a more logical or workable system. The remedy for the first "lack of correlation" is tautological; for the second it is a change in the feelings of value; for the third it is to think clearly.

It is, as we have suggested, by identifying the notion of consistency with the notion of reciprocity, that legal reasoning substitutes logical deduction for feelings of value, and thus accomplishes that "illusion of certainty which makes legal reasoning seem like mathematics." The *valuation* of interests consists in weighing their relative importance. It is a matter of relative human values within a community of interest where the burdens and benefits of limited resources must be shared, and these connot be shared by rules of logic; they are shared according to feelings of value, that is, of relative importance or reciprocity.

There are, thus, accompanying every authorized transaction two pairs of correlatives indicating the authoritative correlation of the two ethical valuations of opposing parties, and these arise from that underlying notion of reciprocity, which is none else than the system of limited, or Austin's "relative," rights and duties. These are the two pairs of correlatives, right-duty and liberty-exposure, backed by their equivalents, power-liability and immunity-disability. Each person at each end of the transaction is authorized, permitted or restrained, according to the dimensions which these correlatives place upon his part in the transaction.

For, a transaction involves the possibility of several acts of either party in consummating it, and the reciprocals and limits pertaining to each party are variously adapted to these possible acts. A person's largest power to put his own will into effect is the area coverd by his rights, for here opposite parties are subject to duties of performance, avoidance, or forbearance, and the superior authority comes to one's aid so that he does not depend alone on his own exertions.

This aid, however, is limited, and at that limit one is exposed to the liberty of opposite parties. Within this field opposite parties may choose performance, avoidance, or forbearance, without committing a wrong. The superior authority simply looks the other way.

This exposure of a person is quite different from the liberty of the same person. The one may be increased without increasing the other, depending on the degree of reciprocity deemed proper by the enacting authority, and the relative physical, economic or persuasive inequalities. For the liberty refers to a different act from the exposure. It is a person's liberty, for example, without committing any wrong, to do any collateral performance, avoidance or forbearance necessary to induce another to act. Whereas his exposure is his danger of lawful damage that may possibly be inflicted by another.

Likewise with one's reciprocal duty. It deducts from his liberty by positive act of government whereas his exposure deducts from his right. Duty implies, by a positive act of government, compulsion on him by the superior authority, whereas exposure implies only lack of assistance from government. Yet the duty of one is not equal to the duty of the other—it is a reciprocal of that duty, depending upon the relative importance, for the transaction, assigned to one and the other by the enacting authority.

In short, these several dimensions, measured off by these variable limits, indicate the attitude and promises of the superior authority towards any party to a transaction. A person's legal right is the positive assistance of government; his exposure is the indifference of government; his liberty is the permission of government; his duty is compulsion by government. And that which applies to the working rules of political government with its sanctions of physical coercion, applies also to the working rules of industrial governments with their sanctions of economic coercion, and to the working rules of cultural governments with their sanctions of favorable and unfavorable opinions of those whose opinions are deemed worth while.

VI. WORKING RULES

We have noticed throughout that the human will is not a lawless capricious force but that it operates within certain limits. Within these limits it has an uncertain range of discretion or freedom of choice. It is these limits of discretion that are usually spoken of as "laws." Yet from the standpoint of a creative and intelligent being who controls more or less the operation of the forces about him, these laws are not something inevitable which he cannot overcome—they are rather certain conditions or forces having strategic or limiting and complementary relations to each other, which a sufficiently intelligent being can manipulate, and thus, although operating upon something that goes on independently of his will, yet its independent operation comes out with results somewhat in conformity with what he intended. These laws or limits within which the will operates may be reduced to the three principles or tendencies which the individual consciously or unconsciously takes into account, and each of which has been set forth by various schools of economists at different times as a ruling principle while the others are taken for granted as the presuppositions of common sense not needing to be formulated in their own rights as factors in the situation.

These three ultimate principles we have designated the Principle of Mechanism, applying solely to the physical or non-living forces of the universe, but including man himself and society as evidently a special case of mechanism; the Principle of Scarcity, applying to the biological, psychological and hence to all human and social phenomena, since scarcity is the relation of living things to limited resources; and the Principle of Working Rules applying to all associations or groupings of individuals which have a continuing existence as an organized movement into and out of which individuals come and go by birth, adoption, death and expulsion.

It is these working rules and the extent and manner in which individuals guide their conduct with reference to them that constitute what is sometimes pictured as a "collective will," a "social mind," a "government of laws and not of men," a "divine" or "natural" order, and so on, although such personification and analogies are merely compendious phrases indicating in reality only a set of working rules which keep on working regardless of the incoming and outgoing of individuals.

Now, as respects individuals, these three principles of mechanism, scarcity and working rules place limits upon the conduct of individuals and thus reduce the will to a certain uniformity of action usually characterized by such words as "reason," "virtue," "ethics," "common sense," where, without this uniformity, the will is characterized by such words as "caprice," "vice," "unethical" or "lunacy." There is a presumable difference between the principles of mechanism and scarcity, on the one hand, and the principle of working rules on the other hand, in that the latter spring from the human will itself whereas mechanism and scarcity are non-human. Yet even this distinction is obliterated if to the term working rules is given, as is proper, a meaning applicable to all communities, packs, herds, colonies, hives, hills, and so on, consisting of a succession of individuals which enter, coöperate and disappear while the community itself goes on indefinitely—in short, the term working rules signifies membership in a going concern. The working rules of human societies have evolved out of the working rules of pre-human societies, and indeed the evolution of individuals is in itself an evolution of capacities to act in concert according to common rules accepted by each individual. Even words and languages are but signs and symbols accepted in common by those who enter and remain with the group, and are, like other working rules, the means of that concerted action which constitutes membership in an organized mass movement.

Languages and many other working rules are accepted by individuals through daily experience and instruction of their elders, thus becoming habits and customs, and this is undoubtedly the origin of the great bulk of them, but many of them, in the course of time, are imposed by way of conquest and permanent subordination of classes or nations of individuals. It was this latter class of rules, taking the form of the absolute will of monarchs or the conscious determinations of legislatures, with correspondingly great abuses, which led the philosophers and economists of the eighteenth century to revolt against all working rules whatsoever as the mere capricious, wicked or insane control of human behavior by arbitrary authority, and to endeavor to set up an ideal society which should have no working rules whatever, except those which might be imposed by such mechanical principles as Newton had made familiar or such as a divine providence acting according to reason, virtue and common sense might impose. In short, the working rules which the rationalists of the seventeenth and eighteenth centuries revolted against in church and state originated from the principles of prerogative based on conquest, whereas the working rules which those rationalists proposed to substitute under such names as reason, natural law, natural order and so on, had originated from the principles of custom and habit, and, in Anglo-American jurisprudence, were known as the common law.

There was a good justification for giving the name of "reason" or "natural law" to these customs of the common law, for the common law did not signify *any* kind of custom or habit whatsoever, but only those customs and habits which had been followed as guides in the decision of disputes and were therefore the approved, good and workable customs to the exclusion of bad and disruptive practices. Hence the kind of "individualism" which the rationalists set up, over against the decrees and statutes of monarchs and legislatures, went on the assumption of individuals whose habits and customs conformed to the working rules of the common law found to be reasonable through centuries of the very commonplace and unobtrusive settlement of disputes between fellow-members of the community. To these, quite obviously, might be given the name of reason, divine providence, natural law, or even an harmonious equilibrium of mechanical forces, according to the theological, metaphysical or materialistic bent of the philosopher who propounded them, although from the more modern and sophisticated bent, which inquires not what a thing *is* but what it *does*, they are, quite as obviously, to be given the name of working rules.

The oversight of the jurists and economists of the eighteenth century proceeded from merely the fact that they did not have the advantage of the modern psychology of habit and custom, but endeavored to assign to reason, intellect, pain, pleasure, or divine or rational guidance, what proceeds from workable habits and customs in the conduct of human affairs. Thus Adam Smith was able to start economic theory with the elimination of all associations, corporations, unions, and almost all of the state itself, with their working rules governing the transactions of individuals, and to substitute, in their place, individual units of self-interest, division of labor, liberty, equality, fluidity in the choice of occupation, and that "invisible hand" or divine providence which was none other than the working rules of an orderly society as understood by Adam Smith in the middle of the eighteenth century.

Starting, as they did, with individuals rather than the working rules of going concerns, both the historical and the causal sequence were reversed. For to the individual the important thing is his rights and liberties protected against infringement by others. Hence the inference is that the working rules were designed by a rational being for the protection of the preëxisting rights and liberties of individuals. But, as a matter of fact, the notion of individual rights is historically many thousands of years subsequent to the full development of working rules, and as a matter of causal sequence the working rules are designed primarily to keep the peace and promote collective action and only secondarily to protect rights and liberties.

The characteristic of all working rules is that they actually do regulate behavior in those dimensions which can, when individual interests come to be asserted in the later development of the race, be given the name of rights, liberties and so on. But primarily, both in history and in causal sequence, the working rules simply say what individuals must, must not, may, can and cannot do, if the authoritative agency that decides disputes bring the collective power of the community to bear upon the said individuals.

Primarily the rules are necessary and their survival in history is contingent on their fitness to hold together in a continuing concern the overweening and unlimited selfishness of individuals pressed on by scarcity of resources. They grow out of the settlement of disputes and the combined action of the group as a mass in offense or defense with other groups. This necessarily means the selection of good habits and practices of individuals as against bad habits and practices that weaken the group as a whole. Out of this ultimate necessity of working rules came secondary rules permitting the division of labor and classification of occupations. Each rule, if it can be depended upon, permits each individual to know in advance what he can, cannot or may do with the help of the group, and what he must or must not do, so that within these limits he knows where security lies. And eventually, when the group is strong enough and its command over resources great enough, the emphasis of the rules turns away from what the individual must or must not do, to what he may and can do, so that the modern liberty and freedom of individuality emerges as the fine fruit of evolving centuries of working rules. It is then that rights and liberties can safely be asserted and allowed.

This assertion of individual claims is facilitated, or rather systematized, by the rise of a profession of lawyers, originally trained in theology, who, with logical acumen above that of other classes, press and resist these claims of individuals and give to the coercive relations resulting from working rules a dialectic formality and persuasive terminology. That which the individual *can* do with the aid of the community is sanctified by the name of right and dignified by the name of power, capacity or freedom. That which he *may* do, because, according to the working rule, other persons are prevented from interfering, becomes his liberty, privilege or immunity. That which he *must* or *must not* do, in that the community will compel or restrain him, becomes moralized under the name of duty, dignified under the name of responsibility, foretold under the name of liability and hallowed under the name of sanction. And lastly, that which he does at his own risk and exposure without protection or help from the community is left with a name that suggests his own disability or incapacity.

These working rules, in all cases, are subject to slow historical change, through the changes in economic, political and ethical conditions which we have indicated. Moreover, they differentiate in a most remarkable fashion, according to the several forms of social organization which separate out from the primitive homogenity of clan, family or tribe. As the church separates from the state, ecclesiasiatical rules separate from political rules. As business separates from church and state then the customs of merchants, the by-laws and practices of guilds, corporations and associations separate themselves from ecclesiastical and political rules. Then, as thousands of voluntary associations arise and flourish, their own peculiar working rules go with them. Labor organizations arise with very different rules in many respects, and it is a significant fact that, out of the peculiar rules of labor unions the modern concept of working rules was introduced into economic theory by the great historians and theorists of the British labor unions, Mr. and Mrs. Webb.[1] They discovered that the unions were endeavoring to set up common rules for the conduct of the industrial processes of modern industry, and that it was these rules, more than the wages and hours of labor, that gave character to the conflict of "capital and labor." Following this discovery of the Webbs, the Swedish economist Cassel generalized the principle of the common rule to apply to all laws of government.[2] In America arose a school of scientific managers or engineers with the professional purpose of systemizing the shop rules of industry, led by Frederic Taylor; and, more recently, the American economist, E. G. Nourse, has set forth a suggestive analysis of the interrelations between the working rules of the thousands of trade organizations in the field of marketing and the supplementary working rules of the federal and state governments.[3]

[1] WEBB, SIDNEY and BEATRICE, *Industrial Democracy*, 560 (1897, 1920).
[2] CASSEL, G., *Der Ausgangspunkt der Theoretischen Oekonomie*, 58 Zeitsch. f. *Staatswirtsch.*, 668 (1902). *Theoretische Oekonomie*, 2d ed. (1921).
[3] NOURSE, E. G., "The Proper Sphere of Governmental Regulation in connection with the marketing of Farm Products." *Proceedings, Amer. Econ. Ass'n*, 1922.

These are a few of the outstanding indications of the recognition during the past twenty-five years of the principle of working rules, always assumed by all economists yet not forced upon their attention until the emergence of new working rules of new associations and unions with their overlappings and conflicts of political, economic and cultural rules growing out of the necessity of deciding disputes and coördinating the individuals of multitudes of concerns into a united mass movement. A complete account of the introduction of the concept of working rules into economic theory would require us to go back to their primitive and later origins expounded in the works of Westermarck, Gierke, Pollock, Pound, as well as in the histories of corporations, trade associations, employers' associations, and labor unions. Our preceding analysis has shown the elementary implication of working rules in so far as the courts have taken them over from the customs of feudal agriculture and modern business. A further analysis of the decisions of the courts in Australia will show the customs and working rules of labor and labor unions in the process of taking over into the same common law of England, and this will be indicated in a later chapter.[1] Suffice to say, at this point, that it is in the principle of working rules with their limits on transactions that is to be found the correlation of law, economics, politics, ethics and modern behavioristic psychology, as well as the omitted factor that accounts for the contradictions of abstract individualism and abstract socialism and the other historic dualisms of individual and society.

It must not be thought that working rules are something external, fixed or compelling, existing apart from the actual behavior. They reveal themselves only as acts, transactions and attitudes—the attitude being a readiness to act in a certain direction rather than other directions. That which entitles them to the name of a rule of action is the principle of anticipation with its sanctions of confidence and caution in view of the expected decisions that will be made in interpreting the rule. No working rule can be stated in such form that it can be said always to be exactly observed or accurately interpreted. It exhibits as many varieties of near or remote accordance as there are individuals interpreting and observing it, and in this is found a principle of differentials which makes possible the gradual change in working rules with the incoming of changing conditions

[1] Below, Chap. VIII.

that tend to shift the behavior in one direction or another, away from the earlier formulation of the rule. A working rule, in other words, is a social process and not a metaphysical entity, a more or less flexible process of acts, transactions and attitudes; yet with a discernible trend; and it is this trend that may be abstracted in thought and formulated in words as a statement of the rule in question. As such it furnishes a guide or mental standard for the decision of disputes as they arise, and it is this expected trend in the decision of disputes that, by anticipation, is the main ground for the voluntary choices that, for the sake of avoiding disputes and retaining the approval of his fellow-members, bring the individual into line with the rule.

There is naturally always a resistance, on the part of those who make the authoritative decisions, against any movement requiring these working rules to be formulated in words and published for the information of all. It is usually contended by them that the rules are so difficult and complex that they can be understood only by experts or those who by long training have become experienced in interpreting them. It was only after a vigorous struggle that the Twelve Tables of the Roman law were published. The Egyptian priests are said to have formulated a principle of the economy of the truth in order to justify their refusal to give out the working rules which they were privileged to interpret. And much the same doctrine is formulated by business men, bankers, financiers, politicians, labor leaders and others who dread the bad use that might be made of the flexible working rules which they administer, or who flatly deny that the rules are anybody's "business" but their own. Yet the publicity of these working rules is the very means by which the ruling authorities in any concern can be held to responsibility for their acts, and the members of the concern can be certain of what they can, may or must do, or not. And in proportion as those who are called upon to obey the rules acquire sufficient intelligence and power, they insist, first, on the publicity of the rules, then upon a voice in formulating the rules, then upon an independent judiciary that shall decide disputes that arise under the rules. This process we have seen in the rise of the business classes of England during the seventeenth century, culminating with the Act of Settlement, and it can be observed in the history of almost any business, religious, cultural or other concern, with the rise of the laborers, the laity, or the so-called "rank and file," into a position of intelligence and power within the concern.

In this way we can see that the evolution of working rules in almost any concern or type of concern, passes through four stages. First the stage of ignorance and confidence, wherein faith, loyalty or submission accepts without protest the working rules as concealed and interpreted by those having authority. Second, the stage of skepticism and protest which is satisfied with the mere publicity of the rules. Third, the stage of resistance, revolt and insistence on a participating voice in amending and recasting the rules. Fourth, a stage of an independent judiciary interpreting the rules as disputes arise.

The foregoing is what might be named the constitutional development of working rules. But a revolutionary development may possibly occur, as in the case of the tyrannies of the Greek cities, of the Roman Empire, and similar dictatorships of later times in politics and industry, wherein the old working rules are wholly overthrown and supplanted by a different set of rules and without the stages of publicity, participation, or independent judiciary.

CHAPTER V

GOING CONCERNS

I. Working Rules of Political, Industrial, and Cultural Concerns

The law books distinguish a "natural person" from an artificial person, the former a human being who exists as a product of nature, the latter a collection of individuals existing only "in contemplation of law." But the natural person is also artificial in contemplation of law, and the artificial person is as natural, in law, as the natural person. Each is a personification and each is a psychological process. Government finds individuals and associations of individuals, each existing prior to, or at least independent of, any act of law. Indeed, it finds them inseparable, for no individual grows out of the animal into the human except through various forms of association with others and various degrees of submission to, and power over, the wills of others. If the individual lives without rights he is, not a person, but a thing, that can be captured, bred, owned and killed without violating any duty towards him. If an association has no rights, it too is an outlaw and its members may be penalized on the ground of conspiracy. What the state does for each is to personify it by granting and imposing rights, duties, liberties, exposures, and if to do this for an association is to create an artificial being so also is it an artificial process to do the same for an individual. It is a process of thinking, and thinking is "artificial." The child grows into the man by a natural process, but government thinks him into a citizen. Even an alien is a part-citizen to the extent that government grants the rights and liberties of citizens. Men associate in families, partnerships, communities, unions, nations, but the law imputes to their association as a unit many of the legal relations that it attributes to natural persons.

The fact that a corporation is not endowed with all the rights of a natural person, and, especially, not endowed with so-called inalienable rights, does not distinguish the artificial from the natural person. Natural persons differ widely in their status, which consists in the rights, liberties, duties and exposures attributed to them, and a corporation in one respect may even be said to have a higher status than the individual, for it may be endowed with that legal perpetuity which is pictured as "immortality." Moreover, neither the rights of individuals nor of corporations are inalienable—they are vested by operation of law and they take effect only on occasion of operative facts recognized by courts, and they are held only on condition, or to the extent, that certain reciprocal duties are lived up to. The quality, common to both, which the courts recognize is the will—the individual will and associated wills. The state imputes to them individually and collectively a group of rights, duties, liberties, exposures, which determine the scope within which the will may operate.

Chief Justice Marshall, following Sir Edward Coke and the ideas of the seventeenth and eighteenth centuries, described a corporation as "an artificial being, invisible, intangible and existing only in contemplation of law. Being the mere creature of law, it possesses only those properties which the charter of its creation confers upon it, either expressly, or as incidental to its very existence. . . . Among the most important are immortality, and, if the expression may be allowed, individuality; properties by which a perpetual succession of many persons are considered as the same, and may act as a single individual." [1]

Here are two notions of intangibility or invisibility mingled with a single notion. The "charter of its creation"—the articles of incorporation—are but the group of promises and commands which the state makes in the form of working rules indicating how the officials of the state shall act in the future in matters affecting the association, the members of the association, and the persons not members. It is these promises and commands, or working rules, of officials which constitute the charter and determine the status of the association. They are the rules of future behavior for its own executives, courts and legislatures, laid down by former officials for future dealings with members of the concern.

But, along with this intangible promised behavior of the public officials is the behavior of that very visible, tangible, living body of men who constitute what has come to be known as "a going concern."

[1] Dartmouth College v. Woodard, 4 Wheat. 518, 636 (1819).

The going concern is animated by a common purpose, governed by common rules of its own making, and the collective behavior in attaining that purpose we distinguish as a "going business." It is this collective behavior of this collective will, this flow of transactions along lines indicated by its own working rules, this going business of a going concern, that constitutes the invisible, intangible being of Marshall's definition. It is not an artificial "creature of law"—it exists prior to the law in the intentions and transactions of its members, and thus exists in the very nature of the human will as well as "in contemplation of law."

This collective, intangible, living process of individuals, the functionaries of the state find already in a trembling existence and then proceed "artificially" to guide the individuals concerned and give it a safer existence. The guidance is made through promising to them a certain line of behavior on the part of public officials, which sets forth the limits on their private behavior and the assistance they may expect on the part of officials. The official behavior is also collective and intangible. The two notions of intangibility are the intangibility of the promised collective behavior of public officials which authorizes private behavior, and the intangibility of the expected collective behavior of the members of the association itself, which is the private behavior thereby authorized. One is the promised behavior of government set forth in working rules for public officials, the other the intended behavior of a going concern set forth in the working rules for its employees, agents and functionaries.

That which holds the going concern together is these two sets of working rules affording an expectation of a gross income to be obtained jointly while it is being distributed among the members. This forecast is based upon business connections, patronage, goodwill, built up in the past and expected to continue or enlarge in the future as long as the working rules continue. If the expectation fails, the immortality fails. While the expectation continues, the corporation is "a going concern." For this reason, the legal form is subordinate. The concern may exist as a partnership, a union, an association, a corporation, a coöperative. The essential thing is the visible, tangible, going concern of persons, with its invisible, intangible behavior of the immediate and remote future stabilized by working rules. Needless to say the modern form of corporation has the peculiar advantage over the others of limited liability of individuals and perpetual succession of individual members without a multitude of legal conveyances needed otherwise to hold them together.

The going concern, whether public or private, whether the state or the corporation, acts, of course, through natural persons, and these, for that purpose, have a double personality. They are officers, agents, employees, whose wills participate in the collective will; and they are individuals acting apart in their other capacities or as members of still other associations and concerns. The stockholders, for example, are the principals or employers in one concern but members of other concerns in their other dealings. While a corporation is usually considered to be the stockholders, this is mainly for the legal purpose of distinguishing between principal, agents and employees. The agents and employees participate in the gross income of the corporation, but their shares are specified or stipulated in advance. The principals, that is, the stockholders, are the residual claimants of the income, and their will is deemed in law to be supreme within limits.

But practically, as an economic institution, the will of the going concern is the composite will of all to the extent that each has any discretion in his acts. The Law may not always actually reflect the reality. The latter includes every person, even the least of the manual workers. He, too, must be depended on for some discretion, else his work could be done by an animal, an idiot or a machine. Participating in the collective will, all of them contribute in different degrees to determine the combined will. The manual worker, acting under orders or shop rules, has a margin of discretion in dealing with the forces of physical nature, where his will modifies slightly the total result. With the foremen, superintendents, managers, salesmen and buyers, who deal with human nature, the discretionary influence on the total result is larger, within the working rules pertaining to them. With stockholders, bondholders, bankers, it is large or small in scope or different in quality or function.

Thus there is a gradation of ministerial and discretionary acts of will, from the manual worker who acts mainly in subjection to the will of others, to the president, stockholder, promoter, banker or financier, who acts within larger limits according to his own views. The collective will is the organized symposium of all the discretionary acts of all participants as they go along from day to day,

according to the rules of the organization. It is an organized mass
movement.

But the collective will is also guided by acts of participants in the
past. Customs, practices, habits, precedents, methods of work, have
been built up and handed down as working rules, which limit discretion in the present. Binding contracts, informal agreements, under-
standings, resolutions of stockholders, perpetuate the working rules
of the past in the behavior of the present. The articles of incorporation, the contracts with bondholders, go back still further and bind
more firmly the present and future acts of will. Over all, the general statute law, the common law, the decisions of courts, in short,
the working rules of the general government, are read into the articles of incorporation and into the transactions of principal and agent,
employer and employee, stockholders, bondholders, patrons, clients,
customers, so that the will of the state, or rather its working rules,
perpetuate the rights, duties, liberties and exposures, within which
the working rules of a subordinate concern are made up and its collective behavior goes along.

Thus the going concern may be looked upon as a person with a
composite will, but this so-called "will" is none other than the working rules of the concern operating through the actions and transactions of those who observe the rules. For every working rule of every
going concern contains, in varying degrees of importance, the four verbs
already indicated for the guidance of the participants to whom the
rule pertains. The rule indicates first what the individual *must* or
must not do. It is thus a rule of compulsion, or *duty*, which the authorities of the concern are supposed to enforce.

The rule tells, second, what the individual *can* do, in the sense that
if he does it the power of the concern will aid him in enforcing his
action in the matter. Here it is a rule of authorization, or *right*,
since, the authorities of the concern will bring its collective power to
assist him in compelling others to obey what he has commanded.

The rule tells, third, what he *cannot* do, in the sense that, though
he is not prohibited from doing it, yet if any damage occurs to him
by virtue of an act of others the power of the concern will not protect him. Here it is a rule of non-authorization, or non-assistance,
that is, he is left in a condition of *exposure* or danger so far as his free
acts may bring upon himself an infliction or loss of any kind proceeding from the permitted acts of others.

Finally, the working rule tells, for the same individual, what he *may* do, in that, although he is neither required to do it, nor is promised the assistance of the concern in requiring his will to be obeyed by others, yet the power of the concern will be used so that others must not interfere with him in doing it. Here it is a rule of permission, that is, of *liberty*, to do as he pleases without interference by others.

These four behavioristic relations of working rules have been described in the preceding chapter. It is sufficient here to note that they constitute the so-called "collective will" of any going concern in the sense of the relations between the conduct of the members and the accompanying conduct of the concern as a whole, and they apply to all concerns, whether it be a family, tribe, business or the state. They say what each member of the concern may, can, cannot, and must or must not do, in so far as the combined power of the concern is deemed to cover his conduct. They give the individual power (right) to act as representing the concern; they give to him liberty to act in that the concern will prevent others from interfering. They limit his power to act for the concern by exposing him beyond that limit to damages that the concern disregards, and they require him to act or not act in certain directions on the sanction of a penalty (duty) if he disregards the rule.

Thus the working rules of a concern necessarily allow to every member a certain amount of discretion or choice of alternatives, consisting in the authority (right) and the immunity (liberty) allowed by the rule in question and limited by the alternatives actually open to him. Wherever an employee is free to choose between two ways of doing a thing, or an agent between two details of a bargain and sale, or an executive, judge or legislator between two lines of conduct, there he is constructing the will, to that extent, of the whole concern. In case of uncertainty a higher-up authority decides, and finally up to the highest official, president, board of directors or Supreme Court who speaks for the collective will of the associated principals, partners or shareholders in the enactment or interpretation of the working rules. Whether it be a strong personality that dominates and gives character to the whole concern, or whether it be the vacillating, indecisive wills of many, the collectivity nevertheless acts like a single will, strong or hesitating, enduring or transient, operating through the instrumentality of many wills, each directing its conduct according to the rules, and, as such, the concern may well be endowed, as it is, with the rights and liberties or burdened by the duties and exposed to the liberties of others, like natural persons.

So that the notion of Coke and Marshall that it is only an artificial convenience of the law to associate individuals together and treat them as a single person, and that therefore the association is only a legal fiction, disregards the fundamental nature of the will, as though the will were an atom unrelated to other atoms. Each individual will is an action and reaction with other wills in manifold variations of collective wills. What the state does is to regulate the form, by determining the limits according to its own rules, in which they act together—it cannot combine them effectively if it tries to do so regardless of the inherent ways in which they act together. They act as principal and agent, as coöperators and members of concerns, as promisor and promisee, as creditor and debtor, as leader and led, and all that the state can do is to specify how far its officials shall go in assisting, compelling, exposing or permitting their transactions.[1]

The state itself is but one of many going concerns, whose sovereign working rules are but a larger collective will, and the behavior of whose officials is a collective behavior. It, too, has its ministerial agents with such slight discretionary powers that they are held in law to be only "employees." It has its discretionary agents, the public officers, whether executives, legislators or judges, whose collective choices determine the policies to be followed from day to day. They, too, have their double personality. They are officers, agents, employees, acting collectively, and they are private persons acting in other capacities or as members of other going concerns. Acting collectively they act according to precedent, custom, judicial opinion, statute law, and, perhaps, those articles of incorporation which make up the written constitution of the state, all of which together constitute its working rules.[2] The state is not "the people," nor "the public," it is the working rules of the discretionary officials of the past and present who have had and now have the legal power to put their will into effect within the limits set by other officials, past and present, and through the instrumentality of other officials or employees, present and future.

[1] *Cf.* BATY, T., "The Rights of Ideas—and Corporations," 33 *Harv. Law Rev.* 364 (1920).
[2] *Cf.* MAITLAND, F. W., *The Crown as Corporation,* 17 *L. Q. R.* 131 (1901); MOORE, HARRISON, 20 *L. Q. R.* 351 (1901); BROWN, W. JETHRO, *The Austinian Theory of Law,* 254 ff. (1912); LASKI, H. J., *"Studies in the Problem of Sovereignty* (1917). These writers generally, however, leave the impression of an entity instead of a bundle of working rules.

The state, through its working rules, has granted to itself, or rather to its discretionary or ministerial agents, certain powers and immunities, and has imposed on them liabilities and disabilities, which limit or liberate their behavior towards each other and towards those whom it deems to be private citizens. It too, is a large person, a collection of wills operating according to accepted rules, a going concern, and, similar to a private corporation with its "going business," so the collective behavior of its officials in dealing with the people and with other states is the "public business."

It is for this reason that we distinguish the "state" and "government" from "society" and "the people." The "state" has developed out of the people as one of several going concerns, in so far as it has taken over the power of violence according to certain rules, which is sovereignty. The "government," on the other hand, is the series of transactions going on between officials and the citizens, and between officials and other officials of the same or other states. The government is not a thing, it is a process according to definite rules. In these transactions which constitute this process, each citizen or official participates in the control of violence. Just as a "going business" is but the series of transactions going on between members of a going concern and members of other concerns in the control of wealth and poverty, so political government is the going business of officials dealing with each other and with citizens in the control of peace and violence. Thus we may employ interchangeably the term "state" and "government." The state is the going concern of persons associated, the government is their going business. One is the persons who participate in sovereignty, the other is their participation.

So with any other loose or compact, temporary or enduring, association of persons acting as a unit. The family, the church, the club, is a going concern, the transactions of its members are its going business, its working rules keep it agoing.

Thus there are three types of persons, the citizen, the private concern and the state, recognized by imputing rights, privileges, powers, immunities and their opposites. They are persons, in that they are more or less free wills, or rather discretionary actors, whose future acts may be directed, controlled, prevented, limited by the imposition of duties and exposures, or rewarded or liberated by the grant of rights and liberties. They are persons, in that they have the qualities and faculties which may be protected, assisted or restrained according to the distribution of rights and duties. They have their internal economy of proportioning transactions; their external relations of opportunity and power; their expectations of the future. The citizen is a person who is a member of many concerns, and his transactions with other citizens constitute, on the one hand, his personality, property, liberty and citizenship, and, on the other hand, his share in the going business and public business of all concerns and of the state.

There is therefore this much of truth in the seventeenth and eighteenth century notions of a corporation, or of the state, as an artificial creature existing only in contemplation of law. Its working rules are likely to leave it in the predicament of an outlaw or conspiracy unless the courts select and give effect to its good rules and reject its bad practices. Marshall took his definition of a corporation from Sir Edward Coke, and Coke along with the common-law lawyers of the Commonwealth, perceived that a corporation existed only as a franchise to be and to act, granted out of the prerogative of the King. It continued to exist only while the King's court continued to recognize the grant of sovereign power and the King's executives to enforce the privileges granted. It existed only in "contemplation of law." So with their notion of the state and the commonwealth. The state also was but a sum total of all individuals, who, in their collective capacity, constituted an abstract entity "the public," or the "general will"; while the commonwealth was but the sum total of all private wealth.

This doctrine of individual liberty and of the individual as the unit of society served, at a later time in the hands of the economists, to split up the state, as well as the corporation, into units of persons and units of wealth which then were added together to constitute the whole, and, for this purpose, could be tied together only by an abstract entity existing only in contemplation of thought. From Coke, in the beginning of the seventeenth century, to John Locke, at the close of that century, from Rousseau and Adam Smith in the eighteenth century down to Herbert Spencer, in the nineteenth century, flowed this individualistic notion of the state as a mere sum total of individuals, on the one hand, and an abstract entity, on the other. And when Spencer destroyed this metaphysical entity there was nothing left for him to hold the parts together except to substitute another entity in the form of an analogy to a biological organism. There was no collective will at all—merely an abstract formula of individual rights by which individuals might hold each other off while a biological analogy held them together. Yet that which held them together was their own working rules.

The dualism arose out of the conflict between liberty and duty in the seventeenth century. The church Fathers, the Pope, the established Church of England, the royalist adherents of the King's prerogative, were all agreed that the unity of Christendom or the unity of the nation could be maintained only on the principle of obedience to a single will.[1] The divine right of Kings, or the divine right of the Pope, were but the religious duty of the subject to obey a single will.[2] Even the iconoclast Thomas Hobbes, who broke down this religious entity, had to substitute, like Herbert Spencer, another one, his monstrous Leviathan in which, by analogy, the citizens were the legs, arms and other members, while the sovereign was the single will that held them together by fear. The philosopher Kant, after dissolving the state into individual wills, had to restore the unity of all by a "Kingdom of Ends," which turned out to be the Prussian monarchy.[3] In more modern times the line of thought is continued by Karl Marx who abolished the individual and found the unity of society in his "social labor power," which turns out to be the "dictatorship of the proletariate" and a new royal prerogative with Lenin and Trotsky on the throne.

Meanwhile, there has been growing up, through the decisions of the courts on cases as they actually arise, the theory of a going concern. This theory has been aided, indeed, by the theory of an artificial entity existing only in contemplation of the mind, and that entity has helped to bridge over the three centuries since Coke and his contemporaries began to shatter the divine right of Kings with their "liberty of the subject" and to shatter corporations and guilds as mere "monopolies" based on privileges enforced by the King's officials. But the going concern is more than an entity, it is collective action; it is mass movement and mass psychology; it is the working rules that decide disputes and keep the mass together in support of the rules. The working out of the theory by inclusion and exclusion of transactions that had to be judicated in the decision of disputes has been necessary in order to do justice to those who had associated themselves together, had built up a business, had assumed responsibilities, had trusted to the credit

---

[1] Cp. Freemantle, W. H., *The World as the Subject of Redemption*, 1888.

[2] Cp. Figgis, J. N., *The Theory of the Divine Right of Kings*, (1896).

[3] Cp. Höffding, H., *A History of Modern Philosophy*, 2:108 (1900).

system, in the hope that their past and present business connections would be permitted to continue in the future. These hopes could not be shattered, else the whole fabric of society would come down. The courts and legislatures find them there, in the customary transactions of individuals, then recognize them, then authorize them, and the authorization is the security of the working rules. New hopes are built on these authorizations, and that which exists in the very nature of man's transactions with his fellows comes to exist also "in contemplation of law."

II. FACULTIES AND OPPORTUNITIES

We have seen the enlargement of the idea of property by means of change in the working rules, from that of ownership of tangible objects to that of ownership of an occupation, a calling, a trade, and even the ownership of one's labor; and the enlargement of liberty from personal liberty to economic liberty. The latter we have seen to consist in choice of opportunities, or choice between two degrees of economic power, and we have noticed two meanings of assets, or expectation, which we have distinguished as two meanings of the expectancies from which assets get their values. One is a part-opportunity, the other is a whole opportunity. A part-opportunity is the expectancy of a single transaction or a series of repeated transactions entered upon in pursuance of the whole opportunity of which it is a part. Capitalized, it is a separate asset, and the expectancy to which it looks forward is a transaction or a series of transactions on either the commodity market or the securities market to which the asset in question is referred. It is an expected sale, purchase, contract, a single or serial transaction, essential to carrying out the purpose of the whole-opportunity. It is a part of the whole.

But the whole-opportunity is that expectancy of a proportioned activity extending over a period of time, expected to yield a net income from the outgo and income of the part-opportunities. It is this whole-opportunity which we find to be identical with what the judges, in their opinions, defined as a "calling," "occupation," "trade," or even "labor," and which is identical with a going concern or a job.

The terms used by the judges, however, may comprehend either a business or a job, as was inevitable at a stage of industrial history when the working man was also a business man. The butchers in the Slaughter House Cases were apparently small butchers owning the physical property with which they worked, working with their own hands and with their employees, buying their materials and selling their products, and consequently the terms "occupation," "trade," "calling," and "labor" included both the business activity of buying and selling by merchants or employers, and the laboring activity of producing a product or otherwise acting for wages under the direction of the merchant or employer. Carrying the analysis thus forward, as it has been developed in business organizations and recognized in the law of principal and agent, master and servant, employer and employee, we distinguish the buying and selling transaction as a "business" from the employee or agency activity as a "job" or "position."

Either a business or a job, in its own field, is a whole-opportunity, and the term "occupation" seems properly to apply to each. An "occupation" is something "occupied," something "taken and held" for one's own use. Originally applied in Roman law to physical things, such as lands or chattels, which, being found or obtained by conquest, were thus "occupied," the term was then broadened out until it signified any intangible or incorporeal thing held for one's own use, and, naturally enough, when one has prepared himself for a trade, a profession, or a business, the term "occupation" is further enlarged, although the thing now referred to is but his own faculties, abilities, or capacities to engage in a line of business or to work at a job or fill a position.

The above opinions of the court, however, distinguished, though indistinctly, between what has come to be known as a "going business" and what may be described as an *intended business*. Those who "had already adopted" the prohibited pursuits in the Slaughter House Cases were engaged in a "going business." They already occupied the whole-opportunity, and to restrain them was to deprive them of a *right to continue in business*. Theirs was a peculiarly strong kind of property, in much the original sense of "occupation," for it was a whole-opportunity already occupied and it needed not the additional right of liberty in order to start the business. Nevertheless they were deprived "as well" of their liberty, in the sense, however, of their liberty to choose the part-opportunities, the particular transactions, necessary to carry on the business as a whole, that is, to "continue in business."

It is different with an *intended* business or job. Here the thing which the person may be said to own is rather the faculties, abilities, or capacities, embodied in his own body, the kind of property which we have just mentioned as also included by the judges in the term "occupation" but in the more personal sense of preparation for a "calling," a "trade," a "profession," or even merely the "ability" to labor, though not yet actually engaged in the occupation.

We see here a still further extension of the meaning of both property and liberty. "Labor" is property. By "labor," of course, is meant not only manual labor, but all of the faculties needed to engage in business or to fill a job or position. It was observed by James Mill that all that man does in the production of wealth is to "move" things and then nature does the rest. Others, including Karl Marx, went further and suggested three aspects of labor, "manual, mental and managerial." It is more appropriate to distinguish these as the physical, mental and managerial faculties to move both things and other persons, and even to move one's own body, by direct physical contact and exertion. The mental faculties are the ability to take a long leverage in moving things and persons by reason of a long look ahead or around, in calculating or inferring the probable results of the action; and, if managerial ability is distinguished from these, it is the ability to induce other persons to move things, usually by that emotional influence of promises, warnings or threats which may be summarized in social psychology as persuasion or coercion, command and obedience.

These physical, mental and managerial abilities are not separate faculties, but they are independent variables, since they differ widely in the proportions in which individuals are endowed with them or have acquired them. However proportioned, they may be considered as a single human faculty of moving things or persons in order that they, in turn, may move things or persons. In this way, they constitute the will of the individual in potential control of his body, prepared, ready or waiting to move things or persons but not yet actually moving them.

This then, appears to be the further extension of the meaning of property implied when it is said that "labor" is property, or that one's "trade," or "calling," or "profession," or even "occupation," (in the sense of preparation for an occupation) is one's property. That which is owned is one's own physical, engineering and managerial faculties incorporated in his body and constituting the expected uses of his body; and that which owns these faculties is that still more inward, inscrutable, more persistent and more important thing, the person himself, the human will.

Thus it is more than a figure of speech that the meaning of property should have been pushed back from physical things to opportunities, and then again to the faculties which make use of the opportunities, and that, in this inner personal recess it should have been identified with liberty. It is simply a recognition, in practice, of that which is known and felt, namely, that back of things, opportunities and even faculties is a central focus of personality, the will, that uses and proportions them all for its own purposes.

The distinction, however, when recognized, should be kept distinct, and this can be done by fixing it in a proper terminology. Property (distinguished from *rights* of property), has two sides, faculties and opportunities, and the connection between the two is acts or transactions. Property is not a physical object but is the relationship which a person necessarily sets up between his personal abilities and the world about. His faculties are his labor-power, rather his man-power, his physical, mental and managerial abilities. He himself is his will-power, his personality, choosing between opportunities, over-coming resistance, submitting to superior power, proportioning both his faculties and opportunities, by means of acts and transactions, for purposes that stretch into the future and are expected to yield what to him at the time is believed to be the largest economy of outgo and income according to his powers, opportunities and character. Property thus becomes human faculties in preparation for, or in occupation of, opportunities.

This relationship, as just now suggested, occurs in two aspects, the intended and the actual or realized. Presumably an intended or pro-spective class of opportunities is indicated by the preparation of the faculties, whether the preparation be the reasoned or casual efforts of self, or of associates, or of superiors. In general, the term "education" covers this activity of self and others in fitting the faculties for intended opportunities. But the actual, or realized, opportunity is the whole-opportunity with its various transactions, namely, the going business or actual job or position occupied.

Hence property is inseparable from the *right* of property. The term "rights," as we have seen, cannot be defined except as reciprocal rights, duties, liberties and exposures. Every so-called right implies all of these dimensions. Thus the so-called "right of liberty" is the right to the absence of compulsion, of restraint or of duty in moving things and persons physically, or inducing other persons to move things and persons. Liberty of access is, of course, essential to connecting up the two sides of property, the faculties and the intended business or job, through the agency of actions and transactions. This liberty is also essential to the choice of those part-opportunities, the thousands and millions of separate transactions which constitute the whole, the going business or actual job.

But since the opposite party has reciprocal liberties, the "right" to a job is exposed to their liberty to deny the right. And, since the opposite party has reciprocal rights, the right to a job is encumbered by reciprocal duties in the realization of the right. Likewise, of course, it is necessary that there be opportunities accessible or actually occupied. Business ability without a going business, labor without a job, is valueless.

III. Assets and Liabilities

By means of the enlargement of the concept of property from things to the exchange value of things, the *rights* of property have also changed from the right to buy, use and sell, a physical thing to the right to buy and sell the exchange-value of the thing. It is this right to the exchange-value of a thing that is known as "intangible property" and is equivalent to the business term "assets."

How is it possible that exchange-value, which is usually thought of only as a ratio-of-exchange at which things are bought and sold, can itself be an object owned and therefore be property? Can a ratio-of-exchange be owned? Is a ratio-of-exchange property? Are there rights of property in ratios-of-exchange?

The solution of the paradox is in the lapse of time. It is not the present ratio-of-exchange which is property; it is the present right to a future ratio-of-exchange. The present ratio-of-exchange is indeed an outcome of the "liberty" to buy and sell property. But the *right* to that future ratio-of-exchange is present property, that is, a present "interest" in the future exchange-value of the thing, and this, in turn, can be bought and sold and has a present value-in-exchange. Of course, then, it is not the *ratio* that becomes private property— private property becomes the right to have in the future the other goods that can be obtained in exchange for the thing now owned. It is a right to the prospective purchasing power of the thing, and this right exists in the present, can be bought and sold, and is property.

It was this paradox that led McLeod to reject both commodities and feelings as the subject-matter of economics and to hold that only *rights* are bought and sold.[1]   The paradox led him to count the same thing in two ways, once as a right to the exchange-value of a thing and once as a *right* to the future income from the thing.   This is also the familiar fallacy of some forms of double taxation, such as the taxation of land at its market value and the additional taxation of a note and mortgage secured by the land, also at its market value.   This was also the paradox that led Karl Marx to the theory of exploitation of labor by capital.   The laborer produces the physical thing, but the capitalist owns its exchange-value, and how can exchange-value produce wealth?

Marx, among other omissions, did not allow for the expected lapse of time.   He thought, like the other physical economists, that value was stored-up labor from the past.   But value lies in the future.   The ownership of value is the present right to the expected exchange-value of things, and it is this right that has a present value-in-exchange.

This, too, is the business man's view of both his property and his capital.   When the courts made the transition from ownership of things to ownership of the expected purchasing-power of things, they followed the practices of business.   The "assets and liabilities" of a business firm are but the present estimated exchange-values of its property and debts on expected markets.   Property is anything that can be bought and sold.   Assets are the present exchange-value of things that can be sold in the future, or whose products can be sold in the future, while liabilities are the present assets of other persons.

"Assets," that is, intangible property, includes everything that can be sold.   It includes physical commodities, such as land and buildings, plant and equipment, materials and supplies.   It includes cash on hand and deposit accounts at the bank.   It includes contracts in process of execution, accounts receivable, stocks and bonds of other companies, patent rights, copyrights, trade-marks, and even goodwill of the business.   Liabilities are assets belonging to other people.   They include every claim against one's own assets to be paid in the future, as well as all other probabilities of deductions from assets.   They include bonds and mortgages, notes payable, salaries and wages due, taxes due,

[1] McLeod, H D.. *Elements of Economics*, 1:153 (1881).

capital stock belonging to stockholders, and even the expected risks of business that reduce the value of assets.

Several facts are noticeable. Assets and liabilities are items which, added and subtracted, give the net assets, and these assets and liabilities are valued with reference to two different markets. Each of these markets is in the future, whether it be an immediate or a remote future. One is the several expected commodity markets for real estate, machinery and other physical products. The other is the expected "money market," or, more properly, the market for debts, where "incorporeal" property, consisting of creditor and debtor relations, such as promissory notes, bank deposits, bonds and stocks are created, bought and sold. These markets are quite distinct. The commodity markets are conducted at every store, every factory, every railroad, theater, warehouse and so on, where commodities or services are bought, stored, enlarged and sold. The money market is conducted mainly at the commercial banks where promises to pay the *prices* agreed upon for commodities are bought, insured, transferred and sold. The money market is a duplication or reflection of prices obtainable on the commodity markets, and it is this that leads to McLeod's and the popular fallacy of counting the same thing twice, once on the commodity markets and once on the money markets. Yet, from the standpoint of the business man, all market values are assets, whether on expected commodity markets or expected money markets.

There is a third class of assets having a peculiar position between commodities and debts, namely, that special case of "intangible" property, consisting of patent rights, copyrights, trade-name, goodwill, business reputation, good credit, the right to continue in business, the right of access to a labor market, the right of access to commodity markets and money markets, all of which have a present value based on expected transactions of buying and selling, borrowing and lending, hiring and hiring out. Their value is simply *exchange-value* itself, the very thing Karl Marx had in mind when he conceived the capitalist as the owner of exchange-value. It is these rights of access to markets, which, in the Slaughter House and Allgeyer Cases, came in under the name of "liberty"; and it is these rights of liberty that are now coming to be known as "intangible property" distinguished from "incorporeal" property. "Incorporeal" property is debts, "corporeal" or "tangible" property is physical things, but "intangible" property is the exchange-value of things and debts.

It is this third class of assets, namely, intangible property, that also gives significance to another distinction to be noticed, namely, that of the value of the assets taken separately on the commodity and money markets, and the value of the going business as a unit. If a business is bankrupt and thrown into the hands of a receiver or otherwise liquidated, all of the assets are sold separately and each has a "realized" market value on the commodity or money markets, which may be different from their expected exchange-value, usually known as their "book value." But, if the business is a "going business," then it is either bought and sold as a unit or the stocks and bonds are bought and sold as shares in its expected income as a unit. It is only a *going concern* that has a valuable "goodwill" or good credit, and hence this is a peculiarly intangible asset.

This distinction between intangible property, or assets, which may be bought and sold separately from the going business, and that more pervasive asset, the goodwill of the going business itself as a whole, calls for a distinction in the ownership of assets. One corporation may own the stocks and bonds of another corporation. To the first corporation these stocks and bonds are intangible property, or assets, to the extent that they have a current exchange-value on the money market or investment market. But, against the second corporation, treated as a unit distinct from its stockholders and bondholders, they are liabilities; as a liability they are the rights of bondholders and stockholders to the entire expected net income of the corporation when once ascertained.

Now this expected net income of the second corporation may be so great that the total value of its stock and bonds exceeds the aggregate value of all its tangible, incorporeal and intangible assets if sold separately. How shall this excess value be accounted for? It may be accounted for by watering the stock and ballooning the bonds. But, since the stocks and bonds are liabilities the corporation will need to show, on the other side of the account, an amount of assets equal to the inflation of stocks and bonds. This may be done in one of two ways, either by overvaluing the other assets or by inserting an item of "goodwill" or similar intangible, valued at the difference between the aggregate other assets and the outstanding issues of stocks and bonds. But this item of goodwill is a peculiarly intangible asset, depending, as it does, on the continuance of the net income, and for this reason, is not, perhaps, properly to be itemized as an asset on the books.[1] It therefore is usually concealed by overvaluing the other assets. But, in any case, whether it appears or does not appear on the books, it is exactly this intangible expectation of net income of the going business as a whole that determines the total value of its stocks and bonds on the markets. If the concern does not have such an expectation of net income, then the total value of its stocks and bonds sinks below even the value of its other assets, in which case the concern is bankrupt and the other assets must perhaps be sold separately and thus realized on the markets. Hence it is this very intangible asset, the goodwill of a going concern, consisting in the expectation of a net operating income, that is bought and sold when the stocks and bonds of the concern are bought and sold. They are simply claims upon its expected net operating income.

Hence we have two overlapping notions of assets. One is that of the tangible, intangible and incorporeal assets owned by a concern, the other is that of the total expected net operating income claimed by stockholders and bondholders. But even this expected net operating income is but a residual part of a gross income obtained by the concern as a whole. This gross income is obtained from day to day and then becomes, at different intervals, a gross income for each member of the concern in so far as he participates. It becomes a gross income for each employee in the form of wages, of each agent and manager in the form of salaries, of bondholders and other creditors in the form of interest and principal, if paid, and of stockholders in the form of dividends. All of them are alike in that each participant has a claim only to a share of the gross income. Each is but a creditor of the going business as a unit, while the going business, as the identical unit, is the debtor. Even the stockholders, as individuals, do not own the separable assets of the business—the lands, buildings and the intangible assets belong to the corporate unit until such time as they are distributed to meet the liabilities of the concern to the several participants.

Neither does the fact that the expected net operating income of the concern belongs to the stockholders, after deducting interest on debts, supported the idea that the going concern exists only in the proprietors and not also in the employees, agents, bondholders and other investors. The stockholders are simply residual claimants

[1] Cp. ESQUERRE, P. J., *The Applied Theory of Accounts*, 244–50 (1917).

on the gross income, while the others, beginning with wage-earners, are priority claimants. The goodwill, therefore, is not the goodwill solely of the stockholders, it is the goodwill of all participants which enables them all together to obtain a gross income as a whole and individually. The stockholders own the residual goodwill, since the others get their share of the proceeds of the joint goodwill before the stockholders get theirs. The value of the goodwill is inseparable from the value of the going business, but it is only the value of the residual goodwill, if any, that can be capitalized and appear in the values of the shares of stock owned by stockholders.

Hence the net income of the concern belonging to the stockholders is but a part of the gross income belonging to the business, and differs not, economically, from the other parts. All of them bear the relation of parts to the whole. The parts may be bought and sold separately, by the concern and by the participants. The gross income as a whole consists in the transactions by which the parts are bought and sold. Since this expected gross income is but the expected profitable transactions in buying and selling the parts which constitute the moving process of obtaining it, we shall name it the Going Business of a Going Concern. The concern "owns" its going business in the sense that it owns the liberty to continue in business through access to markets, and it "owns" its gross income in the sense that its board of directors have power to acquire, use and dispose of that gross income. But when once the gross income is distributed according to priorities the residual net income, as determined by the board of directors, becomes, not an asset of the concern, but a liability of the concern owing to its stockholders.

Hence the going concern owns two types of assets, its physical, incorporeal and intangible assets which are the parts of the whole, and its going business which is nothing else than all of the expected transactions by which the parts are bought, sold and distributed to the several participants. All of the parts are equal to the whole, no matter how great or small, since the residual part belonging to stockholders is merely the difference between the aggregate of the other parts and the gross income of the whole. And it is this gross expected income of the concern as a whole that constitutes its "underlying life," "immeasurably more effective" than all of its physical assets.[1]

[1] Above, Chap. II, p. 18.

All of these assets taken either separately or as a going business, have the common underlying fact that they are present rights to expected exchange-values on the expected commodity and money markets. And, since that expected exchange-value is their power to command a quantity of other objects in exchange, assets are, in substance, the present value of the expected purchasing power of things now owned or used. Consequently, the ownership of exchange-value is more than the ownership of a mere ratio-of-exchange—it is the ownership of expected purchasing power of which those expected ratios of exchange are each a measure of the degrees of power.

But even this expected purchasing power is meaningless except as the business management expects to go upon the markets and actively engage in the transactions of buying and selling. Hence the meaning of property, in the business sense of assets, is a shift from *things* to the *expected purchasing power* of things by way of *expected transactions* on the commodity and money markets. And the meaning of Capital shifts from physical things to the present value of expected acquisitions to be obtained through purchasing power available for use as expected bargaining power on the commodity and money markets. Thus we have four distinct concepts involved in the transition which has occurred in the meanings of Property and Liberty:

One is the concept of physical things which the *physical economists* called commodities or Capital, having their origins in the stored-up labor of the past. But, since in modern economics this is a process and not a thing, we shall distinguish it as a Going Plant.[1]

Second, is the concept of Assets and Liabilities, that intangible aspect of commodities and securities which have their foundation in the future, and consist of the expectations of sales or net income on expected markets, and which both *business men* and some modern economists call Capital, Capitalization, or Value.

Third, is the expected outgo and income of money, that is, of purchasing power, or power of acquisition on expected commodity and security markets, yielding profit, loss, or net income, that which the *accountant* takes account of, and which at any moment of time, appears in the balance-sheet as Assets and Liabilities.

Fourth, is the expected union of all future transactions of buying and selling, borrowing and lending, hiring, firing, leasing, paying

[1] Below, Sec. VI, p. 182.

debts and receiving payment of debts, constituting the expected activities of a Going Concern, with its goodwill, its franchises, its other market opportunities, and its liquidations of indebtedness. This series of transactions is the Going Business, moving along with the Going Plant out of the present point of time where assets and liabilities are measured and the past production of physical goods has accrued, into the future where income and outgo are expected.

The four are tied together as tightly as Things, the Valuation of things and the Reasons for their Valuation. Things are anything that can be bought and sold; assets and liabilities are their valuation, that is, their Capitalization or expectations founded on them; and the reasons for valuing them to the amount that they are valued are the expected other things to be acquired as income by means of them or given up as outgo on account of them, and the expected transactions by means of which the other things are acquired or given up.

These four meanings of Property and Liberty are inseparable attributes of Capitalism, and we shall distinguish them usually as:

1. The going plant, acquiring, producing and disposing of commodities and resources.

2. Expectancies, assets and liabilities, capitalization or present value.

3. Purchasing power, power of acquisition, business resources or prices, and

4. A going business, transactions, bargaining power.

The four meanings, for certain purposes, may be condensed into two: Expectations and Expectancies. Expectations are present assets and liabilities; Expectancies are the things expected in exchange, the purchasing power and bargaining power expected. It will be noted, if this is done, that the distinction between Expectations and Expectancies is quite parallel to that made by Irving Fisher between Capital and Income. But where he speaks of Capital as a "fund" of capital equivalent to capitalization, we speak not of a "fund" but of Expectations, Assets and Liabilities, or Capitalization; and where he speaks of an expected inflow of net income in terms of money, from the accountant's standpoint, we speak, from the legal and business man's standpoint, of Expectancies, which consist in the expected transactions of a going business which determine gross outgo, gross income and net income.

This shift in the meaning of property from things to the capitalization of things as assets and liabilities is a shift from the common-law or feudal-law meaning of physical things held exclusively for one's use to the business-law meaning of property as purchasing power, exchange-value, power of acquisition or prices, available in one's business. It is a distinction between Capital and Capitalization, between things and assets, between things owned and the powers of acquisition residing in the ownership of things, between use-value and exchange-value, between *Eigenthum* and *Vermögen*. The former is things, the latter is the purchasing power of things. But purchasing power is more than a mere passive flow and inflow, it is an active, volitional acquisition of income. It is a process of transactions that bring purchasing power, and a process of transactions is a going business. The shift in meaning, therefore, is a shift from property in things to both property and liberty in the expected acquiring, holding, enlarging and selling of things, and these, as stated in the Allgeyer Case, are "essential parts" of the "rights of liberty and property as guaranteed by the Fourteenth Amendment."

IV. Valuation, Apportionment, Imputation

We saw that the ratio of exchange measures a degree of power in that it is a comparison between the positive cost, or outgo, and the positive value, or income, that accompany a single transaction. The transaction, in that case, occurs between two opposing persons, a seller and a buyer.

Each individual in business, however, is *both* buyer and seller. His net income is derived from at least *two* transactions relating to the same commodity on the way from a primary producer to an ultimate consumer. As a buyer his outgo is a deduction from his assets, as a seller his income is an addition to his assets. His net income of purchasing power is therefore an addition to his assets measured by the difference between his money outgo and his money income. This we may distinguish as the *ratio of profit*. He pays a seller \$1.50 for a given article and sells it to a consumer for \$2.50. The net income is \$1.00 added to assets, and the ratio of profit on the pair of transactions is \$1.00 to \$1.50 or 1 to $1\frac{1}{2}$, or $66^2/_3\%$.

Such a pair of transactions may, of course, be repeated and may thus become an indefinite *flow* of identical transactions. The net income then is an *operating net income* conveniently broken up into units of time, say a year, and determined for a period of time by the difference between the gross operating outgo and the gross operating income. The ratio of profit on this flow of identical transactions remains the same—an operating expense of, say, $150,000 a year, an operating income of $250,000, and a net income of $100,000 with the same *ratio of profit*, $66^2/_3\%$.

The above illustration of a ratio of profit has a certain application in any business, for two reasons. It relates to a flow of identical transactions instead of a flow of *proportioned* transactions; and it is an operating proposition rather than a *capitalization* proposition. The latter signifies a *rate of profit*, rather than a ratio of profit. The distinction will immediately appear.

The business of a going concern is, of course, not a flow of identical transactions, but a continual proportioning and re-proportioning of many limiting and complementary factors, that which Karl Marx named the "organic composition" of capital. The manager does not buy and sell a single article but proportions his outgo among laborers and material of many kinds and prices, in order to proportion his sales to various classes of buyers. For this reason, as an *operating* proposition, the ratio between operating income and outgo is important, in that a change downward is a danger warning and a change upward is a confirmation of his policy. Assuming that prices remain the same, the warning directs attention to a possible poor proportioning of the factors, that is, waste, and a change upward indicates that he has hit on a better proportioning, that is, economy. The best proportioning (markets remaining the same) obtains a maximum net income, the worst proportioning wipes it out.

Whatever the operating net income may be, it is converted, by a process of capitalization, from a *ratio* of profit into a *rate* of profit. Supposing, in the above illustration that the operating net income of $100,000 a year is expected to extend into the future, then that operating net income can be bought and sold in the same way as any piece of physical property. It is not physical property but is the expected expansion and economy of a going business. There may be comparatively little physical property connected with it, as in the case of the goodwill of a firm of lawyers. But whether there is little or much the thing that is actually bought and sold in the process of capitalization is the expected control of the expected opportunities, powers and economies of a going business.

Suppose that the above net income of $100,000 is expected to continue indefinitely into the future. It then is capitalized for the purpose of sale and purchase of the going business. The process is familiar and simple. The expectancy becomes "assets." That which is sold and purchased is the present expectation of a pecuniary net income. There are two convenient but arbitrary expressions of measurement of what is done. One is to say that its present value as assets is a certain *multiple* of its *annual value*. The annual value is the annual net operating income. If the present value is believed to be ten times its annual value, that is, "ten years' purchase," then the total assets, or capitalization, of the concern is $1,000,000. If it is believed to be worth "twenty years' purchase," the assets are $2,000,000. Or, it may be stated that the business is *capitalized* at the rate of 10% in the case of ten years' purchase, or at the rate of 5% in the case of twenty years' purchase.

The two statements mean the same thing. But the first is in the form of a mathematical sum, the present addition of all the expected additions to assets over the total expected period of time. The second is in the form of an annual *rate of profit*, a multiple of the expected addition to assets over an arbitrary unit of time, the year. One method is the reverse of the other. One is the expectation of income, the other the income itself, the expectancy. If the purchaser pays ten times the annual value then his expected rate of profit per year is one-tenth or 10% of what he pays. If he pays twenty years' purchase then his expected rate of profit is one-twentieth, or 5% on the capitalization. What he is actually buying is an expected net income, measured, in the one case, as a *sum* of several expected annual incomes, in the other by a *ratio* of one of those annual incomes to that sum. And the ratio, since it involves a measurement of time as well as measurement of quantity, is rightly named a *rate of profit*, in which form it can then be used to compute the *amount* of profit for any desired period of time.

The conclusions to be drawn from this rather elementary explanation of what happens in the process of capitalization are clouded by two different physical notions of capital and property. Each of them conceives capital to be something fixed, predetermined as it were, and as solidly established as the buildings and lands about us. J. B. Clark, for example, speaks of capital as a "fund of value" transferring itself from object to object, but always a kind of predetermined substantial entity; and interest (or profit) is then a *fraction* of that fund depending on the amount of profit the fund can earn.[1] But if profit is a *fraction* of the amount of capital, then capital is merely a *multiple* of the amount of profit. If, as above, the *rate* of profit is 10% and the *amount* of profit is $100,000 then the "amount" of capital is ten times $100,000 or $1,000,000. If the rate is 5% and the amount of profit continues to be $100,000, then the "amount" of capital is $2,000,000. The so-called "fund" of capital is not a fund but an expectation, and the real thing that determines value is not a "fund" of capital predetermined, but an expectation of future bargaining power which determines it. Clark's "capital," which is really *assets*, or the expectation of income from things, and not the physical things themselves, does not flow out of the past, like a river, and get accumulated in a "reservoir" like a "fund," but his "capital" is the present value of expected opportunity and power on the commodity and money markets. The physical things have, indeed, flowed out of the past and have accrued in the present, but they are not assets of business unless from them is expected economic opportunity and power in the future.

Irving Fisher, on the other hand, has fully demonstrated this proposition that "capital" is the present value of expected net income, but his primitive notion of property as physical things held for one's own use by an owner, led him astray in ascribing the source of that income to physical things. And since the physical things are customers, he was led to the logical conclusion that the business man owns his customers.[2] The same logical conclusion from the ownership of physical things led Veblen to make the business man also the owner of his employees.[3] But modern capital is not capital in the physical sense, but is capital in the behavioristic sense. The behavior is the expected transactions on commodity markets and money markets. It is not corporeal property, but is incorporeal and intangible property. Its name is "assets," the exchange-values of things, and assets are the expected additions to income to be derived, not from physical things, but from expected profitable transactions with persons who are not owned.

What, then, becomes of the physical things, the lands, buildings, machinery, materials, that seem to be the very substance of wealth,

---

[1] CLARK, J. B., *Distribution of Wealth,* 119 (1908 ed.).

[2] FISHER, I., *The Nature of Capital and Income,* 5, 67, 68 (1906). See also COMMONS, J. R., "Political Economy and Business Economy," 22 *Quar. Jour. Econ.* 120 (1907).

[3] VEBLEN, THORSTEIN, *The Theory of Business Enterprise,* 18 (1904); *The Place of Science in Modern Civilization,* 339 ff.

capital and property? We must distinguish between titles of ownership and substance of ownership. If I own a piece of property and
somebody else owns the net income from that property, I hold the
bag and he takes the substance. Things are not the substance; expected behavior is the substance of things. Modern industry has
readily adapted itself to this evident distinction. The stocks and
bonds of a corporation are evidences, not of ownership of the physical
property, but of residual shares in the expected net income. The
corporation itself is erected into a composite person and it is this artificial person who actually owns the physical things (titles), but
the residual net income (substance) is apportioned to bondholders
and stockholders as purchasing power on the commodity markets
and money markets, according to rules of apportionment agreed upon
beforehand. The stocks and bonds are encumbrances on the corporation, arranged according to priorities, and intended to absorb
the entire expected "net operating income" of the corporation, after
the employees, material men and others have absorbed the operating outgo.

If we assume, in the above illustration, that the net income, $100,-
000, is divided in two parts, of which the bondholders' priorities call
for $20,000 and the stockholders' residual is $80,000, then the total
present value, or capitalization, of that net income is likewise divided between the owners of the two kinds of encumbrances. Capitalized at 5%, or 20 years' purchase, the bondholders' annual share,
$20,000, is worth $400,000, and if the total value is $1,000,000 the
stockholders' share is the residual $600,000; or, if the total value
is $2,000,000 the stockholders' residual is $1,600,000.

Similar arrangements are made in business other than corporations. A mortgage is a prior encumbrance on the net income of a
farm, and the farmer's title of ownership is worth only the value of
that residual known in American as "the equity." The mortgagor
and mortgagee apportion the expected net income between themselves, and the total present value of the farm is but the value of the
mortgage plus the value of the equity.

Here the well-known problem of double taxation as well as the
curious theories of Marx, McLeod, and Clark, show an awkward survival of the primitive notions of property and capital. The farm is
physical property. It seems to have substantial value. The farmer
is taxed on that total physical value. But the mortgage also is a

"fund" of value that seems to have a separate existence. It also is
taxed as an additional value. Yet the true situation is evident. The
mortgage is a prior claim, while the "equity," or title of ownership,
is a residual claim, upon the expected net income of the farm. The
total value of both mortgage and title is but the present value of the
expected net operating income, and this is but the expected exercise
of opportunity, power and economy on the part of him who manages
the farm.

In either of these cases, whether that of an incorporated or an unincorporated business, the title of ownership of the physical property
is but one of the several possible methods, and not always the best
method, of adding *security* to the ownership of the expected net income. It is the bag that may or may not hold the substance.

The physical capital—fertility of the soil, buildings, machinery—
thus sink to the level of raw material, not different at all from other
raw material except that its visible life is more prolonged. What is
the difference between a pile of coal or a hundred bushels of potatoes
or a stock of goods, that will last a month or a year in the business,
and a machine that will last ten years, or a building that will last 20
years, or the fertility of the soil that will last 30 years? Each is but
raw material for human labor. Each must be kept up by human
labor. The *depletion* of a pile of coal or a stock of potatoes is not
different economically from the *depreciation* of a machine or building, or the *exhaustion* of the soil. Each is raw material used up rapidly or gradually, and each alike passes over, in its own proportion,
into an indistinguishable part of the whole product of the going concern.

It is this going concern that coördinates the several items of raw
material into what we have distinguished as a Going Plant. Each
kind of raw material is both a limiting and a complementary factor
in the process of turning out a finished product ready for use. Raw
materials, machinery, lands, are the parts, Going Plant is the whole.

Yet these distinctions call for an appropriate classification of assets. As above indicated, we may distinguish the two types of assets
belonging to a going concern, the part-assets and the total assets.
The part-assets consist of three different types. One is *corporeal
assets*, or "*physical* values," consisting in the values of raw materials
taken separately, or the value of the going plant as a whole considered as an operating physical mechansim turning out products for

sale. These are usually designated, by a convenient solecism, as tangible values, or physical values, since they are values-in-exchange of physical things determined by reference to the several commodity markets.

The other is *incorporeal assets*, the value of bills receivable, deposits at the bank, stocks and bonds of other corporations, and similar encumbrances on others owned by the concern. These, by a similar violation of propriety, may be designated *incorporeal value*, since their value is determined on the security or money market.

The third is the value of residual goodwill, of franchises, patent rights, the value of trade-names, and similar opportunities owned by the concern. These may be distinguished as *intangible assets* or *intangible values*.

In each of these cases of valuation of part-assets the valuations are made, not for the purpose of capitalizing the total expected net income, nor for the purpose of apportioning net operating income to stockholders and bondholders, but for the purpose of *imputing* value to the different sources out of which the net income is derived.

We thus have three purposes of valuation which may be distinguished as *valuation proper*, *apportionment* and *imputation*. The purpose of *valuation proper* is that of capitalization, or present valuation, of the total expected net operating income. It gives the value of the going business as a whole. The purpose of *apportionment* is the assignment, according to priorities, of that expected operating net income among bondholders and stockholders. The purpose of *imputation* is that of distinguishing the *sources* of the net income. They are each but a different way of looking at the same things, but for different purposes. The main purpose in valuation proper is the relation between assets and the income expected from assets; the attendant purpose is apportionment of residual income to bondholders and the resulting apportionment of capital value or total assets to stockholders. But, for purposes of buying, selling or public regulation of the business as a whole, the imputation of value to its sources is allowable.

The contrast in the three purposes of valuation may be exhibited as follows, using the preceding figures of operating income and outgo:

1. VALUATION

EXPECTANCY		CAPITALIZATION
Gross Operating Income	$250,000 per year	
Gross Operating Outgo	150,000 per year	
Net Operating Income	100,000 per year	$1,000,000 (@10%) [1]

2. APPORTIONMENT

EXPECTANCY	CAPITALIZATION
$ 20,000 to bondholders....................$	400,000 (@ 5%)
80,000 to stockholders....................	600,000 (@ 13½%)
$100,000 net income......................	$1,000,000 (@ 10%)

3. IMPUTATION

Tangible Value (going-plant, commodity markets)........$	700,000
Incorporeal Value (encumbrances, money markets).......	100,000
Intangible Value (opportunities, money markets)........	200,000
	$1,000,000

V. THE UNIT RULE

If such a thing as a going concern actually exists, distinguishable from physical things, then failure to recognize it perpetrates injustice. In the Adams Express Company Case [2] the Ohio State Board of Assessment had valued the property of the express company for the purpose of taxation at $449,377.60 (capitalization) whereas the value of the tangible property in the state was shown to be only $23,-400 (imputation). The Board had taken into account the value of the entire capital stock and bonds of the company as a unit, under the name of "intangible value" and had apportioned to Ohio a part of that value in proportion to the length of lines within the state. It was contended by the company, and by four dissenting justices of the Federal Supreme Court, that the only "property" in the state of Ohio owned by the company was the horses, wagons, safes and similar tangible personal property; that these should be valued item by item as they always had been valued; that the so-called "intangible value" was but the "skill, diligence, fidelity and success," the

---

[1] The Capitalization figures would, of course, be different if the rate of interest on the money market were different.

[2] Adams Express Co. v. Ohio, 165 U. S. 194 (1897); re-hearing, 166 U. S. 185 (1897).

"reputation and goodwill" of the company, which were not property; that there was no "unity" between the horses and wagons owned in Ohio and those in New York and other states except a mere "unity of ownership;" that while in the case of a telegraph or railway company there was a connected physical plant in all the states, yet in the case of an express company the horses and wagons in Ohio were united to those in New York only by a mere "intellectual fiction," a "metaphysical or intellectual relation," an "imagined thing." The only property of "real intrinsic worth" was the tangible property.

But a majority of the court held that it was not physical unity, nor even unity of ownership, but "unity of use" that gave value to these separate items of tangible property. "Considered as distinct objects of taxation, a horse is indeed a horse; a wagon, a wagon; a safe, a safe; a pouch, a pouch; but how is it that $23,430 worth of horses, wagons, safes and pouches produce $275,446 in a single year?" (165 U. S. 222.) "Whenever separate articles of tangible property are joined together, not simply by a unity of ownership, but in a unity of use, there is not infrequently developed a property, intangible though it may be, which in value exceeds the aggregate of the value of the separate pieces of tangible property." (166 U. S. 219.) "If a state comprehends all property in its scheme of taxation, then the goodwill of an organized and established industry must be recognized as a thing of value." (166 U. S. 221.)

In this opinion the court completed a transition, that had been going on for fifty years, in the meaning of property from that of tangible property owned by individuals to that of a going business owned by a going concern. The tangible property disappears, except as physical instruments, and, in its place, property becomes the personal relations of buyer and seller, creditor and debtor, principal and agents, sovereign and corporation. "In the complex civilization of to-day," said the court, "a large portion of the wealth of a community consists in intangible property. . . . It matters not in what intangible property consists,—whether privileges, corporate franchises, contracts or obligations. It is enough that it is property which, though intangible, exists, which has value, produces income and passes current in the markets of the world." (166 U. S. 219.)

The historical steps in this transition of the meaning of property, in the tax cases, may be roughly indicated as follows. At first the separate items of property were listed and their values added, real estate and goods being itemized and taxed as the property of the corporation, but the stocks and bonds as intangible items in the hands of shareholders and bondholders.

On the other hand, the privilege tax, or franchise tax, on the corporation was at first an arbitrary fixed tax, without accurate regard to its value. Then various attempts were made to tax the value of the franchise. In the case of banks owning government bonds, which were exempt from taxation, it was held, in the year 1865,[1] not to be a tax on the bonds if the bank were taxed on its capital stock, although the *value* of that capital stock depended partly on the income derived from the non-taxable government bonds. The income from all the separate items flows into a common treasury and it is this net income that gives unity and value to the capital stock, distinct from the items like government bonds, which yield the income. The government bonds could not, according to federal law, be listed for taxation as separate items of property, but the present value of the expected income to be derived from them could be taxed with other income as a unit.

A similar result was ultimately reached in the taxation of railway corporations. The gross earnings of a railway are made up, in part, of the separate items of revenue from tolls on freight handled. But if the privilege or franchise tax is laid directly on the separate shipments, item by item, it is a tax on the interstate commerce of the shippers. But in 1891,[2] if the tax is laid on the gross earnings as a unit, derived though they be from the same shipments, it does not restrain commerce and is valid. The distinction turns on the difference between a specific tax on each shipment at the time it is made, which may be shifted to the shipper in a higher freight rate, and a tax on the gross earnings derived from all the shipments, which is a burden, not on the shipper, but on the treasury of the carrier.

The gross earnings tax, however, is unequal as between corporations, since it makes no allowance for differences in cost of operation. It is the amount of *net earnings* that measures the ability to pay taxes. But even net earnings alone are not a true measure. Two companies with the same net earnings may have invested different amounts of capital in the business, so that one is losing money, the other is making a profit, measured by the investment. Moreover,

---

[1] Van Allen v. Assessors, 3 Wall. 573, 593 (1865).
[2] Maine v. Grand Trunk Ry. Co., 142 U. S. 217, (1891).

it is not the *past* net earnings for a single year, but the expected net earnings over a future period of years, that give value to the business of the company. Consequently when these expected net earnings are capitalized, their capitalization is nothing else but the total value of the stocks and bonds. This was the next step. When the "capital stock," interpreted to mean both stocks and bonds, was valued and taxed to the corporation as a unit the tax was sustained. "It is obvious," said the court, in 1875, that "when you have ascertained the current cash value of the funded debt and the current value of the entire number of shares, you have, by the action of those who above all others can best estimate it, ascertained the true value of the road, all its property, its capital stock and its franchises; for these are all represented by the value of its bonded debt and the shares of its capital stock." [1]

These decisions, however, brought about a condition of double taxation, the taxation of the company as a unit on its "capital stock" and the taxation of shareholders and bondholders as individuals on their claims of part-ownership of that stock. But double taxation was held not to be improper, because there were two different persons owning two different objects, the corporation owning its franchise measured by capital stock, and each shareholder or bondholder owning his share of the expected profits. "The corporation," said the court, "is the legal owner of all the property of the bank, real and personal. . . . The interest of the shareholder entitles him to participate in the net profits earned by the bank. . . . This is a distinct, independent interest in property." [2]

Then followed a partial or total exemption of stockholders and bondholders whose intangible property notoriously escaped the assessor, whereas the tax on capital stock already reached them.[3] And this is the "unit rule" of taxation.

Thus the unit rule of taxation, treating the corporation as a going concern, finally tends, as we have seen in the Adams Express Company Case, to be substituted both for the taxation of physical items owned by the corporation and for the taxation of natural individuals owning part claims on the net income of the concern. Physical things and individuals are merged into a going business of a going concern.

[1] State R. R. Tax Cases, 92 U. S. 575, 605 (1875).

[2] Van Allen v. Assessors, 3 Wall. 573, 584 (1865).

[3] Pittsburg Ry. Co. v. Backus, 154 U. S. 421 (1894); Western Union v. Taggart, 162 U. S. 1 (1896); C. & N. W. v. State, 124 Wis. 553 (1906).

There remain, however, vestiges of the primitive notion of physical valuation. In these taxation cases under the unit rule the value of the franchise is sought to be ascertained by subtracting the value of the tangible property from the value of the capital stock, and this remains the practice under all the statutes which follow the unit rule. This practice results in two apparently different kinds of value for the going concern, the "tangible value" and the "intangible value," although, of course, the value of the capital stock as a unit includes both the tangible and the intangible elements. The notions of physical value hang over, even after the thing itself that is valued has changed from physical things to the expected net income of a going concern. But there are, in fact, not two kinds of value, tangible and intangible; there is but one value and it is intangible.

The confusion arises from failure to distinguish between what we have named "valuation proper" and "imputation." Valuation proper is capitalization, which looks to the future. Imputation is analysis of causes and looks to the past. There is but one value proper and it is the intangible expectation of a net income of a going concern. There are several factors contributing to the present expectation, some of which are physical and all of which have a history.

A further important development has occurred, or is occurring, incidental to the development of the unit rule, as will appear in the Adams Express Company Case. The meaning of a corporate franchise has begun to separate itself out into three meanings, which may be distinguished as the "franchise to be," the "franchise to do" and the "going business." The "franchise to be" was the articles of incorporation creating the corporate person with power to act like a natural person, and the legal entity thereby created could exist only in the state which created it. The "franchise to do," in the early corporation laws, was not clearly distinguished from the franchise to be, because corporations were *specially created* for the purpose of doing some special thing. But where the entity was created in one state and the activity occurred in another state, and especially, when the entity came to be created by *general corporation laws* and the special privilege could not be permitted to all such entities, then the "franchise to do" became a separate privilege granted by the same or another state to a public utility corporation, such as a railway or telegraph company, and existed where the tangible property was laid and used. The franchise to do, therefore, was inseparably connected with a stretch of physical property operated as a physical unit, and it was this physical unity that made the transition easy from a tangible thing to the intangible franchise whose value was the value of the capital stock connected with that thing.

But a new situation arose in the Express Company Case. That company, in the State of Ohio, had neither a franchise to be nor a franchise to do, since it was neither incorporated in that state nor did it occupy a stretch of territory in the state. It was but an ordinary private business distinct from the railway corporations over which it operated. To meet this situation the court enlarged the meaning of the "franchise to do" so that it became no longer a special grant or a privilege to operate over a designated stretch of territory, but became also "a combination of franchises, embracing all things which a corporation is given power to do." (166 U. S. 224.) This means, of course, all the things which any individual does in conducting any ordinary business without any special grant of power. In other words, the "franchise to do" becomes the usual rights and liberties open to any individual, except that the individual is now an association of individuals acting as a unit. Both the franchise to be and the franchise to do become identical with a going business of a going concern, as will appear from two of the cases already cited.

The transition in meaning was begun in the State Railway Tax Cases, in 1875. There the court held that the *situs* of personal property, including the franchise, for purposes of taxation, did not necessarily follow the domicile, or main office, of the corporation, but might be distributed by the legislature to all localities where the business was conducted.[1] This territorial diffusion of *situs* was approved in the Adams Express Company Case, so that the residence of a corporation, for this purpose, at least, is no longer the spot occupied by a supposed entity, the soul of the corporation, but the corporation resides wherever it transacts its business. The shift is made from entities to transactions, and going concerns repeat the individual psychology. The philosopher Descartes located the soul of man in the pineal gland but modern psychology locates the soul in what the body does; so the lawyers formerly located the *situs* of a corporation in the state which created it, but now the courts locate it wherever the corporation does its business.

Thus it is that, after the "franchise to be" has widened out from a

[1] 92 U. S. 575 (1875).

special act of incorporation into a universal right of association allowed
to all persons through general corporation laws, the "franchise to do"
also begins to be whittled down from a special grant of privilege not
open to all corporations, and a contrary expansion occurs until it
becomes the ordinary going business of any going concern. The
"going concern," as we have seen, is all of the persons associated and
organized in the concern. The "going business" is the unity and
proportioning of all transactions of the concern. The goodwill is the
expectation of reciprocal benefits to be derived from the transactions.
Thus going concerns are the persons going along together, going business is their transactions, goodwill is the social psychology that keeps
them going.

The explanation of this evolution of the "franchise to be" the " franchise to do" and the "going business" is to be found in the two sources
from which they were derived, namely, the King's prerogative and the
common law. From the prerogative came the articles of incorporation, the "franchise to be" a going concern and to act as a unit. From
the prerogative also came the special privilege of conducting a business, the "franchise to do" what others were not permitted to do.
These sprang from the prerogative which was above the common law,
and exempt from its limitations. They were grants of sovereign powers
and immunities, and not rights and liberties open to all.

But, from the common law, in its evolution into business law, came
the enforcement of contracts—the law of encumbrances—and the
liberty to buy and sell—the law of opportunities. These were open
to all persons, thus constituting the common rights and liberties of a
"going business."

Originally, since the franchises were special privileges, they were
not considered to be property but rather a privileged activity deroga-
tory to and even destructive of the liberty and property of other subjects. They were privileged liberties. In this respect the "franchise
to be" a corporation and the "franchise to do" were at first indistinguishable, for a grant of sovereign power was the grant of a privileged
position to do something. It exempted the holder from the free competition out of which the common law was developing the law of opportunities and goodwill, and, although this exemption had an intangible value it was not property because its value proceeded from a
power to tax the community in excess of what could be obtained by
appealing to the goodwill of the community. But, following the taking

over of the King's prerogative by the legislature and with the incoming of general incorporation laws, beginning in New York at the middle of the Nineteenth Century, the franchise to be a corporation was subjected to the competition of other corporations, through the universal right to incorporate, and its value sank to the mere cost of registration with the secretary of state.

Not so with the "franchise to do," which might be granted to an individual as well as a corporation, and was so granted originally. It retained its privileged character, for it required a special permit, such as a privilege to operate a public utility, like a bank, an insurance company, a tollroad, a railroad, canal or municipal undertaking, with the privilege of making charges or taking tolls not open to business in general. In many of these cases this franchise retained its privileged character on account of physical conditions which prevented access by competitors. Finally, however, even this franchise, in the Adams Express Company Case, is merged into the "going business" of the common law and becomes identical with that "unity of use" which we find is none else than the goodwill of a going business.

SOURCES OF THE LAW OF GOING CONCERNS

Prerogative—Special privileges to be and do.

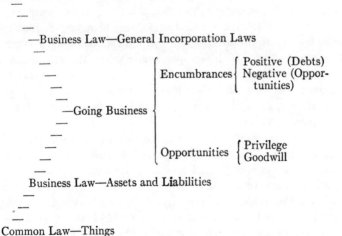

—Business Law—General Incorporation Laws

—Going Business

Encumbrances { Positive (Debts) / Negative (Opportunities) }

Opportunities { Privilege / Goodwill }

Business Law—Assets and Liabilities

Common Law—Things

Thus, up from the feudal common law of things held for use by privileged persons, through the business common law of assets and liabilities determined by the competition of anybody, and down from the prerogative with its exclusive privileges, by way of general incorporation laws, comes the meeting place of goodwill and privilege in the ordinary lawful activity, not, however, of individuals, but of a going concern operating a going business and acting as an individual.

This going business, the outcome and coalescence of the common law and the prerogative, retains its features derived from each. From the common law it derives those encumbrances and opportunities which constitute private property; from the prerogative it derives both powers and immunities of associated persons to act as a unit, the franchise to be, and, in special cases, the power to exercise exclusive privileges not open to business in general, the franchise to do.

It will be noted, from the foregoing, that the concept of a going concern with its going business was developed as a by-product of the effort to secure equality of burdens in support of government. The notion grew, not out of a theory, but out of transactions. It was recognized because failure to recognize it inflicts injustice. But it cannot be recognized in all its attributes *a priori* and in advance of actual transactions. It is recognized piecemeal as its activity begins to impinge on others. Sharing the burdens of taxation is one of these points of impact. The value of property to be ascertained in tax cases is not merely the value of a thing to its owner, but is a value *as between taxpayers*. A certain sum of money is required in order to operate the government, and it must be shared by taxpayers. If one pays less than his proportionate share, the others are compelled to pay more than their share. A taxation case is therefore a litigation between all other taxpayers and a certain taxpayer or class of taxpayers, in order to apportion the expenses of government among them.

The expenses may be apportioned according to either a tax on incomes or an *ad valorem* tax on property. In either case a certain uniform rate of tax is computed and then applied to the amount of individual income or to the value of individual property, in order to ascertain the amount of tax payable by each person. While, in the case of the tax on property, the separate items of property are conceived as having their separate values determined, not by the personal activity of their owners but by the demand and supply of the market, yet, in the case of the income tax the ability of the owner to obtain income through personal activity or management of property is the object taxed. Then, when, in the case of a tax on property, it came to adding shares of stock and evidences of indebtedness to the items listed as property, these too had a value independent of the personal activity of the owner, and they therefore were readily classed with items of tangible property.

It was different with the goodwill of the going concern itself, which is evidently something whose value depends on the "skill, diligence, fidelity, success and reputation" of the persons who compose the concern. The value of the physical and the other intangible assets might go on in the absence of the owner, but the value of goodwill as a whole is a value given by persons actively on the job. Consequently, when the definition of property is enlarged to include the goodwill of a going concern, it passes over from the value of things fixed by demand and supply on the commodity and money markets to the value of personal behavior fixed by "skill, diligence and fidelity."

The connecting link must be looked for not in the mere separable items of assets added together, but in the expected gross income as a unit, to be derived from the combination of the several items into a going business.

It required many years and even centuries to evolve this perfected notion of goodwill and a going business out of the common-law notions of physical property. The outcome is a concept of property, not as the exclusive holding of things by individuals, but as the going business of a going concern yielding an income to all of its members, including a residual net income to its stockholders. Even yet this expanded definition has not been fully accepted. In the case of the *Indianapolis News*, the State Board of Assessment, in attempting to follow the rule in the Adams Express Company Case, added $352,340 as the value of the residual goodwill and Associated Press franchise, to the $47,657 which was found to be the value of the printing presses and other physical assets. The Supreme Court of the State, although the state constitution required "all property not especially exempt to be taxed," yet held that this intangible value was not property within the meaning of that clause. The state court distinguished the Adams Express Company Case and justified its opinion on the ground that the legislature had not specifically provided either that goodwill should be taxed, or that shares in the Associated Press should be taxed, or that the unit rule should be followed.[1] Evidently the principle of a going concern might be made to apply to the taxation of all corporations if the legislatures so desired.

VI. Going Plant and Going Business

Wealth vs. Commonwealth

We have noted that the concept of a going business was developed as a by-product of the effort to obtain justice between taxpayers for the support of government. The going business was there but had not been recognized in the tax laws, owing to the primitive notion that property consisted only in physical things held for one's own use. When, however, the going business was recognized as property, then, not only physical things, but also the "skill, diligence, fidelity, success and reputation" of the persons composing the concern were recognized as property, and property came to consist of the expected profitable transactions of the organized concern.

In a parallel way we shall find that the concept of a going plant operated by a producing organization has been developing out of the effort to establish justice between sellers and buyers. In the cases on taxation, a concept of justice was eventually obtained by abandoning entirely the notion of physical things as property and accepting as a substitute the concept of the present value of an expected income. In the case of a going plant, a remnant of the physical notions continues to clog the decisions under the name of "going concern value." The going plant is a producing organization furnishing a service to the public, but the going business is a bargaining organization obtaining prices from the public. One is the exact reverse of the other, and it is the mingling of these two opposing concepts, under the name of "going concern value," that was injected into the opinions of the Supreme Court by Justice Brewer, beginning in 1892.

The Congress of the United States had authorized the purchase, by condemnation proceedings, of the property of the Monongahela Navigation Company,[2] in order to improve the navigation of the river and to abolish the tolls charged by the private company on the river traffic. In this act the Congress had expressly provided that the franchise of the Company to collect tolls for the navigation of

---

[1] Hart v. Smith, 159 Ind. 182 (1902).
[2] Monongahela Navigation Co. v. U. S., 148 U. S. 312 (1893).

the river should not be considered or estimated in making compensation to the Company for its property. The Supreme Court, by Justice Brewer, held that this proviso of the act deprived the Company of its property without just compensation, since the property of the Company was not merely its physical property but also its franchise to take tolls for the use of that property. "The franchise," said the court, "is a vested right. The state has power to grant it. It may retake it, as it may other private property, for public uses, upon the payment of just compensation. . . . but it can no more take the franchise which the state has given than it can any private property belonging to an individual." (341.)

The court proceeded to notice that the government of the United States in condeming the property, was acquiring the "right" to exact the same prices for service which the navigation company had been receiving. "It would seem strange," the opinion proceeds, "that if by asserting its right to take the property, the government could strip it largely of its value, destroying all that value which comes from the receipt of tolls, and having taken the property at this reduced valuation, immediately possess and enjoy all the profits from the collection of the same tolls. In other words, by the contention this element of value exists before and after taking, and disappears only during the very moment and process of taking." (337, 338.)

This opinion probably reached the modern high tide of the ancient royal prerogative, for the fling at Congress appears to have gone on the assumption that a monarch, Congress in this case, above the common law, had granted to the navigation company a privilege to tax the community for the company's use and then had arbitrarily revoked the privilege in order to tax the community for the monarch's use. A similar issue had arisen between the common law and the prerogative in England, at the end of Elizabeth's reign and the beginning of the reign of James I. The common-law lawyers contended that the franchises, patents, privileges, granted by the sovereigns to the lobbyists of the time, since they were granted to persons "not skilled in the trade," served only to extract private wealth from the commonwealth without increasing the commonwealth; but that the merchants and manufacturers, who became wealthy by their own efforts out of their own private property without aid of the royal prerogative, increased the commonwealth to the extent that they increased their own wealth. On these grounds, the courts, beginning in 1599, declared these patents void, and the parliament, in 1624, abolished them.[1] But now, in 1892, Justice Brewer restores them, partly by putting Congress in the shoes of an absolute monarch and overlooking the intention of Congress to abolish the tolls altogether, and partly by enlarging the definition of property from physical things to franchises, such that the revoking of the special privilege is equivalent to taking private property without compensation. If property is not only a physical thing, but is also a franchise to charge prices for service, then the value of the property is not only the exchange-value of the physical property which the owner has added to the commonwealth, but is also such additional wealth as the owner may extract from the commonwealth over and above what he has added to it. Both are valuable, both are assets and both are property.

But a proper distinction would have recognized *two* values, depending on the opposite person with whom the owner is dealing. As *against other private persons*, a special privilege has a value determined by what private citizens can earn through ownership of the special privilege; but as *against the public*, which, under the common law, retains the power to regulate the prices and has granted the franchise only on condition, express or implied, that the prices be reasonable, the franchise has no value.

The constitution of the United States prohibits the taking of private property for public purposes without just compensation. Just compensation is determined as the amount at which a willing buyer and a willing seller would value the property at the time on the existing markets. Thus the Constitution makes the voluntary transactions of private persons the standard of reasonable measurement of value to be used in the compulsory transaction of taking private property under the power of eminent domain. When the constitution was framed the current definition of property was physical things such as lands and physical chattels. A different clause of the constitution prohibited the impairment of the obligation of contracts, which was the only form of "incorporeal property" then known. The "intangible property," consisting of rights to buy and sell were not known as property in the constitutional sense, until after the Slaughter House Cases. And the Slaughter House Cases, both in the majority and minority opinions, as we have noticed, denied that a grant of a monopoly was private property. The majority opinion

---

[1] Above, Chap. III, p. 47.

held that it was justified only as a police regulation which might be revoked without compensation, as was done and sustained by the court in the later case dealing with the same slaughter houses.[1] Even when the minority opinions became the unanimous opinion of the court, the intangible property recognized was only that which the individual might acquire by his own private transactions and without the aid of a special franchise. The minority opinions, in those cases had held to the original distinction between the common law and the prerogative. A franchise proceeded from the prerogative and was not property. Property proceeded from the common law, since it was only the common law that took the ordinary practices of unprivileged persons and erected them into a system of legal rights, duties and liberties.

But Justice Brewer, in 1892, made this further extension of the definition of intangible property. Now it becomes not only the property which one gets by his own efforts in private transactions, but also the property which he gets by the very grant of sovereign power to operate a monopoly which had been refused the name of property in the Slaughter House Cases, and had been justified only as a revocable exercise of the police power. The franchise in the Monongahela Case [2] did not carry the legal power to take *excessive* tolls, and, if the tolls were reasonable, as the common law required, there would have been no value in the franchise as against the public. The public is not to be presumed to have granted a privilege of extortion. It was, indeed, different when the King granted a franchise—it was a grant of his private power to tax. But this is not to be presumed when the franchise is granted by the public itself. This was evidently the opinion of Congress when the proviso was added that the franchise should not be considered or estimated. Congress was supposed to be the public granting a power to tax itself, in consideration of a service to be rendered to itself.

In support of his opinion, Justice Brewer cited the Dartmouth College Case where it was held that the franchise of a corporation was a contract which could not be set aside by either party to it.[3] But the Dartmouth College Case had to do with a "franchise to be" and not a "franchise to do." It was a grant of power of self-

[1] Above, Chap. II, p. 11.
[2] *Op. cit.*, 148 U. S. 312.
[3] *Op. cit.* 344; Dartmouth College *v.* Woodward, 4 Wheat. 518 (1819).

government within the corporation, the franchise to act as a unit, not the grant of a privilege of taking tolls from the public. The "franchise to be" is, in one sense, of course, a franchise to do, but the kind of "doing" is that internal proportioning of factors which does not concern outsiders and is solely a matter of self-government. But the "franchise to do," in the special meaning attached since the time when general incorporation laws deprived the "franchise to be" of its privileged character, is the expansion of one's resources by means of a special advantage over customers consisting in exclusion of the free competition of third parties. This special franchise to do, at common law, carried the implication that the exercise of the power granted should be reasonable as determined by a jury of the community.

The scope of the Dartmouth College decision was thus enlarged by Justice Brewer from the privilege of self-government into a privilege to tax the community in excess of competitive prices for similar service; privilege was erected into a property-right, analogous to ownership of physical things, as against the common-law theory that it was a grant of prerogative, or against the Slaughter House opinion that it was an exercise of the police power, and not a right of property.

2. Physical Connections

While in the Monongahela Case Justice Brewer expressed his opinion regarding a special franchise then in force, in the Kansas City Water Works Case, two years later,[1] he expressed an opinion regarding a business whose special franchise had expired. Kansas City was required by the legislature, on the expiration of the franchise, to purchase the property covered by the franchise. The company claimed a value of $4,500,000 based on the net earnings. The city, and a lower court, found the value of the physical plant to be $2,714,000 based on the estimated cost of reproduction "put together into a waterworks system as a complete structure, irrespective of any franchise—irrespective of anything the property earns or may earn in the future." (864.)

Justice Brewer, in reversing the lower court and requiring payment for intangible value, agreed that capitalization of earnings would not be fair because it "implies continuance of earnings, and continuance

[1] National Waterworks Co. v. Kansas City, 62 Fed. 853, 865 (1894).

of earnings rests upon a franchise to operate a waterworks," a franchise which in this case had expired. Neither should "original cost" control the valuation, since what they were looking for was "present value." Present value must be the value of an expectancy. It could not, therefore, be found in the "cost of reproduction," which, though it also evidently gives a present value, yet does not give a value based on expectations. The court found this expectancy, not, of course, in the franchise, which had expired, and not in the expected prices to be paid by customers, which, of course, depended on the franchise, but in the physical connections that tied the dwellings of the customers to the plant of the company, even though it was the customers and not the company who had paid for and who owned these physical connections. The cost of reproduction is inadequate, said the court, in that it does "not take into account the value which flows from the established connections between pipes and the buildings of the city. . . . The fact that the company does not own the connections between the pipes in the street and the buildings—such connections being the property of the individual property owners—does not militate against the proposition . . . for who would care to buy, or at least give a large price for, a waterworks system without a single connection between the pipes in the streets and the buildings adjacent? Such a system would be a dead structure, rather then a living and going business." (865.)

These physical connections, by a curious irony, are identified with free choice of opportunity on the part of customers. "Such connections" continued the court, "are not compulsory, but depend on the will of the property owners, and are secured only by efforts on the part of the owners of the waterworks and inducements held out therefor."

This quaint sarcasm of Justice Brewer continues to be the precedent for later decisions. It goes back to John Locke's empty concept of the will. True enough, according to that concept, water works connections in a great city are not compulsory on customers— each customer has the inaccessible alternative of digging his own well.

It follows that the government of Kansas City, as in the Monongahela case, is not the public, but is another private purchaser buying a physical object by means of which it can tax the public for its private use. "The city, by this purchase," said the court, "steps into possession of a waterworks plant—not merely a completed system for bringing water to the city, and distributing it through pipes placed in the streets, but a system already earning a large income by virtue of having secured connections between the pipes in the streets and a multitude of private dwellings." "Who would care to buy or at least give a large price for, a waterworks system" not having these physical connections and pecuniary income? (865.)

In this version Justice Brewer identified a going business operated by the business organization for the sake of obtaining prices for its service, with a going plant operated by a producing organization for the sake of rendering that service. The customers had *physically* connected their property with the physical property of the company, and, by doing so, had *mentally* connected their future patronage with the service rendered by the company and had tacitly accepted such prices as might be charged by the company in the future. Although they cannot readily get away, being physically connected and having no costless alternative, yet the "connections are not compulsory, but depend on the will of the property owners."

In this way, by resorting to a physical notion of property, is retained the primitive notion that property in itself has no economic power through the power to withhold service, and that, the special franchise having expired, there is no legal coercion, therefore no coercion. Indeed, this primitive notion of physical property held for one's own use retained a still more primitive significance, for, in this case, it carried with it also the notion of holding the attached human beings as one's property, just as we have noticed above that Irving Fisher mistakenly supposed. The city, like a private purchaser of an estate with serfs attached, "steps into possession" of "a system already earning a large income" from customers physically attached to the plant. Justice Brewer, by this analogy, applied a physical concept of slavery to a goodwill concept of citizenship, and thus converted the Fourteenth Amendment into an authorization of what Justice Field had named "servitude" as a substitute for slavery.

3. *Lawfulness and Unlawfulness*

While Justice Brewer, in the Monongahela and Kansas City Cases, carried over physical concepts into bargaining concepts, Justice Savage, of the Supreme Court of Maine, gave to the doctrine the legal setting which has been followed by other courts. In the

Water District Case [1] the property of the company and its unexpired franchise were required to be valued for public purchase. Justice Savage, in his instructions to the appraisers, excluded the value of the franchise as such. He saw clearly that the common-law rule against charging "arbitrary rates beyond the power of revision" by the public authorities deprived the franchise itself of value as against the public. This reduced the franchise to merely a kind of certification that the concern is lawfully there, lawfully charging prices for service, and exercising the ordinary equal privilege of anybody to engage in a lawful business. The property was to be valued just as ordinary lawful property would be valued, which required no special privilege.

Yet this ordinary lawfulness itself is valuable. "Even in cases where by statute," he said, "franchises are not to be included in the valuation, we conceive that it must have been implied that the property was to be valued as rightfully where it was and rightfully to be used. For what are pipes in the ground worth as pipes, or reservoirs, or dams, or fixtures, unless they can be rightfully used, and reasonable tolls charged? And these rights are the franchises." (378.) "So far as the structure is maintained and used by virtue of a franchise," the Justice continues, "that fact may add to the value of the structure. One would be likely to pay more for it as a structure if it could be rightfully used than he would if it could not. . . . It is a structure, in actual use, and with a right on the part of its owner to use it, and to charge reasonable rates to customers for services rendered. This is all. It is threefold in discussion but it is single in substance." (376, 377.)

There are thus two concepts of a "dead structure," Justice Brewer's concept of a structure without physical connections, and Justice Savage's concept of a structure without legal authority to charge customers for the use of the service. Without this legal right the concern has no earning value, which is the breath of life that converts the plant into assets. Where Justice Brewer needed mainly physical connections in order to get a going concern, Justice Savage needs also legal sanction in order to get what he called a "going concern *business*." *Without* legal sanction to charge prices it is dead, even though it be a going plant with its producing organization. *With* legal sanction it is also a going business with a business

[1] Water District *v.* Water Co., 99 Me. 371 (1904).

organization, and has a value as assets determined by its expected lawful earning power.

Justice Savage is quaintly correct in his analysis. Ordinary lawfulness is itself valuable. A brewery or saloon in a "dry" country is less valuable than the same brewery or saloon in a "wet" country. A slave loses value for its owner on emancipation. Smuggled goods are less valuable to their owner than the same goods lawfully in the country. A stolen horse has less value to the thief than it has to a lawful purchaser. A waterworks plant lawfully charging tolls is more valuable to its owner than the same plant treated as a nuisance.

This is because *lawfulness* is compared with *out-lawfulness*, instead of comparing *privileged lawfulness* with *equal lawfulness*. It does not follow, as *against other lawful* property, that lawfulness has a value. Competing property is also lawfully there, and this competing property lawfully keeps down the price of other lawful property. Lawfulness is worth having but does not have additional value in competition with others who have equal lawfulness. Equal lawfulness implies *exposure* to lawful competition as well as lawful right to require payment for lawful service. Equal lawfulness is but the legal equivalent of a competitive business, and not something additional to the business. Justice Savage has given a double meaning to lawfulness—the *lawful* exercise of power as *against its unlawful* exercise, and the *privileged* exercise of power as against its *equal* exercise. Privileged lawfulness is none other than the same special franchise to charge arbitrary rates which he had previously excluded from additional valuation. By making equal lawfulness analogous to outlawfulness, he restored what he had excluded when he contrasted privileged lawfulness with equal lawfulness.

Justice Savage then proceeded to construct out of the confusion of use-value and exchange-value the concept of "going-concern-value," by tying together Justice Brewer's physical connections of a going plant with his own privileged lawfulness of a going business. "In the first place, it is a structure, pure and simple, consisting of pipes, pumps, engines, reservoirs, machinery and so forth, with land rights and water rights. As a structure it has value independent of any use, or right to use where it is, a value probably much less than it cost, unless it can be used where it is, unless there is a right to use it. But more than this it is a structure in actual use, a use remunerative to some extent. It has customers. It is a going concern.

The value of the structure is enhanced by the fact that it is being used in, and, in fact, is essential to a going concern business. We speak sometimes of a going concern value as if it is, or could be, separate and distinct from structure value—so much for structure and so much for going concern. But this is not an accurate statement. The going concern part of it has no existence except as a part of the structure. If no structure—no going concern. If a structure in use, it is a structure whose value is affected by the fact that it is in use. There is only one value. It is the value of the structure as being used." [1]

It was this physico-legal compound of Justice Brewer's going plant with its physical connections and Justice Savage's going business with its lawful connections that the Supreme Court afterwards erected into an entity, "going-concern-value," though at first rejecting it under the leadership of Justice Hough, whose illuminating exposure of its fallacies is next in order of time.

4. *Goodwill and Privilege*

In the Consolidated Gas Case, "going-concern-value" appeared under the name of "goodwill value." The municipality of New York had attempted to reduce the price of gas, and the company set up a claim for both franchise value and goodwill value. Justice Hough's reasoning in the lower federal court, where this case first appeared,[2] was the first behavioristic analysis of the distinction between a franchise and goodwill, in this class of cases. Regarding the franchise he said: "Return can be expected only from investment, and he that invests must part with something in the act of investing. . . . It [the company] did not invest in its franchise because it did not pay for it. . . . The investment of property was made, not in the franchise, but under the franchise, and on the faith thereof. The franchise is but a part of the power or privilege of sovereignty, allotted to a private person for the benefit of all, and only incidentally given for private emolument. . . . The franchise has added no producing power to the realty or personalty. It has but authorized their employment in a particular way, and protected the owners while so employing them. . . . I can imagine no more than three

---

[1] P. 376. See also his analysis in a preceding case, Kennebec Water District *v.* Waterville, 97 Me. 185, 220 (1902).

[2] Consolidated Gas Co. *v.* City of New York, 157 Fed. 849 (1907).

ways in which the value of a franchise can be stated. It is valuable
(1) because it authorizes the gainful use of private property in a
particular manner; (2) because once obtained it is often difficult
or impossible to get another like it; (3) because it may be used to
injure or hinder another enterprise, although itself conferring or
securing nothing of value. The third method of statement has
been accurately, though colloquially, described as 'nuisance value,'
and is so obviously illegitimate as to require no discussion. The
second method of statement, when carefully considered, asserts
that because the sovereign has deemed it advisable to intrust a
public work to one citizen or body of citizens, such quasi-monopolistic
grant confers the right to charge for the service more than would
be just or lawful were the occupation open to all. On every private
sale of franchise property the price paid is so much money lost to
the public by official incompetence or worse, and such sale can confer
on the vendee no right to compel the consumer to repay him a price
which should have been paid to the state. For these reasons I believe
that, on principle, a franchise should be held to have no value except
that arising from its use as a shield to protect those investing their
property upon the faith thereof, and that, considered alone and apart
from the property which it renders fruitful, it possesses no more
economic value for the investor than does an actual shield possess
fighting value, apart from the soldier who bears it." (872, 873, 874.)

Justice Hough also excluded the alleged goodwill of consumers from
valuation against themselves as an element in the price which they
should pay for gas. Accepting the definition of goodwill found in
an earlier case [1] as "all that good disposition which customers
entertain towards a house of business identified by a particular
name or firm, and which may induce them to continue giving their
custom to it," he exclaimed, "I cannot perceive how this complainant can possess a goodwill answering that description. . . . It is
required by law to furnish gas to all demanding it within a certain
distance of the mains, service pipes and meters. What induces a
customer to remain with this company? A desire to avoid the 'nuisance of street digging' and the 'beneficially monopolistic character'
of the defendant's present occupancy of the streets." (871, 872.)

From the testimony it appeared that what the company meant
by goodwill was that same "going-concern-value" which we have

[1] Washburn v. National Wall Paper Co., 81 Fed. 20 (1897).

seen to be included in the concepts of both a producing organization and a business organization—in short, the value of a going
business in-so-far as that value is additional to the cost of reproduction of the Going Plant. To this Justice Hough answered, "the
organization itself is but a method of utilizing that which is invested. . . . But goodwill, in the sense of organization for the business
of furnishing gas can have no existence whatever apart or detached
from the franchise conferring the necessary privilege. Would anyone
think of capitalizing goodwill of this kind and distributing its assumed
value in the shape of new shares among shareholders, new or old?"
(872.) This claim of goodwill, he said, "seems to forget that for many
years the price and distribution of complainant's gas has been regulated by law. A citizen is entitled to have a clean street before his
house because he pays taxes *inter alia* for that purpose. . . . I think
it apparent that the conceivable goodwill of a gas company in this
city is about equal to that of the street cleaning department of the
municipal government." (872.)

Notwithstanding this valid reasoning, Justice Hough, in view of
preceding opinions by the Supreme Court, felt himself bound to allow
a franchise value, though not a goodwill, or going concern value.
Considering that his position was that of a trial court, he held that
he could not enforce his own opinion "without doing violence to theories of law and habits of legal thought fairly discoverable in preceding decisions of superior jurisdiction. In this case I am compelled
to the conclusion that it is necessary to allow the discoverable value
of complainant's franchises as part of that capital upon which a fair
return must be allowed, because to refuse would be to disregard
views expressed by higher courts regarding the general nature of
franchises and regulation proceedings. . . . It is my duty to follow
the method of reasoning there clearly indicated, leaving it to higher
tribunals to make distinctions which, if drawn by a lower court, would
in my opinion savor of presumption." (875.) With this protest against
his own decision in the case, Justice Hough felt himself "compelled
to consider franchises not only as property, but as productive and
inherently valuable property, and to add their value if ascertainable,
to complainant's capital account." (877.) "It is a familiar doctrine,"
he said, "that private citizens may acquire vested rights through a
series of even erroneous decisions, rights so firmly vested that it becomes unconstitutional for the court which persisted in error suddenly

to rectify its mistakes to the detriment of those who had securely rested upon the decisions sought to be invalidated." (875.) And he proceeded, by the plainly arbitrary and illogical method of comparison with the increase in adjoining land values, to ascertain a formal value of the franchise.

Yet, so forcible and accurate was Justice Hough's reasoning against his own decision, that, two years later he suffered the satisfaction of seeing the Supreme Court reverse his decision by adopting his reasoning.[1] The reversal, however, consisted only in changing the basis for calculating the value of the franchise and reducing the value of the franchise from that which Justice Hough had arbitrarily calculated to a value which it appeared the legislature of New York, twenty-five years before, had incidently validated when it had approved issues of stock against the franchise value as it then stood. The Supreme Court, however, expressly stated that this peculiar validation by a legislature should not be taken as a precedent for cases where there was no such validation. (47, 48, 52.)

It will be seen that Justice Hough clearly distinguishes goodwill-value from franchise-value. Goodwill and franchise are alike in that the owner thereby is raised above the exposure of competition and obtains ordinarily a residual income in excess of what could be obtained if he were fully exposed. But they differ economically and legally; economically in that the customers, in the case of a special franchise, are not free to go elsewhere and choose an alternative except at an onerous expense which gives to the franchise a value somewhat equal to the cost of the alternative nuisance; but, in the case of goodwill they are free to go elsewhere without additional cost, and consequently the value given to the goodwill by their willing patronage is a value based on what they voluntarily believe to be a superior service. The value of the franchise is a nuisance value, that of the goodwill is a goodwill value. Both of them reflect the prices of products which possess use-value to the customers, but in one case the price is the value of avoiding a nuisance, in the other the value of avoiding an inferior enjoyment.

Legally, also, the two differ, in that goodwill has come up out of the common law of private business transactions, based on what is deemed to be fair dealings between competitors and between sellers and buyers; whereas the franchise comes down from the King's pre-

[1] Wilcox v. Cons. Gas Co., 212 U. S. 19, 42 (1909).

rogative, based on the arbitrary power of a sovereign to grant special privileges to courtiers and lobbyists, protected from competition. Goodwill springs from the common ordinary liberty of competition open to everybody, while the franchise springs from the special favors of the sovereign which reduce the exposures of free competition.

Therefore, basing our terminology on these economic and legal reasons, we shall speak of franchises as privileged values, distinguished from goodwill as unprivileged values; and the value of franchises as privileged assets, the value of goodwill as unprivileged assets. Evidently this is the distinction made by Justice Hough and adopted by the Supreme Court as soon as its attention was called to it. The Supreme Court proceeded at once to eliminate franchise-value, except where a sovereign legislature had mistakenly reverted to the King's prerogative, and to strip off goodwill from the face of special privilege.

5. *Going Concern Value*

But, while the Consolidated Gas Cases disposed of goodwill value and franchise value (unless validated by a legislature) yet the Supreme Court soon resurrected them on Justice Brewer's physical analogy and Justice Savage's legal analogy. This resurrection took the form, first, of distinguishing between cases of rate regulation and cases of public purchase, to the latter of which Justice Brewer's precedent in the Monongahela Case continued to hold, and then obliterating the distinction by merging rate cases into purchase cases.

The first purchase case, following the Consolidated Gas Case, was that of the purchase by the City of Omaha of the property of the Omaha Water Works Company.[1]

Here the Supreme Court, by Justice Lurton, expressly stated that the Consolidated Gas Case was a rate case, and "did not concern the ascertainment of value under contracts of sale." (203.) This distinction had not previously been made. Indeed, in the same year with the Monongahela purchase case, the Supreme Court, led by Justice Brewer's reasoning, had contended that the value for rate-making purposes should be the market value of a railroad's property, the same as for purchase cases.[2] The state of Texas had created a commission to make a valuation of the railroads in that state, and to fix the freight and passenger rates so as to yield a return on that

[1] Omaha v. Omaha Water Co., 218 U. S. 180 (1910).
[2] Reagan v. Farmers' Loan and Trust Co., 154 U. S. 362 (1894).

value. The commission excluded franchises, and valued only the physical property at what it would cost to reproduce it as a going plant. The Supreme Court, by Justice Brewer, said (410), "If the state were to seek to acquire the title to these roads, under its power of eminent domain, is there any doubt that constitutional provisions would require the payment to the corporation of just compensation, that compensation being the value of the property as it stood in the markets of the world, and not as prescribed by an act of the legislature? Is it any less a departure from the obligations of justice to seek to take not the title but the use for the public benefit at less than its market value?" [1]

The same view was taken by Justice Brewer when, in the lower federal court, he overruled an act of the Nebraska legislature regulating railway rates.[2] There he cited the Reagan Case and said that even greater damage was perpetrated in case of regulation than in case of condemnation. When this case came before the Supreme Court,[3] that court unanimously sustained Justice Brewer, although Justice Harlan, in the opinion, added that the "apparent value (*i. e.*, market value) of the property and franchises used by the corporation, as represented by its stocks, bonds and obligations," were not "alone to be considered when determining the rates that may be reasonably charged." (544.)

Evidently Justice Brewer was reasoning in a circle. The market value is the present value of the expected rates. If the rates are unreasonable, so is the market value. Both the rates and the market value depend on the franchise, and if the franchise is valueless, the rates that give value to it are excessive. When it came to the Omaha purchase case, in 1910,[4] the court, having just previously excluded franchise-value from rate cases, now drew the distinction between rate and purchase cases, and created the entity the "going concern value" of Justices Brewer and Savage in place of the franchise-value. The City of Omaha had an option to purchase the plant of the company at the end of twenty years, but with the express proviso in the contract that nothing should be paid for the unexpired franchise of the company. The appraisers fixed the value at $6,263,295 includ-

---

[1] While this language does not use the word franchise, yet franchise was evidently included, since the market value of the roads included any extra value of franchises.

[2] Ames v. Union Pacific R. R. Co., 64 Fed. 165 (1891).

[3] Smyth v. Ames, 169 U. S. 466 (1898).

[4] Omaha v. Omaha Water Co., 218 U. S. 180 (1910).

ing a "going value" of $562,712 against which the city's appraisers protested. The term "going value" was used in the sense of "going concern value." Here, again, the physical structure, although including, but not separately specifying,[1] all the overhead costs of getting a going plant into physical connection with customers and ready to operate, was treated by the court as though it were a dead and unlawful structure in Justice Savage's meaning of the term, and consequently an additional value was given to it because it was physically connected with the houses and was lawfully getting an income from the customers. The court (Justice Lurton) said, "The option to purchase excluded any value on account of unexpired franchise; but it did not limit the value to the bare bones of the plant, its physical properties, such as its land, its machinery, its water pipes or settling reservoirs, nor to what it would take to reproduce each of its physical features. The value in equity and justice must include whatever is contributed by the fact of the connection of the items making a complete and operating plant. The difference between a dead plant and a live one is a real value, and is independent of any franchise to go on, or any mere goodwill as between such a plant and its customers. That kind of goodwill, as suggested in Willcox v. Consolidated Gas Co., 212 U. S. 19, is of little or no commercial value when the business is as here, a natural monopoly, with which the customer must deal whether he will or no. That there is a difference between even the cost of duplication, less depreciation, of the elements making up the water company plant, and the commercial value of the business as a going concern is evident."[2] Such allowance, the court mentioned, was upheld in the Kansas City Case by Justice Brewer. "We can add nothing to the reasoning of the learned justice and shall not try to."

In this opinion, it will be seen, the court, although fully recognizing that the cost of duplication, $6,263,295, included all costs up to the point of readiness to deliver the product to consumers, and that neither franchise nor goodwill were entitled to valuation, yet added a going value of $562,712, thus erecting a going concern value in the place of the franchise-value and the goodwill-value which had been previously rejected.

While franchise-value, or goodwill-value, was thus resurrected under

---

[1] HENDERSON, C. C., "Railway Valuation and the Courts," 33 Harv. Law Rev. 1040 (1920).
[2] Op. cit., 218 U. S. 202-3.

the name of going concern value in the Omaha Case, on the ground that it was a purchase case and not a rate case, the court, for a time in rate cases, followed the Consolidated Gas Case by excluding going concern value, but eventually came around to the Omaha purchase case and included going concern value also in rate cases. That case, however, was not clear, since even if "going value" were included as valid, yet the court held the rates were not reduced low enough to confiscate it.[1]

At the same term of the Supreme Court when the Consolidated Gas Case was passed upon, the court decided the Knoxville Water-rate Case on the similar lines of Justice Hough's reasoning, excluding franchise, goodwill and going value.[2] In the Cedar Rapids Gas-rate Case, two years later, the Supreme Court expressly excluded the "goodwill or advantage incident to the possession of a monopoly, so far as that might be supposed to give the plaintiff power to charge more than a reasonable price." [3] In the Des Moines Gas-rate Case,[4] three years after the Cedar Rapids Case, goodwill and franchise value were excluded and the court held that the alleged "going value" was covered by the "overhead" costs already allowed in the several items, of promotion costs, legal expenses, engineering, insurance, interest, administration, and contingencies during construction. Yet the way was opened by an ambiguous definition of "going concern value" to restore goodwill, franchise, or going value.

This restoration was actually made in the Denver Water-rate Case,[5] three years after the Des Moines Case. In the previous Des Moines Case "going concern value" had been defined in such a way that it might have been interpreted either as "going plant value" in the sense of cost of acquiring an alternative going plant, or "going concern value" in the sense of its future earning value. But in the Denver Case it became not the cost-value of the plant including overhead, but an additional $800,000 based on the rates and the harmonious operation and existence of customers, "doing business and earning money." Yet it is plain, in this respect, that "going concern value" is "sheer duplication of overhead costs of reconstruction.[6]

[1] *Op. cit.*, Henderson, 1039.
[2] Knoxville *v.* Knoxville Water Co., 212 U. S. 1 (1909).
[3] Cedar Rapids Gas Co. *v.* Cedar Rapids, 223 U. S. 655, 669 (1912).
[4] Des Moines Gas Co. *v.* Des Moines, 238 U. S. 153 (1915).
[5] Denver *v.* Denver Union Water Co., 246 U. S. 178 (1918).
[6] *Op. cit.*, Henderson, 1043.

It will have been noted, in the progress of the foregoing cases, that several important steps have been taken away from the physical concept of a commodity, of the early economists, to the concept of a going concern operating both a going plant with a producing organization and a going business with a bargaining organization. We may distinguish these steps, with reference to the meanings of use-value and exchange-value as:

Scrap-Value, the "commodities" of the early economists, containing use-value and exchange-value, yet valued as the dismantled parts of a going plant, and constituting residual business assets that may be realized when sold separately from the plant on existing commodity markets.

Going-Plant-Value, the cost of reconstruction of the physical plant as an operating productive instrument, including its raw materials and products in process and all overhead costs during the estimated period of reconstruction, up to the point of turning out finished products and delivering them to customers who are physically taking them away or consuming them on the spot. As a physical engineering organization the going plant is turning out "social-use-value." As a business assemblage of physical things it constitutes "tangible" assets, valued, not as separate parts, but valued as a complete operating structure, with all of its parts coördinated and actually in operation. It is this that constitutes that "imputed" value, known as physical value or tangible value.[1]

Goodwill Value, the value added by the "skill, diligence, fidelity, success and reputation " of the producing organization that operates the going plant, in so far as this value exceeds the cost of reproduction of the going plant. As a use-value this is indicated in the superior treatment above that of competitors, or the lower prices or higher wages for similar service, which inspires the confidence and holds the loyalty and patronage, whether of customers, creditors, or laborers, who, without compulsion and with the option of costless alternatives, yet willingly contribute to the superior profits of the concern. As an exchange-value this goodwill-value constitutes unprivileged intangible assets.

Political Value, the value added by advantageous treatment from politicians, whether legislators, judges, executives, or administrative boards, in the exercise of the several powers of sovereignty, in so far as

---

[1] Above, Sec. IV, p. 172.

this value exceeds that of the ordinary lawfulness and exposure to competition out of which the value of going plant or goodwill emerges. As a use-value this political value does not usually represent an additional service to customers, creditors, or laborers, inspiring their confidence, loyalty or patronage, but is rather the superior privilege emanating from the blunders, corruption or wisdom of public officials, as shown in the tax exemption bonuses, special franchises, inside information, judicial opinion, and similar exercise of the royal prerogative or the modern sovereignty superior to that received by competitors who enjoy only ordinary lawfulness. As an exchange-value this political value, in so far as it exceeds other values, constitutes privileged intangible assets. Goodwill value and political value, as we have already observed in part, are usually concealed in the going plant value, by inflating those values, in order to make the assets come out even on the books with the value of the going business as a whole.

Going Business Value. Each of the preceding values is derived by a process of Imputation, or the separation of the whole assets into its parts, according to the sources from which each is believed to be derived. But Going Business Value is Valuation Proper, the value of all transactions of all persons upon the markets, whether customers, investors, employees or public officials, so proportioned economically that, in consideration of a gross outgo, a larger gross income is obtained, yielding a net residual income to the stockholders. It is this that is equivalent to the market value of stocks and bonds, or capitalization of expected net income, as seen in the Adams Express Company Case.[1]

Taking up, more in detail, these five processes of valuation, the terms used by the courts for going-plant value seem at times to imply that the court has scrap-value in mind. Yet such is not their intention. The terms "dead structure," "bare bones," "junk," "disconnected plant," "plant-not-in-use," or "plant-not-lawfully-in-use," all of them refer to a going physical plant with its parts coördinated, but abstracted by mental imputation from the going business.

Now, this going plant is "capital" in the productive sense, but not capital in the business sense, since it produces use-values or services, but does not bring in any other values in exchange. Yet at the same time, the going plant is tangible assets of the business. The discrepancy consists in failure to distinguish the process of imputation from

[1] Above, Sec. V, p. 172.

the process of valuation.[1] Imputation refers to the several markets by reference to which an imputed value is assigned to the several types of assets. The value of commodities, as is well known, is determined, not by their original cost of production or the amount of labor stored up in them, as the early economists and Karl Marx would have it, but by the present cost of reproduction in existing condition of depreciation, at existing prices on existing markets. It is this process of imputation that arrives at the "scrap-value" of the several parts of a plant as though they were sold separately on their several commodity markets. They are separable assets, but if the plant is dismantled, then so great is the depreciation of the parts, that, as is well known, scrap-value is reduced to as low as 5, 10 or 20% of the value of the plant as an operating mechanism. It is like a bicycle—a manufacturer finds it embarrassing to foot up the separate parts of a bicycle in a repair-shop at more than, say, 20% of the value of the going bicycle. The parts are commodities—the value imputed to them is a scrap-value. But the bicycle is a going plant with its parts coördinated and turning out a specific use-value. In this case, the bicycle itself is looked upon as a commodity, but so also is a factory, a farm, a store turning out products, to be considered a commodity in the large sense of something that can be bought and sold as a unit. Yet it is a peculiar unit—it is a producing unit, a going plant, with a market value, where the several parts have imputed values.

So with going-plant-value, that which the courts name "junk," or "dead structure." It is also an imputed value when compared with the value of the going business. One item of difference between scrap-value and going-plant value turns on what is imputed to be the "engineering overhead." It is the engineering overhead that augments scrap value into going-plant value, and it includes certain costs not technically engineering costs. For example, the instructions given to the engineers in making this valuation are such as would be given by a prospective purchaser of the going business, who, having the going business or franchise, but not the plant, desires to know how much it would cost him to get the going plant into its present condition of rendering the actual service for which the business is expected to obtain the present prices for service. It includes the total cost of building up the present plant, but not the cost of "building up" the business. As such it includes, in addition to the imputed market

[1] Above, Sec. IV, p. 172.

values of all the separate parts as separate items, also the imputed overhead costs of promotion, construction, installation, such as legal, engineering and business expenses, insurance, allowance for contingencies during construction, interest on the amount of expenditures during construction, and all administrative expenses. These "engineering overhead" expenses were estimated, in the Des Moines Gas Rate Case, at 15% additional to the aggregate costs of the base items.

Thus the same rule of cost of reproduction in existing depreciated condition at existing prices is applied to determining the value of a going plant as is applied to determining scrap-value. Each is a special case of imputation, or what may properly be designated alternative market-value, or cost of reproduction, since it is both an imputed cost and an imputed value. It is an imputed cost to the buyer, since it is outgo for him, and it is an imputed value to the seller, since it is income for him. But it is an alternative market-cost and an alternative market-value, since its value is estimated by reference to what it would cost on an alternative free market at existing prices on the market. It is of the nature of a "nuisance value," or technically, a "disopportunity value," being the alternative price one would have to pay did he not have the existing plant. Going-plant-value, then, is an imputed or alternative market-value, that is, the cost of reproduction imputed to the plant in its existing depreciated condition at existing prices on existing markets.

We thus make the distinction between actual earning-value and imputed, or alternative market-value. The earning-value is the known value of the going business. The alternative market-value is the imputed value of the going plant. Earning-value and alternative market-value coincide wherever an ethical or political question does not intervene. For market-value is none else than the price that buyers and sellers, on a free market, would agree upon in view of the expected earning-value of the property. But when, for ethical or political reasons, the earning-value is called in question, then the actual market-value may disappear altogether and if it reappears as an imputed value it must do so for a different reason. The slave contained earning-value for his master and hence had a market-value for him. But when, for political considerations, the slave was emancipated, his market-value disappeared because his expected earning-value could not be bought and sold. So with a going plant. If private property is abolished then its mere unlawfulness, as Justice Savage innocently observed, destroys both its earning-value and its market-value. If, however, private property is not destroyed, but only its arbitrary power to exact unlawful prices is sought to be abolished, then the essence of private property remains in the imputed valuations that would be obtained on an alternative free and equal market where the buyer is not coerced, since he is free to build or buy an equally good property at existing prices on existing markets, rather than take the one that is offered at the value of its privileged earning power.

This, then, is the issue as regards going-concern-value. Justice Savage, in justifying it, was compelled to rely upon the very earning-value which, for ethical and political reasons, is called in question. As franchise-value, he eliminated it, since it then would appear to spring from unlawful earning value. But as going-concern-value, he restored it, since, of course, it must have earning-value in order to have market value. We have seen, too, how the Supreme Court, in the Knoxville, Cedar Rapids and Des Moines Cases, correctly but temporarily excluded the privileged earning-value of a franchise, and accepted the imputed alternative market-value of the "overhead" as the full allowance for what was claimed as a going-concern-value. But in the later rate cases and in all the purchase cases, the court added a going-concern-value, based on earning power, to the construction overhead, based on alternative cost of reproduction. This allowance was not, indeed, the actual market-value at existing rates, as Justice Brewer had contended it should be, but was admittedly an imputed value constructed out of a curious compound, partly an earning power which if excessive would be unlawful, partly Justice Brewer's physical connections which the company had not paid for, partly Justice Savage's privileged lawfulness contrasted with outlawfulness instead of equal lawfulness.

6. *Uncompensated Service*

We have noticed the interesting contrast that while the economists, since the latter half of the eighteenth century, have been constructing theories of value out of man's relation to nature in the form of commodities and feelings, the courts have been constructing theories of value out of the approved and disapproved transactions of man with man in the form of goodwill and privilege. These processes of valuation are inseparable, but they belong to different orders of thought. Man, as a producer, overcomes the forces of nature in order to satisfy the wants of man as a consumer. Nature furnishes certain "elementary" utilities, the chemical, physical, gravitational, qualities of matter, and man changes these into "form utility," or moves them into "place utility," or stores them up for "time utility," so that he may satisfy whatever may be his wants, wherever or whenever they arise.

These, of course, are fundamental, so much so that they are just as true of other animals. But the human animal, as he emerges into national and world markets, requires something additional. Everything which he consumes passes first through the hands of many other persons, and each person depends on predecessors to select the best of the elementary utilities, to give to them the best form and to bring them regularly to the needful places. As this interdependence enlarges with commerce, the ignorance of each individual enlarges, and each depends more and more on confidence in the honesty, diligence, promptness and good management of others. In short, confidence in others is the largest of all the utilities, for without it each person would need to satisfy his own wants directly from nature or through a small family or tribe whose members he could see and control.

In order to allow for this confidence necessitated by this interdependence, Adam Smith had to assume that man is guided by an "invisible hand," a "law of nature"—his name for divine providence,— which leads man, while seeking his own self-interest to satisfy the wants of others without intending to do so.[1] But experience has discovered that it was exactly this invisible hand that produced adulterations and the "cheap and nasty" goods which consumers had to put up with, and which led Carlyle, Ruskin, Morris and the other romantic economists, to long for a return to the neighborhood production and consumption of the middle ages. Yet, without returning to the past, the courts began to adapt themselves to the uncertainties of the present. As early as 1580 the visible hand of the court had begun to stretch the writ of trespass in order to protect the reputation of a manufacturer who had built up a business on the confidence that he had inspired in customers as to the quality of his goods.[2] He had added an intangible utility to his product—not merely the elementary, form, time and place utilities which the purchaser can see and feel in a commodity, but also the invisible utility of confidence in the implied promises of another, also attached to the commodity which the other had pro-

---

[1] SMITH, *Wealth of Nations*, 1:421 (Cannan's ed.).
[2] Below, Chap. VII, Sec. III.

duced. And, if it may be said that the production of wealth is the production of any and all services that reduce human deficiencies, the greatest of which is ignorance, and that the reliable evidence of that service is the actual behavior, then that intangible utility, the promises that inspire confidence in the good behavior of other persons, also produces wealth. So that the five constituents of use-value are the elementary utilities furnished by nature, the form and place utilities furnished by labor, the time utility furnished by investors, and the confidence utility furnished by human character. In short, confidence in others is a utility "overhead," without which modern society could not realize in sufficient abundance its much needed elementary, form, time and place utilities.

These distinctions enable us to allocate the parts played by a going plant and the producing organization that operates it and to assign these parts to the several branches of science. The going plant is the forces and materials of nature in process of satisfying human needs, under the control of human labor. This relation of man to nature has three aspects distinguishable as art, science and engineering—Art, the purpose of satisfying ultimate consumers by adjusting human and natural forces to their wants and character; Science, the knowledge of those forces according to the processes along which they operate; Engineering, the economizing, or economical proportioning, of those forces so as to bring about the largest accrual of utility with the least outgo of energy. Art and science are wasteful; engineering is economical. Art is purpose and ideals; science is hypothesis and verification; engineering is planning, valuing and executing. Art guides, science understands, engineering executes. Together, these are the field of natural or technological economy, including not only the control of the going plant but also the management of the producing organization that operates the plant. They are the field of human and non-human forces that must be understood before they can successfully be directed towards the production of wealth. And the corresponding sciences through which they are sought to be understood are such as physics, chemistry, biology, animal psychology and that human psychology known latterly as "scientific management" with its "quality" and "quantity" foremanship, and "scientific advertising" with its art of salesmanship. Throughout, the economics of utility is the union of art, science and engineering in the control and proportioning of natural and human forces. It is the economy of a going plant and its producing organization. The plant itself is the forces of nature proportioned according to the qualities, supply and prices of each force; the producing organization is the human forces proportioned according to the supply and prices of their physical, mental and managerial faculties. The business man takes pride in his plant and in his organization. His "good organization," is a good proportioning of human faculties. His efficient plant is a good proportioning of nature's forces. The two are inseparable. The going plant is "a dead structure" without the producing organization. The producing organization is fruitless without the going plant. They are the inseparable relations of man to nature proportioned and economized according to the then state of the arts, the sciences and engineering as understood by the members of the going concern.

But engineering economy, while it produces commodities, does not of itself produce confidence in the commodities. This springs from honesty and good service. So that the production of wealth is the inseparable union of art, science, engineering *and ethics*. Ethics is the field of production of that invisible utility, confidence, without which the tangible utilities are not even produced. The use-value of ethics is confidence in others, and the exchange-value of ethics is the market-value of their goodwill.

Goodwill, like the other utilities of commodities, varies greatly in the proportions which it bears to the other utilities. It diminishes or increases, relative to the other qualities, for various reasons. Mistakes, bad service, dishonesty, false rumors, reduce its value as assets because they reduce confidence. Moreover, the goodwill of customers varies somewhat inversely to their necessities, and hence monopoly, privilege, unfair advantages and other forms of economic coercion, while they diminish goodwill as an asset, correspondingly enlarge the necessities of the public into an asset. For, goodwill is a competitive asset, and diminishes in value with an increase in the supply of competing goodwills. As the level of competition rises through the extension of laws or customs of fair competition, the goodwill of a particular firm sinks into that more universal goodwill which is just ordinary lawfulness, attached to all of the competing commodities. It loses its separable value as an asset, though it may take new forms of superior service and continue to exist above even the higher competitive level.

But goodwill, being a social relation, implies reciprocity. It is the expectation of reciprocal beneficial transactions. It presupposes a contract, express or implied from the behavior of the parties, requiring a compensatory service, and this is none other than the relation of creditor and debtor which is the relation of investment. Even the laborer is an investor in the business until such time as his wages are paid, for he adds the service of waiting to his service of working, and the amount of his investment is the amount of his uncompensated services. On Saturday night the claim is liquidated, and an explicit investor advances the purchasing power, takes over from the laborer the further service of waiting, and so on until final compensation is made in the price paid by the ultimate consumer who is a reciprocal producer.

Thus the going business, while it is a flow of transactions, is built upon the expectation of implied agreements that the transactions shall be the means of compensation for services not yet compensated. It is a process of investment and liquidation implied in the institution of private property which gives to the proprietor power to withhold service until the expected compensation is deemed satisfactory. It is the recognition of this ethical relation between investment and compensation, that in recent years has led to re-definitions of both Capital and Property. A beginning was made by the Railroad Commission of Wisconsin in the Antigo Case[1] and followed in the other cases sustained by the Supreme Court of the state.[2] The financial history of the property was traced out, balancing the original investments, the succeeding deficits and surpluses, and yielding a present total of " unrequited cost " or " net total sacrifice," or " unrequited reasonable sacrifice," [3] considered to be the "sum which the business should be capitalized for in order that the owner should receive a reasonable return on the past investment." [4]

This method of valuation is defective in that it requires a reconstruction of accounts from the beginning, and must establish what

[1] Hill v. Antigo Water Co., 3 W. R. C. R. 623 (1909). WHITTEN, R. H., *Valuation of Public Service Corporations*, 1:520 (1912); 2:1274 (1914).

[2] Appleton Water Works Co. v. R. R. Com., 154 Wis. 121 (1913).

[3] Cp. BAUER, JOHN, "Bases of Valuation—The Control of Return on Public Utility Investments," 6 *Amer. Econ. Rev.* 568, 575 (1916); ALLISON, JAMES, "Ethical and Economic Elements in Public Service Valuation," 27 *Quar. Jour. Ec.* 27 (1912); COMMONS, J. R., Testimony before Interstate Commerce Committee of U. S. Senate (1913); HENDERSON, G. C., "Railway Valuation and the Courts," 33 *Harv. Law Rev.* 902 (1920); RICHBERG, D. R., "A Permanent Basis for Rate Regulation," 31 *Yale Law Jour.* 263 (1922). The conclusions of these writers were apparently accepted in the opinion in Galveston Elec. Co. v. City of Galveston, 272 Fed. 147 (1921) and 42 Sup. Ct. Rep. 351 (1922).

[4] Appleton, W. W. v. R. R. C., 154 Wis. 121, 147, 149.

was a reasonable rate of profit in the past in order to calculate the deficits and surpluses. Whereas, in the past, preceding a statute regulating profit, the expectations of investors were not thus actually limited. The physical plant has been built up partly, perhaps, from profits which, at the time, however excessive, were considered to be the property of the then investors, and partly from new issues of securities. Moreover, this method compensates investors for past deficits, contrary to the way in which competitive business takes its losses in hard times or under poor management. It adds accrual of all deficits to the present capitalization, whereas competitive business would have written off assets.

A more accurate arrival at what the investors actually expected in the past is to ascertain what they actually did put into the plant as they went along from year to year, under the then costs of construction. The plant, as it now stands, is made up of parts, some of which date back to the beginning of the plant, some of which are replacements of earlier parts, some of which are extensions, and all of them are more or less depreciated by time and use. The actual costs of these separate parts at the several dates of installation, depreciated according to the present condition, and including the engineering overhead costs of coördinating the parts, yield what Bauer has called the "net installation cost," [1] or what in the Federal Valuation Act is designated "original cost to date," [2] and represent the measure of confidence of investors, at the time of their investment, in the future of the property as a whole. The total thus obtained at present date of appraisal represents the property-value which investors have put into the business under the expectations held out to them at the time, as they went along. It gives the "closest practical approximation to the direct sacrifice of investors," [3] and is the accrual of their uncompensated service measured by their own ideas of what compensation should be at the time of installation, under all the changing circumstances in the history of the plant.

In short, the net installation cost, or original cost less depreciation, measures historically the goodwill of investors as it actually moved from day to day and year to year in their then attitude toward the business.

---

[1] *Op. cit.*, BAUER, 582, 583.
[2] U. S. Statutes, An Act to Regulate Commerce, Sec. 19a (1913).
[3] BAUER, *op. cit.*, 583.

For goodwill is the uncoerced choice of alternatives by both parties to a transaction. The investor's choice of alternatives is a choice between the expected incomes to be derived from his investment. What he gives up is present purchasing power. What he expects is future purchasing power. The investor's goodwill is the good credit of the business. It depends on confidence in the management and confidence in the reciprocal compensation to be obtained for the product. A monopoly, or privileged market, has rightly been held, as we have seen, to contradict the notion of customer's goodwill, since the customer's freedom of choice is restrained, but the same monopoly or privileged market has strictly an investor's goodwill at the time of investment, for his uninvested capital on the "money market" is the most perfect of all instruments of free choice. If the going concern has his confidence beyond that of alternative investments, he shows it, as an outsider, by the high price he pays for its new securities, thus reducing the rate of interest or profit on his investment, or shows it as a stockholder by declaring only a part of the net income as dividends and leaving a part to be reinvested in the business. In either case the expected net income of the business, at that time of actual construction and reconstruction, is the means of obtaining from investors a larger fund at that time for extensions, replacements and upkeep than a similar net income is able to obtain for a business enjoying less of the confidence of investors. This confidence finds its way into the physical dimensions and conditions of the plant as original costs of construction, and into the quantity and quality of the service rendered, and is none other than the original cost of each existing part of the plant at the date when it was actually installed.

Wages and salaries in the past have compensated all the members of the producing business organization for their services, at the then accepted rates of compensation. They have no further claim on the business. Interest and dividends in the past have compensated investors at the then accepted terms and risks on which investments were made. They have no further just claim for deficits, if such occurred in the past, because they tacitly agreed to accept them, just as no claim can justly be made against them for surpluses obtained in the past, because it was the expectation of surplus that induced them to take the chance of deficit. Thus the operating income and outgo of the past and the compensation of investors in the past need not be inquired into in order to ascertain the accrual of uncompensated service. Whatever it may have been, it was the actual choice of alternatives made by all parties under all the conditions and expectations of the time of actual construction or reconstruction, exactly as competitive business induces choices to be made. Out of these choices of the past, at the prices paid in the past, there survives the going plant in its existing condition of depreciation, measured by original cost less depreciation, representing what the investors have actually left in the business of their own free choice.

Thus we see that the "going concern" begins to separate itself into three notions, each distinguished by an amount of value, in terms of assets, ascertained by different methods for different purposes.

First, is the going plant, a physical thing whose "structural value," "physical value," "tangible value" is an imputed value estimated as the cost of reproducing in its existing condition a similar plant connected up and delivering its product to customers. Its valuation as assets is guided by that competitive-cost principle of the classical economic theory, holding that the exchange-value of a thing is determined, not by its original cost of production, but by its present cost of reproduction, applied, however, not to separate commodities, but to that enlarged commodity, a complete operating plant with all of its tangible parts coördinated. The valuation or inventory of a going plant, is its imputed "present value" in the sense of the price a buyer would now pay for it in its existing condition, if he owned the business or franchise but did not have the plant and had to construct it anew at present prices.

Second, is the going business, a coördination of tangible, incorporeal and intangible assets, whose "going-concern-value," or rather going-business-value, is the value of expected transactions. Its valuation is guided by that *anticipation* principle, first given its psychological basis by Böhm-Bawerk in Austria and stated in its complete psychological and business form by Fisher in America.[1] This concept also yields a "present value," but it is not guided by cost of reproduction but by the present value of expected bargaining power, that is, the anticipation in the present of the net income expected in the future.

Third, is the actual investment, the "original cost to date," the "actual cost," the "net installation cost," the "unrequited reasonable

---

[1] Böhm-Bawerk, Eugen v., *Positive Theory of Capital* (tr. 1891); Fisher, Irving, *Nature of Capital and Income* (1906).

sacrifice," whose procedure of valuation is guided by that *ethical* principle which looks to the relation between service and compensation. It gives, too, a "present value," but the value is an accrual of uncompensated services, services rendered in the past, but as yet uncompensated by customers and ultimate consumers.

These three aspects of a going concern are, in effect, also three notions of Capital. First, the classical notion of capital as physical things held for future production and income, but whose exchange-value, under a system of free competition on the commodity markets, could not exceed the cost of reproduction. Second, the more comprehensive business notion of capital as the purchasing power of assets, tangible, intangible and incorporeal, having a present market price as a going concern determined by capitalization of expected net income. Third, the ethical notion of capital as the accrual of uncompensated services of those who have devoted their property in the past to the future use of others and are entitled to reimbursement in the future. According to the first notion, capital is the present market prices of physical things; according to the second, capital is the present value of future bargaining power; according to the third, capital is the present value of uncompensated service.

A similar shift occurs in the notion of property.[1] According to the first notion, property is physical things held for production and sale; according to the second, property is expected bargaining power; according to the third, property is the service rendered in expectation of future bargaining power relied upon at the time.

There is no necessary identity of the several values of capital and property obtained by the guidance of these three principles of valuation and imputation. If value were a fixed external object, having a physical existence, there could be but one value of a thing at one time and place. But if value is a *process of valuing* then the *purpose* of the valuation determines what the value shall be.[2] If the purpose is that of setting forth an ethical relation between buyer and seller, creditor and debtor, employer and employee, sovereign and citizen, expressed in prices, then there might conceivably be as many values of the same thing as there are varieties of these elementary human relations. For price is then a measure of justice and injustice, as well as an effect of

---

[1] Not "property-rights."
[2] Below, Chap. IX. Cp. FRIDAY, DAVID, "An Extension of Value Theory," 26 *Quar. Jour. Econ.* 197 (1922).

demand and supply, and when price comes to be largely controlled by governments and by associations of capital or labor it becomes increasingly a measure of justice and injustice as well as an effect of demand and supply.

Two inheritances of the past stand in the way of accepting this ethical concept of Capital and Property. One is the individualistic, physical, concept of value as the cost of reproduction determined by free competition. The other is the business concept of value as the present value of a going business. The two are closely connected. Cost of reproduction is conceived to be the cost of reproducing, not only the going plant but also the going business. But the going plant and the going business belong to two different and even opposing systems. The going plant is the producing organization turning out service to the public. The going business is the business organization bringing in income to producers. One is service to other persons, the other is power over them. One is the means of rendering service, the other is power to get a price for the service. Consequently the valuation of the two proceeds on two different social relations and from two different standpoints.

The cost of reproduction is figured out as measuring the price to be agreed upon in the pursuit of their private purposes between a seller and a buyer. What would it cost a buyer to reproduce the plant and the business rather than buy it as it stands? The value to him is the estimated alternative sacrifice, the alternative market price, the "nuisance-value" which he would incur in order to get the plant if he had the business without the plant, or to build up a similar plant and business if he had neither. What he capitalizes, in either case, is the cost to him of getting a similar income in the future instead of buying the income in question which belongs to the seller. He capitalizes the business at its nuisance-value.

But when the state steps in, representing, not the buyer and seller, but the commonwealth, with its public purposes, it does so because the very income itself is called in question on the ground that it no longer is conceived to spring from goodwill but from privilege. The attempt is then made to restore the relation to what it would have been had consumers been free to choose between producers. The consumers have little or no freedom of choice, but the valuation of the property is made as a claim against them. They are implied debtors, and the valuation of the property is the value of the expected prices they will owe for the service. If the going business as it stands is capitalized against them then their unwillingness is valued against them, whereas only their willing patronage is the reasonable measure of the price they should pay.

Goodwill, indeed, is like privilege in that it is a differential advantage over competitors and yields therefore a larger profit on the actual investment. It differs, however, in that it is a fragile advantage and must be maintained by constant attention to service. The practical question then is, shall the element of goodwill be recognized in the form of capitalization or in the form of a rate of profit? Valuation of the property sets up a permanent claim against consumers regardless of the service that may be rendered thereafter. But a fluctuating rate of profit sets up no permanent claim against them, since it fluctuates both with general business conditions and with the rise and fall of goodwill. This goes to the heart of the attempt to regulate private business. Goodwill cannot properly be capitalized for rate regulation. It is an asset depending on expected service. The more precise method, consistent with the nature of goodwill, is to adopt a sliding scale of prices and profits, such that, if the concern reduces prices, the profits may be increased, and if the concern advances prices the profits are correspondingly reduced. The practicability and detail of this method cannot here be considered.[1]

---

[1] Cp. Sliding scale systems described in Civic Federation Report on Municipal and Private Operation of Public Utilities, 1:24 (1907).

CHAPTER VI

THE RENT BARGAIN—FEUDALISM AND USE-VALUE

Mr. Orth has conveniently assembled many of the legal definitions of property, going to show a bewildering variety. Among them are the "right to improve, use, hold, enjoy and dispose of a thing"; the "right to protect one's property by all lawful means"; "every valuable right or interest"; "everything to which the right of ownership can be attached, no matter how insignificant"; "everything that has exchange value," whether "corporeal or incorporeal," "tangible or intangible," "visible or invisible," "real or personal," including "labor and right to labor," "easements and franchises," "mortgages," "mining claims"; "every right and title to realty," "liens and options on real property," "money, goods, chattels," "fire insurance applications," "insurance policies," "choses in action," "solvent credits," "shares of stock," "patents" and "products of the mind." [1]

This variety of meanings of both property and liberty is the outcome of centuries of legal history, and we should therefore expect that they might fall into a semblance of order only if we arrange them in historical sequence and observe the different sources from which the notions are derived. The comments in the foregoing chapters suggest two sources of the modern notions. One is the royal prerogative, the other the common law. The two have evolved together and are inseparable in fact. The prerogative originated in conquest, the common law in the customs and beliefs of the people. But these customs and beliefs were interpreted by the judicial agents of the King and were given effect by his executive agents. William the Conqueror and his lawyers did not distinguish his property from his sovereignty.[2] Both were possessions rather than property. He was both landlord and King. The soil belonged to him by right of conquest, and the people were his subjects. Property and sovereignty were one, since both were but dominion over things and persons.

---

[1] ELY, *Property and Contract*, 855 (1914); also BOUV. 2750.

[2] MAITLAND, F. W., *Domesday Book and Beyond*, 102, 168, 169 (1907); HOLDSWORTH, W. S., *A History of English Law*, 1:10, 3:354 (1903); JENKS, EDW., *Short History of English Law*, 26.

Similar notions of ownership and lordship prevailed throughout the descending ranks of freemen. We have spoken of the primitive notion of property as the exclusive holding of things for one's own use and enjoyment. But this "use and enjoyment" were more than a materialistic possession of things. They were a control of the behavior of subject persons. Property was lordship by virtue of possession.[1] It was a personal relation of command and obedience. "In medieval English one spoke of the *lord* of a beast or other chattel,"[2] and Blackstone, in his day, could speak of property as "the sole and despotic dominion which one man claims over the external things of the world, in total exclusion of the right of any other individual in the universe."[3]

But in the early days this "sole and despotic dominion" was not merely dominion over things, it was more really dominion over a part or the whole of human behavior. Land, serfs, villeins went together. Control over them was shared in an ascending scale from the lowest freeman up to the King. Each freeman was both owner and lord of the services contained in the share, which belonged to him, of the personal services of others, and those personal services were paid in the form of physical products.[4] The primitive mind could with difficulty comprehend anything but physical objects and individual persons, and, indeed, in this it but reflected the facts. In an age of violence the will of powerful individuals was the government, and in an age of serfdom and villeinage physical control over persons was scarcely distinguishable from exclusive holding of land and movables. There was as yet no money economy by which rents could be converted into a price; and little or no personal liberty of the worker, by which lordship over persons has been separated from lordship over things; and no automatic enforcement of contracts by a stabilized government, such that one does not need to exercise personal command in order to obtain what belongs to him, but it flows in by mere right of the creditor and duty of the debtor. By these later reforms the more materialistic notions of holding physical things for one's own use and enjoyment become distinct from the more human notion of lordship with its command and obedience. But in either case whether it was personal

---

[1] POLLOCK and MAITLAND, *History of English Law*, 1:149 (1911). There pointed out that the medieval mind was concerned with the physical possession of things, and could scarcely comprehend what became the later distinctions of "property" and "ownership" without physical possession.

[2] *Ibid.*, II, 4.

[3] 2 Bla. Com. 2.

[4] POLLOCK and MAITLAND 2:145, 148, 181.

service or physical products, the dominant fact of Feudalism and the Rent-bargain was use-values and not exchange-values.

Seven hundred years after the Norman Conquest Blackstone defined prerogative as "that special preëminence which the King hath over and above all other persons, and out of the ordinary course of the common law, in right of his royal dignity." [1] But in the Eleventh Century the common law, a law common to all freemen, arising from their customs and protecting their property and liberty, was unknown. There were local customs and jurisdictions but no common law with force enough to restrain the prerogative and thus make it an exception to the "ordinary course." The prerogative was the source of power. It showed itself partly in the grants of sovereign powers and immunities by the King to his subjects, partly in the powers which he exercised through his own agents. We have already suggested the two principal forms in which he granted economic privileges, namely, grants of lands and grants of those franchises or "liberties" which afterwards became grants of exclusive markets and corporate franchises. The main economic prerogatives which he retained, or tried to retain, in his own hands were the control of taxes and currency.

The grants of lands, markets and corporate franchises differed but little in the conditions on which they were granted. Each was sold or given to his subjects individually by a kind of private bargain. He could sell privileges and franchises just as he could sell the royal lands.[2] Each grant carried with it a promise of sovereign powers and immunities. The powers were the promise that the King's courts and executives would exclude other persons from the land or the market, if necessary, thus giving to the grantee the economic power to fix rents and prices. The immunities were the promise that the King's courts and executives would not interfere with the grantee in the exercise of that power. Each grant carried with it, too, express or implied, a consideration of loyalty and service to the King, and the terms of this consideration could be changed arbitrarily, for the King could not be tried in his own courts.

Consequently the subject had no enforceable *right* either to lands or liberties as long as the monarch could exercise the power to withdraw them or change their terms at will. They were *promises*, not *rights* of property. The barons, in Magna Carta, endeavored collectively to

---

[1] 1 Bla. 239. Cp. CHITTY, JOSEPH, *Prerogatives of the Crown* (1820).
[2] Above, Chap. III, p. 48.

convert these promises into rights. They induced King John, on the field of battle, to agree that no freeman should be "taken or imprisoned or disseized of his freehold or liberties or rights of levying tolls and taxes . . . except by the lawful judgment of his peers or by the law of the land." They then set up a standing committee of their own, intended to be superior in power to the King, to decide and act against him in case of dispute over this agreement. To this the King also agreed. Every claimant of land or "liberties" should have his claim passed upon, not by the agents of the King, but by the equals of the claimant; and the standing committee of the barons and their successors should have an army to impose a penalty on the King in case he broke his promise, by seizing any of his lands and holding the same until redress was obtained. [1]

It is known that this crude attempt to convert the royal prerogative into rights of property by collective action was not successful. The royal prerogative actually grew and expanded until it reached its culmination in the absolute monarchy of Henry VIII and Elizabeth.

Meanwhile, beneath the prerogative was growing up the common law, the law of private property and personal liberty of freemen, though not of bondmen. Early English law, before the Conquest, was formulated in popular assemblies of freemen meeting frequently in the assemblies in the county. Without written records they relied on memory and living testimony of custom in deciding cases, and these had to do mainly with the physical acts of assault, trespass and theft. These assemblies were at one and the same time legislatures, courts and executives, and the judicial procedure was not separated into the functions of judge, jury, witnesses and counsel.

The Norman Conquest largely reduced the Anglo-Saxon freemen to the position of tenants and bondmen of the conquerors, abolished their popular assemblies and set up assemblies of landlord and tenants, since the holding of land as a tenant or subtenant of the King carried with it criminal and civil jurisdiction for trial and decision of disputes among the tenants. Tenancy was inseparable from government; each fief or holding was both an agricultural and a governmental unit. An estate with its various levels of freehold and copyhold tenants, like a plantation with its slaves, had both an economic unity as a going agricultural concern, and the governmental unity of a central authority with its band of retainers. But the feudal estate differed from

[1] McKECHNIE, *Magna Carta*, 467; above, p. 481.

the slave plantation in that the free tenants had certain customary rights, often inherited from pre-Conquest times, but more often they had contract rights of service on the one side and of protection on the other, which became custom in post-Conquest times. And the determination of these rights came before the private courts of the lords of various degree, from the King downward, each governing his immediate tenants. They were limited agricultural monarchies, where a slave plantation was an absolute agricultural monarchy.

It was not until the second half of the twelfth century that Henry II sent out his circuit judges to hold court in the counties. They assembled certain of the freemen, and thus they originated the jury, not, as once was asserted, out of the customs of the people, but at the command of the King, to assist his justices in determining both the customs of the neighborhood and the rights claimed by individuals under those customs. The juries were witnesses, both to the customs of the people and to the possessions, claims, assaults and trespasses of individuals.[1] To them were put questions both of law and fact. Later, when the King's justices began to protect tenants against their landlords, they inquired also, What are the customary rents and rent-practices of this neighborhood and this landed estate? This was the most important power of the King's justices—the power to take a tenant's suit against his landlord out of the private court of his landlord and to give justice to the tenant on the findings of his neighbors.[2]

These private feudal courts died hard. Powerful nobles intimidated the King's common-law courts. The King's Chancellor began to take cases out of their hands and to decide civil cases where the great men were too great for the local courts.[3] Not until the wars of the barons of the fifteenth century ended in the destruction of the nobility and the triumph of Henry VII (1485) was it possible for the King to go to the root of their power by prohibiting the nobility from maintaining armed bands of retainers. This was accomplished by creating the Star Chamber and the Court of Requests to supplement the civil jurisdiction of Chancery by an extraordinary criminal and civil jurisdiction in summoning and condemning the great barons.

The economic focus of this agricultural monarchy was the rent bargain. The land of England was held in descending scales of tenancy from the sole owner, the King, through chief tenants, sub-tenants, freehold tenants, servile and semi-servile tenants. In each descending

---

[1] POLLOCK and MAITLAND, 1:138.   [2] *Ibid.*, 1:147.   [3] Holdsworth, 3:176.

level no distinction was made between ownership and government. The King was both landlord and sovereign. So with the barons and sub-barons. Each was both landlord and a combined legislature, executive and chief justice of his baronial estate.

Hence the rent-bargain was two-fold, economic and governmental. One was rent, the other was taxes. As yet undifferentiated, they took the form of, and were in fact, a contract between superior and inferior, graded, however, in degrees of coerciveness according to the two main divisions of "free" and "unfree" tenures. Loyalty to the overlord was the essence of free tenure, with its contract and oath of fealty and its ceremony of homage.[1] Attendance on the lord's court or assembly of vassals was mandatory. The military tenants, the Knights, held from their overlord on condition of furnishing a certain number of esquires, or men-at-arms. Below them were the villeins, the later copyholders, the purely agricultural tenants, paying the rent for their land in their personal services and products for the landlord. Above all was the sole landlord and sovereign.

By gradual stages the governmental rent was extracted from the economic rent, by the process of changing from use-values to exchange values through the introduction of money. As between the chief tenants and the King, the process consisted in depriving them of their armies of retainers and creating a King's standing army; and in taking over by the King's courts from their baronial courts the determination of the customary rents of their tenants, as well as all other civil and criminal jurisdiction.

Having taken over the army the King required funds for the support of the army and the government. These were obtained in various ways from the chief tenants, often under the form of more or less arbitrary payments under the name of "aids," "benevolences," "reliefs," "wardships" of infants and women, compensation on occasion of marriage or sale of the land, etc. Various efforts were made to commute these arbitrary incidents of the rent bargain into fixed and regular payments of money. The attempt was made in 1610, by the proposed "great contract," to buy up and commute these arbitrary payments into cash, but King James proposed a cash rental which was unsatisfactory to the landlords.[2] Finally, the parliament of 1660, controlled by the landlords, proceeded to abolish the military tenures,

---

[1] JENKS, 32.
[2] JENKS, 237; GARDINER, *History of England*, 2:106; DOWELL, *Taxation*, 1:187.

altogether without compensation to the King, but they substituted in lieu thereof, a perpetual hereditary excise on the drink of the people.

This abolition of arbitrary rents by commuting them into money, Blackstone might well say, "was a greater acquisition to the civil property of this Kingdom than even *Magna Carta* itself; since that only pruned the luxuriances that had grown out of the military tenures, and thereby preserved them in vigour; but the statute of King Charles extirpated the whole, and demolished both root and branches." [1]

Indeed the royalist tenants of the Restoration, by this act of Parliament, truly created modern landed property, for, by commuting the sovereign's arbitrary rentals into pecuniary taxes they resolved themselves from tenants into owners, and gave to themselves that "sole and despotic dominion" over external things which constitutes both sovereignty and property.

Thus the right of private property in land emerged from the struggle of 450 years between the sovereign as landlord and his vassals as tenants, over the rental value of land. The collective bargaining over rents, begun with Magna Carta in 1215 and ending with the Restoration and a limited monarchy in 1660, transferred dominion from the will of the sovereign to the will of the tenant, by the simple device of making fixed and certain, in terms of money, instead of arbitrary, in terms of commodities and services, the rents owed by the tenant to the monarch. Private property emerged from the rent bargain carried on collectively in terms of money between the supreme landlord, the King, and his tenants. The duty to pay definite taxes in cash, determined collectively by monarch and the representatives of the taxpayers, was substituted for the indefinite duty to pay rent in commodities and services, determined individually by the chief landlord. As long as the King could arbitrarily fix rents, whether in services or money, he was truly the owner as well as the sovereign. When the rents were fixed collectively in cash, he became only the sovereign and his tenants became the owners. The separation of sovereignty from property was the commutation of individual rent-bargains into a collective rent-bargain and the shift from use-values to exchange-values, such that the arbitrary will of the sovereign became regulated by an annual pecuniary bargain in parliament; and the tenants, instead of the sovereign, became the landlords. The collective rent-

[1] 2 Bla. Com. 77. Text of the act in ADAMS and STEPHENS, *Select Documents of English Constitutional History*, 442.

bargain in terms of money is the land-tax, private property is the residuum of power in terms of use-value or exchange-value left for the landlord after the tax is paid.

It was not necessary, of course, to change the nominal title of ownership, which, in England remained in the King. But the real owners, nevertheless, are the tenants, because the rent charges are definite taxes in terms of money, but the indefinite residuum which marks the real ownership, because it marks the orbit where the will is free, is transferred to the nominal tenants. So that, speaking historically, land taxes are commutations of physical rents into money-rents, and taxes are not something taken from private property by the sovereign, but property is sovereignty taken collectively from the King by his tenants. The result was that pecuniary taxes became the governmental rent of land, and landed property became assimilated to the law of business freedom and security, so that, eventually, like movables, it could be bought and sold in expectation of its money values.

Beneath the chief tenants and the lesser barons, who bargained directly with the King, were the freehold tenants, who, when military service had been commuted in the fourteenth and fifteenth centuries for a money rent, paid that rent to the immediate lord instead of the King, to whom their military service had been due.[1] This created eventually the yeomen, the farmers, subject only, on the governmental side, to the King's call to arms, but subject, on the economic side, to rents payable in services, products, or money, to their immediate landlord. Their condition was materially reduced in the course of centuries, until it approached that of the copyholders.

Lastly, were the villeins, later become copyholders, the great bulk of the workers, whose services were mainly agricultural, but who had no access to the King's courts against the arbitrary power of their lords. Their personal services had been in part commuted for fixed cash rentals in the fourteenth and fifteenth centuries. Eventually, however, when the landlords, in the sixteenth century, after the general rise in prices, began wholesale evictions of these tenants and increased their rentals, new courts, other than the common-law courts, were set up by the King, and these began to restrain the landlords by the rule that "a lord could not at his will and pleasure change the customs attached to lands held by a

[1] JENKS, 33.

particular tenure . . . the lords were compelled to respect the customs of the manor and the terms of the tenure." [1] Even the customs
themselves were refused recognition if they seemed to the judges to be
oppressive and servile.   In this way the common law gradually assimilated the law of copyhold tenure to the law of free tenure, and the
tenure of copyhold became, like free tenure, a form of land-ownership
without servile taint.[2] So that, when Coke wrote his "Compleate
Copyholder" in the early years of the seventeenth century he could
say, "But now copiholders stand upon a sure ground, now they weigh
not their Lord's displeasure, they shake not at every suddaine blast of
wind, they eate, drinke, and sleepe securely; onely drawing a speciall
care of the maine chance (viz.) to performe carefully what duties and
services soever their Tenure doth exact, and Custome doth require;
then let Lord frowne, the Copy holder cares not, knowing himselfe
safe and not within any danger, for if the lord's anger grow to expulsion, the Law hath provided severall weapons of remedy; for it is at his
election either to sue a Subpena or an Action of Trespasse against the
Lord.   Time hath dealt very favorably with Copy holders in divers
respects." [3]

Thus, in the end, the common-law courts were able to become the
people's courts, protecting the free and even the servile tenant against
his landlord in his possession of land and his rent bargain, so that in
the reign of Elizabeth it was possible for her great secretary and am-
bassador, Sir Thomas Smith, to describe England as a "Common
Wealth" (res publica) rather than a "host of men," or as instruments
for the will of one man.   "A common wealth," he said, "is called a
society or common doing of a multitude of free men collected together
and united by common accord and covenauntes among themselves,
for the conservation of themselves as well in peace as in warre.   For
properly an host of men is not called a common wealth but abusively,
because they are collected but for a time and for a fact: which done,
each divideth himselfe from others as they were before.   And if one
man had as some of the old Romanes had (if it be true that is written)
V. thousande or X. thousande bondmen whom he ruled well, though
they dwelled all in one citie, or were distributed into divers villages,
yet that were no common wealth: for the bondman hath no communion

---

[1] HOLDSWORTH, 3:178.
[2] *Ibid.*, 179.
[3] COKE, *Compleate Copy-holder*, Sec. 9 (1641) quoted by HOLDSWORTH, 3:180.

with his master, the wealth of the Lord is onely sought for, and not the profit of the slave or bondman. . . . A bondman or a slave is as it were (saving life and humane reason) but the instrument of his Lord, as the axe, the sawe, the chessyll and gowge is of the charpenter. . . . And though one husbandman had a great number of all those and looked well to them, it made no common wealth and could not so be called. For private wealth of the husbandmen is onely regarded, and there is no mutual societie or portion, no law or pleading betweene thone and thother. . . . Wherefore except there be other orders and administrations amongst the Turks, if the prince of the Turks (as it is written of him) do repute all other his bondmen and slaves (him selfe and his sonnes onely freemen) a man may doubt whether his administration be to be accompted a common wealth or a Kingdome, or rather to be reputed onely as one that hath under him an infinite number of slaves or bondmen among whom there is no right, law nor common wealth compact, but onely the will of the Lorde and segnior." [1]

And Thomas Smith divided this Common Wealth of agricultural England among four classes of people, three of whom participated in it and one did not. The three participating classes were the "barons or estate of Lordes;" the "Knightes, Esquires and simpely gentlemen," who "live idly without manuall labor;" and the "yeomanrie." [2]

The yeomen are they who "have the greatest charge and doings in the common wealth, or rather are more travailed to serve in it than all the rest." They are the farmers—the "fermors unto gentlemen" who, by agriculture, "get both their own living and parte of their maisters." [3] They are the "tenauntes of their Lorde," the archers and footmen who excelled the horsemen, for, in the wars, the Kings of England fought always amongst them, rather than among the horsemen, thereby showing, "as a man may guess, where he thought his strength did consist." [4]

Finally, the "fourth sort or classe amongst us," said Smith, were what the old Romans called the proletarii or workers, the "day labourers, poore husbandmen," "lowest and rascall sort of the people," "yea merchantes or retailers who have no free lande, copiholders, and all artificers, as Taylors, Shoomakers, Carpenters, Brickemakers,

---

[1] SMITH, SIR THOMAS, *De Republica Anglorum* (1567), reprint in 1589 under the title *The Common-Wealth of England*, 20, 21 (1906).

[2] *Ibid.*, at 31.

[3] *Ibid.*, at 43.

[4] *Ibid.*, 31–47.

Bricklayers, Masons, etc.," who have "no voice nor authoritie in our common wealth, and no account is made of them but onelie to be ruled, not to rule others, and yet they be not altogether neglected." [1]

Thus, in the time of Elizabeth, the common law, springing from the customs of the people in so far as seemed reasonable to the King's justices, had erected an agricultural commonwealth, by depriving the barons of their private courts and armies and substituting the common-law courts of the King, and these created, for the farmers, property and liberty, by changing the economic foundation of Society from bargains in terms of use-values to bargains in terms of exchange-values.

[1] SMITH, at 46.

CHAPTER VII

THE PRICE BARGAIN—CAPITALISM AND EXCHANGE-VALUE

I. *The Commonwealth*

Sir Thomas Smith, in his account of the Commonwealth, barely mentions "citizens and burgesses" as "next to gentlemen," yet it was these citizens and burgesses, who, since the reign of John,[1] had been obtaining collective powers and immunities, also known as "liberties," and who, within a third of a century after Smith wrote, would, like the landlords, begin to be deprived of the monopolistic and governmental features of their franchises. The gild franchises of the merchants and manufacturers gave to them a "collective lordship" similar to the private lordship of the barons, for their gilds were erected into governments with their popular assemblies, their legislatures, their courts, their executives, and even with authority to enforce fines and imprisonment of violators of their rules. Their most important sovereign privilege granted by the King was that of binding all the members by a majority vote so that they could act as a unit. These merchants' and manufacturers' gilds, at the height of their power, were not only legalized "closed shops" but also legalized governments. Within their jurisdiction no person could compete who was not authorized by the gild, and within the gild no one could compete except on the terms of fair competition which their rules imposed. They maintained standards of quality of product and of qualifications of competitors designed both to protect the public and prevent destructive competition.[2] They even required members to share with each other the raw material and any exceptional good bargains that one might come across. They enforced the contracts of their members. Associated together they even gained control of the borough governments, and their chief men became mayors and aldermen.

---

[1] Gross mentions 24 charters granted to merchant gilds prior to 1215. Gross, Chas., *The Gild Merchant*, 9–16 (1890).

[2] Cp. Commons, J. R., "The American Shoemakers," 24 *Quar. Journ. Econ.*, 39 (1909); *Labor and Administration*, 219 (1913).

Thus the gilds were the spots, here and there, where capitalism had its origin. Surrounded by feudal landlords they obtained immunity as small peddlers and artisans only by obtaining from a feudal superior privileges which enabled them to act as units and to make and enforce their own by-laws. The gilds were Defensive Capitalism. But they grew in wealth and power. Their defensive privileges became exclusive privileges in proportion as markets and commerce advanced over militarism and agriculture and increasing numbers of people depended on buying and selling for a living, where formerly they depended on command and obedience.

Beginning in 1599, by that line of notable decisions referred to by Justice Field in the Slaughter House Cases,[1] the highest court of the common law, the King's Bench, deprived them of their closed-shop privileges in so far as those privileges depended on enforcement of penalties by the King's executives. In France they were abolished by the Revolution; in Germany they lived over to the nineteenth century; in England they lived on as voluntary organizations but without sovereign power physically to enforce their rules.

In 1599 the Merchant Tailors of London were the first to lose their legalized closed shop. The King's Bench, in that year, declared that a by-law of the Tailor's Society was unlawful in requiring every "brother" of the society to give to another brother who "exercised the art of clothworker," at least as much of his cloth to be worked up as he might give to any clothworker not a member of the society, upon pain of forfeiting ten shillings, and providing enforcement upon his goods. This by-law, although authorized in the charter granted from early times to the Society and confirmed by successive Kings and Parliament, was nevertheless adjudged against the "common right and public good," and "against the common law," because, being a monopoly, it was "against the liberty of the subject," and "against the commonwealth." [2]

This argument was even more clearly and forcibly made in the Case of Monopolies, in 1602, at the close of Elizabeth's reign.[3] This case concerned but one of the many patent monopolies which Elizabeth had granted for the upbuilding of the country, for the development of new resources and the encouragement of new importations from

[1] Above, Chap. III, p. 46.
[2] Davenant v. Hurdis, Trin. 41 Eliz., Moor (K. B.) 576 (1599); commented on by Coke in Case of Monopolies, 11 Co. 86 a, b.
[3] Darcy v. Allein, Trin. 44 Eliz. (1602), 11 Co. 84 b.

abroad.[1] Indeed, as Unwin has said of the similar monopolies granted by Elizabeth's successors, James and Charles, "It was not merely that such grants seemed to afford the easiest way out of the Crown's growing financial difficulties. The spirit of corporate monopoly which pervaded all classes engaged in commerce and industry, from the richest to the poorest, made it possible, perhaps with sincerity, to represent the grants, not as a hateful but unavoidable expedient for raising money, but as part of a great and beneficent scheme of national policy." [2]

Elizabeth had, however, yielded to the outcry against monopolies, had revoked the most unpopular patents, and left the rest to the decision of the judges. Darcy's case was the monopoly of sale, manufacture and importation of playing cards. Popham, the Chief Justice, and the entire court declared that it was void, as against the common law and acts of parliament, for four reasons:

1. All trades which prevent idleness, "the bane of the commonwealth," and increase the substance of themselves and families to serve the Queen when occasion requires, "are profitable for the commonwealth." 2. "The inseparable incidents to every monopoly against the commonwealth" are, increase in price, inferior quality, and impoverishment of mechanics and their families, because "the patentee, having the sole trade, regards only his private benefit and not the common wealth." 3. The Queen was deceived in her grant, for she intended it "for the weal public," but "it will be employed for private gain of the patentee, and for the prejudice of the weal public." 4. "It cannot be intended that Edward Darcy, an Esquire, and a groom of the Queen's Privy Chamber, has any skill in this mechanical trade of making cards; . . . To forbid others to make cards who have the art and skill, and to give him the sole making of them who has no skill to make them, will make the patent utterly void."

Thus the basic principle of the commonwealth, stated clearly by the chief justice of the common-law courts at this early day, was the principle—Let any person get rich in so far as he enriches the commonwealth, but not in so far as he merely extracts private wealth from the commonwealth.

Other similar decisions were given during this critical period. In 1519 Henry VIII had granted to the physicians of London a charter of

---

[1] Cunningham, W. E., *The Growth of English Industry and Commerce*, 2:58, 287n. (1903).
[2] Unwin, George, *The Gilds and Companies of London*, 300 (1908).

incorporation, confirmed later by Parliament, giving to them authority to pass upon the qualifications of physicians within the city and suburbs, and to prohibit the unqualified from practicing, on penalty of fine and imprisonment, prosecuted before the governors and censors of this company of physicians. Under this authority Dr. Bonham, in 1608, was imprisoned by agents of the company, and brought his action of false imprisonment. The court, Coke being then Chief Justice, decided that the censors and wardens had not that power, and, in this case he went to the extreme point of squarely overruling an act of parliament. For, said he, "in many cases the common law will controul acts of parliament and sometimes adjudge them to be utterly void: for when an act of parliament is against common right and reason, or repugnant, or impossible to be performed, the common law will controul it, and adjudge such act to be void." [1]

This was followed by the Ipswich Tailors in 1615.[2] This society had been incorporated by Henry VII and confirmed by parliament in the year 1504, with power to make and enforce ordinances. The company brought an action in debt against a tailor who came to the town and practiced his trade without proof that he had served an apprenticeship for seven years, and without being admitted by the master and wardens as a sufficient workman. It was resolved by the court that, at common law, "no man could be prohibited from working in any lawful trade;" that the youth ought "to learn lawful sciences and trades which are profitable to the common-wealth;" that the restraint was "against the liberty and freedom of the subject," and "all this is against the common law, and the common-wealth."

Thus the common-law courts accomplished, in the case of the gilds, what they had accomplished in the case of the barons. They abolished the private jurisdictions with their private courts,[3] and the way was thenceforth open for them to build up, for the Kingdom, a common law of the price-bargain, just as they had built up a common law of the rent-bargain. The business man now, like the Yeoman and copyholders, could have his customs inquired into by the King's justices, and his rights and privileges asserted against private jurisdiction of both gilds and barons. Capitalism entered upon its offensive stage, intent on controlling the government whose aid it had petitioned dur-

---

[1] Bonham's Case, 8 Co. 114 a, 118 a (1610).
[2] 11 Co. 53 a.
[3] Certain decisions in the 18th century seem to have supported the claims of the gilds. See HOLDSWORTH, *History of English Law*, 1:352. They were abolished in 1853.

ing its defensive period. Eventually its petitions became its rights. The next hundred years, until the Act of Settlement in 1700, was substantially the struggle of farmers and business men to become members of the Commonwealth, whereby they might have courts of law willing and able to convert their customary bargains into a common law of property and liberty. The King's courts themselves had been impotent after Chief Justice Coke, the great champion of the common law, had been removed from office by King James in 1616,[1] and consequently the farmers and business men turned towards collective control through parliament, towards raising an army, and even, for a period of ten years, abolishing both King and House of Lords and converting the Kingdom literally into a commonwealth. Although the Kingdom was restored and the very name of Commonwealth stricken from the records, yet, after 1700, the courts were made independent of the King, and the common law of business was incorporated into the common law of agriculture. The name of commonwealth was moved to America, and, under new auspices, is resurrected in the Commonwealth of Australia.

It will thus be seen that the notion of a commonwealth, as expounded by Sir Thomas Smith in the middle of the sixteenth century, differed from the notions of the Wealth of Nations expounded by Adam Smith's followers, more than by Adam Smith himself, in the eighteenth and nineteenth centuries, in that it explicitly included both the economic and the political aspects in a single concept. It was a notion both of common-weal and of participation in that weal through the possession of rights and the corresponding power to enlist the officials of government in one's behalf. The classical economists tended to separate the wealth of nations from the commonwealth, making the wealth of nations identical with the prosperity of but a single class within the commonwealth, the business men, upon whom all other classes depended for prosperity. But the notion of a commonwealth which arose with Thomas Smith in the sixteenth century and led to the two revolutions of the seventeenth century was a notion of participation by each freeman in both the government and the wealth of the nation. The difference between Thomas Smith's notion and the notion of Coke, Selden, Littleton, the common-law lawyers and their successors of the seventeenth century, extended only to the degree to which merchants, manufacturers and farmers

[1] GARDINER, S. R., *History of England*, 1603–1642, 3:27 (1890).

should actively participate in the commonwealth along with barons, monopolists, gilds and the other beneficiaries of the King's prerogative. The literal "commonwealth" of 1640 went further and abolished both the monarch and the House of Lords. The reaction which followed gave to the landlords an even more powerful participation than they had before, and it has required more than two additional centuries and the growth of the then inferior merchants and manufacturers into the new world-power of capitalism to bring attention back to the original notion of the commonwealth as it struggled for recognition in the reigns of Elizabeth, James and Charles.

Yet the original participants in the King's prerogative were trying to do what needed to be done, and had to be done in other ways when the power of the prerogative to protect them was weakened. The abolition of the legal power of the gilds required the courts both to take over the rules of fair competition and to enforce the contracts which had grown out of their customs and had been enforced in their own courts. We shall see how, in 1580 and 1620, the common-law courts began to take over, and to enact into law for the whole of England, certain of the regulations of the gilds whose private authority they were then abolishing. The first of the goodwill decisions enforcing a contract to sell a going business (1620) and the first of the trade-mark decisions enforcing a claim for damages against the use of a competitor's name in business (1580) were but the legal adoption on a national scale of the very rules of fair competition which the gilds adopted within their own exclusive membership. The court which abolished the power of the gilds began to take over the work of the gilds. Their private jurisdiction became a public jurisdiction. And the very customs which the gilds endeavored to enforce within their ranks became the customs which the courts enforced for the nation. The monopoly, the closed shop, and the private jurisdiction were gone, but the economics and ethics remained. Much later, in the modern commonwealth, other functions of the gilds, such as protection of the quality of the product and the qualifications of practitioners, have also been taken over by courts or legislatures. Beside the chartered gilds there were other less formal courts at the fairs where merchants came with their goods (piepoudre) and there were the practices of merchants in drawing bills of exchange upon each other calling for money, which the common-law courts, at about the same period, began to take notice of and to interpret according to the customs of merchants. The common law became the law of property, liberty *and business*.

But neither business expectations nor the expectations aroused by the law of property and liberty could expand as long as the prerogative of the monarch was above the common law. The struggle, begun with Magna Carta, did not reach its crisis until the rise of protestantism and commerce. The former asserted a new right, the right to equality, liberty and security of worship, the latter the right to equality, liberty and security of business. Business could not be free and secure while the prerogative exercised capricious control, especially over currency, franchises and rents.

Arbitrary alterations of the currency were not repeated after Edward VI,[1] and money thenceforth became a comparatively reliable standard of value and medium of exchange, a universal representative of the value of products, a trusted instrument of inducement and compensation, and therefore a solid foundation for the credit system. Franchises were not taken from the personal control of the monarch until the victory of parliament in the civil wars and not completely until the Act of Settlement in 1700, which confirmed the Case of Monopolies of 1602 and the Statute of Monopolies of 1624. Taxes were not made certain until, after 1689, they could be levied only by consent of Parliament. By these measures business, based on predictable prices, was permitted to develop unhampered by arbitrary interference of the sovereign.

Even these stabilizing reforms of currency, franchises and rents, which prepared the way for a business economy based on prices, could not be rendered permanently secure until the Revolution of 1689, and especially the Act of Settlement of 1700, which took from the monarch the power to remove the justices of the courts. When James I succeeded Elizabeth, in 1603, the prerogative, besides including the power to appoint judges of the common-law courts and of the highest of those courts, the King's Bench, included also a number of other courts, or rather a number of other agents of the King appointed and removed at his pleasure. Greatest was the Star Chamber, the personal council of the King sitting as a court in the Star Chamber, exercising civil, criminal and political jurisdiction wherever great questions of state or great and powerful personages, or violations of the King's prerogative, were called in question or litigated. The most

[1] CUNNINGHAM, *Growth of English Industry and Commerce*, 2:127 (1903).

significant function of the Star Chamber was its position as an administrative court by means of which the King's officials were exempt from trial in the common-law courts.[1]   A similar jurisdiction existed in the Court of Exchequer where all cases between taxpayers and the crown were tried, as well as cases in which revenue officers themselves were tried.   It, too, had power to remove cases from the common-law courts.[2]   Then there was the Court of High Commission with inferior ecclesiastical courts, having authority to try cases of religious doctrine and ritual, and to remove the clergy from the jurisdiction of the common-law courts.[3]   Finally was the Chancellor, a member of the King's Council and the highest personage next to the King, who kept the King's seal which alone authenticated the King's acts, and exercised likewise the King's prerogative power of issuing injunctions restraining parties from bringing their cases to the common-law courts, or, if they had already done so, from enforcing judgment.[4]

The parliament of 1640 and the revolution that followed abolished these prerogative courts or limited them, while the Act of Settlement in 1700 [5] made the judges as well as the chancellor independent of the King and appointed for life.   Henceforth came about that peculiar and outstanding feature of Anglo-American law, the subjection of officials as well as citizens to the jurisdiction of the ordinary courts of law.   It was this that made it possible for Francis Lieber, in 1853, to say "The guaranty of the supremacy of the law leads to a principle which, so far as I know, it has never been attempted to transplant from the soil inhabited by Anglican people, and which, nevertheless, has been in our system of liberty, the natural production of a thorough government of law as contra-distinguished to a government of functionaries," [6] and for English and American courts to say, ours is a "government of laws, and not of men."   It is such because officials and citizens are each subject to the same courts, interpreting the same due process of law.

But the American constitutions went much further.   While the Act of Settlement made the judges independent, yet parliament retained the power to overrule the courts.   But in America, as is

---

[1] HOLDSWORTH, *History of English Law*, 1:276.
[2] *Ibid.*, 104, 105.
[3] *Ibid.*, 375 ff.
[4] *Ibid.*, 246.
[5] ADAMS and STEPHENS, *Select Documents of English Constitutional History*, 475–479.
[6] LIEBER, FRANCIS, *Civil Liberty and Self-government*, 91 (1853); TAYLOR, H., *Due Process*, 608 (1917).

well known, under written constitutions, the Supreme Courts are the
final interpreters of the constitution and of the powers and responsibilities of officials, as well as the rights and duties of citizens. In this
respect, as is brought out by Haines,[1] America went back to the doctrine of Sir Edward Coke, who would have made parliament, as well as
the King, subordinate to the common-law court of King's Bench over
which he presided as Chief Justice. But with a difference. Coke
would have made the King and parliament subject to the common
law. The supreme courts of the United States make legislatures,
executives and judges subject to the common law and equity. The
common law is historic custom, precedent, and the ancient law of the
land; equity is conscience, reason, and the law of God or nature. The
two are in fact inseparable. King James had said that "he thought
the 'law' was founded upon reason, and that he and others had reason,
as well as the judges." "True," said Coke, "God had endowed his
Majesty with excellent science and great endowments of nature. But
his Majesty was not learned in the laws of his realm of England, and
causes which concern the life, or inheritance, or goods, or fortunes of
his subjects, are not to be decided by natural reason, but by the
artificial reason and judgment of law, which law is an act which requires long study and experience, before that a man can attain to the
cognizance of it." The King ought not, indeed, to be under any man,
but under "God and law"—yet not God's law, as James and the
Church contended, but the common law.[2] Furthermore, contended
Coke, when an act, even of parliament, "is against common right and
reason, or repugnant or impossible to be performed, the common law
will control it, and adjudge such act to be void."[3] Thus Coke interpreted the common law as not only the customs and precedents of
ancient law but also as the rule of "right and reason," interpreted by
the common-law judge. In this respect he distinguished it from
equity, which at that time was the arbitrary power of the sovereign,
and agreed with his great contemporary, John Selden, who likened
equity to the Chancellor's foot.

Meanwhile, the common law also, under the influence of Lord
Mansfield in the eighteenth century, had itself widened out with
principles of natural justice drawn from Roman law and from equity,[4]

---

[1] HAINES, C. G., *The American Doctrine of Judicial Supremacy* 25 ff. (1914).
[2] *Prohibitions del Roy*, 12 Co. 64-65 (1608); HAINES, 28.
[3] Bonham's case, 8 Co. 118 a., b.,; HAINES, *op. cit.* 31.
[4] HOLDSWORTH, 1:253; JENKS, 234 ff.

thus adapting itself to the change from a feudal economy to a capitalist economy. It required another century, in England, before the parliament, in 1873, consolidated the common law and equity courts in a supreme court of judicature,[1] a consolidation which was effected in America by the Constitution of 1787 making the judicial power of the federal government extend to all cases at law and equity under the Constitution, while the state constitutions began the similar consolidation with New York in 1840.

The evident advantage of the equity process over the common-law process is in its control over conduct in advance of action instead of punishment after action. The proceedings do not require the prolonged investigation, indictment and jury trial of the common law, but both the injunction and punishment for its violation are expeditious. For the Court of Chancery had the peculiar faculty of commanding specific behavior by mandamus or injunction, on mere allegations and affidavits of a complainant, without waiting for the slow processes of a suit for damages, as in the common-law courts. It commands first, and finds out afterwards what are the law, the rights and the facts; whereas the common law finds out first what are the law and facts and afterwards issues its commands. This one feature alone would have required the equity courts to intervene with the injunction, or else would have required the extension, by the common-law courts, of their writs of mandamus and prohibition, in order to create those intangible property rights of modern business which have made the transition from physical property to intangible property. By means of the injunction the court can, in advance, enter into the most minute detail of behavior needed to recognize new rights and protect new definitions of persons and property.[2] The common law was able to deal effectively only with physical things and to punish *after* the event,—equity deals with the most intangible values, for it commands directly, *before* the event, the very performance, avoidance or forbearance on which value depends. Equity looks on property as behavior claimed of other persons; the common law looks on it as a thing owned by a person.[3]

[1] JENKS, *op. cit.* 408.
[2] "This capacity of moulding a decree to suit the exact exigencies of a particular case is indeed one of the most striking advantages which procedure in chancery enjoys over that at common law, and must have been one of the elements which contributed in no small degree to the origin and growth of equitable jurisprudence." BISPHAM, *Principles of Equity,* 9 (8th ed., 1909).
[3] AMES, J. B., *Lectures in Legal History,* 108 (1913).

Indeed, the first important field of equity was that of creating uses and trusts, which distinguish physical things from the expected transactions growing out of things. And since value does not reside in things but in these expected transactions, equity procedure at once extracts from the common-law procedure the very substance of value. Hence flowed the whole range of behavioristic values by way of the relief which equity afforded against the rigidity or inadequacy of the common law, such as the remedying of accidents and mistakes, the controlling of accounts, partnerships, and every detail of corporation law. The remarkable expansion of the equity jurisdiction in the Eighteenth Century reflected the rise of capitalism based on pecuniary expectations, and the corresponding subsidence of feudalism and the prerogative based on physical power. Thereafter it became possible for the courts to build up the law of business in proportion as business itself developed.

II. Incorporeal Property—Encumbrances

1. *Promises*

The law of credit instruments passed through two stages, first, the stage of enforcement of contracts, the second the authorization of the supplementary buying and selling of the contracts themselves. The first may be distinguished as the stage of enforceable promises, or incorporeal property; the second the stage of negotiable promises, or intangible property. The first stage was practically completed by the latter half of the sixteenth century; the second begins with the first recorded opinion on bills of exchange at the beginning of the seventeenth century. The distinction between the law of intangible property, which we name the law of opportunities, and the law of incorporeal property, which we name a special case of the law of encumbrances, turns on the question whether the opposite party has or has not liberty of choice between alternatives.

If the opposite party has no liberty of choice, in the particular behavior at issue, then, to that extent, he is burdened by an encumbrance, or duty, of performance, forbearance or avoidance. If, however, the opposite party is at liberty to choose an alternative then the relation between them is one of opportunity. The law of encumbrances on behavior is the law of right and duty; the law of opportunities for behavior is the law of liberty and exposure. An encumbrance indicates the psychological relation of command and obedience. The first party issues a command, the opposite party obeys, or is compelled to obey. He has no option. But an opportunity indicates the psychological relation of persuasion or coercion. The opposite party is free to choose alternatives rather than obey. Instead, therefore, of a command and obedience, the first party must resort to that kind of inducement which consists in setting up, or taking advantage of, alternatives between which the opposite party may choose. If the alternative is onerous so that the choice is a hard one, the opposite party still improves his condition, as perceived at the time, by selecting the better alternative. He always gains by choosing, and persuasion and coercion do not differ in kind but in degree. A hard alternative, where taken advantage of, is coercion; an agreeable, or not disagreeable alternative, is persuasion.

Command and obedience are thus legally different from persuasion or coercion, although psychologically they may look alike, for in the one relation the opposite party has no lawful option. He must obey. But in the other relation he has an option; he is free to accept or reject. Command and obedience imply the juristic relation of duty of the opposite party, which therefore we name encumbrance. Persuasion and coercion imply the juristic relation of liberty, which we understand by choice of opportunities. Command and obedience, that is, encumbrances, are sanctioned by legal rewards and penalties; persuasion or coercion, that is, opportunities, are sanctioned by economic advantage and disadvantage. Each is expected to be beneficial to the first party, but encumbrances are beneficial in that they are mandatory acts required of an opposite party; opportunities in that they are optional transactions with an opposite party. Encumbrances, completely defined, are expected, beneficial, one-sided mandatory actions; opportunities are expected, beneficial, reciprocal optional, transactions.

Now, the law of incorporeal property is a special case of the law of encumbrances, in that it imposes only a "positive" duty, the duty of performance, whereas the "negative" duties of forbearance and avoidance are the encumbrances peculiar to the law of intangible property. Incorporeal property turns on the duty to pay a debt but intangible property turns on the duty to avoid or forbear in the exercise of physical, economic or moral power. The two are insep arable in fact, the distinction between the two being made at the point of time when an enforceable promise is deemed to come into effect. *Before* the promise is made the parties are in the position of choosing between opportunities; *after* the promise is made there is no further choice if the promise is enforceable in law. Yet both before and after the promise comes into effect, there exist duties of forbearance or avoidance on the two parties and all third parties. It is the gradual historical change in all of these encumbrances on behavior, whether of performance, avoidance, or forbearance, that marks the evolution of both incorporeal and intangible property and the shift back and forth from one to the other.

Since, therefore, the special case of a duty of performance is the peculiar attribute of incorporeal property, we may take for granted the presence of the necessary supporting duties of forbearance and avoidance and may speak of the law of encumbrances as the law of "positive" encumbrances of performance and therefore equivalent to incorporeal property in that it is the law of creditor and debtor relations; while the law of opportunities is the law of intangible property, in that it deals with the relation of buyer and seller in its various forms of purchase and sale, lending and borrowing, hiring and hiring out, leasing, and so on.

The law of positive encumbrances may be said to have had a two-fold development, distinguishable as the law of labor encumbrances, and the law of investment encumbrances. The law of labor has historically unfolded as the law of owner and slave, landlord and serf, master and servant, employer and employee, principal and agent, with perhaps subordinate divisions of parent and child, husband and wife. The law of investment is mainly the law of landlord and tenant, lessor and lessee, creditor and debtor. Each of these shows an evolution of the notion of property from the ownership of visible things to the ownership of invisible encumbrances on behavior and opportunities.

The law of employment and agency sets up the creditor and debtor relation until such time as wages or salaries are paid, and then slides informally into the law of specific investment. The investor proper of modern industry emerges as a specialist who takes over, at pay-day, from the employee or agent, the burden of waiting for compensation until that time when the ultimate consumer makes compensation for all of the preceding services. He may be a formal or an informal investor. As an informal investor he enters by investing his own money in his own business.

The bargain which the formal investor makes is a sale of present purchasing power in exchange for future purchasing power. This occurs, in modern business, under many forms and includes shares of stock, as well as bonds and promissory notes. In either case, the essential transaction consists in selling present purchasing power and accepting a promise or expectation of future purchasing power. The one is money, the other is credit.

In selling present purchasing power he sells that part of his liberty which consists in control over the purchasing power which had been his, so that his field of liberty, for the time being, is thus limited by a duty of avoidance. He accepts, in return, a promise of future purchasing power, an encumbrance on the debtor or the going concern, and it is this investment encumbrance, or incorporeal property, that has emerged out of the primitive notion of holding physical things for one's own use.

The law of investor's encumbrance started, under the common law, with the idea of property in physical things and with corresponding legal actions for the recovery of tangible goods and even specific money coins, wrongfully deforced, detained or held, from their owner; and also with actions against violent trespass on lands, chattels, or persons, until it gradually became, about the middle of the Sixteenth Century, the enforcement of a mere promise, express, or implied, written or unwritten, accepted formally or even acted upon without a formal promise, as though it had been promised

Thus, for example, the "writ of right" and the "writ of debt" indicated similar ideas and procedure, the one being a remedy for forcible detention of land, the other for forcible detention of physical chattels. The writ of right, addressed by the King to the sheriff bade him to require the defendant A to render to the plaintiff B a piece of land, which A had unjustly taken from B.[1] This merely gave to B a better right of possession than to A. It gave possession but not property.[2] Yet, eventually, out of this remedy grew the complete remedies of the judgment *in rem*, affirming the absolute right of property against all the world with its various remedies applicable to title and ownership of all physical things, whether land goods, or even paper instruments serving as evidence of ownership.

[1] JENKS, 56 (1912).   [2] POLLOCK and MAITLAND, 2:77.

The "writ of debt" was scarcely different from the writ of right except in the physical object claimed by the plaintiff. It, too, bade the sheriff to require the defendant A to render to the plaintiff B not land, but, say, one hundred specific pieces of coin which A owed B. The defendant was to restore the very coins lent. Afterwards this became, not the specific coins, but the amount of the debt.[1] Even where a personal obligation of the debtor to perform a certain act was recognized, it had to take objective form in a sealed bond, made with formality in the presence of witnesses or the court,[2] and it was not so much the promise of the debtor that constituted the ground of his debt as the bond itself with its huge seal.[3]

But the modern simple, or parol, contract, a written or unwritten promise, with its recognition of a personal liability of the debtor, got its recognition, not by way of enforcement of a promise, but by way of physical damage done to the person or property of the creditor. "The gist of the Writ of Trespass was an allegation that the defendant had, with force and arms, and against the peace of our Lord the King, interfered with the plaintiff's possession of his body, land, or goods."[4] Next by authority of Parliament in 1285[5] the writ of trespass was permitted to be extended to analogous cases, and came to be known as "trespass on a similar case," then as "trespass on the case," then simply as "action on the case," or merely "case." Under this authority it was extended to "malfeasance," or damage to a physical object owned by the plaintiff, as early as the year 1374; then extended to "non-feasance," in 1424, or the damage caused by mere nonfulfillment of a promise without fraud or deceit; then to "misfeasance" or deliberate fraud of the defendant in breaking his promise though not involving physical damage (1433); then, including "assumpsit" and limited by the doctrine of "consideration," or "value received," it established the modern form of contract in the latter part of the Sixteenth Century.[6]

Thus the promissory note or even a simple promise by word of mouth or only implied in the conduct of the parties, was slowly legalized through the period of the sixteenth century, and the court

---

[1] JENKS, 57, 58, 59.
[2] AMES, *Lectures on Legal History*, 123 (1913).
[3] JENKS, 135-6 510.
[4] *Ibid.*, 137; POLLOCK and MAITLAND, 182 (contract) 510 (The Trespasses).
[5] Westm. 2, 13 Edw. I, c. 24 (1285).
[6] POLLOCK and MAITLAND, 2:511.

recognized the essential notion of a credit instrument, the modern incorporeal property, where protection was something distinct and widely different from the older notions of protection against trespass on the body, land, or goods of a plaintiff.

Not that there had not been in the feudal period a type of incorporeal property, but that property was not the modern relation of voluntary agreements between equals, but was lordship over physical things, or the physical products of the soil or of labor. The "rents" of land were even a part of the lordship over lands and tenants. "The landlord who demands the rent that is in arrear is not seeking to enforce a contract, he is seeking to recover a thing." [1] It was only in course of time, and with the modern freedom of labor and money economy, that this "medieval realism," [2] became the modern obligation of contracts between equals. The law of landlord and tenant unfolds into many varieties of the law of lessor and lessee, a special case of the law of creditor and debtor. The lessor turns over to the lessee the control of his property, and accepts, for the period of time, the economic relation of investor and creditor, the lessee that of business man or going concern and debtor.

We need not delay to consider the informal investor, the business man, who puts his own property or money into his own business. He does so, of course, not on a formal promise, but on an implied expectation of something roughly in excess of what is promised in similar cases. He takes chances on expected opportunities.

2. *Legal Tender*

It has been the practice in economic theorizing, since the reaction of the Physiocrats and Adam Smith against Mercantilism, to eliminate money from consideration and to get back to the realities of physical commodities and human wants. Money was simply a measure of value and a medium of exchange, and, while important, its importance belonged to the category of weights and measures of transportation. The government should provide an authentic unit of measurement of value just as it provided a unit of length, weights or cubic content, and it should provide a smooth administration of coinage and banking, since what it provided was Adam Smith's "great wheel of circulation." In these respects the value of

---

[1] POLLOCK and MAITLAND, 2:126.

[2] *Ibid.*, 2:181, on Ownership and Possession.

money was simply nominal value, containing nothing more in itself than a yardstick or an empty basket. The real thing back of
it was the production, exchange and consumption of quantities of
commodities, whose measurement and transfer money facilitated.

These views obviously took the individualistic or private standpoint, as against Mercantilism which had taken the public or rather
monarchical standpoint. What the individual wants is commodities, not money,—satisfaction, not prices. When the public standpoint was needful it was brought in as a servant or administrator
operating " a great wheel of circulation," [1] rather than a judge deciding disputes, or brought in as a " natural order " and beneficent purpose of nature or deity, rather than a common-law judge enforcing
private contracts. Obviously it followed that, when the history
of money was traced out of the customs of primitive society, showing the evolution of the material of money from beads, cattle, to-
bacco, to iron, copper, silver, gold, and bank credit, it was the *mechanism* of money and credit, rather than the behavior of judges in
interpreting and enforcing promises, that attracted attention.

This attitude conformed to the general attitude imposed on both
economists and publicists by the constitutional struggles of three
hundred years between monarchs and parliaments which made it
appear that government signified only the executive and legislative branches of government rather than the judicial branch. Hence
they sought for the legal attributes of money in the proclamations
of the prerogative or in the statutes of the legislatures rather than
the common law. Yet it is out of the common law, the law that
standardized the customs of the people, that the legal tender quality
originated, and the function of the prerogative or legislature came
in afterwards to direct the judges as to the lawful standards of weights
and measures, including money, which all of them should employ
uniformly throughout the land in deciding disputes and enforcing
promises.

This oversight of the Physiocrats, of Adam Smith and the classical economists, is explicable in the fact that what they mistook for
the order of nature or divine providence was merely the common
law silently growing up around them in the decisions of judges who
were quietly selecting and standardizing the good customs of the
neighborhood and rejecting the bad practices that did not conform

[1] Cp. VEBLEN, *Place of Science*, 66.

to the accepted rules of reason.   Legislatures and monarchs are dramatic, arbitrary and artificial; courts are commonplace and natural.

It is also explicable in the fact that economic theory has consistently taken the point of view of individuals on the one hand and commodities on the other hand, instead of the point of view of transactions between individuals.   Our analysis of a transaction has shown that there is always a third party to every transaction, the judge who decides or is expected to decide every dispute upon the principle of the common rule applicable to all similar transactions. The business man is not concerned, directly, in his daily transactions, with what the legislatures or the state or monarch does—he wants to know what the judge and the sheriff will do.   This judge, however, necessarily takes a public point of view, since his decisions must conform to what other judges have decided in similar disputes and to what the customs or laws of the community authorize and support.   In applying the common rule he is conforming to public purpose.   Hence the public point of view is inherent in every transaction, and just as much so in primitive society as in a credit economy.

Money originated, indeed, out of the habits and customs of individuals in their transactions, but whenever a dispute arose between individuals as to the price, or the payment of a deferred price, agreed upon, it is evident that the judge, chieftain, headman or king, exercising the controlling power of the community, had to decide upon the quantity and quality of the circulating medium which the seller or creditor should be required to accept.   This decision settled the dispute, stopped private vengeance, liberated the debtor or buyer and restrained the creditor or seller.   Then when markets and fairs appeared, the same process automatically appeared, and the impromptu pie poudre [1] courts of early England testify to the inherent function of the judiciary in interpreting and enforcing accepted customs even of the most transitory and individualistic of itinerant peddlers.

Consequently there is another custom to be taken into account in the history and origin of money—the custom of judges in deciding disputes according to the principle of the working rule, and thereby determining what is "lawful money" or "lawful tender" in the settlement of claims.   The fact that these judges presumably followed the

---

[1] The "dusty feet" courts of traveling merchants; cp. POLLOCK and MAITLAND, 1:467; HOLDSWORTH, 1:300, 302, 309.

custom of the community in making their decisions is simply the universal fact of the common law which consists in selecting the good and approved customs and eliminating bad practices in the decision of disputes.

This custom of courts led to the next stage when conquest or federation had brought together tribes under a sovereign with many local courts and many private coiners and minters of money. Ethelstan, Edgar and Canute, in Anglo-Saxon times, issued proclamations condemning and threatening punishment of those who corrupted the coinage; Edward I proclaimed that "no subject should be compelled to take in buying or selling or other payment any money made but only of lawful metal, silver or gold"; and Henry II is said to have selected the coins of a set of foreign merchants from Flanders, the Esterlings, and proclaimed their " sterling " alloy to be the standard for all goldsmiths, coiners,[1] and obviously also for the itinerant justices whom Henry was the first to send out on the circuits. Thus it came to be settled, at common law, that the King, "by his absolute prerogative" might make foreign or any coin "lawful money" in England,[2] and that an obstinate creditor had no remedy by the common law to have payment " because it shall be accounted his own folly that he refused the money when a lawful tender of it was made to him." [3] The records of the pie poudre court at St. Ives in the year 1300 contain a decision by merchants requiring a fellow merchant to pay in "lawful money"—legali moneta—since the "crocards and pollards" in which he promised to make payment had meanwhile been "prohibited by the lord King throughout all England." [4]

Evidently the King was directly concerned in stabilizing the coinage, since by impairing the coins the King lost his revenues, forfeitures and subsidies, the coercive debts of his subjects. Then when the modern banking system arose, with its bills, notes and deposits, the expectation of what the judges will do in deciding disputes becomes the all-important standard for all private transactions. The "customs " of business men and bankers are still the foundations of money, but these private practices must conform to the customs of the courts if business promises are to be secure. It is this legal tender

---

[1] 2 Coke Inst. 576.

[2] 5 Co. Rep. 114a, Wade's Case; Trin. 43 Eliz. (1601).

[3] Co. Litt. 207, a. b. 208, a; Pong v. Lindsay, 1 Dyer, 82a, Hil. 6 and 7, Edw. VI; 1 Bla. Com. 276; Viner Abr. "Tender."

[4] 23 Selden Soc. 80.

medium of payments, including governmental paper money, the "greenbacks,"[1] required by the custom of courts which, in American practice, is known as "lawful money," the common-law term that goes back to Anglo-Saxon times.

There is thus always a public purpose in every system of money, even the most primitive, as soon as there is an authoritative decision of disputes respecting the means of payment. The public purpose develops along with the growth of population, the practices of the people, the form of government and the motives of the governor. In early times it might go no further than the purpose of keeping the peace; but soon it becomes the purpose of obtaining a revenue for the sovereign; then, with the development of modern capitalism and the predominance of business in the counsels of government, it became Adam Smith's purpose of providing "the great wheel of circulation," truly "an organ of the economic commonwealth."

Soon the question had to arise as to whether the legal tender standard itself had been designed to accomplish accurately the purpose of a "great wheel of circulation," and then a critical examination ensued as to the relative importance of different purposes from the public standpoint. Since the time of John Locke the dominant purpose for the sake of modern world commerce has been that of settling upon a single standard of value that should be undisturbed by the ignorance or interests of monarchs who controlled its issue. This standardization of gold and silver came in with the overthrow of absolutism in England in 1689 and the control of government by the constitutional methods of parliamentary representation. Here the public purpose was simply that of providing a simple uniform medium of exchange for both domestic and foreign trade.

A hundred and fifty years after the settlement of this as the dominant purpose, a new public purpose began to be suggested as the ideal, namely, a stable level of prices, in order to prevent injustice between creditors and debtors. This purpose was based upon a new device of statistics, namely, the tabular standard or index number of prices, suggested, in 1822 by Joseph Lowe, the London merchant, and renewed in 1833 by C. Poulett Scroupe, the politician and publicist.

Malthus, in 1821, had previously suggested another practical pur-

---

[1] Hepburn v. Griswold, 8 Wall. 603 (1869); Legal Tender Cases, 12 Wall. 457 (1870); Juillard v. Greenman, 110 U. S. 421 (1884).

pose from the public standpoint, namely, that of preventing the oscillations of prosperity and depression, overemployment and underemployment, which he had connected with the oscillation of the general purchasing power of money.[1] This public purpose has now come to the forefront as a criterion for determining the legal standard of value and the operations of the banking system, which are the means instituted by government for furnishing and withholding credit.[2] If the governing officials are changed, or the existing officials change their minds in conformity with this new criterion, as was the case when John Locke addressed himself to them at the close of the Seventeenth Century, then the public purpose, as revealed in the behavior of officials and judges, will also advance another step and adopt a stable price level as well as a single standard of value as its criterion.

Thus it is not so much the material out of which money is made, nor the mechanism of money and credit, as it is the behavior of judges in deciding disputes, that determines the measure of value and medium of exchange. It is not gold, but the legal tender attribute of gold attached to it by the courts, that determines the prices that business men shall pay for commodities, for it is that that determines the enforceability of contracts, the liquidation of debts, the assets and liabilities of a going concern. Prices are indeed " nominal values"—they are the expectations of judicial behavior in the enforcement of promises. And modern economics is not a *barter* economy or a *truck* economy as the Physiocrats and classical economists would have it, nor is it a pleasure and pain economy of production and consumption, as the hedonic economists would have it, but it is a *price* economy, as the customs of business and the custom of courts actually have it. For business is not an *exchange* of commodities—it is a *purchase* and *sale* of commodities. It is an economy of buyers and sellers, borrowers and lenders, not one of truck and barter. Its essential quality, before anything else can be done, is transfer of titles and the liberation of debtors from encumbrances through the tender of lawful means of liquidating their promises. It is strictly, in the fullest sense of the word, a " credit " economy, for it is a transfer of goods and services for a mere promise to pay a price, whose reality is none other than confidence in the expected behavior of citizens, judges

---

[1] MALTHUS, T. R., *Principles of Political Economy*, 397, 398 (1821).
[2] *Cf.* COMMONS, McCRACKEN, and ZEUCH, "Secular Trends and Business Cycles," 4 *Rev. of Ec. Stat.*, 6 (1922).

and legislatures. Back of this insubstantial and delicate process of the mind with its purely nominal values or prices, is the great reality of production and consumption, prosperity and poverty, private wealth and commonwealth. We cannot, however, clearly see the connection between promises and reality, between prices and welfare, until we have seen another and most remarkable quality of this mental process, by which the courts have made mere promises actually to look and act like a commodity—the quality of negotiability.

III. INTANGIBLE PROPERTY—OPPORTUNITIES

1. *Negotiability*

We have described the change in meaning of the term property from the common-law meaning of physical things to the business-law meaning of the prices of things. The expected prices are imputed as a present value and become the assets, or expectations, which the business man entertains, of future transactions on the commodity markets. An even more momentous change from the common law to the business law was that which converted the mere promises of one person to another into commodities that could be bought and sold on the money and securities markets. " If it were asked," says McLeod,[1] " what discovery has most deeply affected the fortunes of the human race it might probably be said with truth—The discovery that a debt is a saleable commodity. When Daniel Webster said that credit has done more a thousand times to enrich nations than all the mines of all the world, he meant the discovery that a debt is a saleable commodity, or chattel; and that it may be used like money; and produce all the effects of money."

There were two circumstances which prevented the primitive common law from enforcing the assignment or negotiability of contracts,

---

[1] McLeod, H. D., *Theory and Practice of Banking*, 5th ed., 1:200. Further references on negotiability and assignment are as follows: Morse, John T., Jr., *Banks and Banking*, 4th ed., 1903; Holdsworth, W. S., "Origins and Early History of Negotiable Instruments," 31 *L. Q. R.* 12, 173, 376; 32 *L. Q. R.* 20 (1915–16); Jenks, Edward, "Early History of Negotiable Instruments," 9 *L. Q. R.* 70 (1893); Greer, F. A., "Custom in the Common Law," 9 *L. Q. R.* 153 (1893); Carter, A. T., "The Early History of the Law Merchant in England," 17 *L. Q. R.* 232 (1901); Ames, James Barr, "History of Assumpsit," 2 *Harv L. Rev.* 1, 53, 377 (1888); *Selected Essays in Anglo-American Legal History*, 3:259; Holdsworth, W. S., *A History of English Law*, 302 (1909); Pollock and Maitland, *History of English Law*, 2:226 (1911); Page on Contracts, 2343 *et passim* (1919); Pound, Roscoe, "Liberty of Contract," 18 *Yale Law Jour.* 454 (1909); Browne, J. H. B., *The Law of Usages and Customs* (1875).

namely, the concept of property as tangible objects and the concept of contract as a personal relation. The concept of tangible objects arises from man's dealings with physical nature; the concept of personal relations arises from the character and confidence imposed in individuals. While the business law in the 17th century was converting man's dealings with nature into the assets of a going concern, the same business law was eliminating the personality of individuals by converting their debts also into the assets and liabilities of a going concern.

The primitive mind could not conceive of property apart from physical possession. "Property" is really an intangible relation depending on the promises of government, such that a person may own an object that he cannot see. But "possession" is, in its original meaning, a physical relation of seeing, touching and holding tangible things. And if the thing cannot be physically handled yet that physical handling can be symbolized by another physical object which can be handled. Hence a class of promises embodied in such paper documents as deeds and bonds, the so-called "specialties," drafted in the presence of witnesses with great solemnity and loaded with the formidable seal of the grantor, symbolized physically to the owner and all others his direct holding of a physical object, in the case of a deed, or his indirect holding of the same to be delivered to him, in the case of a bond. The primitive mind could not grasp the underlying promise with its unseen foundation in the expected behavior of courts that enforce the promise, but must grasp it in the paper instrument with its huge decorated seal.

Survivals of this primitive materialism continue to the present day. In distinguishing the paper symbol of a deed, which had been altered and modified, from the "substance" of the promise contained in the deed, which had not been modified, Justice Holmes, in 1901, pointed out that, under the primitive law, "the alteration was a cancellation of the deed, having the same effect that tearing off the seals would have had. This rule comes down to us from a time when the contract contained in a sealed instrument was bound so indissolubly to the substance of the document that the soul perished with the body when the latter was destroyed or changed its identity for any cause." [1] And, in distinguishing a debt from the paper instrument which was merely an evidence of the debt, Justice Holmes also said,

[1] Bacon v. Hooker, 177 Mass. 335, 337 (1901).

in another case, " The debt is inseparable from the paper which declares and constitutes it, by a tradition that comes down from more
archaic conditions. Therefore, considering only the *place* of the property, it was held that bonds held out of the state could not be reached.
. . . But it is plain that the transfer does depend upon the law of
New York, not because of any theoretical speculation concerning the
whereabouts of the debt, but because of the practical fact of its power
over the person of the debtor . . . What gives the debt validity?
Nothing but the fact that the law of the place where the debtor
is will make him pay. Power over the person of the debtor confers jurisdiction." [1]

Thus has judicial analysis continually been called upon to go behind the primitive notions of physical things as the " substance " or
symbol of property and to find the reality of property, not in things
but in the promises of individuals supported by the promises of courts
to hold individuals responsible for the execution of their promises.
This outcome is a result of the several centuries of experience required
to work out the principle of the simple unsealed promise, made without formality which we have seen in the preceding section, and especially to work out the devices by which such promises could be bought
and sold.

There was another fundamental reason in primitive society ac-
counting for the non-negotiability of promises. Promises, express
or implied, are the foundation of human society. This is the root of
the doctrine that society originated in contract. But the contract
was not an original formal contract made once for all at the beginning of society and then interpreted afterwards by each individual,
but is a process of implied promises inferred from daily behavior according to the approved way of doing things at the time.[2] When a
person enters a room with others, he promises, by his very act of entrance, that he will not trespass, but will fall in line with the custom of that kind of gathering. Such promises are personal. They
are made between the persons then living and acting together. But
while personal, they are not individual. They are collective. An
injury to one is the concern of all who are acting together. In primitive society these collective expectations absorbed the individual

---

[1] Blackstone *v.* Miller, 188 U. S. 189, 205, 206 (1903).
[2] "It is custom that writes out slowly from generation to generation the terms of the social compact." GREER, F. A., "Custom in the Common Law," 9 *Law Quar. Rev.* 153 (1893).

in the group, such that the violation of express or implied promises must be atoned vicariously by other members of the group and by the children of the wrongdoer, while the recompense accrued not alone to the individual injured but to his group and his children. Thus the blood feud, hereditary serfdom, fixed status of individuals, and communism, followed the primitive notions of collective responsibility and collective power to enforce responsibility.

When the individual emerged out of the group it was by stages and by classes of individuals, first the landed proprietors by conquest, second the capitalists by participation in sovereignty, third the laborers. This emergence consisted in the equality and liberty of the individuals constituting the class, retaining superiority and command over individuals of classes not yet participating in sovereignty. Between superior and inferior the promise was the involuntary one of protection and obedience, and its enforcement was in the hands of the superior. Between equals the promise was the voluntary one of reciprocal service, and its enforcement was accomplished, as we have seen, by the judiciary, who took away from individuals the power of private enforcement while recognizing the binding character of the promise.

Such recognition of the promises of reciprocal service between equals consisted in allowing equal liberty to make individual promises and the accompanying individual responsibility to fulfill the promise. As such, the resulting contract did not bind a successor of the one who promised nor did its benefits accrue to a successor of the one to whom the promise was so made. Likewise, the liability to make redress for violation of the custom could not be vicariously transferred to another, neither could the one to whom redress is owed transfer his claim to another, but the compensation must be rendered in person by the wrongdoer and satisfaction must be obtained in person by the sufferer. Neither may the liability survive the life of the wrongdoer nor the claim to redress survive the life of the injured individual, else it ends in blood feud, or in the hereditary relation of slavery and serfdom which nullifies the equality and liberty of individuals in the same class. The law of equality and liberty of the individual is, then, the law of non-transferability and non-survivorship of both the right to recompense and the duty to make recompense, while the law of slavery or status was the law of transferability and survivorship of the rights of the superior and the duties of the inferior.

Thus it was that, after the law of creditor and debtor had been perfected in the sixteenth century, it required still another century to convert the personal relations of creditor and debtor between equals, as conceived in the common law of liberty and equality, into the property relation of assets and liabilities. This consisted in inventing the transferability and survivorship of promises freed from the personality of the parties to the promise. And so substantial has been the transformation that these mere promises between equals, which constitute the debts of the credit system, can themselves be treated, in law and popular thought, like commodities, to be bought and sold like other commodities, though they are neither commodities nor slaves nor serfs treated like commodities, but are a mental expectation arising out of confidence in the promises of governments, courts and business men.

The essential requirement of business practice was to convert these promises of freemen into something as nearly like money as possible. Primitive buying and selling was barter—the direct exchange of movable products. Even when money was introduced the exchange for money was but a barter of coins for products, and both were chattels. This constituted strictly a money bargain as distinguished from a credit-bargain or price-bargain. No credit-bargain was recognized, the "action of debt" being an action to recover coins or chattels unlawfully held, just as the "action of right" to land was an action to recover land forcibly detained.[1] They were actions to recover physical property, not actions to enforce promises. In so far as mere promises were enforced, involving no idea of unlawful assault, trespass or theft, they were matters of conscience or honor, and the court to which appeal could be made was only either the priest in the confessional or the wager of battle to ward off dishonor.

It was similar with the relation of landlord and tenant. Being a personal relation, the rent bargain and its resulting contract could not be transferred by either the landlord or the tenant to another landlord or tenant, without the consent of the other party. The King's tenant could not alienate his tenancy without consent of the King; and the sub-tenants down the line could not alienate without consent of their immediately superior landlord.

The same was true of other contracts. A contract, being a personal relation between creditor and debtor, could not be sold by the creditor to a third party, nor assumed on behalf of the debtor by another

[1] Above, p. 238.

debtor, without the consent of the adverse party to the original contract. Being personal promises of oath and fidelity, or of reciprocal personal service of equals, the common-law lawyers could not see how other parties not originally bound to each other in good faith could become so unless they also personally pledged themselves to each other in a similar confidence.

Thus, at common law, the assignment of contractual rights, being the voluntary promises of two parties equal and free, was of no effect if the opposite party did not consent to the assignment. The relation between the two was a personal relation arising out of personal confidence, and not a property relation arising out of the transfer of the physical things. Wherever this personal relation continues, indeed, to prevail at the present day, the contract continues to be non-transferable. A promise to marry cannot be assigned by the promisee to a third party, nor negotiated upon the market. A promise to perform any special service depending on the contingencies of character or skill of the promisor cannot be transferred.

The highest and most complete type of assignability is negotiability, which consists in a promise to pay a definite sum of money, without condition, at a definite time and place. Here the personal element is as nearly eliminated as possible, so much so that a third party to whom the promise is legally transferred, can bring suit in his own name as though the promise were made to him personally. And in doing so, he is free of all defenses of fraud or offsets which the debtor might have set up against the party with whom the contract was actually made. The bearer of certain negotiable paper takes even a stronger title than that possessed by the original creditor, for he takes it free from defect in title and free of equities against the creditor from whom he received it; and the anomaly is created of authorizing a person to sell more than he owns. The debtor must pay and then bring suit against the original creditor who has presumed to sell more than he owned.

It was this anomaly that persisted in the minds of the common-law judges until the legislature was compelled to intervene. As late as 1704, Chief Justice Holt refused enforcement of the promissory notes of the goldsmiths of London, payable to bearer on demand, and constituting the modern bank note. These promissory notes, he said, "are only an invention of the goldsmiths in Lombard street who had a mind to make a law to bind all those that did deal with them; and sure to allow such a note to carry any lien with it were to turn a piece of paper, which is in law but evidence of a parol contract, into a specialty; and besides it would empower one to assign that to another which he could not have himself; for since he to whom this note was made could not have this action, how can his assignee have it?" [1] It required an Act of Parliament to reverse this common-law theory of Justice Holt.[2]

While the negotiability of promissory notes was thus long delayed, it had been a rather simple matter to bring about recognition of the negotiability of bills of exchange, including their modern development, the checks drawn by a depositor on the bank. A bill or check is an order by a creditor upon his debtor to pay to a third party designated, or even to any third party, "the bearer," a part or the whole of the debt owing. The first recorded case recognizing the negotiability of bills of exchange in England was decided in 1603.[3] This related to a foreign bill of exchange, and negotiation was easily allowed since international trade was distinct from domestic trade and came under a mercantile custom common to merchants of all lands. But once started in this direction, the negotiability of inland bills was afterwards slowly allowed. At first, both for bills and notes, it was necessary to set out and prove the custom of merchants, but after 1695 and 1704, the courts began to assume "judicial knowledge" of the custom and hence a mere declaration of the custom was good.[4] At first the courts applied the law only to those who were actually merchants, then it was extended to all traders and dealers, and finally, in 1689, an acceptor who was not actually a merchant was forbidden to deny that he was.[5] Thus, by a process extending through a hundred years, aided by equity and legislation, of gradually taking away the defenses which at common law the debtor could set up against paying his debt, the bona fide holder of the debtor's promise could not only sue in his own name even though the promise had not been made to him personally, but could even have a stronger case at law than that of the original creditor; and that which had been a personal relation between definite individuals became the assets and liabilities of a going business,

---

[1] Buller v. Crips, 6 Mod. 29 (1702). But see McLEOD, *Theory and Practice of Banking*, 1:224 ff., who contended that Justice Holt was wrong and that promissory notes were negotiable at common law. This contention overlooks the decisive fact that Lord Holt was one of the most eminent of the common-law lawyers.

[2] 3 and 4 Anne c. 7, 1705.

[3] Martin v. Boure, Cro. Jac. 6 (1603).

[4] Williams v. Williams, Carthew, 269 (1693); Bromwich v. Lloyd, 2 Lutw. 1582 (1704).

[5] Sarsfield v. Witherly, Carth. 82 (1689).

independent of the persons, past, present or future, who might actually constitute the concern.

It can be seen, therefore, why it is that modern capitalism begins with the assignment and negotiability of contracts. They accomplish two purposes, a low rate of interest and a rapid turnover of capital. The two operate together. Capitalism could scarcely survive on a 10% or 20% rate of interest and a turnover once or twice a year. It has survived on a 3% to 6% rate of interest and a turnover three to five times a year. The difference is cumulative. Ten per cent a year on capital turned over once a year means an overhead cost of obtaining capital ten times as great as 5% a year on capital turned over 5 times a year. The same amount of capital does five times as much work at one-half the rate of interest.

Shortly after the middle of the 17th century in the year 1668, when the legal process of assignment and negotiability above mentioned was half-way accomplished in England, Sir Joshua Child, the great English exponent of Mercantilism, compared the advantages which Holland enjoyed contrasted with England, where the current rate of interest was 3% in "peaceable times" compared with a legal rate of 6% in England, and the turnover of capital was twice or thrice that of England. This "turnover," as it now would be named, was accomplished in Holland, said Child, by "the law that is in use among them for transference of bills of debt from one man to another; this is of extraordinary advantage to them in their commerce; by means whereof they can turn their stocks twice or thrice in trade, for once that we can in England; for that, having sold our foreign goods here, we cannot buy again to advantage, till we are possessed of our money; which it may be we shall be six, nine or twelve months in recovering: and if what we sell be considerable, it is a good man's work all the year to be following vintners and shopkeepers for money. Whereas, were the law of transferring bills in practice with us, we could presently after the sale of our goods dispose of our bills, and close up our accounts." [1]

And Sir Joshua proposed a cumbersome piece of legislation authorizing assignment, equivalent to the modern "acceptance," which, however, was, within the next thirty years accomplished, as we have just noted, by the simple method of judicial recognition and

[1] CHILD, SIR JOSHUA, "A New Discourse of Trade," original, 1668. See *Dict. of Pol. Econ.* (6th ed. of 1804).

enforcement of the customs of merchants. "The great advantage," he said, "that would accrue to this kingdom by a law for transferring bills of debt from one person to another, is sufficiently understood by most men, especially by merchants. The difficulty seems not to be so much in making of a law to this purpose, as reducing it to practice; because we have been so long accustomed to buy and sell goods by verbal contracts only, that rich and great men for some time will be apt to think it a diminution of their reputation to have bills under their hands and seals demanded of them for goods bought, and meaner men will fear the losing of their customers by insisting upon having such bills for what they sell." These compunctions of the great and the meaner men have long since given way, as we know, before the greater economy of buying and selling short-term promises at the commercial banks. Twenty years after the perfection of negotiability of promises, by the Act of 1704, the rate of discount at the Bank of England had fallen to 2½%, and has since fluctuated between 2% and 7% according to business conditions.

2. *Commodity Tickets and Price Tickets*

This remarkable innovation of negotiability, which took an entire century for its accomplishment from the first decision on bills of exchange in 1603 to the parliamentary reversal of Lord Chief Justice Holt in 1704, while it established modern capitalism, yet introduced the most disturbing confusion between primitive notions of physical commodities and the new notion of a promise acting like a commodity. Stock-jobbing frenzies for the first time seized upon the minds of Englishmen in 1792,[1] the Mississippi Bubble and the South Sea Bubble overwhelmed France in 1716 and England in 1718, and a recurring cycle of inflation and contraction, prosperity and depression set in for two hundred years so regularly that learned men ascribed it to the sun, to Venus, to human nature, to human depravity, until, in more recent times, it is seen to be the workings of the clever invention of negotiability of promises. What negotiability actually introduced was the phenomena of two opposite markets, two opposite classes of legal claims to commodities or services, and two opposing concepts of value. The two markets are the commodity markets and the money markets; the two classes of legal claims may be contrasted as commodity tickets and price tickets, and the

[1] MACAULAY, T. B., *History of England*, 4:256. (1856).

two concepts of value are the real value assigned to commodities or labor and the nominal value expressed in prices.

Every productive enterprise carries on these two lines of business, the business of buying, storing, enlarging and selling quantities of real value or real wealth in the form of commodities and labor, and the business of creating, buying, selling, offsetting and cancelling promises to pay the nominal value or price of that real value or real wealth. The former kind of business is carried on at factories, retail and wholesale stores, railroads, theatres, warehouses, produce exchanges, farms, real estate markets, where people deliver commodities or labor power and transfer the titles to them. Every factory is a kind of warehouse in which raw material and labor are "deposited" to reappear in a few weeks or months as a finished product. Every wholesale or retail store is a warehouse where finished goods and the labor of salesmen are bought and stored to be sold in a few days or weeks. So with every farm, every railroad, every workshop, every theater, and so on. These are the commodity markets and labor markets of the country, and the operations there going on constitute that process which we have named a going plant with its producing organization, creating the real values and real wealth of the country.

But the business of creating, buying, selling, offsetting and cancelling the promises to pay the *prices* which are negotiated on the commodity markets is conducted at commercial banks which are the money markets of the country. The "going business" of any concern connects its commodity market and its money market, for it is the business on the commodity markets, of buying and selling, hiring and hiring out, renting and leasing, and the business on the money market of borrowing and lending, discounting and depositing promises to pay the prices of commodities in lawful money within 24 hours to 90 days.

Historically the legal transition is the transition from bailments, which are commodity tickets, to debts, which are price tickets. The Bank of Amsterdam and the Goldsmiths of London began their "banking" business as warehouses for the storage of gold and silver and the issue of warehouse certificates to depositors for the amount of the commodity, gold or silver, which they had stored. The survival of that warehouse business is seen in the American gold and silver "certificates." Latterly, finding that all of this commodity in storage was not called for at any one moment, they violated their pledge of storage, loaned their depositors' money to other people at a profit, and issued their commodity tickets in excess of the quantity of commodity on hand. This violation of a pledge, if practiced by an ordinary warehouseman, would constitute an unlawful conversion of bailment, since, in such a case, the deposited commodity, such as wheat or gold, is not the property of the warehouseman to loan or sell to others, but is the property of the depositor. In order that this unlawful practice of the goldsmiths might become lawful, it was necessary for the courts to substitute a *sale* of gold to the banker for a *deposit* of gold by the customer, and to substitute a *debt* of the banker to the customer for a *bailment* of the customer to the warehouse. The warehouseman now became the owner of the commodity instead of a bailee, and the former owner became a creditor, owning a bank note, instead of a depositor owning the commodity. This was the unlawful "invention of the goldsmiths in Lombard street who had a mind to make a law" different from the common law, that stirred the wrath of Chief Justice Holt and required an act of parliament to overrule him.

Yet the names "deposit" and "depositor" were retained in banking practice in order not to break with that conservative materialism of the human mind which insists on tangible evidence, although the depositor had changed from owner of a thing to creditor of the bank. This retention of the primitive materialism was convenient under the practice of bank checks, although the depositor now deposits not a commodity but his own or his customer's promise to pay, and the bank, through the device of negotiability, becomes, not the warehouseman, but the owner of that promise. "Money" now becomes, not a corporeal property, gold or silver, but bank credit, having the two legal qualities of incorporeal property, the demand-promise of the banker, and intangible property, the exchange-value of that promise on the markets. And this kind of money becomes elastic since its volume changes with the prices that business men agree to pay for commodities. Thus the transition is accomplished from a commodity ticket, or bailment, calling for a specific corporeal property, gold or silver, to a price-ticket, or bank credit, calling for any commodity at its then exchange-value.

The commodity ticket is, in effect, a title of ownership of corporeal property, the price-ticket is a negotiable promise. The significance of commodity tickets is originally that of corporeal property, the ownership of physical things, even real estate, whose ownership does not pass by physical delivery, but by recording the ticket which is the title of ownership. So with all commodities, that is, chattels. I hand you physically a bushel of potatoes, but I do not pass the title to you unless there goes with it an evidence which the law acknowledges as transfer of ownership. Thus all titles of ownership are commodity tickets authorized by government, being evidences of ownership regardless of changes in the value of the thing owned.

These titles of ownership slip over into that huge class of bailments, wherein something of a personal nature is delivered to another to be held but not owned and to be returned to self or delivered to third parties, the evidence being recorded on such tickets as warehouse receipts, dock warrants, bills of lading and those original deposits of the Bank of Amsterdam and the goldsmiths of London, or even not recorded, as in the case of goods hired or left for repair.

Bailments, which are promises to deliver *things*, shift into what may broadly be designated *futures*, which are promises to deliver the *values* of things—as when an iron manufacturer promises to deliver a quantity of iron or its value, or when a banker promises to deliver gold or its equivalent checking account, which is, in reality only an account set off against other debtors of that or other banks. But it has therefore the great value of liquidating debts.

These specific futures slide into speculative futures, to which the name "futures" is usually attached, where either party, not having the thing itself, expects to buy or borrow it on the market or to deliver the then market price as of the date of delivery, or at least the "margin" between the agreed and the then market price.

But commodity tickets themselves finally comprehend even the entire range of incorporeal and intangible properties as well as corporeal property, since, with the device of negotiability, stocks, bonds, debentures, warrants, bills of lading and so on have been rendered as nearly like money as possible, and may be passed readily from hand to hand along with their titles of ownership.

There remains, however, in all these transactions, the distinguishing character of commodity tickets, whether they be claims to real estate, chattels, bailed goods, futures, or even all incorporeal and intangible properties, namely, that the commodity ticket changes in value exactly as the value of the thing itself to which the ticket lays title. But it is different with the price-ticket, money. Money is power to obtain in exchange, not a specific thing, but power to obtain *anything* at the then price of anything. A warehouse receipt calls for a *given number* of bushels of wheat stored in an elevator; but a price-ticket calls for *any* number of bushels of wheat at the then price of wheat. If the wheat rises in price the price-ticket obtains a smaller number of bushels; if the wheat falls in price the price-ticket obtains a larger number of bushels.

Hence it is that, although the two kinds of business of every concern on the commodity markets and the money market are inseparable, yet they are likely to move off remarkably in different directions with very different social effects. I sell to you 1,000 tons of pig iron at $20 per ton and you promise to pay me $20,000 in 60 days. I take your promise to the bank and the bank gives me a deposit of $20,000, less the discount. The bank writes down on its books under the heading "loans and discounts" $20,000 *receivable* in 60 days, and under the heading "deposits" $20,000 *payable* on demand.

But suppose I sell that thousand tons of pig iron at $40 per ton. You now promise to pay me $40,000. I now take your promise to the bank and get a loan and a deposit of $40,000. It is the same quantity of pig iron. There is no change in the commodity. It is deposited in a warehouse or converted into stoves or steel. I have transferred the title or bill of lading to you—have given to you a commodity ticket that calls for 1,000 tons—and have taken from you a promise that calls for $20,000 or $40,000, as the case may be, in lawful money in 60 days. The bank then underwrites that promise by agreeing that that price was a going price, that you and I are good for that price in 60 days, and by issuing to me its own negotiable promise to pay that price on demand. This "deposit" is a price-ticket, good at any bank in payment of debts.

The significance of it is that the commodity ticket and the price-ticket move off in different directions, since they are independent variables on different markets. If a warehouse company promises to deliver 1,000 tons of real value on demand, in the form of pig iron which has been "deposited" at the warehouse, it receives and delivers 1,000 tons regardless of whether the nominal value changes meanwhile from $20,000 to $40,000 or from $20,000 to $10,000. But if a bank promises to deliver the *price* of that pig iron on demand it does so irrespective of whether the $20,000 will, within the same 60 days, purchase 1,000 tons or only 500 tons. The warehouse deals in commodities regardless of changes in their prices; the bank deals in prices irrespective of changes in the quantity of commodities. The commodity ticket calls for 1,000 tons of pig iron regardless of whether or not its price changes from $20,000 to $40,000. But the price-ticket calls for a price of, say, $20,000, regardless of whether the price afterwards will purchase 1,000 tons or only 500 tons.

A commodity ticket is good at a warehouse, a factory, a farm, because it is simply a title of ownership, a bill of lading, a warehouse receipt, a claim to a seat or standing room in a theater or street car, which calls for a *given quantity* of commodity or service. But a price-ticket is good at a bank because it is a check drawn on a "bank deposit" at one of the banks for a *given price* of that commodity or service. A valid commodity ticket is good on its specific commodity market. A properly authenticated price-ticket is good on any commodity market and any money market. A commodity ticket follows the specified commodity with every change of ownership, regardless of changes in its price. But a price-ticket petrifies the price of that commodity on a given day at the bank and then circulates that price around from bank to bank for 30 to 90 days, regardless of changes in the quantity of that commodity which that petrified price meanwhile will purchase.

It is here that the public purpose of that negotiable promise, a price-ticket, or bank deposit, may be discovered. The two kinds of business on the commodity markets and the money markets correspond to two ways of getting rich or making a profit in business. One is by increasing the quantity of products or reducing their costs without raising prices; the other is by getting higher prices without increasing the quantity of products. The first method is that of increasing the quantity of commodities with a stable level of prices; the second is that of marking up the level of prices without increasing the quantity of commodities. The first is an increase of output, the second is relatively a restriction of output. The first is the *productive* method of making a profit by increasing the welfare of the community. The second is a *speculative* method of making a profit by taking it out of other people whose prices are not moving up as fast and hence without furnishing to them a corresponding increase of real wealth.

The commercial banks themselves do not clearly distinguish this public point of view from this private point of view, for two reasons: they are interested in the solvency of borrowers and they are interested in their own reserves of lawful money, and not in the movement of the general level of prices. In other words, they have no common rule of public policy to guide them. A pig-iron producer is perhaps as good a risk for a bank deposit of $40,000 when the *price* of pig iron moves up from $20 to $40 a ton if his customer's prices for their products are also moving up, as when the *quantity* of pig iron, which he sells, moves up from 1,000 tons to 2,000 tons at $20 per ton. In either case the bank can perhaps safely lend the producer $40,000 and thereby create "new credit," which is equivalent to creating "new money."

But there is a great difference in the public consequences of the two methods of creating new money. The first method creates new money because prices are being marked up. The second creates it because real wealth is being enlarged. In the second case the bank guarantees the public, in effect, that the quantity of real wealth has been doubled. But in the first case the bank guarantees only that the *price* of that wealth has been doubled. This is because the marking up of nominal values, or prices, by the business community is accompanied by the marking up, on both sides of the bank's books, of approximately just that amount of increase in the total volume of bank loans and bank deposits, or price tickets. It is simply a marking up of promises by business men ratified by a marking up of promises by bankers.

This is the second reason for the banker's private point of view, namely, the ratio of his reserves of lawful money to the volume of checks which he has promised to pay on demand. Were it a matter of a barter economy or a metallic money economy, there would be little or no elasticity in the supply of the commodity which the producer furnishes. But the bank is not dealing in commodities, it is dealing in promises to pay lawful money. And the volume of its promises to pay on demand may be as great as the risks it is willing to take on the chance of having enough lawful money on hand to meet a run of outgoing checks presented by customers and other banks in excess of the run of incoming checks deposited by customers and drawn on other banks. If the two are about equal, then the bank merely offsets one promise on its books by other promises, and its total liabilities remain constant.

But if it has greatly increased its volume of demand promises by guranteeing an increased volume of price-agreements between business men, then the volume of outgoing checks increases without a corresponding increase in the volume of incoming checks. And, since the volume of lawful money, constituting the reserves which it has promised to pay on demand, is like the volume of other commodities in that it cannot be increased merely by issuing more promises but must be increased only by buying or producing more commodities, then the ratio of lawful money to the volume of demand promises falls, the risks are increased, and the bank begins to withhold its issue of promises. From the bank's point of view, this is the process of inflation and deflation—inflation is the increase of deposits relative to bank reserves of lawful money, deflation is the decrease of deposits relative to bank reserves.

But from the public standpoint, inflation is a general rise of prices without a corresponding increase in the quantity of products, and deflation is a general fall of prices without a corresponding decrease in the quantity of products.

The reconciliation of the two points of view is to be accomplished by the adoption of a working rule stabilizing the general level of prices, such that price-tickets calling for nominal values, shall always call for as nearly as possible the same quantity of real values, and such that banks will not insure business men in making profits on the mere rise of prices to be followed by a general collapse, but will insure them in making profits on an increase in the quantities and a reduction in the costs of commodities to be followed by a general increase in public welfare.[1]

3. Goodwill and Privilege

Every social relation involves, for our present purpose,[2] at least three parties, who may be named the first, the second and the third party. The first party is self. The second is an opposite party, say a debtor, an agent, an employee or a bargainer. The third party is a possible disturber of the relation between the first and the second party, say a trespasser, an intruder, a competitor, an infringer.

Furthermore, every act, for our present purpose,[3] is either a positive act which we name a *performance*, or a negative act (an "omission," negative performance), which we name an *avoidance*.

---

[1] Practicable details are discussed by IRVING FISHER, *Purchasing Power of Money* (1911) and *Stabilizing the Dollar* (1920); by G. CASSEL, *The Nature and Necessity of Interest* (1903); *The Money Market and Foreign Exchange after 1914* (1922); *The World's Monetary Problems* (1921); and by R. G. HAWTREY, *Currency and Credit* (1919) and *Monetary Reconstruction* (1923); FOSTER and CATCHINGS, *Money*, (1923).

[2] Above, Chap. IV, Sec. I, p. 66 ff.

[3] Above, Chap. IV, Sec. II, p. 78.

An encumbrance, then, may be either positive or negative, that is, a performance or an avoidance, and it is proper to name it an encumbrance in either case, because it limits the field of liberty of him upon whom it is enforced. If the encumbrance is positive, that is, a performance, it means that the *opposite* party is required positively to perform an act, to pay a debt, to obey the commands of the principal or the employer. He has no option. It is this form of encumbrance which we have distinguished as the labor encumbrance and the investor encumbrance, or incorporeal property.

If the encumbrance, however, is negative, that is, an avoidance, it means that a *third party* is restrained from committing an act, for example, to trespass, intrude, or compete, and therefore is constrained to direct his behavior elsewhere. Each deducts from the field of free behavior of another party. The duty of performance deducts positively from the field which the second party already controls; the duty of avoidance constrains a third party to push elsewhere the boundaries of his field of control, if he can.

If the matter at issue is a positive encumbrance, the relation of debtor and creditor, then the duty of performance imposed on the second party implies a duty of avoidance imposed on all third parties. An encumbrance is thus two-fold: a duty of performance which deducts from the liberty of the *second party* and a duty of avoidance which deducts from the liberty of any *third party*.

Now, opportunities differ from encumbrances in that the *second party*, a bargainer, is burdened by no duty either of performance or avoidance within the field where the transaction occurs. He may be, and is, encumbered, at other points of the matter at issue, by a duty of avoidance. He must not carry his liberty too far beyond the limit of allowable deception or coercion. But beyond that limit he is free to negotiate, to offer alternatives, to persuade or coerce, to withhold or yield, bound by no encumbrance either of performance or avoidance, just as the first party is also free. Within this field of opportunity the relation between the first and second party is that of liberty, the absence of duties.

But a third party, the possible trespasser or competitor, is burdened only by a duty of avoidance. Up to a certain point he must not intrude between the first and second parties to the potential bargain. Up to that point he must avoid physical disturbance, or trespass, and competitive disturbance, or infringement.

For the sake of brevity of discourse it is not customary to state explicitly the part played by third parties either in the case of encumbrances or opportunities. Third parties are usually "all the world," and it is usually enough to take for granted the negative encumbrance, the avoidance, or duty to not-do something, which is imposed upon their liberty of action. Generally, we shall speak of the second party as the *opposite* party, since the duty of avoidance is imposed on third parties for the sake of the transactions with opposite parties. The terms encumbrance and opportunity therefore will be usually employed with reference only to the transactions between first and second parties. Thus limited, but with third parties always implied and taken for granted, an encumbrance is a positive duty of the opposite party; an opportunity is an absence of both the positive duty of performance and the negative duty of avoidance.

But third parties cannot always be taken for granted. Individuals emerge out of "all the world" as specific persons at critical points. It is, for example, a third party (possible competitor) who sells his liberty to compete when he sells the goodwill of his business, or who is restrained from unfair competition or fraud when the court protects the goodwill or trade-mark of the first party. In either case there is imposed upon him, as a third party, not a general, but a more specific and limited duty of avoidance that originates the law of goodwill and privilege.

The law of goodwill was tardier in its development than the law of encumbrances. It was not until the year 1620 that what appears to have been the first decision was handed down to the effect that a person might lawfully sell his liberty along with his business. The opinion was given in the highest court of the common law, and then was appealed to "all the justices and barons of the Exchequer." That the matter contained a doubt is revealed in the dissent of one of the justices. The opinion aroused great interest and was recorded by all of the reporters of that day,[1] for it legalized a restraint of trade by stretching the common law at the very time of intense excitement over those restraints of trade which the sovereign had been exercising by stretching his prerogative.

A merchant had sold his stock of goods at a price in excess of their inventory value, and, in selling, had agreed not to set himself up in

---

[1] Jollyfe against Brode (1620–21), Cro. Jac. 596; Noy, 98; 2 Rolle, 201; W. Jones, 13. Referred to in Taylors of Exeter, 3 Lev. 241 (1686).

competition with the business of the purchaser. He violated his promise, suit was brought against him by the purchaser for damages, and decided in the latter's favor. Prior to that time contracts in restraint of trade seem uniformly to have been held void and even criminal, and the only case on record in which an English judge is reported to have resorted to profanity in rendering his decision was in the case of a dyer in the year 1417 [1] who had agreed under bond not to practice his craft within the town for a certain period of time. The bond was declared void and the dyer was absolved by the court from compliance. So the decisions had uniformly run against agreements in restraint of trade from the year 1417 until, in 1620, this exception was made, thus laying one of the cornerstones of the modern law of goodwill.

At about the time when it was thus first decided, in 1620, that a person could lawfully sell a part of his liberty, reference was made, in a different case,[2] to an earlier case in 1580 which, however, had not been reported, in which it was alleged to have been held that a competitor might lawfully be deprived of a part of his liberty to compete, even though he had not consented to it. In the year 1580 it was said, a clothier alleged that "he had gained great reputation for his making of his cloth, by reason whereof he had great utterance to his great benefit and profit, and that he used to set his mark to his cloth, whereby it should be known to be his cloth; and another clothier perceiving it, used the same mark to his ill-made cloth on purpose to deceive him." He brought suit against the infringer and the case was decided on the question of extending the writ of "trespass on the case" so as to afford a remedy for injury to business. The court now decided, in 1580, that the "action did well lie." The development of this form of action has already been mentioned in connection with the law of *enforcement of contract;* [3] here we note the way in which it split off into the law of bargaining, the law of *liberty of contract.* In the latter case it indicates the gradual and scarcely perceptible enlargement of the law from the protection of physical property to the protection of intangible property after the latter had emerged with the extension of markets. The ancient "writ of trespass" had

---

[1] Year Book, 2 Hen. V, fol. V, pl. 26 (1417) Judge Hull said: "By God, if the plaintiff were here he should go to prison until he pay a fine to the King."

[2] Poph. 144 (1618) referring to an opinion said to have been given in 22 Eliz. See Wigmore, Select Cases on the Law of Torts, 1:318.

[3] Above, Sec. II, p. 239.

been a form of action at common law, based on an allegation of violence done to the body, or a forcible entrance on the plaintiff's lands or chattels.   Then the term "trespass" was so extended as to include every species of wrong causing an injury.   This made it possible for the common-law courts to expand the law of torts along with the expansion of markets, so that, by easy steps from the Act of Parliament in 1285 [1] to the trade-mark case in 1580, injury to physical property became injury to business, violence became unfair competition, trespass became infringement.

Thus the two cornerstones of the law of goodwill were laid, in 1580 and 1620, in the action to recover damages to intangible property and in sustaining a voluntary sale of one's liberty along with one's business.   It is significant as already suggested, that this first recorded case in which a voluntary agreement in restraint of trade was enforced by the court occurred in the decade following the great decision which nullified both the monopolies and the involuntary restraints of trade by the gilds under patents and charters granted by the Crown.   In the Case of Monopolies, already referred to, two of the three grounds on which the Queen's patent to Lord Darcy was held to be against the common law were the increase in price and the decrease in quality of the product, for, said the court, the patentee is not "skilled in the trade" and must turn over the actual making of the playing cards to artisans, whereas, he himself, "having the sole trade, regards only his private benefit and not the common wealth." [2]

Likewise in the Case of the Merchant Tailors of London (1599) the by-law requiring members to share their bargains with fellow-members was adjudged a monopoly and void under the common law, although the by-law was authorized under a charter long before granted by the King. [3]

These decisions from the King's Bench established, against the King's prerogative, a common-law rule against monopolies and charters in restraint of trade, on the ground, partly, of the power of oppressing the public, that is, "the common wealth," which the King thereby had placed in private hands.   With these privileged restraints cleared away it became possible to clear the air for the en-

---

[1] Above, Sec. II, p. 239.

[2] Above, p. 227.

[3] Another by-law of the Tailors of Ipswich (11 Co. 53 b. 1615), was nullified on similar grounds, but by-laws to enforce a "custom" were held good. The cases are distinguished in Mitchell v. Reynolds, below.

forcement of such unprivileged restraints as did not oppress the commonwealth. Notwithstanding the prices charged might be even higher than those charged by competitors yet the test of whether the customer received a commensurate benefit was left to be determined by the customer himself on the assumption that he was free to go elsewhere if not satisfied.

Nearly a hundred years after the transaction of 1620, Justice Parker, in 1711,[1] stated the law regarding voluntary restraints of trade as it had evolved meanwhile, and his opinion is the recognized guide for all subsequent opinions. He distinguished voluntary from coerced restraints (the latter being always unlawful) and "general" restraints from "particular" restraints. Voluntary restraints, by agreement of the parties, are void if they are "general" in extent, that is, if they extend throughout the Kingdom, and this is so even if a consideration is paid in exchange for the agreement not to compete.[2] "No man can contract not to use his trade at all," "since the public interest requires that he should not remain in idleness." "Particular" restraints are those limited to places or persons, and these are also void if there was no consideration, but are lawful if "made upon a good and adequate consideration, so as to make it a proper and useful contract." Even "a particular restraint is not good without just reason and consideration." Although the law presumes in favor of liberty, yet, just as a man may part with his property, so he may part with a part of his liberty, if "by his own consent, for a valuable consideration." And, having accepted compensation for his promise not to compete he will be compelled by the court to keep his promise, if within the particular limits.

But it was not until the year 1743 that the term "goodwill" first crept into the decisions, and then only by way of illustrating a different matter.[3] Again, in the year 1769, the term was used in the copyright case, by Justice Yates, in order to show, by illustration, that a common-law copyright could not be held to be property. Good-

---

[1] Mitchell v. Reynolds, 1 P. Wms. 185–189 (1711).

[2] This limitation has been enlarged in later times by the rule that it may extend to the area of the entire country if the business that is sold extends actually that far. However, it is doubtful whether the purchaser can insist that the vendor retire completely from his kind of business, though this depends on the extent to which the court resists the tendency to monopoly or the encouragement of idleness on the part of the seller. Nims, Unfair Competition, 2d ed. 38 ff. (1917); 1 Page on Contracts (1905), 589 ff.; Nordenfeldt v. Maxim-Nordenfeldt Guns and Ammunitions Co., App. Cas. 535 (1894).

[3] Gibblett v. Read, 9 Mod. 459 (1743); below, p. 274.

will, he said, was not property because the purchaser "has no power to *confine* it to himself," since the customer may withdraw the next day if he pleases. Furthermore, he cannot "use any power to *prevent other people* from gaining the custom." In this opinion Justice Yates adhered to the common-law notion of property as pertaining only to physical things, though the majority, in that case, took a different view as respects copyright.[1]

It was not until the beginning of the Nineteenth Century that the meaning of goodwill had broadened out to cover the whole field of competition, so that the Chancellor, Lord Eldon, in 1803, could give to it the first indication of its more modern statement of the law of "fair" and "unfair" competition. Lord Eldon, while usually charged with limiting the term to what may be termed "location" goodwill, recognized two other types which may be distinguished as personal goodwill and business goodwill, or the goodwill of a going business.[2] Location goodwill, he said, is "nothing more than the probability that the old customers will resort to the old place." In this respect it was merely a special case of land value, and the enjoyment of the benefits of location could not be enjoined by a court of equity without interfering with the owner's legitimate use of his land.

But fraud, or unfair competition, presented a different case. If there is fair competition, there is no damage or injury. The injunction is granted by Lord Eldon, not to prevent the "fair course of improving a trade in which it was lawful to engage," but to prevent representing it to be the trade of an established business built up by another.[3]

But goodwill, after all, begins as personal goodwill. It is built up by the efforts of individuals. The individual may sell his location goodwill or his business goodwill, but still carry his personal goodwill with him. In order that this too may be sold he must agree to contract away his future liberty. Indeed, what the vendor sells is not a physical thing but a market opportunity which yields a certain net income, and in order to give effect to the sale he must part with his liberty to do certain acts which diminish this income. The "physical" part of this opportunity is apparently only the bodies of his customers whose patronage he has obtained and which is expected to

[1] Below, Sec. IV, p. 277.
[2] Hogg *v.* Kirby, 8 Ves. 215 (1803); Cruttwell *v.* Lye, 17 Ves. 335, 346 (1810).
[3] 8 Ves. (1803).

continue. What he has actually sold, however, is not his customers, but his liberty to sell commodities to his customers. And what the purchaser of the goodwill buys is not commodities, but is an exclusive right to the liberty of selling certain commodities to customers. He has truly bought something intangible. He has bought the right to control the supply of commodities through buying an expectation that government will restrain the bodies of competitors if they attempt to supply that particular commodity. The mere ownership of land, physical capital, or commodities has no significance for a business economy unless accompanied by access to a market, and access to a market has no significance without power to control the supply and fix the prices of things offered on the market. Historically, as we have noticed, the right of access to a commodity market began as a special privilege, granted to merchants, merchant gilds, craft gilds, money lenders, or favored courtiers in the form of patents, charters, or other special protection by the sovereign. These special privileges were done away with, not by abolishing the privileges, but by making them universal—by extending the right equally to all citizens, and eventually, by treaties, to aliens.

This then became the universal, equal right of access to markets, the personal right to economic liberty. But, as such, it is without value because exposed to free competition. Not until it could legally be separated from the person and sold to others did it have a value which could constitute the assets of a business.

This separation of business goodwill from personal goodwill began with the trade-mark case of 1580 and the legalized voluntary restraint of trade in 1620. The object now owned and protected by law became merely the probability of beneficial transactions, and the justification became the expectation which one might reasonably entertain if he has devoted his efforts or possessions to a service that satisfies those who come freely upon that market. By protecting this mutually beneficial expectancy and giving to it the attribute of negotiability the law converts a valueless personal right into a valuable property right.

Thus the protection of goodwill is not the protection of property in physical things, it is protection of power to control the supply of physical things against the price-exposure of unlimited competition. Hence the separation of business goodwill from personal goodwill is also the separation of control over supply of things from ownership

of the things. Where the thing is itself physically limited in supply, the separation, in so far as thus limited, cannot be made, and
business goodwill dissolves into forms of special privilege. Thus
"location goodwill" is but a special case of land values. Lord Eldon
defined it, in 1810, as "nothing more than the probability that the
old customers will resort to the old place."[1] When the land is sold,
or the rent is raised by the landlord, the business goodwill is, in so far,
absorbed by the land value. Goodwill has given added value to that
site, and in so far as that added value, or rent, is permitted to eat up
the business income, so far has business goodwill been absorbed by
privileged site value.

This can occur only in the custom-order or retail-shop stage of industry. When industry passes over into the wholesale-order, wholesale speculative, merchant-capitalist or industrial-capitalist stages,[2]
then business goodwill separates itself out, independently of situation, and broadens out into almost anything that can be ascribed
either to the attitude of the public or the activity of the concern that
conduces to business success. Commenting on Lord Eldon's remark
as to location goodwill the Supreme Court of Wisconsin, by Justice
Winslow, said: "The habit of people to purchase from a certain
dealer or manufacturer, which is the foundation for any expectation
that purchases will continue, may depend on many things besides
place. . . . Goodwill is a sort of beaten pathway from the seller to
the buyer, usually established and made easy of passage by years of
effort and expense in advertising, solicitation, and recommendation by
travelling agents, exhibition tests or displays of goods, often by ac-
quaintance with local dealers who enjoy confidence of their own neighbors, and the like."[3] And the Supreme Court of the United States
could say, in 1877: "Suppose the latter has obtained celebrity in his
manufacture, he is entitled to all the advantages of that celebrity,
whether resulting from the greater demand for his goods or from the
higher price the public are willing to give for the article, rather than
for the goods of the other manufacturer, whose reputation is not so
high as a manufacturer." And Justice Story, carrying the content
of goodwill still further, could describe it, in 1841, as "the advantage

---

[1] Crutwell v. Lye, 17 Ves. 335-346 (1810).

[2] Regarding these successive stages See COMMONS, "The American Shoemakers—1638-
1895—A Sketch of Industrial Evolution," 24 Quar. Jour. Econ. 39 (1909); reprinted in
Labor and Administration, 219 (1913); Doc. History Amer. Industrial Society, Vol. III.

[3] Rowell v. Rowell, 122 Wis. 1, 17 (1904).

or benefit which is acquired by an establishment, beyond the mere value of the capital stock, funds, or property employed therein, in consequence of the general public patronage and encouragement which it receives from constant or habitual customers, on account of its local position, or common celebrity, or reputation for skill or affluence, or punctuality, or from other accidental circumstances, or necessities, or even from ancient partialities or prejudices."[1]

In one respect Justice Story went too far when he included the "necessity" of the customer as one of the factors in goodwill, if by necessity is meant the absence of costless alternatives. Under modern conditions of industry, developed since the time of Justice Story, with the growth of great public service corporations occupying limited and strategic positions for the sale of their products, location goodwill has taken on a new importance and has dissolved business goodwill into monopoly privilege, and the freedom of customers into their necessities. When, in 1907, the Consolidated Gas Company of New York, claimed the right to charge its customers a price high enough to earn interest on "goodwill and franchises," Justice Hough in the federal court disallowed the claim as respects goodwill, on the ground that the company enjoyed a monopoly in fact, and the customer had no choice except to remain with the company. And the Supreme Court adopted this view, saying, "The complainant has a monopoly in fact, and a consumer must take gas from it or go without. He will resort to the 'old stand' because he cannot get gas anywhere else."[2]

And Justice Savage, of the Supreme Court of Maine, in a case where a water company had set up a valuation of the goodwill of customers as a valuable asset, said, " Goodwill is inappropriate where there can be no choice. So far as the defendants' system is 'practically exclusive' the element of goodwill should not be considered."[3] And similarly the Wisconsin court excluded goodwill as assets in the case of a monopoly like that of a water supply.[4]

In one respect Justice Yates, in the copyright case, while denying that goodwill was property, yet asserted the essential attribute of goodwill. The owner has no right whatever against the customer. Rather is the owner exposed to the liberty of the customer, for good-

[1] Story on Partnership, 139 (1841).
[2] Above, p. 191.
[3] Kennebeck Water Dist. v. Waterville, 97 Me. 185, 217 (1902).
[4] Appleton Water Works v. Railroad Com., 154 Wis. 121, 147 (1913); above, p. 207.

will is the customer's freedom to choose an alternative without additional cost to himself. Goodwill is not a positive right, like the right to have a debt paid. It is a "negative" right, the right of avoidance against third parties.

Thus goodwill is a by-product of liberty, and should be looked for where liberty ripens. The first and most perfect instrument of economic liberty is money. A dollar is a bundle of options both between different classes of commodities and different producers of the same class. Money affords the largest liberty known to man, although within the limits of the amount of money possessed and the number of alternatives accessible. As these alternatives enlarge with the extension of markets and the variety of products, so does the freedom of choice enlarge, and the owner of money is further and further removed from the limit of coercive alternatives. In proportion, too as subordinate classes receive their compensation in money, at shorter intervals and without obligations attached to its expenditure, the range of economic liberty is enlarged, their goodwill must be obtained, and they rise literally to the level of "patron" where previously they were "clients."

For, goodwill is good action, not necessarily a virtuous will or a loving will, or a sentimental goodwill, but a will that is free to go elsewhere and does not go. Goodwill is property, not love, sympathy or loyalty. But the good act is good, not for anything or anybody, but for each of the two persons who are willing to accept and pay the price, and thus to convey reciprocal benefits though not compelled to do so. Goodwill is reciprocity. It is evidence, not of the good or bad quality of the will of either party, but of agreement between opposing wills. It is "good" because it overcomes competition and because it yields consent, not that the motives or intentions are good or bad, but that it is the "meeting of wills" in action. It is the meeting of wills not compelled to meet, and this signifies, not the meeting of metaphysical "free wills," but of free choices under actual circumstances, the meeting-place of wills within the limits of limited resources and alternative opportunities.

Consequently goodwill is pleasurable, not because it is that individualistic pleasure, or subjective utility, of economic theory, but because it is the pleasure of being persuaded instead of being coerced. It is the pleasure of economic liberty, of power and wealth, against the pain of economic necessity, impotence, or poverty.

It is also the social psychology of persuasion, and implies the right to be informed before choosing. No individual, however free or powerful, makes up his mind and decides out of his own unaided will. His right to liberty of choice is his right to be informed of all the alternatives open to him, for ignorance of alternatives is absence of alternatives, and the right to liberty is the right to be persuaded by free speech, a free press, free advertising, free assembly. The more narrowly the individual is tied down to the alternatives offered by a single person the more nearly does he become the private property of that person. It is this that Justice Field distinguished as servitude, in contrast with slavery.[1] It is this that distinguishes goodwill from loyalty and duty. The slave is loyal to his master if he serves him devotedly, but the master does not rely on his goodwill, else he would emancipate him. The laborer is loyal to his employer if he looks out for his employer's interest under fear of losing his job, but the goodwill of the workman is his willingness to renew the contract after he has been released from its obligations. Loyalty is duty and fear; goodwill is liberty and hope. Goodwill in business is liberty to go elsewhere. In proportion as alternatives diminish, goodwill diminishes, until with the disappearance of all alternatives, goodwill disappears in the loyalty of vassal or slave.

Hence goodwill, as a business asset and a property right, is not limited to commercial goodwill—it is also industrial goodwill, the willingness of employees to work for one employer as against competing employers.[2] And what is "good credit" but the goodwill of investors? The willing investor lends his savings in larger amounts and at lower rates of interest, so that the goodwill of investors is the largest asset of business, without which all others are unavailing.

Liberty is, as it were, the common property of citizens; goodwill is the private property of a definite person or concern. Liberty is unlimited in supply, hence without value, hence common property; goodwill is limited in supply, an expectation of income, hence private property, determined by the amount of expected income. Liberty is common property in that it is an unexercised option, always in the future, never appropriated, gone as soon as exercised. Goodwill has a past, a present and a future—a history of past performance,

[1] Above, Chap. II, p. 12, 13.
[2] Below, Chap. VIII, p. 295; COMMONS, J. R., *Industrial Goodwill* (1919). See also the important article by C. J. FOREMAN, "Economics and Profits of Good-will," 13 *Amer. Econ. Rev.* 209 (1923).

of options exercised in the past, of investment accrued in the present; and it has a future of expected income, commuted and capitalized, negotiable in the present. Liberty is a valueless right to choose, goodwill is a valuable right of continuous choosing. Hence the protection of liberty is the common right to engage in any business or enter any occupation; it is the right to do business or the right to work. But the protection of goodwill is protection of the individual right to follow a business previously entered or a job already held— the right to continue in business or to continue at work.

Thus goodwill is an asset, but an extraordinarily evanescent asset. It is held only on good behavior. Of all kinds of property it most of all demands watchfulness. Good reputation slips away with a few little mistakes left uncorrected. The British law of partnership arbitrarily capitalized the expected income from goodwill at only "two years' purchase," a capitalization at the rate of 50% where bonds and lands will capitalize automatically on the market at twenty years' purchase, or 5%. Goodwill requires too much effort, thought, ability and attention to business. No wonder capitalists endeavor to convert it into bonds, land and monopolies.

For it is the most highly creditable of all assets. It survives only while it renders what is deemed, by those who receive it, to be an equivalent service. It is the one measurable evidence that the owner is becoming wealthy in proportion to his contributions to the common-wealth, for it is measured by that only behavioristic test, the willing patronage of those who are free to choose. Hence it is that goodwill is so often honored by that tribute which vice pays to virtue, and monopolies, special privileges and economic oppressions hide their transactions under the name of goodwill.

That goodwill should not have found its place in the economic theories of value while it is the crux of legal theories of value and the principal asset of business must probably be explained by the individualistic materialism and hedonism of those theories which sought to eliminate the will as something capricious. Yet goodwill can be seen and felt—seen not in commodities, but in the transactions of business; and felt, not in consumption and production, but in the confidence of patrons, investors and employees.

4. COPYRIGHT AND PATENTS

The transition from concepts of physical things to concepts of business assets, could not be fully completed until the idea of ownership was shifted from the holding of physical things to the expectations of profit from the transactions of business. The foregoing discussion has had to do mainly with the instruments devised to *protect* that ownership, not with the thing itself, the *subject-matter* of ownership. And it was with considerable difficulty that the courts of England in the Eighteenth Century bridged this gap from property in the sense of ownership of physical things to property in the sense of ownership of so invisible a thing as expected profits to be derived from beneficial transactions with other people.

The question arose, in 1743, of the disposition of that part of an estate represented by shares in the profits of an unincorporated business. It is difficult, said the Chancellor, Lord Hardwicke, "to define the various natures of property, yet it may, notwithstanding, be transmissible to representatives. . . . All things of this sort ought to be taken according to the known nature of the dealing, and the method of the parties considering these matters and carrying them on. . . . It would be a deceit and a fraud on the parties if this court did not consider things on the same foot as purchasers of a thing of this sort did. . . . There are many cases where no property of a testator has been employed or made use of in carrying on the business, and yet the executor has been accountable for the profits of the business as the testator's personal estate. The case put of physical [1] secrets or nostrums, where everything was carried on by the materials purchased after the testator's death, and yet the nostrum is part of the personal estate of the testator. . . . Suppose the house were a house of great trade, he must account for the value of what is called the goodwill of it." [2]

These references indicate that, by the middle of the Eighteenth Century, the expectation of profits distinct and separable from the ownership of tangible things had become assimilated to the notion of property in its aspects of exclusive holding for one's own use, of purchase and sale, and of transmission to representatives. Goodwill, whose foundations, we have seen, were first laid in the decisions of 1580 and 1620, was first mentioned by that name in this case of 1743,

---

[1] *I. e.* medical, physiological.   [2] Gibblett *v.* Read, 9 Mod. 459 (1743).

and then only by way of illustrating a recognized species of property. It was not until 1803 that a legal definition of goodwill began its separate evolution. However, the substantial but intangible thing underlying goodwill, and especially the difficult and even treacherous step which was taken in shifting the meaning of property from physical things to expectations of profit, are better shown in the copyright cases that came to a head in the year 1774.[1] These cases were critical turning points in the progress from the primitive common-law meaning of property to the modern business-law meaning, and for that reason the points at issue deserve attention.

The question that came before the highest court of the common law in the case of Millar v. Taylor, in 1769, was whether an author and his successors had the same common-law right to the perpetual exclusive printing and publishing of his writings that the owner of tangible property, his heirs and successors, have to the exclusive perpetual use and selling of a tangible thing and of the products yielded by that thing. The copyright statute of Queen Anne, in 1709,[2] as an exercise of the *prerogative*, had granted this exclusive privilege for a period of twenty-eight years to authors who registered under the act, but the issue in 1769 was that of a book published forty-two years before but *not registered* under the copyright statute, and consequently the question was whether the *common-law* action of "trespass on the case" could be brought by the legal successors of the author, some forty years after the first publication, against a competing publisher bringing out an unauthorized edition.

The court of King's Bench, the highest court of the common law, divided on the question, the majority supporting Lord Mansfield, who went to the furthest possible extreme in his identification of the right of exclusive copying and selling the *copies* of one's manuscript with the right of exclusive holding and selling physical things and their products. Had his opinion and that of the majority with him prevailed afterwards in the House of Lords, copyright would have become, like the ownership of physical objects, the perpetual property of the author, his heirs and assigns forever. This outcome Mansfield expressly contemplated, saying, "property of the copy thus narrowed [*i.e.*, defined as a common-law right] may equally go down from

---

[1] Millar v. Taylor, 4 Burr. 2303 (1769); Donaldson v. Beckett, 4 Burr. 2408, 2 Bro. P. C. 129 (1774).
[2] 8 Anne, c. 19.

generation to generation, and possibly continue forever." (2397.) This conclusion was vigorously protested by Justice Yates, the only dissenting justice, saying, "This claim of a perpetual monopoly is by no means warranted by the general principles of property." (2367.)

But Mansfield's opinion did not permanently prevail, owing, apparently, more to its consequences than its logic. Five years later the issue came before the House of Lords,[1] and that highest tribunal, although the majority agreed with Mansfield that the common law gave a perpetual copyright, yet wisely held that the copyright statute of 1709 should be interpreted, by implication, as having taken away that common-law right, and having substituted an exclusive privilege for a period of only twenty-eight years, a point which Mansfield had expressly denied. (2406)

What almost happened in these cases was an extension into perpetuity, by merely enlarging the definition of property, of that extension of the common law in the restraint of trade which had begun with the sale of goodwill in 1620 and the trade-mark case of 1580. In the goodwill cases the restraint of trade could, in the nature of things, extend only to the duration of the life of the merchant or clothworker, or the life of his going business. In this case, however, it would extend to the author's assigns or descendants forever, just as the ownership of lands or other physical things extends to them forever. It was, perhaps, with such consequences in mind, that Thomas Jefferson, in 1788, exclaimed: "I hold it essential in America to forbid that any English decision which has happened since the accession of Lord Mansfield to the bench, should ever be cited in a court; because, though there have come many good ones from him, yet there is so much sly poison instilled into a great part of them, that it is better to proscribe the whole."[2] And the opinion of Justice Yates in the copyright case as against Mansfield's was afterwards, in 1834, approved by the Supreme Court of the United States as one that displayed "an ability, if equalled, certainly not surpassed."[3] Jefferson's opinion of Mansfield's method of reasoning by analogy became the opinion of the Supreme Court of the United States.

That which Mansfield appealed to, first of all, was the sense of justice, and in this he introduced the theory of John Locke, first pro-

---

[1] Donaldson v. Beckett, 2 Bro. P. C. 129, 4 Burr. 2408 (1774).

[2] *Jefferson's Works*, 2:487.

[3] Wheaton v. Peters, 8 Pet. 593, 655 (1834).

pounded in 1695, and repeated by Adam Smith in 1776,[1] that the source of the right of property is not in the will of the sovereign but in the natural right of a person to his own labor and the fruits of his labor. Neither did the rights of property spring from immemorial usage, but from the sense of justice. "From what source, then," asked Mansfield, "is the common law drawn? . . . From *this* argument—because it is *just* that an author should reap the pecuniary profits of his own ingenuity and labor. . . . It is fit that he should judge when to publish, or whether he ever will publish. It is *fit* he should not only choose the time, but the manner of publication; how many; what volume; what print. (2398.) The whole, then, must finally resolve in this question, 'Whether it is agreeable to natural principles, moral justice and fitness, to allow him the copy, after publication, as well as before. (2399.) . . . The general consent of this Kingdom, for ages, is on the affirmative side." (2399.)

It was, likewise, upon this inner sense of fitness rather than the correctness of his logic, that Justice Yates differed from Lord Mansfield, and this difference expressed itself in Yates' definition of property. Physical things, lands and chattels, go on forever or according to their physical structure; their ownership is transferred from hand to hand, is transmitted to descendants, in a perpetual succession of owners. Not so with these intangible things which it was now proposed to extend into perpetuity. "The goodwill of a shop, or of an ale-house," said Yates, "and the custom of the road (as it is called among carriers) are constantly bargained for and sold *as if* they were property. But what are these? Nothing more than the goodwill of the customers, who may withdraw from them, the very next day, if they please. The purchaser of this custom, or goodwill, gains no certain property in it; he has no power to confine it to himself nor can he use any power to prevent other people from gaining the custom. It is an advantage . . . as it gives the purchaser a *priority* for custom. And so it is in the case of the publication of a book: it gives a *priority*, and gets a set of *first customers*. But none of these cases can establish an absolute, perpetual, exclusive property." (2369.) "The mere fact of usage," he said, "will be no right at all, in itself. . . . No usage can be a part of the law or have the force of a custom that is not immemorial." (2368.)

Differences in their sense of fitness not only produced differences

[1] LOCKE, JOHN, *Two Treatises of Government, Works*, 5:354, 421 (11th ed., 1812).

between Mansfield and Yates in their interpretation of the common law, but also in their interpretation of the prerogative. They agreed, indeed, that the stretch of the prerogative from the time of Henry VIII to the end of the Stuarts could not be cited as precedent to justify the stretch of property from physical things to expected profits. The monarchs of that period had incorporated the Stationers' Company as a gild, with exclusive rights of publication of books to be registered with that Company, and with drastic powers of search and seizure of unauthorized books. Mansfield, however, contended that the practice of the Stationers was based on a notion of private property in the "copy," which, on the strength of that practice, he defined as "the exclusive right of publication of somewhat intellectual." He thus was reading into the word "copy" what Yates contended was the fallacy of an "equivocal use of the word 'property' which sometimes denoted the right of the person, sometimes the object itself." (2362.) These exclusive privileges of the Stationers' Company, based on the King's prerogative, Yates rightly declared, were really a denial of the right of property in an author or his representative who was not a member of that Company. (2377.)

But it was not on the exercise of the King's prerogative in the hands of the Stationers' gild, which he admitted was obnoxious and overthrown by the Revolution of 1689, that Mansfield based his right of property in the "copy," but on an analogy which made the *prerogative* the *private* property of the King. The King had the exclusive publication of the English Bible, of the statutes, the Year Books, the common prayer-book, because he had paid for them out of his own pocket. (2403, 2405.) And, by parity of reasoning, "whatever the common law says of property in the King's case, from analogy to the case of authors, must hold conclusively, in my apprehension, with regard to authors." (2406.) Thus it was not the King's prerogative but the King's private property that gave him the exclusive right of publishing these privileged books, and that also is the right of an author or his representative independent of prerogative. (2402.) To which Yates replied that this right of the King was not grounded on "property" but on what would now be known in America as the *police power* of the "head of the Church and the political constitution," "founded on reasons of religion or of state." (2382, 2383.) "The King does not derive this right from labor or composition or any one circumstance attending the case of authors." (2384.)

All of the justices agreed that "literary property was not the effect of arbitrary power, but of law and justice, and therefore ought to be safe" (2314), but Yates contended that neither was it founded on the *common law* nor an extension of the *common-law* definition of property, but solely on the copyright statute of 1709, which was an exercise of *prerogative* in its widened form of sovereignty, which limited the duration of the grant to a term of years roughly corresponding to an author's life expectancy. In short, according to Yates, the judiciary should not create this right of property by enlarging the *common-law* definition of property but should leave it to the legislature in exercising the King's prerogative.

Yet neither Justice Yates nor the majority were quite clear as to exactly what was the thing for which was claimed this perpetual right of ownership. Mansfield and the majority seemed to think that it was the *ideas;* Yates thought it was only the *manuscript.* It required later legal opinions to reveal that the object claimed and owned is merely the *expected behavior* of other people to be obtained through expected restraint of competition and control of supply of the book.

Mansfield spoke of "intellectual ideas or modes of thinking" and of "property in notion" as though the object to which a person has an exclusive right of ownership is his own ideas, his "modes of expression," his "somewhat intellectual," which he might give out or keep to himself. And even if he gives them out, that is, "communicates them by letters," or sells them in a book, he does not give to others any property right in those *ideas*, nor does he turn them over to "common ownership" unless he shows a definite intention to do so. He retains the right to control the correctness of their expression, to prevent additions, to amend, retract and prevent their further publication, just as he is the master of the use of his own name. (2398.)

This holding, withholding and selling one's *ideas*, replied Yates, may have a distant analogy to holding, withholding and selling one's *physical property*, but it was the latter alone that was included in the common-law notion of property. In the case of an author the physical property is merely the *manuscript*, a kind of property that may, indeed, be acquired, like other physical property, by labor. But "ideas" and "thoughts" are not thus tangibly produced and held for one's own use, like the manuscript. "The invention and labor," he said, "which are ranked among the modes of acquiring specific property in the subject itself are that kind of invention and labor which are known by the name of occupancy." [1]   In that sense, Yates continued, "invention is defining and discovering of a vacant property; and labor is the taking possession of that property and bestowing cultivation upon it. Property is founded upon occupancy. But how is possession to be taken, or any act of occupancy to be asserted, on mere intellectual ideas? . . . The occupancy of a *thought* would be a new kind of occupancy indeed." (2357.)

Applying these primitive notions, Justice Yates could recognize but three species of property, that is, real estate, goods and debts (2384), distinguishable as "corporeal" and "incorporeal" property. But this new property, which we now define as "intangible property," or the right to an opportunity to sell and to control the supply of the thing sold, this right to Mansfield's "sole printing and publishing of somewhat intellectual," did not fall under either of these species. It was unknown to the common law, for, of course, it consisted not in the exclusive holding for self of lands, goods or services, nor in the enforcement of contracts, but in a field of market opportunities and control of supply, free from competition. The only "property," in this case, that fitted the primitive notion was the manuscript. This was, indeed, a species of "goods"; it was "corporeal," had "visible substance," was "capable of actual possession." But "mere intellectual ideas," these were "incapable of any distinct separate possession."

"The author's *unpublished manuscript*," said Yates, "will indeed very properly fall under this class of property because that is corporeal; but after publication of it, the mere intellectual ideas are totally incorporeal; and therefore incapable of any distinct, separate possession; they can neither be seized or forfeited or possessed." (2385.) They have become common to all the world; title to them has been renounced; they have been "abandoned" and may be taken up, but not held nor "occupied" exclusively, by anybody who comes along. "Nothing can be an object of property which is not capable of a sole and exclusive enjoyment." (2362.)

It was this distinction between the *manuscript* and the *publication* of the manuscript that furnished the clue to what afterwards be-

---

[1] "Occupancy is the taking possession of those things which before belonged to nobody. This . . . is the true ground and foundation of all property, or of holding those things in severalty, which by the law of nature, unqualified by that of society, were common to all mankind." 2 Bla. Com. 258.

came the settled law, not only of copyright, but also of patents, trade secrets, and even of every going concern in business. The later decisions on copyright have turned on drawing the line at the point at which publication occurs, yet the line has not been drawn between the physical *manuscript* and the *utterance of the ideas*, as contended by Yates, but between the *class of persons* with whom the author is dealing. As decided in later cases, "publication" denotes "those acts an author which evidence a dedication to the public." But "the public" is the "general public," not those persons who bear what we have described as the internal relation of "economy," such as the relation of friendship, agency, employment, or privacy. The acts which indicate a "dedication to the public" are such as take it out of this field where the will of the author remains supreme and bring it into the field which we have described as "expansion," where other persons, the general public, are free to exercise their own will. The printer may print the book but he has no right of publication (unless previously stipulated), since the author or his representative may store the copies or order them to be stored instead of published. If the author loans the manuscript to a friend to read and return, he has not dedicated it to the public, and the publication may be restrained by injunction. There may be also a "limited publication," or "a restricted or private communication of its contents" under conditions "expressly or impliedly precluding its dedication to the public." A lecture delivered orally is not thereby "published." Even a printed book, leased to a subscriber for his own use but not for the general public, is not thereby published.[1] And an immense business has grown up on this distinction, for it includes an associated press franchise, the use of stock exchange and market reports, the use of great systems of business forecasting, all of them belonging to that intangible property which is far more important and valuable than the underlying physical property.

The similar principle has been worked out in the law of patents and trade secrets. A secret process or invention, not yet given to the public nor patented, remains by operation of common law, the exclusive property of the inventor, and his secret cannot be wrested from him by fraud or communicated to or used by others through breach of confidence. Yet "whenever the inventor permits the invention to pass beyond the legally defined limits of his exclusive pos-

[1] 6 R. C. L. 1134, and cases there cited.

session, his right to it ceases and the right of all mankind to it begins." [1]

In other words, the old distinction between the *possession of physical property* and *liberty of contract* becomes the distinction between the behavior of those persons who are subject to command and obedience and the behavior of those persons who are subject only to persuasion or coercion. "Economy" is the exclusive holding for one's own use, according to one's own will, but the thing now held for one's own use is not a physical thing, the manuscript, nor even the printed book, nor the physical objects embodying an invention, but is the behavior of persons over whom the owner retains the power of command and obedience, since they are his employees, agents, friends, who are bound to obey his commands in their use of the manuscript, book, or secret process. On the other hand, "expansion" relates to the behavior of the general public, the outsiders, who have liberty of choice of opportunities or exercise of economic power, the field of persuasion or coercion.

[1] Robinson, W. C., *Law of Patents*, secs. 24–40 (1890).

CHAPTER VIII

THE WAGE BARGAIN—INDUSTRIALISM

I. Individual Bargaining

We have seen, in the Slaughter House Cases, that the minority opinions defined a man's "calling," "occupation," "trade", and his "labor" as his property, as well as the physical things he might own; and his right to choose an occupation or trade, that is, to choose the direction in which he would exercise his labor, was defined as a part of his liberty. The authority for the definition of labor as property was found, not in earlier decisions of the courts, but was ascribed to Adam Smith, who had said, "The property which every man has in his own labor, as it is the original foundation of all property, so it is the most sacred and inviolable." [1] And the authority for including the right to choose a calling, *i. e.*, "to live and work where he will," was found in the change of meaning given by Coke and the lawyers of the Commonwealth to the "liberties" of the barons in Magna Carta. One of the liberties of these barons had been the privilege of holding lands and the serfs attached to the land against the power of the chief landlord, the King. So that the enlargement of the terms liberty and property, as used in the constitution, from physical liberty and property to economic liberty and property, was the reflection, in the minds of the judges, of the business revolution that followed the extension of markets and the political revolution that liberated the slaves.

Under this new definition of labor as the property and liberty of the laborer himself it is not quite clear what is meant by "labor." It evidently does not mean the physical body of the laborer. In an imperfect sense his body is his property, since it was the property of the slaveowner, or his parents, which has been transferred, by purchase, or confiscation, or age, to the laborer. But since he cannot by law transfer the title to his body, he cannot sell it and it has no exchange-value as business assets. His ownership of his body is im-

---

[1] Smith, Adam, *Wealth of Nations*, Book I, Chap. X, Pt. II.

perfect since he has only the right to use it and not the right to sell it.

But neither can he sell the use of his body. Its uses are its muscular motions as used by himself for purposes which only he himself directs. Thus used they are his "manual, mental, and managerial" faculties, employed to move things and persons. These are his "labor." What he sells when he sells his labor is his *willingness* to use his faculties according to a purpose that has been pointed out to him. He sells his promise to obey commands. He sells his goodwill.

But even this promise has no exchange-value. When the business man sells his goodwill he promises to stay away and not compete. His goodwill is a separable asset attached to his going business and transferred to another. Likewise, when the laborer sells his physical *product* he sells his promise to stay away and not exercise his will upon the product. But when he sells his labor he sells his promise to stay on the job with it. This is usually a valueless promise, not because he will not stay on the job, but because the law, in recent times, refuses to compel him to stay. The indentured servant, the former contract laborer or apprentice, the peon, even perhaps the slave, had sold his promise to work, and the law enforced the promise by punishing him for the crime of running away, or permitted the purchaser to punish him for disobedience. The laborer's promise was an enforceable contract, a legal duty to work. But the Thirteenth Amendment to the Constitution forbids involuntary servitude of every kind except as punishment for crime of which the person must duly have been convicted in a court of law.[1] Hence the laborer can lawfully change his mind without penalty inflicted upon his body. And, to change his mind is to violate his promise.

But if his body can no longer be offered as security for the fulfillment of his promise to work, his separable assets, his tools, houses, furniture, animals, are security that may be levied upon in damages. Yet even these, by statute during the past eighty years, have been so liberally exempted from execution that a suit to recover damages for breach of contract by laborers is, in fact, an empty remedy.[2]

Hence, the free laborer is employed at will—no obligation arises on the part of the employer to keep him, and no obligation on the part of the laborer to continue at work. Under no ordinary circumstances

---

[1] Clyatt v. U. S., 197 U. S. 207, 218 (1904).
[2] Cp. COMMONS and ANDREWS, *Principles of Labor Legislation*, Chap. II (1920).

can the laborer be enjoined from quitting work,[1] nor the employer from dismissing him. And, under no ordinary circumstances can either obtain damages for failure to fulfill his promise. The labor contract therefore is not a contract, it is a continuing implied *renewal* of contracts at every minute and hour, based on the continuance of what is deemed, on the employer's side, to be satisfactory service, and, on the laborer's side, what is deemed to be satisfactory conditions and compensation. As stated by a writer in the *Yale Law Journal;* [2] "It is true that wherever C is in B's employ, his relationship is often called a contract of employment. But it is submitted that there is often no effective contract at all between them, or at most there is only a contract from day to day or from week to week. Neither of the parties is under a contractual duty as to succeeding days and consequently no third person can induce a breach thereof. . . . Despite the fact in the case put that there is no contractual relation between B and C some courts are inclined to treat it substantially as if there were. This is doubtless due to the origin of this kind of action. Originally its basis was in tort for the seduction of C, causing a loss of C's services to B. Even though this seduction theory is properly exploded, there seems to be a vestige of it still remaining in the minds of the courts." Consequently the relation between the two is not that of a right and duty—neither the right of the laborer to the particular job and the corresponding duty of the employer to retain him, nor the right of the employer to have the laborer remain on the job and the corresponding duty of the laborer to remain—but the relation between the two is that of liberty and exposure—the liberty of the laborer to quit and an equivalent exposure of the employer to damage on account of the possible exercise of that liberty; and the reciprocal liberty of the employer to dismiss him and the corresponding exposure of the laborer to the damage of possible unemployment.

The relation, thus, is not that of a positive encumbrance on the liberty of either, which we have seen distinguished as "incorporeal property," but is that of an opportunity to buy and sell, which is distinguished as "intangible property." The labor contract is not a contract, it is a continuing renewal of a contract at every successive moment, implied simply from the fact that the laborer keeps at work and the employer accepts his product. Such a relation, we saw, is

[1] Arthur *v.* Oakes, 63 Fed. 310 (1899).   [2] 30 *Yale Law Jour.* 618, 619 (1921).

not that of an encumbrance, but is that of an opportunity, either goodwill or privilege—goodwill if the alternative open to either is deemed to be good; privilege if there is deemed to be no alternative or if the best alternative is deemed to be onerous.

Hence it is that when it is said that "labor" is property, what is intended is that the laborer owns an expectancy dependent upon the goodwill of his employer. He does not own the job—his employer is under no duty to keep him—he owns the liberty to be continuously bargaining with his employer to be kept on the job by virtue of continuously delivering a service which the employer continously accepts, thereby impliedly renewing continuously the contract.

The contract at the beginning of his employment is therefore not a contract—it is a usage, a custom, a habit—it is an understanding between the two, that, at each point in the continuous flow of impliedly renewing the contract, the terms of renewal shall conform to what was understood, but without any duty on either side to renew or conform. The laborer is thus continuously on the labor market— even while he is working at his job he is both producing and bargaining, and the two are inseparable. His bargaining is his act of producing something for the employer and his producing something acceptable is his method of bargaining.

This bargaining, therefore, is continuously a choosing of opportunities. It is well known that, in hard times when jobs are scarce, the laborer works more energetically than in good times when alternative jobs are plentiful. And in good times when laborers are scarce, compared with jobs, the laborers take advantage of the employers' absence of alternative laborers by demanding more pay for less work. And *vice versa*. The two are continuously upon the labor market. The job is the laborer's going business, consisting in his continuing transactions of offering a product in exchange for compensation and choosing between alternative opportunities. And the jobs are a part of the going business of the employer, consisting, on his side, of the identical transactions. Hence, if the laborer's labor is his property, it is equally his employer's property, for in each case it is the expectation of those reciprocal beneficial transactions which constitute goodwill or privilege according to the degree of damage imposed by reason of being required to choose the best available alternative. The goodwill of the employer is the laborer's property and the goodwill of the laborer is the employer's property, since each is valuable as a means of acquisition. And, likewise, if one is privileged and the other unprivileged, in that the one is not dependent on the goodwill of the other but only on the other's absence of alternatives, then the one is merely the owner of privileged, the other of unprivileged property.

Sometimes the legal language seems to imply that the laborer's "product" is his property. But the wage-earner's product is not his property. By virtue of the understanding on which they operate, his product is his employer's property—he works in his employer's plant, with his employer's machinery, and on his employer's raw material—he merely adds use-value to the employer's property.

Again it is sometimes implied that the laborer's "wages" are his property. These are, indeed, his property, but they are "incorporeal property." The laborer goes to work on Monday morning and is paid his wages on Saturday night. During the interval the relation between him and his employer is the "intangible property" of liberty and exposure. Neither possesses any encumbrance on the future behavior of the other requiring the relationship to continue. But during the week an accrual of indebtedness in consideration of an accrual of product transferred to the employer, takes place. The laborer adds use-value to the employer's plant or product, and the employer adds a stipulated debt in terms of money to his other liabilities. Even where there is no agreement as to his compensation, "the law implies a promise from the employer to the workman that he will pay him for his services as much as he may deserve or merit," that is, as much as similar labor would be paid on the labor market at the time.[1]

The laborer's accrual of use-value to the employer's product is the laborer's accrual of an encumbrance on the property of the going concern. The employer becomes a debtor, the laborer a creditor. Hence the laborer during the week is an investor in the business; usually, since the inauguration of mechanics' and laborers' liens beginning in 1829,[2] he is a priority investor. At the end of the week he is paid his wages, not in product, but in that universal intangible property, money, which is his liberty to go upon the commodity markets and purchase the things he wishes. A formal investor, or an informal investor, the employer, or the banker, takes his place, and his temporary investment is liquidated.

[1] BOUVIER, article "quantum meruit" and cases cited.
[2] COMMONS and ANDREWS, Principles of Labor Legislation, 60 (1920).

Thus the laborer's job, while it lasts, is that inseparable union of incorporeal and intangible property, a special case of a securities market, where the period of investment, however, is so short that a rate of interest is not formally calculated. It is "intangible property" in that it is the relation of liberty and exposure upon the labor market. It is "incorporeal property" in that it is the relation of creditor and debtor upon the investment market. And it is periodically converted into nominal wages, or money, another "intangible property," being the liberties and exposures of the various commodity markets where are found the food, clothing, and shelter that constitute the real wages for his labor.

II. Associated Persons and Associated Property

As stated by the Oregon court in the case referred to above, the justification of a law restraining the power of property in the matter of wages turns on the protection of health and morals.[1] In this respect the justification differs from that of the Munn Case where no question of morals or health was involved, and only the question of sheer power. The labor cases in which this issue of power, stripped of other issues, has come before the Supreme Court of the United States, are the cases where Congress and the state legislatures had attempted to protect employees in the right to belong to labor organizations. In the Adair Case the court denied that authority to Congress, under the Fifth Amendment, and in the Coppage Case denied it to the states, under the Fourteenth Amendment, as depriving persons of liberty and property without due process of law.[2]

The Congress of the United States, in order to carry out its purpose of providing voluntary arbitration of labor disputes on railways had prohibited such corporations and their agents from refusing employment and from discharging or threatening to discharge workmen, if done solely on the ground of membership in a labor organization. The state of Kansas had enacted a similar law, except that its operation was not limited to railways or corporations, but extended to employees of corporations generally. Similar laws had been held unconstitutional by six state courts, including an earlier opinion of

---

[1] When the Oregon ten-hour law for men and women came before the court, including provision of time-and-one-half wages for overtime, the court treated the wage-feature as a kind of penalty and said (in the syllabus) "whether the law could be upheld as a regulation of wages is not considered or decided." Bunting v. Oregon, 243 U. S. 426 (1916).

[2] Adair v. U. S., 208 U. S., 161 (1908); Coppage v. Kansas, 236 U. S. 1 (1915).

the Kansas court,[1] but when a second law of this kind was enacted in Kansas the state court sustained it,[2] and appeal was taken to the United States court.

The ruling in the Adair Case was followed by the Supreme Court in the Coppage Case, for, said Justice Pitney,[3] if the federal government is prohibited from "arbitrary interference with the liberty of contract because of the due process provision of the Fifth Amendment, it is too clear for argument that the states are prevented from the like interference by virtue of the corresponding clause of the Fourteenth Amendment."

The Kansas law had made it unlawful for any firm, company, or corporation, its members, officers or agents, to coerce, require, demand or influence any person not to join or become or remain a member of any labor organization or association, as a condition of securing employment or continuing in employment. Coppage, a superintendent of a railway company, had requested Hedges, a member of the switchmen's union, to sign such an agreement, at the same time informing him that if he did not sign it he could not remain in the employ of the company. Hedges refused to sign or to withdraw from the union, and Coppage discharged him. The provision of the Kansas law prohibiting such action by Coppage, declared Justice Pitney for the majority (Justices Day, Holmes, and Hughes dissenting), was a deprivation of liberty and property without due process of law. For, he said, "Included in the right of personal liberty and the right of private property—partaking of the nature of each— is the right to make contracts for the acquisition of property. Chief among such contracts is that of personal employment, by which labor and other services are exchanged for money or other forms of property." [4]

There were two questions involved in this case, one as to whether economic coercion in itself can be permitted to be made unlawful by the legislature, the other as to whether the legislature can be per-

---

[1] State v. Julow, 129 Mo. 163; (1895), Gillespie v. People, 188 Ill. 176 (1900); State ex rel. Zillmer v. Kreutzberg, 114 Wis. 530 (1902); Coffeyville Brick Co. v. Perry, 69 Kan. 297 (1904); People v. Marcus, 185 N. Y. 257 (1906); State ex rel. Smith v. Daniels, 188 Minn. 155, (1912).

[2] State v. Coppage, 87 Kan. 752 (1912).

[3] 236 U. S. 1, 11. For a discussion of these cases see COOK, W. W., "Privileges of Labor Unions in the Struggle for Life," 27 *Yale Law Jour.* 779 (1918); POWELL, T. R., "Collective bargaining before the Supreme Court," 33 *Pol. Sci. Quar.* 396 (1918).

[4] 236 U. S. 14.

mitted to create and protect a right of association of persons as against an association of property-owners.

The first issue was dismissed by citing the four hold-up cases to which we have referred above,[1] where, as we have seen, the court does not recognize mere inequality of property, or the power to withhold from others, as coming within the definition of "coercion." In those and similar cases there must be some inequality of personal relations in order to render the act of the superior person coercive. This issue appeared and was decided in the Coppage Case as follows: Hedges, as a member of the switchmen's union, "was entitled to benefits in the nature of insurance to the amount of fifteen hundred dollars which he would have been obliged to forego if he had ceased to be a member." But if Coppage "was otherwise within his legal rights in insisting that Hedges should elect whether to remain in the employ of the company or to retain his membership in the union, that insistence is not rendered unlawful by the fact that the choice involved a pecuniary sacrifice to Hedges."[2]

And it is unlawful for the legislature to attempt to enlarge the definition of coercion to include protection against mere economic power. The Kansas legislature had attempted to create a criminal offense out of the circumstances that in "dealing with Hedges, an employee at will and a man of full age and understanding, subject to no restraint or disability, Coppage insisted that Hedges should freely choose whether he would leave the employ of the company or would agree to refrain from association with the union while so employed. . . . The state of Kansas intends by this legislation to punish conduct such as that of Coppage, although entirely devoid of any element of coercion, compulsion, duress, or undue influence, just as certainly as it intends to punish coercion and the like. . . . It is equally clear that to punish an employer or his agent for simply proposing certain terms of employment, under circumstances devoid of coercion, duress, or undue influence, has no reasonable relation to a declared purpose of repressing coercion, duress, and undue influence. Nor can a state, by designating as "coercion" conduct which is not such in truth, render criminal any normal and essentially innocent exercise of personal liberty or of property rights." (15, 16.)

The Kansas court had said the "employees as a rule are not financially able to be as independent in making contracts for the sale of

[1] Chap. III, p. 59.   [2] 236 U. S. 8, 9.

their labor as are employers in making contracts of purchase thereof." To this the Supreme Court said, "No doubt, wherever the right of private property exists, there must and will be inequalities of fortune; and thus it naturally happens that parties negotiating about a contract are not equally unhampered by circumstances. . . . Since it is self-evident that, unless all things are held in common, some persons must have more property than others, it is from the nature of things impossible to uphold freedom of contract and the right of private property without at the same time recognizing as legitimate those inequalities of fortune that are the necessary result of the exercise of those rights." (17.)

The second question, that of protecting a right of association of individuals as against an association of owners, is inseparable from the first, for the "inequalities of fortune" to which Justice Pitney referred, were not the inequalities of Hedges and Coppage, but of Hedges and the railway company. This question, however, was not even presented to the court, much less passed upon, although the Kansas law was limited to firms, companies, and corporations. The explanation, apparently, resides in the fact that, for the purposes of the Fourteenth Amendment, a corporation is deemed to be a person and not an association of persons.

The meaning of a corporation, like the meaning of property and liberty, has been changing during decades and centuries, and when a corporation appears in court it takes on a variety of shapes derived from different parts of its history. It is not a citizen within the meaning of the Federal Constitution but is a "person" within the meaning of the Fourteenth Amendment.[1] At one time it appears to be an *association* of persons, at another time *a person;* at one time it is an independent existence separate from its members, at another a dummy concealing the acts of its stockholders.[2] At one time it is a fiction existing only in contemplation of law and limited strictly to the powers granted in the act that created it; at another it is a set of transactions giving rise to obligations not authorized expressly by the charter but read into it by operation of law.[3] To Hedges it might appear to be a

---

[1] 1 Cook on Corporations, 94 (7th ed.).

[2] *Ibid.*, 32, 33; 7 R. C. L. No. 4.

[3] *Ibid.*, 12. "The theory of a corporation is that it has no powers except those expressly given or necessarily implied. But this theory is no longer strictly applied to private corporations. A private corporation may exercise many extraordinary powers, provided all of its stockholders assent and none of its creditors are injured. There is no one to complain except the state and the business being entirely private, the state does not interfere."

Leviathan controlling twenty thousand jobs, but when he gets into court it is only Coppage, a person like himself. With this elastic ability to change its shape and slip out of your hands when you think you have it, the definition of a corporation is truly intangible.

Roscoe Pound has said that the personality of a corporation is not an entity but a convenience. But it is a safe convenience only if, while defined as a unit it is also defined as an association acting as a unit. Yet this very unity is two-fold, a union of property and a union of persons.

As a union of property the corporation has expanded from the primitive notion of physical objects held for one's own use to the notion of a going business operated by an association of persons in dealings with other persons. In this respect it avails itself of all the laws of creditor and debtor, principal and agent, employer and employee, buyer and seller, which have emerged out of the history of the common law, aided by equity and statutes, and have built themselves up on the primary protection of title and possession of physical objects.

As a union of persons the corporation is the descendant of that royal prerogative which granted a portion of the sovereign's personal power to his subjects. While many of the personal privileges then granted, such as monopolies and the various feudal "liberties" previously mentioned, were abolished outright during the Seventeenth Century, or rather transferred to Parliament, this one, the corporate franchise, was held over until the Nineteenth Century at the disposal of Parliaments and legislatures. Corporate franchises had been bestowed, like the others, through individual or special bargains between the sovereign and the subject. When the legislature succeeded to the King, this bargaining continued in the form of lobbying, political influence and corruption, until, about the middle of the Nineteenth Century, through the enactment of general corporation laws, first in America, this special privilege was opened to any group of citizens, regardless of personal influence, who should bind themselves together by contracts conforming to general rules and then register their intentions with the secretary of state. Thus a personal privilege, conferred on individuals by the sovereign, becomes a universal right of association open to all persons, by which they may erect themselves into a unity unknown to the common law.

The corporate franchise prolongs the life of the association beyond the expectations of any individual. It binds a minority, without their consent, if necessary, to act as a unit with the majority. It relieves individuals of responsibility beyond a certain limit, and limits the total responsibility to the amount of property owned by the corporation. Immortality, self-government, and limited liability are thus the sovereign powers and immunities granted to persons, collectively and individually, in order that a single will may act through agents in dealing with the rest of the world. Thus the unit of property, a going business, is separated from individuals and is given an independent existence, an industrial government of its own, and a capacity of growth unknown to the natural person.

If, now, this expanding unit of property retains the primitive meaning of property it is but an empty title to possession of physical objects devoid of value for business. Even if it is enlarged to include that liberty of passive choice of opportunities contended for by Coke in the Case of Monopolies in 1602, and by the minority in the Slaughter House Cases in 1872, it is even yet ineffective. But when the meaning enlarges to that exercise of economic power revealed in the Munn Case in 1876, the Holden-Hardy Case in 1898, the Bunting and Stettler Cases in 1916 and 1917, it is because this child of privilege has become a privileged association of men.

That this expanding meaning of property should have halted in the Adair and Coppage Cases seems to be owing to the circumstance that in these cases the Congress and the legislature proposed to set up an agency, the labor union, to accomplish what in the other cases was made the duty of governmental factory inspectors. Justice Pitney could see no public purpose in a labor organization. "They are not public institutions, charged by law with public or governmental duties, such as would render the maintenance of their membership a matter of direct concern to the general welfare."[1] Distinguishing Holden v. Hardy and similar cases, he said that in those cases there was a public purpose, such as health, safety, morals, or public welfare "beyond the supposed desirability of leveling inequalities of fortune by depriving one who has property of some part of what is characterized as his 'financial independence' . . . . The mere restriction of liberty or of property right cannot of itself be denominated 'public welfare' and treated as a legitimate object of the police power; for such restriction is the very thing that is inhibited by the Amendment."[2]

[1] Coppage v. Kansas, 236 U. S. 1, 16 (1915). [2] Ibid., 18, 19.

This absence of a public purpose seems also to have been the underlying reason for the opinion in the Hitchman Case.[1] In that case a union and its agents who were attempting to unionize the mines of a coal company in West Virginia, were enjoined against even persuading the employees from joining the union in pursuance of a plan to unionize the mines by means of a strike, if necessary. The employees had been taken back at the end of a lost strike some years before on condition that they should agree not to belong to a union while working for the company, and all employees taken on afterward had been required to agree to this condition. In the Adair and Coppage Cases it was the Congress and state legislatures that were forbidden to prohibit employers from insisting on such conditions in the contract of employment. In the Hitchman Case it was the labor union that was forbidden to interfere with such contracts.

The majority of the court in the Hitchman Case (Justices Brandeis, Holmes and Clarke dissenting) while conceding the right of workingmen to form unions and enlarge their membership by inviting other workingmen to join, could see no just excuse in the intention of the union to inflict damage on the company by means of a strike in order to induce it, through fear of financial loss, to consent to the unionization of the mine as the lesser evil. The company was entitled to the goodwill of its employees irrespective of the fact that, being employed at will, the relation of employer and employee was terminable by either party at any time. It did not appear to the court that the union might also be entitled to build up a goodwill of its own in competition with the goodwill of the corporation, a kind of asset which is built up only by inducing customers to leave one concern and patronize another concern, thus inflicting damage on the first concern by enlarging the patronage of the competing concern.

The goodwill of a concern is ordinarily maintained and enlarged by persuading customers, who are free to terminate or refuse their patronage at any time, to continue the same in spite of the persuasion of competitors. Goodwill is competitive persuasion, and if competitors are enjoined from offering customers alternative attractions, then the customers are held, not by their goodwill but by ignorance of alternatives, which is absence of alternatives, and therefore, privilege instead of goodwill. There is thus a public purpose underlying the doctrine of goodwill since that first case in 1580 when the court

[1] Hitchman Coal & Coke Co. v. Mitchell, 245 U. S. 229 (1917).

prohibited a competitor from attaching the plaintiff's trade-mark to his "ill-made cloth," but the purpose consists in the liberty of customers to decide for themselves, without fraud, coercion, or obligation, but with opportunity to obtain knowledge as to the attractiveness of competing offers.

That which is offered, on the one side of a labor dispute, is, as stated in the minority opinion, "a reasonable effort to improve the condition of working men engaged in the industry by strengthening their bargaining power through unions, and extending the field of union power." [1]

That which is offered on the other side, as stated by the majority, is "the reasonable probability that, by properly treating its employees, and paying them fair wages, and avoiding reasonable grounds of complaint, it will be able to retain them in its employ, and to fill vacancies occurring from time to time by the employment of other men on the same terms." (252.)

Here, apparently, is a competition for the goodwill of workingmen, enlarged by analogy to the competition of merchants for the goodwill of customers. "The plaintiff," said the majority opinion, "was and is entitled to the goodwill of its employees, precisely as a merchant is entitled to the goodwill of his customers although they are under no obligation to continue to deal with him. . . . The pecuniary value of such reasonable probabilities is incalculably great, and is recognized by the law in a variety of relations." But, not recognizing that the customer is under no obligation or contract to continue to deal with the merchant and may be presuaded by a competitor to transfer his patronage, the court fell back on the old law of master and servant, saying, "the right of action for persuading an employee to leave his employer is universally recognized." (252.) Apparently there is a confusion here of liberty with duty and goodwill with servitude. Goodwill is liberty; a contract is duty; the enforcement of a contract is servitude. The employer is under no duty to keep the laborer, the laborer is under no duty to remain, and to prevent him from obtaining knowledge of alternatives is servitude.

It would seem that not all of the doctrine of goodwill has here been carried over from the customer to the employee, apparently because the liberty of the laborer to choose between alternatives,

[1] Hitchman Coal & Coke Co. v. Mitchell, 245 U. S. 223, 268 (1917).

although employed at will, is not conceived to be of as much public importance as that of the customer who patronizes at will. Consequently the labor union, which attempts to persuade a laborer to leave, is damaging business without a good excuse, whereas the competitor or employer who similarly persuades the customer or laborer to leave, has a good and lawful excuse.

Apparently, also, there is another, but inseparable, reason. The Hitchman Coal Company appears in court as a single individual rather than an association of individuals who have combined their property into a unit, with an industrial government, with limited liability and with corporate immortality; whereas the union appears as a conspiracy of individuals, holding conventions, without property, and merely inflicting damage on property by withholding the supply of labor until the terms of the contract can be agreed upon. (241, 253.) But, if labor is property, it would seem that associated labor is also property; that the right to act together as an industrial government is a property right, and that the property need not be tangible coal mines, but is the expectation of income to be obtained through bargaining power and apportioned to its members according to rules agreed upon, an expectation similar to the goodwill of a business.

According to this distinction of the court, as we have already seen, a unit of property has no power; it is an inert mass, no matter how large its dimensions; but a union of persons *is* power, and the reason why the corporation does not have power is because it does not appear as a unit of persons but as a unit of property. The opposite of this, we have seen, was approved in the Munn Case.

This appears to be the legal doctrine of conspiracy. The essence of conspiracy is in the duress, or coercion, exercised over an individual by a combination of individuals, as is evident in the fact that that which may be lawful for a single individual, such as refusal to buy or sell or work, may become unlawful when done in concert by a combination of individuals. The illegality of a conspiracy is in the *concert* of action, and not in the act itself, which might be perfectly legal if performed without concert by the same number of individuals, since the combination may exercise a greater power than is possible for the faculties of a single individual.

But a combination of *property*, distinguished from a combination of human faculties, is not deemed to exercise greater coercive power than a single person, else it would be deemed unlawful for a corporation to do what the isolated individual might legally do. The corporation, by the grant of sovereign power, is looked upon as a single person like other persons and may lawfully refuse to buy or sell or lease or hire, just as other persons may lawfully refuse. Like them, of course, it might unlawfully join in a conspiracy with other persons or other corporations, in which case, however, the unlawful duress or coercion is still deemed to be the concerted acts of persons, one of whom is this corporation considered as a person. But in so far as it is merely a unit of physical property, that is, a going plant although owned by a combination of persons, it is not deemed to exercise duress or coercion in its dealings with individuals, whether buyers, sellers, employees, borrowers, or lenders. Coercion and duress spring from combinations of persons, not from the combined ownership of things.

This distinction between legal coercion and economic coercion and between an association of property owners and an association of persons without tangible property, was brought out in the dissenting opinion in the Hitchman Case. Justice Brandeis said, "It is also urged that defendants are seeking to 'coerce' plaintiff to 'unionize' its mine. But coercion, in a legal sense is not exerted when a union merely endeavors to induce employees to join a union with the intention thereafter to order a strike unless the employer consents to unionize his shop. Such pressure is not coercion in a legal sense. The employer is free either to accept the agreement or the disadvantage. Indeed, the plaintiff's whole case is rested upon agreements secured under similar pressure of economic necessity or disadvantage. If it is coercion to threaten to strike unless plaintiff consents to a closed union shop, it is coercion also to threaten not to give one employment unless the applicant will consent to a closed non-union shop. The employer may sign the union agreement for fear that *labor* may not be otherwise obtainable; the workman may sign the individual agreement for fear that *employment* may not be otherwise obtainable. But such fear does not imply coercion in a legal sense. In other words, an employer, in order to effectuate the closing of his shop to *union* labor, may exact an agreement to that effect from his employees. The agreement itself being a lawful one, the employer may withhold from the men an economic need—employment—until they assent to make it. Likewise, an agreement closing a shop to *non-union* labor being lawful, the union may withhold from an employer an economic need—labor—until he assents to make it. In a legal sense an agreement entered into, under such circumstances, is voluntarily entered into." (271, 272.)

This being the case, the preference is given by the court to that association of persons deemed to be of the greater public importance. The corporate franchise, with its powers and immunities, is granted to the coal company because the public, as consumers, is interested in the mining of abundance of coal. Whether or not the increased bargaining power in dealings with labor, that goes with the franchise, is also a public purpose depends on the relative importance attached to unions of capitalists and unions of laborers. The majority opinion saw no public purpose subserved by the labor union in the Hitchman Case, as they had seen no such purpose in the Coppage Case. The minority saw a public purpose in strengthening the bargaining power of labor. The purpose of interfering with the employees of the Hitchman Company who were employed at will, said the minority, "was confessedly in order to strengthen the union, in the belief that thereby the condition of workmen engaged in mining would be improved; the bargaining power of the individual workingman was to be strengthened by collective bargaining; and collective bargaining was to be insured by obtaining the union agreement. It should not, at this day, be doubted that to induce workingmen to leave or not to enter an employment in order to advance such a purpose is justifiable when the workmen are not bound by contract to remain in such employment." (273.) But it is *doubted*, not as a matter of logic but as a matter of beliefs and this belief is none other than the habitual wish of the judge who decides and who, in three hundred years since the beginning of the business revolution, can always find precedents and logic to back up what he wishes. It is the judge who believes in the law and custom of business and not the judge who believes in the law and custom of labor, that decides.

III. CUSTOM AND LAW

Two apparently opposite theories of law have been formulated, the one tracing its lineage through Hobbes and Bentham to John Austin.[1] The other through Coke and Blackstone to its American statement by James C. Carter.[2] According to the one view law is

[1] AUSTIN, *Lectures on Jurisprudence*; BROWN, W. J., *The Austinian Theory of Law* (1906).
[2] CARTER, J. C., *Law; Its Origin, Growth and Function* (1907).

made by the command of a superior to an inferior. According to the other, law is *found* in the customs of the people.

Austin defined law as "a rule laid down for the guidance of an intelligent being by an intelligent being having power over him." Carter defines the unwritten law, which is the main body of our law, as the "rules springing from the social standard of justice, or from the habits and customs from which that standard has itself been derived."

Carrying out the theory of Hobbes, Bentham and Austin, the lawgiver by a proper study of the passions of men might reconstruct society according to his standards of justice and welfare. Carrying out the theory of Coke, Blackstone and Carter, the lawgiver is but an investigator and systemizer of the existing habits of the people. He does not make law—he finds it and registers it.

Neither party, of course, carries out its theory to the logical limit, and, as a matter of historical fact, the one is looking at the prerogative, the other at the common law. The one leads to the written law formulated by the monarch or legislature, or constitutional convention; the other to the unwritten law formulated piecemeal by the courts. The two are inseparable. Yet, by looking mainly at the written law, the one ends by proposing to substitute a code of laws, or a socialistic utopia, or a dictatorship of the proletariat, for the customs of the people; the other, by looking at the unwritten law, ends by deriving standards of justice from those customs and erecting the standards into the voice of Reason or the voice of God. The codes, the utopias and the dictatorships have been attempted and have broken down or been interpreted by double meanings of words. Statute law or constitutional law is a dead letter where it does not fit the customs. It is made, as Carter points out, by a single person or by a few persons, and "necessarily exhibits the imperfection and error which attaches to all such works." But, according to Carter, the unwritten law, though formulated by the courts, is made by God or Beneficent Nature. It is "self-existent, eternal, absolutely right and just for the purposes of social government, irrepealable and unchangeable. It may be justly called Divine; for being identical with custom which is the form in which human nature necessarily develops conduct, it can have no other author than that of human nature itself." (231.)

Customs are, indeed, the raw material out of which justice is constructed. But customs differ, customs change, customs are good and bad, and customs conflict. They are uncertain, complex, contradictory, and confusing. A choice must be made. Somebody must choose which customs to authorize and which to condemn or let alone. Carter maintains his thesis only by distinguishing "custom" from "bad practice." (255.) "Custom" is *good* custom; "bad practice" is *bad* custom. Who shall say? Is it the voice of God? Is it the law of Nature? Is it universal reason, or the *vox populi?* Carter criticised the Supreme Court because, in a railroad consolidation case it did not authorize the modern custom of business in consolidating corporations and eliminating competition. (210–213.) Apparently that custom is the voice of God. Others approve the Supreme Court when it condemns the modern custom of labor organizations in boycotting employers whom they deem unfair. Apparently that custom is not the voice of God.

Somebody must choose between customs. Whoever chooses is the lawgiver. The policeman chooses certain customs, rejects others, and, within his limits of power and immunity, he is the prerogative in action. He both finds the law and makes it—*finds* it by choosing the desirable customs of his bailiwick and rejecting the undesirable customs; *makes* it by choosing the direction in which the power of the state shall be brought against those who violate the desired custom, or practice the undesired one. The court does the same in a larger field of power and immunity. And the legislature, in its field, finds bad customs which it penalizes, good ones to which it lends the power of the state, and indifferent ones which it lets alone. This is discretion, and official discretion is choice of customs.

For customs are customary behavior, and behavior is the flow of transactions between persons. In this they differ from "habit." Habit is the customary acts of an individual. Custom is the customary *transactions* of similar classes of individuals under similar circumstances. The economic transactions with which historically we are concerned are the transactions of landlord and tenant, creditor and debtor, employer and employee. In Anglo-American history, each of these began as custom; the approved customs became a common law, unwritten because written piecemeal in the decisions of courts; the common law was then pieced-out by the two arms of the prerogative, equity and statutory or constitutional law; finally, to some extent, in certain departments, the whole was codified. So that, out of the rent-bargain and its custom of landlord and tenant evolved the common law of agriculture, serfdom and slavery, with its rights of tangible property in lands, chattels and human beings. Out of the price-bargain and its customs of merchants and manufacturers, evolved the law merchant and the common law of business and liberty with its rights of intangible and incorporeal property.

The law of business, as thus developed, is as different from the old common law as is a going business from an acre of land, or a promise from a horse. Yet, as we have seen, by fiction, by new meanings for old words, the old slid into the new so easily that there was no serious break except at the points in the seventeenth century when the revolutions of 1640 and 1689 subjected the officials of the monarch to the same courts and to similar rules of law as the private citizen. The power of the courts, especially on the equity side, thereupon unfolded to meet the unfolding conditions of business, and never more vigorously than in the past forty years when business is confronted by labor, as feudalism was confronted by business in the Seventeenth Century.

The customs of labor and of labor organizations are as different from the customs of business, as the customs of business were different from the customs of feudal agriculture. For the definition of custom is not complete when it is left as the mere instinctive, impulsive, unthinking habit of uniformity in action. It is this inadequate definition that underlies Sir Henry Maine's notion that the progress of society is from *status* to *contract*,[1] as well as the notion that the common law can be displaced by a code or a constitution. According to Maine, "status" was the fixed position of the individual in society, tied there by fixed customs. But "contract" is his liberty to break away from the customary way of doing things, and to fashion for himself, by negotiation with others, a changing position in society. Status, custom, and the common law derived from them, were static; but contract, statutory law and codes of law are dynamic.

Rather are customs the common-sense activities of people in planning for the future on the experience of the past, and contracts are themselves customs. The binding power of custom is its security of expectations. What has happened before may be expected to happen again, and he who arbitrarily disappoints expectations must be restrained or punished. And customs are not fixed from time im-

[1] MAINE, SIR HENRY, *Ancient Law*, 173-4 (1861 ed., Pollock).

memorial but are continually changing and continually being formulated in assemblies or groups while dealing with violations and
deciding disputes as they arise. Not until a government is erected
above these loose assemblies, and an official class of judges, executives, law givers, or business managers, sets to work to deal with
violations and decide disputes, do the customs emerge as common
law binding on all the different local assemblies according to the precedents set down in decided cases. Then it is that approved customs,
found in one place, begin to be extended to similar situations found
in other places. This indicates conflict, choice and survival of customs, according to the changing political, economic and cultural
conditions and governments.

The two great economic changes that have brought in new customs are the change from agriculture to traffic, and the change from
isolated to collective industry; and the two accompanying political
and legal changes are the change from slavery or serfdom to liberty
or business, and the change to liberty of labor. The first brought
in or enlarged the new transactions of creditor and debtor, seller and
buyer, with the apparent change from status and custom to liberty
and contract. But the change was rather from the customs of agriculture to the customs of business. For contracts require interpretation in case of dispute; there could arise no security of business
without uniform interpretation, and uniform interpretation is customary interpretation. The customs of business are but the customary way of drawing up, interpreting and enforcing formal contracts, and reading into the behavior of parties implied contracts
according to the custom implied. And the change from status to
liberty was the accompanying political and legal change from the
customs and law of landlord and tenant to the customs and law of
buyer and seller, creditor and debtor.

Likewise with the change from isolated to collective industry, and
from buying and selling things to buying and selling labor. To enforce contracts in the case of propertyless laborers resulted in compulsory labor or imprisonment for debt; and, with the abolition of
these, there is not only a change from status to liberty and contract
but a still further change from contract to *liberty to violate contracts*.
Hence, no binding contracts are made, since they are not enforced.
Hiring and hiring out,"firing" and quitting, are at will. These are
not a substitution of contract for status or custom, but are a new cus-

tom of making contracts. The labor contract is made according to an understanding, a usage, a custom. It is a custom based, not on expected enforcement of contracts but on expected non-enforcement, and hence on continuous renewal of contracts.

The wage-bargain reverses completely the first principles of the credit-bargain, for it substitutes non-enforcement of contract for enforcement. The wage-earner is a tenant-at-will of either party. He can quit without giving a reason and the employer can discharge him without giving a reason. The theory of the law-merchant, however, still hangs over, in that it is held illegal to break a contract, and that, if it is broken, the right to institute a suit for damages immediately accrues to the party damaged by the violation. But both law and custom nullify this remedy in the case of the wage-bargain. The laborer is granted liberal property exemptions and he cannot be condemned by law to involuntary servitude. Neither can he bring a suit against his employer for unlawful dismissal, for, by custom, he is hired at will. Hence the remarkable ambiguity in that the courts do not recognize the customs of the wage-bargain, since they hold it unlawful to break the contract, yet they are prohibited by law and prevented by custom from enforcing the contract. The capitalist system has been built up, as we have seen, on the enforcement and negotiability of contracts, and it is as difficult for the lawyer of today to appreciate the custom of employer and employee in breaking labor contracts as it was for the lawyers of the Sixteenth and Seventeenth Centuries to authorize the custom of merchants in enforcing promises and buying and selling them. While the violation cannot be penalized against either the employer or the employee, yet the theory that it is unlawful rises up on occasion to penalize or enjoin third parties who induce the violation, although the only effective liberty of the wage earner is the alternative opportunities offered by those third parties.

This defect goes back, as we have seen,[1] to a theory of the will itself. For the will is not an empty choosing between doing and not doing, but between different degrees of power in doing one thing instead of another. The will cannot choose nothing—it must choose something in this world of scarcity—and it chooses the next best alternative. If this alternative is a good one, then the will is free, and can be induced only by persuasion. If the alternative is a poor one, or if there

[1] Above, Chap. IV, Sec. II, p. 69.

is no alternative, then the will is coerced. The will chooses between opportunities, and opportunities are held and withheld by other wills which also are choosing between opportunities, and these opportunities are limited by principles of scarcity.

This economic coercion, as we have noted,[1] finds with difficulty a place in legal concepts because the precedents by which the law of property and liberty was constructed had to do only with immunity from physical coercion. Property and liberty consist in protection against force and violence, whether that force and violence be the assaults and trespass of private persons or the commands of officials with authority to exercise the organized violence of the King or sovereign. But the property and liberty for which laborers seek to get protection, while they include protection against violence, include also protection against economic coercion. Precedents, indeed, may be found for protection against economic coercion, but, as we have seen, they have usually been constructed by avoiding the notion of economic power and passing it off as either a special privilege granted by a sovereign or a violation of confidential or other relations of legal superiority and inferiority. Economic superiority and inferiority, as distinguished from personal or legal superiority and inferiority, have had no recognition by the courts on their own initiative, and have found a place only to the extent that the court has yielded to the views of the legislature, as was done in the case of Munn *v.* Illinois, and Holden *v.* Hardy. And, in cases where the court has not yielded and has either declared the law unconstitutional or nullified it by definition, there the court has had adequate precedents to sustain the position that economic coercion cannot be made illegal, since it is not force and violence.

It is this economic coercion upon which is built industrial government, for its extreme penalty and inducement to obedience is that fear of poverty which varies greatly in its many aspects from fear of bankruptcy to fear of unemployment. And consequently, what may be distinguished as the common law of labor springing from the customs of wage earners, as distinguished from that historic common law springing from the customs of merchants and manufacturers, consists in those practices by which laborers endeavor to achieve their ideals through protection against the economic power of employers.

These ideals and customs are quite peculiar and differ in important

[1] Above, Chap. III.

respects from those of business. Primarily they spring from that insecurity of jobs and positions which has a double aspect, namely, the limited supply of jobs and the control of that supply by capitalists. Out of this conviction that there are not enough jobs to go around, and the knowledge that the jobs themselves are owned by capitalists instead of laborers, arise many peculiar ideas and corresponding customs. One is the idea that the individual who gets more work or works faster than the others, is taking the bread out of their mouths. This goes along with the idea of stretching out one's work to make it last, or of sharing the work with others, and this leads to that severe reprobation and condemnation of those who violate the custom and refuse to be bound by these notions of solidarity in a field of limited opportunities.

This, of course, is exactly opposite to the ideals and customs of business which the courts have been defining and classifying for some 300 years, and is similar to the ideals and customs of business when it was contending with feudalism by means of its little gilds of merchants and manufacturers. Initiative, enterprise, ambition, individual success, are quite contrary to the rules of solidarity and fair competition that characterize gilds and unions, and naturally the courts do not comprehend and sanction such customs, any more than do the capitalists. They are not, in the words of Carter, to be regarded as "customs" but as "bad practices."

For individual success consists in rising out of a lower class into a higher class—from the laboring class to the professional, managerial, capitalistic, or official class—and it is difficult to distinguish this kind of success, which increases one's income by augmenting the income of others, from that other kind of success which takes a larger share for self from the limited supply of opportunities for all. One is success, the other is fair competition. Success consists in rising above the class, fair competition consists in rising with the class. The laborer is in an ambiguous position. If he increases his individual product he, by reducing its exchange-value, diminishes the share which his class of laborers gets of the national product. To his fellows in the same functional class, he seems to be a "hog," for the very act by which he augments both the total national product and his own compensation, reduces the exchange-value of the units of that product and thereby reduces both the share of the national product which his own class secures, and ultimately his own compensation.

This is, of course, also the familiar and well-known resentment among business men against the price-cutter and the cut-throat competitor, as it is among laboring men against the "swift," the "hog," the "scab." It is a by-product of division of labor and exchange-value. When business men call upon laborers to "produce," and criticise them for restricting production, they are calling upon them to do that which they themselves do not. For they, like the laborers, produce, not indiscriminately, but they produce in limited quantities, in order to maintain the price in their market. Their call for more product from labor is a call for labor to reduce the exchange-value of the joint product of labor and capital in that occupation. And when the value as thus reduced approaches the profitless point, the capitalist restricts the output by laying off the laborers. Restriction of output is practiced by both, but in one case it seems "natural" and therefore right, because there is no profit; in the other case it seems arbitrary and therefore wrong because it places a limit on national wealth. To the laborer, however, it looks different. To lay off workmen is wrong because the previous profit ought to have been considered; and to spread out the work steadily over the year is right because there is no stored-up wages to tide over the lay-off.

The difference proceeds from a different psychology springing from different experiences and different hopes and fears. The business psychology is speculative—high profits at one time are equalized with losses at another time, through reserve funds of various kinds, and interest and dividends are paid out of the funds at the end of the year. The laborer's psychology is conservative—high wages at one time do not offset no-wages at another time. He has no convenient place to invest his savings and no inducement or security to acquire a means of livelihood by borrowing, if a period of no-wages may happen to eat up his savings to pay his debts. The laborer lives from day to day, the business man from year to year. Speculation demoralizes the one but vitalizes the other, and what seems natural and right if it vitalizes is contrary to nature and wrong if it demoralizes.

IV. INDUSTRIAL GOVERNMENT

It was, as we have seen, identically the same restrictive and regulative rules just mentioned that characterized the merchants' and manufacturers' gilds during the period when business was weak and struggling to make for itself a place under the régime of feudalism.

And when the common-law courts, beginning in 1599, began to strike off the closed-shop and fair-trade rules of the gilds, the same courts and especially the reformed equity courts began to build up that property-right in a going business which became the law of fair and unfair competition. So history repeats itself on new levels. Just as the prerogative courts of the Sixteenth and Seventeenth Centuries could not comprehend and yield to the demand for liberty and power on the part of the small but aggressive merchants and manufacturers outside the gilds, so the courts of to-day do not comprehend and yield to the demand for new definitions of liberty and power on the part of the aggressive laborers. History repeats itself, and the Supreme Court takes over the protection of the liberty and power of business, just as the prerogative courts protected the privileges of the monarch and his party. The injunction gets a new importance which it has not had since the chancellor Lord Ellesmere was sustained by King James in his contest with Coke and the latter was removed from his position as Chief Justice of the common-law courts. The reasons and precedents then were on the side of Ellesmere and James. And so it is to-day. The reasons and precedents are on the side of business, and the liberty and power demanded by labor is as contrary to precedent as the liberty and power demanded by business was contrary to the precedents of feudalism or the King's prerogative or the special privileges of gilds or the common law of agricultural England. The prerogative of to-day is the prerogative of business, and the common law of to-day seeking recognition is the customs of propertyless laborers developing in their own assemblies and industrial courts. And, while the courts, when overruling the closed-shop privileges of the gilds, began to take over the fair-competition rules of the gilds, yet, in nullifying the closed-shop privileges of the unions, they do not take over the protection of labor against the "unfair employer." Apparently, a "new equity" is needed—an equity that will protect the job as the older equity protected the business.

When new conditions appear, equity can immediately respond. This elasticity of equity is seen in its enlargement towards the prevention of criminal acts whose punishment had previously been thought to belong only to the common law through indictment by a grand jury. The indictment is punitive, the injunction is preventive, and hence is far more efficacious in preventing strikes when they are deemed unlawful by the court.

In many cases this unlawfulness, in the case of strikes, is patent, since it is accompanied with violence or threa s of violence. Under such circumstances the court, as in the Debs Case,[1] responded to the appeal of the executive to issue an injunction and thereby to order what it was the duty of the executive to do anyhow. In other cases the unlawfulness depends mainly upon the judge's opinion of the public policy involved in the case, for where there is no "compulsion of violence," the only influence which a union can have in a strike towards inducing an employer to agree to its terms is that "compulsion of motive "[2] through the economic power of inflicting pecuniary loss on the employer. If the judge feels, in such a case, that the public importance of the property interests to which the employer belongs is greater than that of the organized employees, he grants the injunction. If he feels that the public importance of the union is greater than that of the employer he refuses the injunction. In either case a damage is about to be inflicted, either by the union on the business of the employer, or by the employer on the jobs of the employees. And the judge, acting for the state, chooses the damage which he considers less, in the interest of the public, and enjoins that which he considers greater or more obnoxious.

This conclusion was reached by Justice Holmes in one of the early cases, where the majority of the Massachusetts Supreme Court approved an injunction prohibiting the union from employing any "scheme or conspiracy " whatever to bring pressure on other workmen to keep them from entering the employment, whereas Justice Holmes would have enjoined them only from using violence or threats of violence. Said Justice Holmes, in that case:

"In numberless instances the law warrants the intentional infliction of temporal damage because it regards it as justified. . . . The true grounds of decision are considerations of policy and of social advantage, and it is vain to suppose that solutions can be attained merely by logic and the general propositions of law which nobody disputes. Propositions as to public policy rarely are unanimously accepted, and still more rarely, if ever,

[1] In re Debs, 158 U. S. 564 (1895).

[2] Sir Thomas Erskine, in his defense of Lord George Gordon, in 1787, on an indictment for assembling a multitude and petitioning parliament to repeal a law which had removed certain disabilities of Roman Catholics, said in addressing the jury, "You must find that Lord George Gordon assembled these men with that traitorous intention:—you must find not merely a riotous illegal petitioning,—not a tumultuous indecent importunity to influence parliament—not the compulsion of motive, from seeing so great a body of people united in sentiment and clamorous supplication—but the absolute, unequivocal compulsion of force, from the hostile acts of numbers united in rebellious conspiracy and arms." 21 How. St. Tr. 486, 594.

are capable of unanswerable proof. They require a special training to enable any one even to form an intelligent opinion about them. In the early stages of law, at least, they generally are acted on rather as inarticulate instincts than as definite ideas for which a rational defense is ready. . . . It has been the law for centuries that a man may set up a business in a country town too small to support more than one, although he expects and intends thereby to ruin someone already there, and succeeds in his intent. The reason, of course is that the doctrine generally has been accepted that free competition is worth more to society than it costs and that on this ground the infliction of the damage is privileged. . . . If the policy on which our law is founded is too narrowly expressed in the term free competition we may substitute free struggle for life. . . . Free competition means combination. . . . Combination on the one side is patent and powerful. Combination on the other is the necessary and desirable counterpart, if the battle is to be carried on in a fair and equal way." [1]

Again, with the enlarged definitions of property and liberty, the injunction itself is enlarged to protect not only property rights but to protect what formerly were considered personal liberty or civil rights, but now are property rights. The court had said in 1888,[2] "The office and jurisdiction of a court of equity, unless enlarged by express statute, are limited to protection of rights of property. It has no jurisdiction over the prosecution, the punishment or the pardon of crimes," and had quoted Chief Justice Holt of the common-law court of Queen's Bench saying, in 1704, that his court would "break" any injunction granted by Chancery in a criminal matter then under examination in the law court and would "protect any that would proceed in contempt of it."[3]

But now, with the definition of property enlarged so that, in 1915, it was deemed to include the right of an alien to a livelihood and to continue in employment, and with the supreme court having power to declare unconstitutional any law infringing that property right, the court enjoined a criminal prosecution in the state of Arizona, saying: "equitable jurisdiction exists to restrain criminal prosecution under unconstitutional enactments, when the prevention of such prosecutions is essential to the safe-guarding of rights of property."[4]

Finally, with the two-fold fact of modern corporations and modern trade unions extending over the breadth of a nation, the injunction when directed towards the thousands of agents, employees, members, sympathizers, of either the corporation or the union, without men-

---

[1] Vegelahn v. Guntner, 167 Mass. 92, 105, 107, 108 (1896).
[2] In re Sawyer, 124 U. S. 200, 210 (1888).
[3] Holderstaffe v. Saunders, S. C. 6 Mod. 16 (1704).
[4] Truax v. Raich, 239 U. S. 33, 37, 38 (1915).

tioning the names of all individuals or serving notice upon them, becomes in fact as truly an act of legislation as any that ever was adopted by a legislature. The easy steps by which the "blanket" injunction was finally approved, from its implied notice to all agents of the party enjoined, until it included "any and all other persons associated with them in committing, etc.," may be traced in the cases and need not here be shown.[1] Suffice to note the futile protests of dissenting Justices as the process advanced. Justice Harlan, dissenting in the Standard Oil Case in 1911, above referred to, said, "The court by its decision, when interpreted by the language of its opinion, has not only upset the long-settled interpretation of the act, but has usurped the constitutional function of the legislative branch of the government."[2]

And Justice Caldwell, dissenting in 1897, said, "Courts of equity have no jurisdiction to enforce the criminal laws . . . It is said by those who defend the assumption of this jurisdiction by the federal courts that it is a swifter and speedier mode of dealing with those who violate or threaten to violate the laws than by the prescribed and customary methods of proceeding in courts of law; that it avoids the delay and uncertainty incident to a jury trial, occasions less expense, and insures a speedier punishment. All this may be conceded to be true. But the logical difficulty with this reasoning is that it confers jurisdiction on the mob equally with the chancellor . . . It can make little difference to the victims of shortcut and unconstitutional methods, whether it is the mob or the chancellor that deprives them of their constitutional rights. It is vain to disguise the fact that this desire for a shortcut originates in the feeling of hostility to trial by jury—a mode of trial which has never been popular with the aristocracy of wealth, or the corporations and trusts. . . . Against the exercise of this jurisdiction the constitution of the United States interposes an insurmountable barrier. . . . ' The trial of all crimes, except in cases of impeachment, shall be by jury.' (Const. Art.3) ' In all criminal prosecutions the accused shall enjoy a right to a speedy and public trial by an impartial jury. Id., Art. 6. . . . With the interpolations essential to support government by injunction, the constitution would contain the following further exceptions to the right

---

[1] Amer. St. & W. Co. v. Wire Drawers' Union, 90 Fed. 598 (1898); In re Reese, 107 Fed. 942 (1901); Union Pac. R. Co. v. Ruef, 120 Fed. 102 (1902); High on Injunctions, par. 1443 (4th ed.).

[2] Standard Oil Co. v. U. S., 221 U. S. 1, 83 (1911).

of trial by jury: 'And except when many persons are associated together for a common purpose, and except in the case of members of
trade unions and other labor organizations, and except in cases of
all persons 'of small means.' " [1]

On the other hand, the answer to these dissents and charges of
usurpation is made by Justice Ricks.[2] "It is said the orders issued
in this case are without precedent. Every just order or rule known
to equity courts was born of some emergency, to meet some new
condition, and was, therefore, in its time, without a precedent."
And he found support in quoting the assertion of Justice Brewer:
"I believe most thoroughly that the powers of a court of equity are
as vast, and its processes and procedure as elastic, as all the changing
emergencies of increasingly complex business relations and the
protection of rights can demand."

The King's prerogative, thus inherited by the courts of equity,
was not the absolute authority of a single person, and the King was
not a person above and apart from the clash of private interests,
but the King was the chief of the court party, the party of courtiers,
feudal lords, gildsmen, holders and expectant holders of privileges
or monopolies, derived from the prerogative. And what we have
distinguished as the prerogative courts as against the common-law
courts were the agents by which the prerogative party exempted
themselves from the same common law that defined the rights and
duties of those not privileged. Then the contest took place between
the prerogative courts of the King and the common-law courts,
both of which were eventually brought under the same rule of constitutional government, and it then became possible for the common
law of business to unfold out of what were deemed to be the reasonable
customs of business men.

Likewise, with the customs of labor and with the prerogatives of
Capitalism and its agents, the superintendents and foremen. The
restraints which laborers place on free competition in the interests
of fair competition, begin to be taken over by employers and administered by their own labor managers. Even organized labor achieves
participation with the management in the protection of the job,
just as the barons and the capitalists achieved participation with
the King in the protection of property and business. A common

---

[1] Hopkins v. Oxley Stave Co., 83 Fed. 912, 921–940 (1897).
[2] Tol. A. A. & N. M. Ry. Co. v. Penna. Co., 54 Fed. 746, 751 (1893).

law of labor is constructed by selecting the reasonable practices and rejecting the bad practices of labor, and by depriving both unions and management of arbitrary power over the job. An amendment is gradually worked into the constitution of industrial government: "No employer shall deprive any employee of his job without due process of industrial law, nor deny to any employee within his jurisdiction the equal protection of the common law of labor." [1] Even statute law begins to add its part by imposing duties upon employers in the safeguarding of jobs against accidents, against sickness, against long hours, inadequate wages, and insecurity of employment. Out of the wage-bargain a constitution for industrial government is being constructed by removing cases from the prerogative of management and the arbitrary power of unions and subjecting the foremen, the superintendents and the business agents to the same due process of law as that which governs the laborers.

[1] COMMONS and ASSOCIATES, *Industrial Government*, chapter on "Due Process of Law," by MALCOLM SHARP (1921).

CHAPTER IX

PUBLIC PURPOSE

I. Concerns and Positions

The foregoing historical sketch from the time of the Norman Conquest to the Twentieth Century, indicates the three historical stages in the evolution of Anglo-American systems of Value and Valuation, the agricultural, commercial, and industrial stages. Each stage proceeds by the evolution of customs and the formulation of customs into working rules by a government. The customs are customary transactions, and these have the twofold aspect of authorized and authoritative transactions, the one being transactions between equals, the other between superior and inferior. The agricultural stage proceeds out of the relation of landlord and tenant, and the transactions are those which determine the rent-bargain of the feudal system. The commercial stage proceeds out of the relations of creditor and debtor, and the transactions are those which determine the price-bargain. The industrial stage is the relation of employer and employee, and the transactions are those which determine the wage-bargain and the wage system. Out of the rent-bargain was developed, on the authoritative side, the system of constitutional government, or sovereignty, and on the authorized side the institution of tangible property and personal equality and liberty of property owners. Out of the price-bargain was developed the system of banking and financiering, or the money power, with its institutions of incorporeal and intangible property and its equal liberty of contract and enforcement of contracts. Out of the wage-bargain has been developing, on the authoritative side, a system of industrial government, and on the authorized side the institution of jobs or positions in industry with their liberty but non-enforcement of contracts.

Each of these historical stages implies a threefold expansion in the fields of economics, jurisprudence and politics. In *economics* it implies the expansion from use-value or "real" values, to exchange-values, from production and consumption to buying and selling, from things to prices. The use-values, that is "real values" of physical things proceed from the direct control of lands, chattels and human beings in both the production and consumption of wealth. Exchange-values, or prices, spring up between the primary producers and ultimate consumers, through a nation-wide division of labor, a credit system and freedom in bargaining. Upon the foundation of use-value was built feudalism; upon nominal values or prices, capitalism and industrialism. In *jurisprudence* this expansion is reflected in the expansion of the common law from the protection of tangible property and persons in an age of violence to the protection of business and positions in the peaceful expansion of markets. In *politics* it is the mass movements of individuals, organized or unorganized, which bring about the transitions from prerogative to sovereignty, from personal government to the collective bargaining of King, landlords and merchants, then of corporations and coöperatives, then of employers and employees. Together, these made possible the further evolution, in the Eighteenth and Nineteenth Centuries, of those incorporeal and intangible properties whose value consists, not in their physical uses but in the going business and jobs of a going concern.

In the agricultural stage the relation of owner to slave or serf conformed to the primitive notion of property in that it was the exclusive holding and dominion over a physical object for one's own use. The slave or serf was a thing, without liberty to choose alternative opportunities, and the relation was that of owner to thing owned. In proportion as freedom of choice was recognized and protected by law the relationship was evolved through intermediate stages until it reached its modern dimensions of master and servant, employer and employee, principal and agent. The outcome consists, not in the elimination of command and obedience, but in the liberty of bargaining as to the terms or limits within which obedience shall be rendered. The employee or agent, indeed, is not permitted to sell his physical body, which would carry with it all of his liberty, but he is permitted to sell his willingness to obey commands within certain limits. In this respect he sells a part of his liberty, and submits to the will of the employer or principal. The terms on which he will sell are a matter of persuasion or coercion, for he is free to sell or reject the offer, but, once accepted, the relation which he assumes is that of command and obedience.

A subordinate distinction is the modern one between agent and employee.[1] The *agent* deals with people, and must therefore rely on persuasion or coercion, since they have legal liberty to choose alternatives. It is this relation that constitutes a going business. But the *employee* deals with physical and animal forces of nature not deemed to have rights and liberties, and his relation with them is analogous to that of command and obedience, constituting what we distinguish as a going plant. But, in either case, the agent or the employee executes the will of his principal or employer, and is lawfully permitted to choose for himself only within those limits set by the agreement or by the working rules of labor or agency. If he does not obey, within the field of his agency or employment, he renders himself liable to dismissal and even damages.

If he does obey, then, by contract or by operation of the rules of law, he sets up a counter-encumbrance against the principal or employer to the extent of the hourly and daily accrual of compensation designated for his service. He becomes a creditor, the employer a debtor, to the extent of his uncompensated services. In this respect he is, for the time being, an investor in the business, waiting for compensation until pay-day.

The rules of law in respect to encumbrance have thus evolved, in respect to the law of labor, from that of physical property in the sense of holding the body of the laborer with its compulsory obedience to all commands, until it becomes that intangible property of voluntary obedience, and that incorporeal property, the right to compensation.

The early goodwill and copyright cases have been dwelt upon at length because they show the actual steps by which the primitive notion of tangible property passed over to the modern notion of intangible property.

The first needful step was that of dealing with competition as a kind of trespass. This step was taken on the procedural side, presumably in the year 1580, by enlarging the common-law writ of trespass so as to permit a suit for damages to be entertained, not only on the ground of physical violence, but also on the ground, first of fraud, and then, with the help of equity, on the ground of "unfair competition." By this means a property-right was created and protected, not in the exclusive holding of things, but in the expected purchasing power to be obtained from future bargains with customers. Tangible

---

[1] The term "servant" may mean either agent or employee.

things, with their expected use-values, become intangible opportunities with their expected prices.

The next step was to make these expectations saleable like things. This step was taken in 1620 when, apparently for the first time, a voluntary restraint of one's liberty to compete with a purchaser of his going business was legalized and the contract enforced. A person was now permitted to sell a part of his liberty just as he could sell his physical property, and thus to convert both into assets.

The third step was that of recognizing the expectation of future transactions as personal property to be held exclusively for one's own use, like any visible piece of land or chattel. This recognition by the court is perceptible, in 1743, when shares in expected profits are separated from the tangible property and passed over as personal property to the executor of an intestate, in conformity with the various ways in which expected profits, independently of tangible things, were already being bought, sold, and transmitted by will as personal property. The intangible expectation of a future net income of purchasing power to be derived from bargaining was thus placed on the same footing as property-rights in things.

Along with these conversions of physical things into expectancies of purchasing power, came the evident necessity of converting them into liquid assets, as nearly like the commodity, gold, as possible, in order that they might be realizable on the markets as promptly as possible, in terms of the legal tender standard of value. Hence a parallel development occurs establishing the negotiability of new forms of intangible and incorporeal property as rapidly as they emerge.

Since the various forms of intangible and incorporeal property cannot be created except by imposing new legal duties and new restraints on the liberty of individuals, questions were continually arising as to the reasonable scope and duration of these restraints. Here a fine point of dispute emerges, for goodwill slips readily into privilege or monopoly, since each is a restraint of trade, and can be distinguished only by good judgment as to the point where goodwill ends and special privilege begins. With this in view Justice Parker, in 1711, correlated the various cases on restraint of trade, and, while the general principles then laid down remain to the present day, their application varies with the judgment of the courts and legislatures as to their proper scope and duration.

In all cases an ambiguity arose out of the survival of physical concepts of property injected into the intangible concepts. It has always been necessary to clear up this ambiguity, and one of the steps is that of distinguishing reasonable and unreasonable restraints of trade when proceeding from the mere enlargement of the common-law definition of physical property. An instance of this was the decision of 1774 reversing the copyright decision of 1769. It was then decided that the analogy to rights of property in physical things should not be carried so far as to create a perpetual exclusive ownership in expected income to be derived from a perpetual restraint of trade, and that, where a time-limit should be set on the future prolongation of property, the matter had to be arranged by legislative statute and not by judicial definition of property.

The dissenting opinions in those cases pointed to the true limits within which the common-law definition of property might be extended by analogy from the holding of a physical thing for one's own use to the holding of expected profits for one's own use. The new line was drawn, not where subjective ideas are distinguished from their external embodiment in things or manuscript, but at the point where it was deemed fit that the owner's will should have exclusive control over other persons, and beyond which other persons should be deemed to have liberty of choice in dealing with the owner or his representative.

This point we have found to be a point which can be stated differently according to the branch of learning which we have uppermost in mind, although these branches are inseparable in fact. Stated in terms of social psychology it is the limit where command and obedience stop and persuasion or coercion begins. Stated in terms of economics it is the point where the aspect of economy, or mere proportioning of natural and human factors, is distinguished from the aspect of expansion, or enlargement of control over other persons through choice of opportunities and exercise of power. Stated in terms of law it is the point where the law of privacy, of privileged communication, or the law which binds an agent, or employee, or servant to execute the will of his principal, employer, or master, becomes the law that governs the dealings of self or agent with the general public who are not bound by those obligations of privacy and obedience to commands. Or, stated in terms which seem to combine psychology, economics, and law, it is the point where positive encumbrances merge into opportunities.

It will be seen, in this historical sketch, that the distinction between property and contract has been merged into that of property, promises, and opportunities. Property, in its original sense of physical possession, refers to physical things; promises are the restraints on liberty agreed to by the parties; opportunities are the alternatives present when the agreements are made. The constitution of the United States forbids any state to enforce a law "impairing the obligation of contracts." This prohibition is largely nullified by the law of freedom, which prevents the enforcement of promises in so far as they impose involuntary servitude. So with laws forbidding imprisonment for debt, and with the many wage-exemptions, homestead exemption and insolvency laws. They prevent the complete enforcement of the obligation of contracts, by liberating the debtor from a part or the whole of his debt. So with public utility regulations. The rates charged may be changed by the legislature even in apparent conflict with promises previously entered into either between the state and the corporation, or between the corporation and patrons. When these and similar cases arose, the court held that no obligation of contract can defeat lawful governmental authority, or conflict with public policy. Hence, because the strict enforcement of obligations of contract is deemed to restrain liberty where liberty is deemed to be the more important, there the liberty to violate contracts is substituted for the duty to fulfill contracts.

These distinctions have required attention to two inseparable aspects of economy, namely, the engineering economy of a going plant and the business economy of a going business. Engineering economy relates to the physical things of the universe, the relationship of "man to nature." This field has, indeed, its dimensions similar to those of business economy, and for that reason is not always distinguished from the latter. It has its dimensions of economy, or the proportioning of nature's forces, or materials, for the sake of the largest use and enjoyment of self. It has its dimensions of choice between physical objects, and since these choices run along the line of what is deemed to be the least resistance or greatest power, they indicate expansion of control over nature, in contrast with more economical proportioning of items within that control. It has also its time-dimension of expected use and enjoyment, inducing present action.

The distinguishing mark, however, regarding this nature-aspect of economy, opportunity, power, and expectancy, is the fact that the external objects, even though they are human beings, are not deemed to have any will of their own to be considered. They are merely instruments of one's own will, and therefore, to that extent, the branches of science dealing with them are properly to be distinguished as engineering economy, or scientific management. We have distinguished this relationship of man to nature as a going plant with its producing organization.

It is different at the point where these things are deemed to have a will protected by rules or principles of ethics or law, for then they begin to have those relationships of rights, duties, liberties, and exposures which constitute what we have distinguished as encumbrances and opportunities, thus constituting a going business. Since these encumbrances and opportunities are determined by a higher authority whose will is superior to that of the parties concerned, it is this superior authority that transforms engineering economy, business economy, and scientific management into political economy.

What has happened to the notion of property, can now be seen. To the original notion of holding physical things for self is first added the enforcement of mere promises, and thus, in the early Sixteenth Century, the law of contract, or positive encumbrances on others, starts its modern career. Then, in the early Seventeenth Century, the law of opportunity or negative encumbrance, springing partly from contract, partly from tort, begins to be added. Meanwhile the mere arbitrary prerogative and capricious will of the monarch is in process of being stabilized under the form of constitutional government, or working rules that declare the collective will of the state, completed by the Act of Settlement at the beginning of the Eighteenth Century, and thereupon the courts are free to develop the law of contract and tort, with the help of equity, in its modern shape of encumbrances and opportunities. Finally, by the middle of the Nineteenth Century, this stabilized prerogative completes the development of that special privilege, a corporate franchise, and opens up, by general corporation laws, to all comers, the privilege of binding themselves together by contract into a going concern.

With these delegations of sovereign power, property expands into an industrial government of its own, treated as a unit and even a person, although it is not a person but an industrial government. The economic power of this government begins to be recognized by the highest court in the latter part of the Nineteenth Century in the public utility and labor cases, but when its power is challenged by another industrial government, the labor organization endeavoring also to obtain sovereign powers and immunities, the court is divided. A majority cling to the recently developed ideas of property as a union of property and liberty, summarized in the law of goodwill; a minority sees in this union an emergence of economic power.

The division of opinion turns on the definition of property and the scope of contract. Physical things of themselves are powerless. Even liberty to choose between opportunities is passive and ineffective. But power to withhold opportunities is economic power, and associated power is government. When therefore liberty of contract is merged with property, it adds the liberty of persons to the exclusive holding of things. And this liberty operates in the several directions of liberty to combine their property into an industrial government and to act as a unit, not only in proportioning their resources economically but also in choosing opportunities, in commanding obedience, in persuading or coercing, and in planning for the expectations of an indefinite future. Liberty of contract becomes economy, opportunity, power, expectancy, *and* industrial government. In short, through the law of contracts and the law of torts the modern concept of property has evolved from the holding of things to the control of the supply of things through controlling the transactions of persons, so that it signifies the four personal relations of buyer and seller, creditor and debtor, competitors, and governors and governed. Property emerges from physical things into assets and liabilities, and liberty emerges from personal liberty into the positions and jobs of a going business operated by a going concern.

We have seen that these going concerns may be classified according to the kind of sanction or penalty which they employ in obtaining the obedience of members. Going concerns are but organized mass movements with a common purpose and common rules designed to permit the concern to act as a unit. Each concern springs up out of the body of society as a whole, through a process of differentiation. In early times they were unseparated, and there was no division between the "state" employing the sanction of physical violence, and the business concern employing the sanction of bankruptcy or poverty and the cultural concerns employing the sanction of the mere common opinion of those deemed worth while. But, with the business revolution of the Seventeenth Century both the business concerns began to separate off from the political concern through the separation of ownership from sovereignty, and cultural concerns began to separate off from both business and politics through the newly established principle of toleration and freedom of worship.

Each concern is, indeed a government, employing its peculiar sanctions, and each individual holds a position or job in many governments. He is a citizen of the state, a principal, agent, employee, creditor, debtor, of a business concern, a father, son, brother, fellow-communicant, comrade, and so on, of the various cultural concerns. Since these concerns, with their group psychology, act as a unit through agents or representatives, and especially since they must necessarily establish and enforce common rules in order to avoid disputes and dissolution, there emerges in all concerns, from primitive times to the present, the principles of a common purpose and a corresponding set of working rules holding the members together. Each concern has its different sanctions, but its enforcement of those sanctions in particular cases is in the hands of those who primarily exercise the functions of a judiciary. It is therefore in the decision of the judicial functionaries of each concern in interpreting their working rules that the economist must look for the concern's purpose, that is the "public" purpose of the concern. In the Anglo-American political concern, this public purpose has been evolved under the names of classification and due process of law.

II. CLASSIFICATION

The notable fact of Western civilization is the increasing control over nature's forces by an increasing population, yet without improvement in the brains of individuals. Could the babies of our Teutonic ancestors have been lifted over from the German forests two thousand years ago into modern civilization they could, in their lifetime, have carried it on as efficiently as we do. Indeed, a good case can be made for a decreasing efficiency of individuals along with an increasing efficiency of going concerns. In a hundred years the population of the United States has increased tenfold, but it is probable that the services for ultimate consumers have increased forty-fold. One hundred years ago it took seven farmers' families to feed eight families, now seven feed twenty-one. Yet it is doubtful whether farmers and farm workers are more brainy than they were a hundred years ago. Compositors in printing offices turn out to-day five times as many columns of type in an hour as they did forty years ago, but the printer, as such, is less efficient, for now he can learn his part of the trade in three months, then it took three years. Yet the printer, by means of his trade union, has brought his hours of labor down from eleven and twelve to seven or eight a day, has doubled his wages per day, while the employers make more money than they did, the inventors and manufacturers of the linotype become wealthy, the price of newspapers comes down from five cents to two cents for two or three times as much reading matter, and the efficiency of the entire nation is multiplied by a wider diffusion of knowledge.

The steel industry is probably five times as efficient per man-hour of all its workers as it was forty years ago, but, with the labor organization destroyed, the hours were increased to twelve, the week to seven days, the workers individually are more ignorant and less efficient, but enormous fortunes have been made and every industry in the nation is multiplied in its efficiency by the one factor of cheap and widespread use of steel. Many illustrations could be added—decreasing efficiency of individuals and yet an increasing efficiency for all of them and an increasing income for each of them according to their ability to pull a larger share out of the total increasing national efficiency.

So it has been at every step from the forests of Germany in the time of Cæsar to the industries of America in 1923. Nature seems to have finished the development of brains by the struggle for existence in a cold climate, and then started out to multiply the efficiency of collective brains. This fact so impressed Karl Marx that he attributed the whole historic process to a Social Labor Power in which the individual was nothing but a brain.

It does, indeed, spring from that universal economy of nature which accomplishes marvellous results merely by re-proportioning the factors more advantageously without enlarging them individually. A nation is not an addition of atoms but a multiplication of complementary by limiting factors. But the limiting factors, in this case, are not blind—they have each individually a purpose of its own.

Karl Marx conceived that, at any given period, there were but two classes, the property owners who produced nothing, and the propertyless who produced everything. But in a system of limiting and complementary factors where each is necessary to the total result but in a diminishing importance according to its supply, it is impossible to simplify the issue in this way. There are as many classes as there are classifications of factors contributing to the total national welfare. At different periods and under different circumstances one or more classes are more important than others, because, at the time, the total command over nature is relatively limited by their ability to perform their part of the total economy. All of the other classes, at such a time, yield to the pre-eminence of that class, both willingly amd unwillingly. The warrior and priestly class were preëminent and greatly admired, when the fear of violence was the limiting factor in men's minds and paralyzed their other faculties. With the fear of violence once regulated, the business class became preëminent, for the fear of poverty, which they alone knew how to circumvent, became the paralyzing factor in national efficiency. With the fear of poverty regulated by industrial government, the laboring class becomes a limiting factor, for their unwillingness to work when not pushed to it by fear, and their resentment against coercion through fear of unemployment, looms up as a factor retarding all others.

Thus the proportioning of factors in a national economy is not the blind proportioning of blind forces of nature, but is the proportioning of inducements to willing and unwilling persons.

Starting with Adam Smith's ideas of property, liberty, self-interest, division of labor, and divine providence, economic theory worked out a mechanistic proportioning of factors according to laws of supply and demand. If too much of a certain factor is produced its value falls and its producers then shift to other products. If too little is produced its value rises and producers shift to it. Producers, led on by an "invisible hand," are shifting towards the limiting factors whose value is high, and away from the complementary factors whose values are low, thus proportioning the factors by equalizing the incomes of individuals towards a "normal" or "natural" or harmonious standard of wages, interest, or profits for each class.

Yet this mechanistic economy of nature, as Smith sorrowfully acknowledged, has been greatly interfered with by the collective power of political and industrial governments. Protective tariffs have limited the supply of certain factors and increased their prices. Taxes on property, on income and on commodities have changed prices and the directions of industry. Labor legislation has imposed burdens on employers and changed the direction in which profit is obtained. Great corporations fix prices of commodities or labor, and the individual does not bargain with them—he takes it or leaves it. Labor organizations, authorized or permitted by government, have interfered with nature's laws. Had property and liberty developed as Smith hoped, it might have turned out differently. But even his ideas of property and liberty would have required action by government to prevent any individual from holding more property than he could physically use and to prevent individuals associating in corporations and unions.

Natural economy continues to operate. Mechanism cannot override scarcity. "Demand and supply " cannot be eliminated, for it proceeds from the limited supply of nature's resources and the proportioning of human effort through division of labor. But collective action of political and industrial governments has reproportioned considerably the limiting and complementary factors, and obtained a different national result from that intended by nature as interpreted by Adam Smith.

Smith had hoped to reduce collective power to its lowest limits and thereby raise the individual to the highest power. But it has happened differently. The wealth of nations did not start with the French Revolution. The property and liberty of that period were but a passing result of governmental proportioning and reproportioning of inducements, and that reproportioning has kept on according to the purposes of those who controlled the governments. Not Adam Smith but William the Conqueror was the founder of Anglo-American political economy. Adam Smith started the theory, but William started the economy. Nor did Smith start the whole of the theory. It was started by Coke, Littleton, Seldon and the other theorists of the time preceding the Commonwealth. Just as Adam Smith identified private wealth with commonwealth, so William and his lawyers, as we have seen, identified his private property with his sovereignty. William was the public. His "weal" was the "public weal." His private purposes were public purposes. His will was the collective will. Not until the time of the Commonwealth did the notion of public purpose get clearly separated out from the private purposes of the sovereign. Clinched by the Act of Settlement, this separation of property from sovereignty, of private wealth from commonwealth, signified a field where the will of the individual should be final, and another field where the collective will should be final. One was the field of property, the other of sovereignty. One was private wealth, the other common-wealth. The latter, however, owing to the objectionable way in which it was asserted by Cromwell, came to be known by other terms, such as "common good," the "weal public," "common right," "public policy" and "public purpose."

What it signified was a considerably different proportioning of inducements to willing and unwilling persons, according to the operations of the collective will. Certain classes of subjects—merchants, manufacturers, tenant farmers—hitherto looked down upon, were now able to have the collective power of the nation exercised in their behalf under the name of Freedom; while under the name of Liberty they were exempt from duties to their landlords and sovereign, and under the name of Immunities were exempt from the collective will itself. This was the field of private wealth, apportioned to individuals as their share of the commonwealth, the field of property and liberty as their share of the public power, the area of private will assigned by the collective will.

New apportionments have followed, as we well know, in England and America. The widening of the suffrage introduced additional participants in formulating the collective will. The definitions of property and liberty were enlarged to include both the private will of the propertyless laborer and the collective will of corporations and other going concerns, each defined, supported and enforced by the collective will of the nation. So that the apportionment has not been that of property in the physical sense of lands and buildings, but has been the apportionment of property and liberty in the behavioristic sense of encumbrances and opportunities limiting and widening the transactions and expectations of persons. It is the proportioning of inducements to act, by imposing encumbrances in certain directions and liberating opportunities in other directions, always with reference to what is deemed that public policy which is the commonwealth.

Public Policy, said the English jurist, "is a very unruly horse, and when once you get astride of it you never know where it will carry you."[1] It is, indeed, unruly for it lives in the feelings rather than logic, the field of values rather than mathematics. Every individual, every judge and every official of government has a different set of habits and emotions from every other individual, and the resulting emotions of value are the very center of individuality. Quite cor-

[1] Burroughs, J., 2 Bing. 252 (1824).

rectly here, as elsewhere, the courts endeavor to escape this unruly horse by seeking some external rule fixed in the nature of things that does not change with changing valuations. But try as they may they cannot escape valuing consciously or unconsciously, by logic or habit, the relative importance of the human interests at stake. Every transaction is weighed at every point according to what is deemed to be a public purpose. The public policy, for example, requires the judicial branch of government to decide whether a contract is freely and intelligently made, but liberty is a matter of the degree of coercion, and the definition of liberty is a definition of the allowable amount of pressure that may be employed in order to induce action, and this proportioning of permissible persuasion or coercion, command and obedience, depends, in turn, on the relative importance assigned to persons and classes of persons.

But, even if a contract is freely and intelligently made, yet, if it "bind the maker to do something opposed to the public policy of state or nation, or conflicts with the wants, interest or prevailing sentiment of the people, or our obligations to the world, or is repugnant to the morals of the time, it is void, however solemnly the same may be made." [1] "The inquiry must, in each instance, where no former precedent had occurred, have been into the tendency of the act to interfere with the general interest." [2] "If there be any doubt what is the law, judges solve such doubts by considering what will be the good or bad effects of their decision." [3] In all cases the question of whether the collective power shall come to the aid of the individual in enforcing contracts turns on the relative human values attributed to the persons or classes of persons involved.

The same is true when the other great determining powers of the state, the taxing power, the power of eminent domain, the police power, are employed by the legislative branch of government to reproportion the inducements to individuals and classes. The taxing power "may not be used for private purposes." But it always is used for private purposes and can be used in no other way, for its effect is to reduce the field of freedom and liberty for the taxpayer and enlarge the field of freedom and liberty for all who are benefited by the tax. The question always is, not, *What* is a private purpose

---

[1] Greenhood, Pub. Pol. 1 (1886).
[2] Lord Lyndhurst, 4 H. L. C. 161 (1853).
[3] 4 H. L. C. 146 (1853); 3 Bing. 590.

over against a public purpose? but, Is the private purpose *also* a public purpose, or *merely* a private purpose? Will the behavior of the persons benefited prove to be, in the direction of that benefit, also a public benefit? Are they a limiting factor, at that point, in multiplying the total welfare of the nation, and should their field of action be enlarged by restricting the field of others? Are they valued as a part of the public respecting that particular transaction, or are they valued as instruments to carry out the will of private persons? In the words of Lord Coke in reporting the case of Monopolies, Is the " increase " of their "substance " "profitable for the common-wealth? " [1] Will their private wealth be also a commonwealth?

Thus each individual is a "public utility" to the extent that the public powers are employed in his behalf against others, and a public "disutility" to the extent that the public powers are employed against him in behalf of others. The term "public utility," has, in recent years, come to signify a special class of private business, like railways, highways, water supply, and so on, peculiarly affected by a public interest. But all private business and jobs are affected with a public interest in so far as the collective powers are directed to their protection or furtherance against superior power of others. What is signified by this recent meaning of "public utility" springs rather from the idea that, to a certain extent, the business is a peculiar public *disutility* and is therefore sorted out for special restraint by imposing on its owners new duties of performance, avoidance, forbearance, in the interest of those who are deemed "the public." Every private business or job has, in fact, the qualities of both public utility and public disutility, depending on the current economic and human valuations. And it is in restraining the behavior believed to produce public disutility, by imposing new duties, that the opposite behavior of other persons believed to produce public utility is protected and liberated.

For neither public utility nor private utility is in physical things. It is in the expected transactions of persons using physical things as instruments in serving others and thereby inducing them to render service in turn. While the above physical objects, as going plants, have acquired the name public utilities, it is rather the potential or expected transactions of their owners, employees, managers, that constitute the utility in question, and it is their expected behavior

[1] 11 Co. 84 b (1601); above, Chap. VII, Sec. I, p. 227.

that is useful or disuseful to the public. The owners have devoted their property to a "public use." So have their employees and managers devoted their faculties to a public use. In either case their property is their expected share in the national wealth to be obtained through transactions with other persons. "The public," in these cases, is the expected consumers or users of their intended services, and it is through transactions with them that their share of the commonwealth is obtained.

It is only by way of historical accident that these businesses have been sorted out as public business distinguished from private business. At the beginning of modern market development, as shown by Adler,[1] every person who held himself out "to deal with persons indifferently for profit," as distinguished from those who followed their occupation for their own use or the use of a particular landlord or patron, was considered as devoting his skill or occupation to the use of the public, and therefore subjecting himself to duties to the public. The term "common employment" meant employed by "persons indifferently," that is, by the public; "common" meant simply "business" as distinguished from production for self or landlord or master; and the term "private business" is a "contradiction in terms." The person engaged in business requires new and enlarged assistance of the collective power, as against the assistance needed to follow his occupation for private use, and this carries reciprocal new and enlarged duties to the public which assists him. Not until the time of Adam Smith did this notion of duty give way to liberty, not perceiving that liberty carried exposure with it, and it has required another hundred years to swing back again from liberty to duty.

But the public need not be all of the public. It may be a particular individual. The Supreme Court declared that a single farmer in Utah might exercise the power of eminent domain to carry enough water for his use alone.[2] But he was granted that power not as an individual—he was granted it on account of the expected public purpose he would serve, by augmenting the national resources. He was granted it as a *class* of individuals, though he happened to be the only member of the class

The public is not any particular individual, it is a classification of

[1] ADLER, E. A., "Business Jurisprudence," 28 *Harv. Law Rev.* 135 (1914); "Labor, Capital and Business at Common Law," 29 *Harv. Law Rev.* 241 (1916).
[2] Clark v. Nash, 198 U. S. 361 (1905).

activities in the body politic deemed to be of value to the rest of the public, rather than a classification of individuals. Anybody who comes along "indifferently," and gets himself into a position where he might perform that class of activity, is the public. His private interests, when he gets in that position, are deemed identical with the public interest. When this identity is recognized by the functionaries of government, then to him is granted a certain share of that collective power which he did not enjoy before, and, correspondingly, the owners of the public disutility which places undue limits on that activity are subjected to duties of avoidance, performance or forbearance which they did not obey before.

This is the process of classification and reclassification according to the purposes of the ruling authorities, a process which has advanced with every change in economic evolution and every change in feelings and habits towards human beings, and which is but the proportioning and reproportioning of inducements to willing and unwilling persons, according to what is believed to be the degree of desired reciprocity between them. For, classification is the selection of a certain factor, deemed to be a limiting factor, and enlarging the field of that factor by restraining the field of other limiting factors, in order to accomplish what is deemed to be the largest total result from all. It is the process of political economy, which enlarges what is deemed to be the commonwealth by merely proportioning the factors that compose it. Thus, when the hoped-for welfare of women or children comes to be believed to be a limiting factor in the national economy, their hours of labor are reduced or their minimum wages raised, by imposing new duties on employers or parents, under the belief that merely this new apportionment of freedom or collective power, regardless of other changes in the quantity of labor, or of national resources, or of individual efficiency, will increase the national welfare. So with all other legislative and judicial decisions which determine Freedom in one direction by imposing liability in the opposite direction. Each is but a classification of persons according to beliefs in their public value, with the intention of reproportioning the national economy and thus enlarging the commonwealth.

It is often charged against legislation that the state does not create wealth—only private activity is wealth-producing. The charge is, of course, true. Legislation only classifies activities and proportions the inducements to wealth-producers. Individuals do the rest. But so might it be said of other economies. Economy is merely proportioning the factors by limiting some and expanding others. Yet the total product of the combined factors is enormously increased if the best possible proportioning is obtained, or it disappears altogether if a bad proportioning is adopted. The business man's principal business is not that of working with his hands, but is that of proportioning the different kinds of work, materials and machines, so that, within his given resources and markets, certain kinds of work are not over-supplied and therefore wasted by diminishing their value, and other kinds are not under-supplied and therefore also wasted by not taking advantage of their higher value for his purposes. So it is with legislation and judicial decision. They do nothing but proportion inducements, and individuals do the rest. But they may waste the commonwealth by bad proportioning, may enlarge it by good proportioning.

Since the time of Elizabeth, the limiting factors have been thought, on the whole, to be "capital," or rather investors' savings and business ability. Land and labor seemed to be complementary factors furnished by nature, but investment and enterprise were limiting factors requiring the power of the state to induce their potential owners to act. Latterly, it began to be felt that the proportioning in this direction was being overdone, and that land and labor also were not merely forces of nature but were the *owners* of land and *owners* of labor whose inducements were also being proportioned by the very laws which proportioned the inducements to investors and business men. Consequently, labor in its various classifications came to be looked upon as limiting factors and as such came to be liberated by imposing duties and enlarging exposures on owners of land, investments and business ability. In all cases the principle of classification has been the good or bad proportioning of behavior by proportioning inducements to contribute to what is believed to be the commonwealth.

Whether these various apportionments of collective power serve to augment the total welfare is a matter of opinion and judgment, and depends on the relative human values attributed by the determining officials of government, at the time, to those who are benefited and those who are burdened. Opinions clash, and it never can be expected that those who are burdened will look at the process in the same light as those who are benefited. For this reason the history of Anglo-American jurisprudence is a history of efforts to work out fundamental principles of classification which shall permit new proportioning of the national economy without unduly disturbing the old. This history is epitomized in the largest term known to jurisprudence, "due process of law," which was identified by Coke and Littleton with the "law of the land" as used in Magna Carta. Said Littleton in his argument preceding the Petition of Right in 1628, "'Law of the land' must of necessity be understood in this nation to be by due process of law, and not the law of the land generally, or otherwise it would comprehend bondmen (whom we call villeins) who are excluded by the word '*liber*'; for the general law of the land doth allow their lords to imprison them at their pleasure without cause, wherein they only differ from the freemen in respect of their persons, who cannot be imprisoned without a cause."[1] Thus "due process of law" became identical, not with the total "law of the land" but with the law of freemen. It is the law of citizenship, and citizens are the only "persons" known to law.

The term appears negatively in the American constitutions and amendments. Neither the federal government nor the state governments are permitted to deprive citizens of life, liberty or property without due process of law, or deny to any citizen the equal protection of the laws. Stated positively, the government *may* deprive persons of life, liberty or property *with* due process of law and *with* equal protection of the laws. In other words, the officers of government are limited by due process and equal protection, but, within those limits they may reproportion the national economy by a reclassification of persons for the purpose of assigning to them what is deemed a proper share in the expected burdens and benefits of the commonwealth. Due process of law thus signifies the classification of persons according to what is deemed their public value. Due process is due classification, and classification is a rearrangement of the working rules of going concerns.

III. The Working Rules of Going Concerns

Throughout the history of legal theories in all countries there has been a notable double meaning of words. Words are symbols or signs by which men convey to each other not only interesting ideas but also inducements to act. It was late in Anglo-American history

[1] 3 How. St. Tr. 86.

before the word "law" was separated by Austin into the two meanings of justice and commands.[1] One is related to the ethical idea of that which is right as against that which is wrong. The other is a working rule of a going concern, laid down by authority. One is a purpose of obtaining justice—the other is a process of command and obedience. Similar ambiguities afflicted the Roman *jus*, the German *recht*, the French *droit*. They signified either justice and right as against injustice and wrong, or rules and regulations as against the unruly and unregulated.

There was, of course, a certain pragmatic advantage in this confusion of purpose and process under the same sign. Purpose springs from the intentions of benevolent or malevolent beings, whether gods, devils or men, but process is the mere behavior of men. If the process can be justified by reference to a benevolent or ethical purpose it loses that stigma of arbitrary or despotic commands of a sovereign or proprietor which otherwise might provoke unruly conduct. In the early history of any concern the justification proceeds on accepted lines of authority derived from a superior being without question. But where this authority begins to be questioned, for any reason, there philosophical discussions ensue which turn on the distinction between the purpose of law and the process of law. Yet the distinction is not clear on account of the double meaning of the word law itself. Kant defined right or law (recht) in such a way as to include in the same definition both the abstract purpose of individual liberty and the abstract process of universal law. Hegel gave to this definition an evolutionary growth as the unfolding of the "idea" of liberty through the unfolding of the "idea" of law.[2] Law was looked upon, not as the working rules of a going concern adopted by the participants in a world of limited resources according to the principle of scarcity, but as a mechanical unfolding of ideal concepts of liberty, justice and law. The individual was the unit, liberty the goal and law the mechanism. Yet every concern must have its working rules, which are its laws. These spring from authority, custom, habit, initiative, or what not. They are the common law, the statute law, the equity jurisprudence of the concern. The state, the business concern and the cultural concern are alike in their depend-

---

[1] AUSTIN, JOHN, *Lectures on Jurisprudence*, 5th ed. 100. Although Austin is justly criticised for overlooking the part played by custom in the origin of law yet the two meanings of justice and custom are likewise separable.

[2] Cp. POUND, ROSCOE, *Interpretations of Legal History*, 28, 46 (1923).

ence on these working rules, the difference being mainly in the kind of sanctions, whether physical, economic, or moral, which they can bring to bear in enforcing the rules. And the declarations and enforcement of the rules create a complete outfit of rights, duties, liberties and exposures of each member occupying each position in the particular concern.

The unfolding of these rules is an historical process brought about through the decision of disputes between members of the concern, and it is this unfolding of decisions that necessitates at all times, but especially at times of great economic or social change, the distinction to be made between the purpose of the working rules and the process of making and enforcing them. The change has been wrought out by the American courts by changing the definitions of "due process of law." This change has occurred during the past forty years along with the changes in definition of property and liberty. If we notice this change in the concept of working rules brought about in that coercive concern the state we shall be able to understand the similar process in industrial concerns and cultural concerns.

Prior to the Civil War due process of law signified *due procedure* of law. Now it signifies also *due purpose* of law. The change in definition was worked out in the great case of Hurtado v. California,[1] against the protest of Justice Harlan who clung to the old definition. According to the common law, the "law of the land," no person could be put in jeopardy of life except by way of indictment by a grand jury. The state of California changed this procedure by authorizing the district attorney merely to present an information. Hurtado was charged with murder, not by a grand jury, but by the prosecuting attorney. The Supreme Court held that "due process," the ancient "law of the land," did not require any "particular form of procedure," provided the tribunal which decided the case had jurisdiction and the proceedings were such as to get all of the facts before the tribunal, so as to maintain "those fundamental principles of liberty and justice" for which procedure is only the instrument. Law, said the court, approving the words of Daniel Webster, is " the general law, a law which hears before it condemns, which proceeds upon inquiry and renders judgment only after trial," so " that every citizen shall hold his life, liberty, property and immunities under the protection of the general rules that govern society." [2] In so far as

[1] 110 U. S. 516 (1884).   [2] Hurtado Case, at pp. 535, 536.

procedure is deemed necessary for these general purposes it resolves itself into that minimum of procedure by which all of the facts are brought before the court, including opportunity of the defendant to be heard through counsel, with all that that implies of notice and approved judicial methods of investigation.

Prior to the Hurtado Case, in the first case in which the meaning of due process of law was elaborately discussed,[1] the court had held to the original meaning of due process. It observed that the constitution contained neither a description of the processes, nor a declaration of the principles, which it was intended to allow, forbid, or apply, in construing the phrase. It, however, asserted that "the words ' due process of law ' were undoubtedly intended to convey the same meaning as the words ' by the law of the land' "; and there was a difference between "legal process" and "due process." "The warrant in question is legal process," said the court. "It was issued in conformity with an act of Congress. But is it 'due process of law'?" [2] The case was that of an executive officer exercising judicial functions by summary procedure without notice or hearing, under an act of Congress, in the collection of a "debt owing the government by another government official." The question was whether a levy on lands by an executive officer without hearing or trial was due process of law. In answering the question, the court reviewed the customs and statutes of England and the colonists, and found that that same executive process had been used in similar cases. It found, not perhaps an underlying principle, but at least a distinction between this and ordinary cases, in that, while private persons might not be deprived of property without judicial inquiry, yet "imperative necessity" forced a distinction in the procedure between claims against them and claims for moneys owed to government by a collector of customs. (275, 278.) Here the subject-matter of the case was the line of demarkation between the legislative, the executive and the judicial branches of the federal government, and due process of law was decided to be immemorial usage.

Thus the opinion in the Murray's Lessees Case in 1855 looked for the meaning of due process in the intention of the framers of the constitution, and it looked for evidence that those usages were not

---

[1] Murray's Lessees v. Hoboken, etc., 18 How. 272 (1855). Cp. McGEHEE, "Due Process of Law," 23 (1906).

[2] *Ibid.*, 18 How. 276.

unsuited to the civil and political condition in this country by inquiring whether they had been acted upon by the colonists after the
settlement of this country and even after the adoption of the constitution.   This method has been more or less followed, the court
saying in 1896, "Whether the mode of proceeding, prescribed by this
statute, and followed in this case, was due process of law, depends
upon the question whether it was in substantial accord with the law
and usage in England before the Declaration of Independence, and
in this country since it became a nation, in similar cases." [1]   But in
1876, the court had foreshadowed a different view when it said that,
while the common law furnishes forms of procedure, "a person has
no property, no vested interest, in any rule of the common law.   That
is only one of the forms of municipal law, and is no more sacred than
any other." [2]

But in the case of Hurtado v. California, in 1884, the question was
whether a state legislature could dispense with the grand jury selected
from the people, the most important feature of the common law in
protecting the citizen against arbitrary action of officials, and could
allow a prosecution for murder to be made on a mere information
filed by a prosecuting attorney.   Here the court enlarged the meaning of due process to include procedure not found in the "settled
usage" of England or this country.   In explaining away Murray's
Lessees v. Hoboken, Justice Matthews said that although the procedure in that case was exceptional, "as tested by definitions and
principles of ordinary procedure," nevertheless it had been "immemo-
rially the law of the land and, therefore, is due process of law."   But,
said the court, "it by no means follows that nothing else can be due
process of law."   Grand juries are by name specifically required in
the federal courts by the Fifth and Sixth Amendments, and the question in the Hurtado Case, was whether they were required in state
courts under the due process clause of the Fourteenth Amendment.
The court, in the opinion rendered by Justice Matthews, reached the
following conclusions: [3]

1st. If we follow the immemorial usages and customs of England
back to the earliest times, we find that they then justified practices
which now would be considered cruel and superstitious.   "It is

[1] Lowe v. Kansas, 163 U. S. 81, 85 (1896).
[2] Munn v. Ill.. 94 U. S. 113, 134 (1876).
[3] Hurtado v. California, ibid., 528–535.

better not to go too far back into antiquity for the best securities for our ancient liberties."

2d. There are other lands besides England which have "ideas and processes of civil justice," and "it was the characteristic principle of the common law to draw its inspiration from every fountain of justice."

3d. If we go back to Magna Carta we find that it contained nothing that can rightly be construed as a "broad charter of public right and law," but was wrung from the King by the barons for their own purposes and contained nothing to protect the people against the barons; so that "the omnipotence of Parliament over the common law was absolute, even against common right and reason." But in our country, written constitutions protect the rights and liberties of the people broadly and against "all the powers of government, legislative as well as executive and judicial."

4th. Particular forms and modes of procedure which in England might be used to restrain the executive precisely and in detail might prove obstructive and injurious when "imposed on the just and necessary discretion of legislative power." This kind of restraint would, however, be enforced by the court against the legislature, but only where the constitution contains "express and specific injunctions and prohibitions."

5th. In other cases, where the constitution imposes only a "general principle or maxim, founded on the essential nature of law as a just and reasonable expression of the public will and of government, as instituted by popular consent and for the general good," these ancient forms of procedure "can only be applied to cases coming clearly within the scope of its spirit and purpose, and not to legislative provisions merely establishing forms and modes of attainment."

6th. But legislative powers are not absolute and despotic. "Law is something more than mere will exerted as an act of power." Applying the language of Webster, quoted above, the court excluded, as not due process of law, acts of attainder, bills of pains and penalties, acts of confiscation, acts reversing judgments, acts directly transferring one man's estate to another, legislative judgments and decrees, and "other similar special, partial and arbitrary exertions of power under the forms of legislation."

7th. On this account law is progressive and can break away from ancient procedure and can adapt new procedure to new conditions.

Procedure itself is but the embodiment, at the time, of fundamental principles of personal liberty and individual right. "It follows that any legal proceeding enforced by public authority, whether sanctioned by age or custom, or merely devised in the discretion of the legislative power, in furtherance of the general public good, which regards and preserves these principles of liberty and justice, must be held to be due process of law," and due process of law "must be held to guarantee not particular forms of procedure, but the very substance of individual rights to life, liberty and property." It is not particular forms that make up our civil and political institutions, but "those fundamental principles of liberty and justice " which lie at their base.

Justice Harlan wrote a vigorous dissent [1] to these opinions of the majority in the court, and showed that no case could be found in the law of England where indictment by grand jury was dispensed with in cases where the life of the defendant was at stake. The court had not merely allowed the common-law rule to be modified—it had abolished it altogether so far as the requirement of due process of law was concerned. He distinguished "equal protection" from "due process." Conceding the principle of general laws which thereby secure equal protection, he held that by the same reasoning trial by jury could be dispensed with by general laws applying equally to all capital offenses. "It is difficult," he said, "to perceive anything in the system of prosecuting human beings for their lives, by information, which suggests that the state which adopts it has entered upon an era of progress and improvement in the law of criminal procedure." (553.)

Yet, notwithstanding Justice Harlan's protest, the great and important change was made in the definition of due process of law. It now becomes due purpose distinguished from due procedure. The term "procedure" becomes the orderly, regulated behavior of the courts; the term "purpose" becomes the public purpose towards which that behavior is believed to be directed. This great distinction runs through all of the cases which, since the Hurtado Case, have turned on the meaning of due process of law. One of its large points of significance is the distinction drawn between property right and personal right, the former having to do with the exchange-values of property, the latter with rights that do not immediately involve exchange-values, or prices. At some points property rights are deemed

[1] Hurtado v. Cal., 538–553.

to be more important, at other points personal rights, and the difference of opinions between justices is largely a difference as to which, in the particular case, is the more important for the *due purpose* of law. This distinction will appear in the following majority and minority opinions.

What the court decided in the Hurtado Case was that the requirement of a grand jury in federal courts does not apply to state courts. Under the Seventh Amendment no person may be tried for felony in a federal court except on indictment by a grand jury. This, in so many words, incorporated the common-law procedure into the federal constitution. The Fourteenth Amendment would have made the same procedure mandatory on the states had the court defined due process of law as due procedure. Defining it, however, as *due purpose*, the states are free to abolish or modify the common-law procedure, although the national legislature is not thus free. Following the Hurtado Case, Justice Harlan's prediction has been fulfilled. The court had already, in 1875, prepared the way by holding that the Fourteenth Amendment did not require the first ten amendments (which had to do with procedure and constituted the Federal Bill of Rights taken over from the common law) to apply to the states. The Seventh Amendment guarantees the right of trial by jury in federal courts, but in that year the Supreme Court held that it did not apply to civil cases in state courts. The "states are left to regulate trials in their own courts in their own way." [1]

The right to trial by a jury was the right to trial by a jury of twelve persons and this was so held in federal cases under the Seventh Amendment. But in 1900, the court declared that a conviction and eighteen years' imprisonment decided in a state court on information filed by the prosecuting attorney and a finding made by a jury of eight persons, instead of twelve, did not deprive the defendant of equal protection of the law and due process of law. [2] To this, again, Justice Harlan dissented. "If," he said, "prior to the adoption of the Fourteenth Amendment it was one of the privileges and immunities of citizens of the United States . . . how can it be that a citizen of the United States may now be tried . . . by eight jurors when the amendment expressly says, 'No state shall make or enforce any law which shall abridge the privileges or immunities of citizens of the

---

[1] Walker *v.* Sauvinet, 92 U. S. 90 (1875).
[2] Maxwell *v.* Dow, 176 U. S. 581 (1900).

United States.'" [1]   Referring to railway and taxation cases previously decided, where the court had vetoed the state legislature in its attempt to regulate and tax private property,[2] Justice Harlan said, "If, then, the 'due process of law' required by the Fourteenth Amendment does not allow a state to take private property without just compensation, but does allow the life and liberty of the citizen to be taken in a mode that is repugnant to the settled usages and the modes of proceeding authorized at the time the constitution was adopted, and which was expressly forbidden in the National Bill of Rights, it would seem that the protection of private property is of more consequence than the protection of the life and liberty of the citizen." [3]

In 1904 the court decided that the common-law rule, required by the Sixth Amendment in federal courts, that defendants in criminal cases had the right to be confronted by witnesses and could not be convicted on written testimony, did "not apply to proceedings in state courts," if all defendants in all cases were equally deprived of the right. [4] To this again Justice Harlan dissented.

In 1908 the court decided that the exemption from self-incrimination guaranteed by the Fifth Amendment in federal courts, did not apply to state courts, provided self-incriminations were equally enforced on all defendants under similar circumstances.[5] Justice Harlan again dissented, saying, "As I read the opinion of the court, it will follow from the general principles underlying it, or from the reasoning pursued therein, that the Fourteenth Amendment would be no obstacle whatever in the way of a state law or practice under which, for instance, cruel or unusual punishments (such as the thumb screw, or the rack or burning at the stake) might be inflicted. So of a state law which infringed the right of free speech, or authorized unreasonable searches or seizures of persons, their houses, papers or effects, or a state law under which one accused of crime could be put in jeopardy twice or oftener, at the pleasure of the prosecution, for the same offense." [6]

In 1915 the Supreme Court refused the writ of *habeas corpus* on the appeal of a defendant convicted of murder in a state court, the defend-

[1] Maxwell *v*. Dow, 176 U. S. 612.
[2] C., B. & Q. R. Co. *v*. Chi., 166 U. S. 226 (1896); Norwood *v*. Baker, 172 U. S. 269 (1898).
[3] *Op. cit.*, 176 U. S. 614.
[4] West *v*. Louisiana, 194 U. S. 258 (1904).
[5] Twining *v*. New Jersey, 211 U. S. 78 (1908).
[6] *Ibid.*, at p. 125.

ant alleging mob domination of the court and jury, and involuntary absence of the prisoner during a part of the trial. The ground of the refusal by the Supreme Court was that the state Supreme Court had heard the case and refused the writ. "Since," said the court, "a state may abolish trial by jury so also may it limit the effect given to error in the trial and may permit the prisoner to waive presence at the trial." [1] The line of dissenting opinions from Justice Harlan having ceased with his death, the dissent was now taken up by Justices Holmes and Hughes, who, declaring that the federal Supreme Court had only recently overruled the procedure of a state Supreme Court in the case of property rights [2] where the state court had observed the *forms* of due process and equal protection but had not protected the *substance*, added, "We see no reason for a less liberal rule in a matter of life and death. . . . To maintain this immunity [of local courts from outside control by a mob] it may be necessary that the supremacy of the law and of the federal constitution should be vindicated in a case like this. . . . It is our duty to act upon them now and to declare lynch law as little valid when practiced by a regularly drawn jury as when administered by one elected by a mob intent on death." [3]

The foregoing cases, from Hurtado in 1884 to Frank in 1915, indicate the different meaning given to due process of law when the term applies to the federal government under the first ten amendments and when it applies to a state government under the Fourteenth Amendment. The federal courts in federal cases are held to the common-law procedure; the states are permitted to change and abolish that procedure.

This difference in meaning began, as we have seen, with the majority and minority opinions in the Slaughter House Cases in 1872 and completed its double meaning with the unanimous opinion in the Allgeyer Case in 1896. In the Slaughter House Cases the majority of the Supreme Court refused to define due process of law, as used in the Fourteenth Amendment, so as to take over by the national government the protection of property and liberty of contract against the acts of state governments. To this definition the court has adhered in the cases of criminal procedure, where the rights of life and personal liberty are at stake, and has left the states to regulate criminal trials

[1] Frank *v.* Magnum, 237 U. S. 309 (1915).
[2] Simon *v.* So. Ry. Co., 236 U. S. 115 (1915).
[3] *Op. cit.* 237 U. S. 347, 349–50.

in their own way. But in the case of property rights, as we have seen, a different definition of due process came in with the Minnesota Rate Case in 1890. The court then determined that due process signified a *right* purpose, and that, even though the procedure was right, yet the federal courts should have jurisdiction to ascertain whether the corporation was deprived of the reasonable value of its property. The *purpose* must be right, as well as the procedure.

This view was finally rounded out and given its complete statement in the case of the C., B. & Q. Ry. Co. *v.* Chicago, in 1896,[1] the same session with the Allgeyer Case,[2] which decided that liberty of contract was property. In the Railroad Case the court defined due process, as applied to property rights, as a process not satisfied with the mere form of procedure, including notice and hearing, but requiring also substantial justice to the property interests involved. The definition of due process, as drawn from that case, is formulated by McGehee as "the administration of equal laws, according to established rules, not violative of established rights, by a competent tribunal, having jurisdiction of the case, and proceeding upon notice and hearing."[3] This definition, however, is not quite adequate, for it is couched in terms of *procedure*, and overlooks the new meaning of *purpose* which the court was formulating. It should read as follows: Due process of law is the equal administration of laws, according to established rules, not violative of established rights *that are deemed important by the court*, by a competent tribunal having jurisdiction of the case, and proceeding upon notice and hearing.

Under this amended definition the court completed, in 1896, the change in definition of due process in the cases of property rights, just as it completed, in the Allgeyer Case in the same year, the change in definition of property and liberty. Liberty, in the Allgeyer Case, came to mean the liberty of business to buy and sell, and due process, in the railway cases, came to mean the reasonable value of the property bought and sold. Neither of these, any longer, are to be left to the states to be determined in their own way.

Thus the double meaning of due process of law is completed. In the case of property rights it signifies *an important purpose* as well as *procedure;* in the case of personal rights it signifies any pro-

---

[1] 166 U. S. 226 (1896).
[2] Allgeyer *v.* Louisiana, 165 U. S. 580 (1897).
[3] McGEHEE, *Due Process of Law*, 1.

cedure and a less important purpose. In the case of property rights the federal courts determine *both* whether the procedure is right and the purpose is important; in the case of personal rights the federal courts inquire *only* whether the procedure is right because the purpose is less important. The *procedure* is tested by equal protection of the laws. It is right if it deprives all persons of property and liberty equally under similar circumstances. The *purpose* is tested by the *value* of the deprivation. It is not right if it deprives them of established rights that are deemed important.

If the rights of which they are deprived are sufficiently important, then due process of law signifies that they shall have the protection of the federal government against the states; if not sufficiently important, then the states may take away the procedure if they do it equally to all persons in the same classification. The distinction was clearly expressed by Justice Moody, in the Twining Case, above referred to, when he said that "salutary as the principle [immunity from self-incrimination] may seem to the great majority it cannot be ranked with the right of hearing before condemnation, the immunity from arbitrary power not acting by general laws and the inviolability of private property." [1] And the distinction was equally well expressed by Justices Holmes and Hughes in the Frank Case where they said, "We see no reason for a less liberal rule in a matter of life and death."

Thus property rights are deemed to be so important for national purposes that the Fourteenth Amendment authorizes the federal court to protect them against the states. But personal rights, including, as they do, the rights of workingmen and others where property interests are negligible, are deemed to be less important for national purposes and may be left to the states. And it came about that while, prior to the Hurtado Case, due process of law had been identified with common-law procedure, now it comes to mean "whatever process seems due to the demands of the times, as understood by the judges of the time being." [2]

IV. Due Process of Thinking

If, in the last jeopardy of life and death the grand jury and other procedure of the common law, which had been erected for the sole

---

[1] 211 U. S. 113.

[2] Hough, C. M., "Due Process of Law To-Day," 32 *Harv. Law Rev.* 218, 233 (1919).

purpose of protecting the individual's life and liberty against the arbitrary power of the crown, can be dispensed with, then in the lesser jeopardy of economic liberty and property, other procedure of the common law may be dispensed with, provided liberty and exchange-value of property are protected. So, administrative commissions have been set up in great variety, and authorized by the Supreme Court, to regulate prices, wages, markets, competition, with power to investigate, to enter on private property, to compel testimony, to weigh the facts, to issue orders and to prosecute violators of their orders before the courts. American constitutions had separated the legislative, executive and judicial functions, but the new definition of due process amended the constitution by merging somewhat in these commissions legislative, executive and judicial procedure. Not the procedure is important, but the *purpose* in the procedure.

For procedure is but the authoritative behavior of officials dealing with each other and with citizens. It is the working rules of government which determine the direction in which the collective power shall guide behavior. Certain directions are deemed beneficial, others detrimental. In the beneficial directions transactions are authorized, in the detrimental directions, restrained. Purpose governs the working rules.

What, then, is beneficial, and what is detrimental? The answer is inseparable from the procedure. The procedure is the authoritative purpose of the authoritative actors. It is the transactions by which their purpose is attempted and accomplished. Having eliminated working rules deemed unnecessary for the purpose, the actor may choose the procedure deemed to conform to the purpose. The common law had built up a rigid set of working rules, partly because the primitive mind could not weigh the purposes back of the procedure, and partly because a rigid rule of procedure prevented the crown and its agents from injecting their autocratic purposes into the transaction. Thus it had subordinated purpose to the working rule. Just as the primitive mind could comprehend only physical objects so it comprehended only objective usages, customs, fixed procedure. True to the dualisms that afflicted it, procedure was something tangible, objective, customary, fixed, natural; but purpose was subjective, capricious, willful. And, just as the primitive definition of property passed over, in recent times, from tangible objects to expectations of conduct, so did the definition of due process of law pass over from orderly behavior to the purpose in the behavior.

The two are inseparable, provided the actor is permitted to choose his procedure. Procedure is the working rules of transactions, purpose is the ideal embodied in the transaction. By eliminating what is deemed unessential behavior, the actor chooses that procedure which he deems valuable for his purposes. And thus when the Hurtado decision and its many successors in many fields permitted choice of working rules they changed the meaning of due process of law from historic procedure to subjective purpose—from behavior to the valuation of behavior. No wonder the higher courts now began to inquire, in the case of property rights, What is the *purpose* of the legislatures, of the executives, of the authorities? Their procedure has been reduced to its lowest elements, that of investigation of all the facts. Now the question is, Have they given *due weight* to the facts?

This is the purpose of classification. Some facts are important, others are not. Each fact does not count for one. Some of them count for much more than one, some for much less than one. Facts are the qualities, the faculties and transactions of persons and things. There is no thinking without classification, for classification is the sorting out of qualities, faculties or acts that are similar and distinguishing them from others that are dissimilar. And the reason for sorting them out is in order to value, choose, and act. "Classification," said Justice McKenna,[1] "is essentially the same in law as it is in other departments of knowledge or practice. It is the grouping of things in speculation or practice, because they 'agree with one another in certain particulars and differ from others in those same particulars.' Things may have very diverse qualities and yet be united in a class. They may have very similar qualities and yet be cast in different classes. . . . Human beings are essentially alike, yet some individuals may have attributes not possessed by others, which may constitute them a class. But their classification—indeed all classification—must primarily depend upon the purpose—the problem presented. Science will have one purpose, business another, and legislation still another."

For science is but systematized thinking. In all thinking it is a search for truth. But truth is not part-truth—it is whole truth. Classification, by its very process of sorting, is part-truth; a complete

[1] Billings *v.* Ill., 88 U. S. 97, 102 (1903).

classification would yield the whole truth. Each part-truth is weighed as well as counted, and its weight is its importance in making up the whole truth. It is not merely *added* to other truths—it is a fraction, and the whole truth is a multiple of part-truths. Each classification of part-truth is a limiting factor in the total economy of truth, for truth is but a reflection of the economy of nature and man.

But classification in jurisprudence has an additional pragmatic value. Its purpose is not only truth—but also justice. After due process of law had become due purpose of law, it became, *in form*, identical with that other clause of the Fourteenth Amendment, "nor deny to any person within its jurisdiction the equal protection of the laws." Never has this signified that individuals are equal or that they have equal rights. It signifies simply that all individuals belonging to the *same class* shall be treated equally, while treating differently, but equally within the class, individuals of different classes. It signifies, no individual shall be treated solely as an individual but always as belonging to a class of individuals. "If the purpose is within the legal powers of the legislature," continued Justice McKenna,[1] "and the classification made has relation to that purpose (excludes no persons or objects that are affected by the purpose, includes all that are), logically speaking, it will be appropriate; legally speaking, a law based upon it will have equality of operation."

Neither the Fourteenth Amendment nor any other amendment, said Justice Field, in an earlier case,[2] "was designed to interfere with the power of the state, sometimes termed its police power, to prescribe regulations to promote the health, peace, morals, education, and good order of the people, and to legislate so as to increase the industries of the state, develop its resources, and add to its wealth and prosperity. . . . Regulations for these purposes may press with more or less weight upon one than upon another, but they are designed, not to impose unequal or unnecessary restrictions upon any one, but to promote, with as little inconvenience as possible, the general good. . . . Class legislation, discrimination against some and favoring others, is prohibited, but legislation which, in carrying out a public purpose, is limited in its application, if within the sphere of its operation it affects alike all persons similarly situated, is not within the amendment."

And Justice Brewer added, in 1899, "It is the essence of classifica-

[1] *Op. cit.*, 88 U. S. 103.   [2] Barbies *v.* Connolly, 113 U. S. 27, 31 (1885).

tion that upon the class are cast duties and burdens different from those resting upon the general public. . . . The very idea of classification is that of inequality, so that it goes without saying that the fact of inequality in no manner determines the matter of constitutionality." [1]

Thus arose the grand importance of precedent in Anglo-American jurisprudence. For precedent is the instrument of classification. A dispute arises and is brought before the court for decision. The court seeks first for precedents. How were similar transactions previously decided? The quest for precedents is guided by the desire to treat this case like all similar disputes. The search for precedents is both the scientific process of thinking straight, and the juristic process of granting to the citizen the equal protection of the laws. Precedent is classification, and classification is the equal treatment of all who belong to the same class. This is the strictly judicial process of dealing with individual disputes as they arise, and assigning the plaintiff and defendant to the class of transactions to which similar transactions have previously been assigned. The judicial process is equal treatment of individuals by classification of their transactions.

But no dispute that comes before a court is exactly similar to any preceding one. Each case presents certain facts which, in their junction with the other facts of the case, have never before been exactly passed upon. The new combination of facts requires a new proportioning and weighing of each in order to ascertain the whole truth of the case.

Thus every classification has two dimensions, the *inclusion* of all facts that are similar, along with *exclusion* of all that are dissimilar, and the *weighing* of each fact in order to determine its degree of similarity. This is the process of definition, and classification is definition.

The courts rightly refuse to give fixed, *a priori* definitions to the terms which they use. They proceed by the truly scientific device of description rather than definition, and description is the judicial process of inclusion and exclusion as cases arise, according to whether

---

[1] A., T., etc., R. Co. *v.* Matthews, 174 U. S. 96, 106 (1899). Cases cited showing that while the court had at times been divided on questions of classification, "The division in all of them was, not upon the principle or rule of separation, but upon the location of the particular case one side or the other of the dividing line," that is, upon the weight to be given to the facts in the case. On this point see the historical note on principles of classification, Truax *v.* Corrigan, 257 U. S. 312 (1922).

the facts are deemed important or unimportant. In this they consciously differ from both the untutored and the metaphysical notions of definition. The common mind conceives that a horse is a horse, and that is the end of it. The metaphysical notion abstracts a concept of horseness, and, like Plato, fills the sky with a world of ideas that come down and embody themselves in things; or, like Hegel or Karl Marx, finds the "idea" of "liberty" or of "social-labor-power" embodied in primitive society and struggling to unfold itself through the centuries. But the judicial mind perceives that a horse is a horse for some purposes and something else for other purposes, that liberty is good in some circumstances and not in others. For the physiologist a horse is a life process, for the farmer the horse is is horse-power, for the lawyer the horse is property, for the business man the horse is the price of the horse. The horse is an object of infinite qualities, faculties, possibilities, and is classified differently for different purposes, with a different *class name*, which is a different definition. Thus definition is a collecting, by the purpose of inclusion, of qualities that are deemed similar, and an eliminating, by the process of exclusion, of qualities deemed dissimilar, always with reference to their fitness in attaining the purpose of the one who does the classifying. In this respect, definition is classification according to importance of the facts.

Thus definition is also valuation. A quality or faculty is known only by its behavior. Even for strictly logical purposes a term cannot be defined except with reference to the context of other terms with which it is associated. Its meaning depends upon the meaning of the other terms defined along with it. It shades off into different meanings in order to fit itself to their meaning. So much the more does its importance vary when the quality or faculty is seen in action along with other qualities and faculties also in action. Then it operates with different degrees of power according to its part in the total of complementary qualities and faculties. "Legal definitions, for the most part, are generalizations from judicial experience. To be complete and adequate they must sum up the results of all that experience." [1] Ambiguity is a quality attaching not to words isolated from all context, but "to words *as used in assertion and reasoning*." [2]

[1] Bouv., 817 and cases cited.
[2] SIDGWICK, ALFRED, *The Application of Logic*, 123 (1910).

In the case of Smythe *v.* Ames,[1] dealing with the valuation of public service corporations, the court illustrated this process. It enumerated a list of facts many of them contradictory, each of which, if abstracted and taken alone, would lead to an abstract conclusion consistent only with that class of facts. Taken together, each was but a fraction playing its part in the total transactions of a going concern, past, present and expected. Certain classes of facts looked toward the expected bargaining power of the corporation, such as "the amount and market value of its bonds and stocks," "the sum required to meet operating expenses," "the probable earning capacity of the property under the particular rates prescribed by the statute." Other facts looked toward the past transactions of the corporation, such as "the original cost of construction," and "the amount expended for permanent improvements." Others looked at "the present condition of the property compared with the original cost of construction." Still other facts, said the court, might need to be included if the valuation of the property was to conform to the definition of due process of law, that is, due purpose of law. All of these are "matters for consideration, and are to be given such weight as may be just and right in each case," in order to arrive at a system of reasonable prices.

Thus the facts must not only be classified, they must also be *weighed*. *All* of them must be weighed, each in its relation to the others, and to each must be given its due weight. This is a process as true of logical definition where the "meaning," that is, the value, depends on the context, as it is of economics or ethics where value depends on social relations.

Weighing the facts is not a mere statistical enumeration of them. The facts, when they come before a person, do not automatically seek their own specific gravity. Weighing is not a mere intellectual process of distinguishing the various qualities or faculties of objects or persons. Nor is it a logical process of abstracting a certain class of qualities and arranging them in a system. It is also an emotional valuation of qualities and faculties in the process of social life. Some of the facts may seem important to one person as reasons for the total result, and unimportant to another person. By giving undue weight to unimportant facts a different conclusion is reached than in giving due weight to all the facts. The facts are collected. This

[1] 169 U. S. 466, 547 (1898).

is a statistical process. But they are also assorted and selected by inclusion and exclusion. This is classification. Classification is also definition, for it is a sorting of similar facts under the name of a concept or idea on which to string the facts. But this implies a purpose for which the facts are selected. Some are useful for one purpose but not for other purposes.

And this is not enough. The immediate purpose of definition is instrumental to an ultimate purpose. The ultimate purpose is the total of all the expectancies to which each fact or class of facts contributes. This may be good or bad, worthy or unworthy, desired or undesired, important or unimportant. This is the ultimate feeling of value, the emotional process of valuation that tinges all definitions, the place where the feelings exercise the power of choice by including the facts which are felt to be important and excluding those deemed unimportant, thus converting truth into belief, and facts into opinions regarding facts.

Thus we may say, based on our study of the behavioristic psychollogy of judges,[1] that the process of thinking, which is also the process of arriving at the working rules of a going concern, resolves itself into the purposes which guide believing. Purpose is anticipation of the future, and pulls forward. Believing is in the present. Purpose and procedure together resolve themselves into the distinguishable but inseparable attributes of the human will, namely, habits, ideals, definitions, investigations, classifications, valuations, choices, behavior.

1. Habits are the sub-conscious setting of body, nerves and brain on the basis of past experience and ready to set off in accustomed directions when touched by stimulus from outside. "Habit is energy organized in certain channels."[2] When habits emerge on the threshold of consciousness they seem to be the intuitive or instinctive sense of fitness or unfitness leading the actor to choose without thinking. When checked and balanced by that hesitating process which we call "thinking," it is because a mental habit of acting on words and symbols intervenes between the impulse from without and the physical response to the impulse. If a "meaning" is identified with these words and symbols we call that meaning an "idea."

2. Ideals are ideas projected into the future by means of symbols.

---

[1] Cp. ISAACS, NATHAN, "How Lawyers Think," 23 *Col. Law Rev.* 555 (1923).
[2] DEWEY, JOHN, *Human Nature and Conduct*, 76, *passim* (1922).

They are the ideas of self, of others, of the nation, ideas of duty, right, wrong, liberty, justice, ideas of persons, ideas of prices, of things or anything—not as a passing flash of pain, pleasure, or sensation, but as a continuing experience with an unfinished future projecting forward out of the present where the past has been finished, and leading on. They proceed from the power of choice. Whatever is chosen is to that extent the ideal, or part of the ideal. All *ideas* as such are alike; they are mere intellectual constructs; but the *idea chosen* is the *ideal*, because there is purpose in it, as well as intellect. Ideals are ideas felt to be important for future purposes.

3. Definitions are the description of ideas. Definition, as such, is the pure intellectual process of forming abstract concepts or principles and giving identification marks to them, so that they can be recognized again and serve for strings on which to hang items of fact as they come along. As "concepts" they are class-names, for they are the names of qualities, faculties or acts common to objects, and not the feelings of pain, pleasure, sensation, arising from contact with the objects. As "principles" they are relations between concepts, conceived as existing or operating uniformly like a "drift" or tendency or habit, and ranging all the way from axioms, maxims, or "first principles" intuitively accepted without hesitation, to elaborate descriptions of concepts and relations expressing truth or belief. Definition is defining, and defining is embalming ideas in symbols, and the three great types of symbols are words, numbers and prices.

4. Classification is sorting, describing and selecting the items of fact by including those that are deemed similar, excluding those deemed dissimilar, and preparing them for definition and symbols. Classification is investigation, enumeration, definition, according to a concept or principle common to items of fact, with the intent of choosing the class of items that is important for the purpose and excluding the class that is unimportant. Classification and definition are idealization of facts for the purposes of the future.

5. Investigation is the statistical process of seeking, finding, watching the items, to be thereby sorted out and strung up on classifications and definitions. All thinking is investigating, for it is hesitating about classification, definitions and ideals, distinguished from intuitions which size up situations without hesitating. Investigation is the "instinct of curiosity" in action.

6. Valuation is the feeling of relative importance for the future,

not of ideas, but of the expected behaviors which are their content; it is the feeling of hesitation while thinking, and of preference while acting. It is inseparable from that which is both the feeling and the intuition of dependence, security, power and fitness, of independence, insecurity, importance, unfitness, attributed to items while in the very process of investigation, classification, definition, idealization and choosing for the purpose of the future. It is valuation that gives meaning to words, numbers and prices.

7. Choices and behavior cannot be separated. They are one and the same. "Discretion" is choosing alternatives, and behavior is the process of choosing. Behavior is the outward transaction, the procedure, the process of moving the muscles in conformity with the habits, ideals, definitions, classifications, investigations, valuations, and choices leading on to further behavior in the reach for purposes yet unattained.

All of human behavior, therefore, resolves itself into this sevenfold process of thinking. And due process differs from other process of thinking and acting in that it is guided by sympathy and limited by duty. It is the process of personification, where, without sympathy and duty, it is merely the process of capitalization. For this reason it introduces ideas of willing and unwilling subordination to others where mere process of thinking is indifferent to the will and wish of others. Due process passes judgment upon all the processes of thinking and acting, moved by sympathy, antipathy and duty. Its purpose is the purpose of government and personality, the purpose of employing superior power to induce subordination. It passes judgment upon the use of power in suppressing or liberating personality. Its procedure is coercive, authoritative.

For this reason due process of thinking scrutinizes the purposes and distinguishes correct habits of thought from the incorrect; right ideals from wrong ideals; distinguishes the honest, truthful correct definition from the ambiguous and crooked definition; the complete investigation which seeks all the facts from the partial and blind investigation; the reasonable classification guided by right ideals from class legislation; the reasonable value, that weighs all the human interests, from confiscation that gives undue weight; the reasonable exercise of discretion, or choice, in place of arbitrary caprice; the just behavior from the unjust. So that, while mere process of thinking is the process of habits, ideals, definitions, investigations, classifications, valuations and behavior, *due process of thinking, which is due process of law*, is the process of correct habits, right ideals, true definitions, sincere investigation, reasonable classification, reasonable value, and justice; whereas its opposite, undue process, is perverse habit, wrong ideals, double meanings, partial investigation, class legislation, confiscation and injustice.

It is only by means of this concept of due process of thinking that mankind, as well as judges, is able to get away, on the one hand, from that solipsism, or absolute egoism, which makes the universe exist only for each individual as he thinks it exists, and, on the other hand, from its opposite extreme which makes the universe a substance, a set of entities, souls, wills, or *noumena*, a *ding an sich*, apart from the *phenomena* which each individual experiences differently from every other individual. The first makes each individual a law unto himself, makes value the pleasures and pains of the individual, makes the will caprice. The second makes law an unknowable entity, makes value intrinsic, makes the will universal reason, or universal force irrespective of individuals.

But the concept of due process of thinking, to be derived from the reasoning of the courts because they deal with actual cases as they arise and at the same time seek to explain and justify their opinions in the public interest, is neither a concept of caprice nor of universal reason. It is the truly pragmatic process of inclusion and exclusion of facts as they arise, of classifying the facts as they themselves and other judges have classified them, of investigating and valuing all of the facts through listening to arguments of interested parties. In short, due process of law is the *collective* reasoning of the past and the present, a process of reasoning to which the just judge feels himself as firmly bound as though it were a superior bodily presence commanding him. Even when he changes the definitions of words, by new inclusions and exclusions to meet new conditions, he laboriously searches the precedents and the books and is convinced that he finds, not his own capricious will, but the collective judgment of those who command confidence. It was a fine remark of Lord Eldon, who had spent his judicial life in stabilizing the rules and principles of equity in the Court of Chancery, when he referred to what John Seldon had said, two hundred years before, in the reign of King James. "Equity," said Seldon, "is a roguish thing. . . . For *law* we have a measure. . . . Equity is according to the conscience of him who is Chancellor, and as that is larger or narrower, so is equity. . . . 'Tis all one as if they should make the standard for the measure a Chancellor's foot." [1] To this, Lord Eldon replied, in 1818: "The doctrines of this Court ought to be as well settled, and made as uniform, *almost*, as those of the common law, laying down fixed principles, but taking care that they are to be applied according to the circumstances of each case. I cannot agree that the doctrines of this court are to be changed by every succeeding judge. Nothing would inflict on me greater pain, in quitting this place, than the recollection that I had done anything to justify the reproach, that the equity of this Court varies like the Chancellor's foot." [2]

Yet, as we have seen and shall further see, new conditions require new inclusions and exclusions, and Lord Eldon, in turn, has been reproached for adhering so closely to precedent that he reduced equity to a system as rigid as the common law itself. In making these new inclusions and exclusions there must be more than precedent—there must be choice of new alternatives presented in the present and leading on to new consequences in the future.

V. DISCRETION

Thus it was that the court declared that, even if the procedure conformed to an investigation of all the facts yet that was not enough. The legislatures, executives and courts are further bound by the due purpose of the law; and due purpose is not what is or has been, but what *ought* to be the law of the land. The officials are not bound by the procedure taken over from England at the time when the constitution took effect. That would deny any power to adapt the law to new conditions. This was settled by the Hurtado Case. But their power is not unlimited. They are bound by ideals. Due process is ideal process. It is what *ought* to be rather than what *is* or *was*. Regard must be had to the *substance* rather than the *form*. The form is the procedure. Procedure is "the mode by which the purpose of the law may be effected." [3] But the substance of the law is its purpose. "Substance" is not an outside entity back of things and persons, but substance is in the mind, form is in the behavior. Substance

---

[1] HOLDSWORTH, *A History of English Law*, 254 n.
[2] *Ibid.*, at 255; Gee *v.* Pritchard, 2 Swanst. 402 414 (1818).
[3] Jenkins *v.* Ballantyne, 8 Utah, 245 (1892).

is in the future, form is in the present. The one is *due purpose* of law, the other *due procedure*, and the two together are *due process* of law.

Where, then, shall we find the substance of the law? We shall find it in the habits and ideals of those whose definitions are final in determining the law. This is Discretion. The field of Discretion is the field of Power and Immunity—of Power, the "freedom" of the actor to determine the direction of the collective power; of immunity, the absence of responsibility and liability to the collective power for the results of that freedom. It is within this field of power (Freedom) and immunity that every individual is free to act as he thinks, both citizen and official. It is there that his behavior puts into effect his ideals, definitions, classifications, investigations, and valuations. And he who is clothed with official power is merely clothed with a more conclusive power than the private person in directing the collective power toward his ideals. His views may not be very "idealistic" in the opinion of other people, but that is because their habits and ideals are different from his. They are idealistic *for him*, for they are in the unfinished future that he is bending towards.

The framers of the American Constitution, under the influence of Eighteenth Century psychology, attempted to separate sovereignty into three departments corresponding to three faculties—will, intellect, behavior. The will resided in the legislature or people; the intellect, or reason, in the judiciary; behavior, or the execution of the will, in the executive. In the legislature alone, representing the people, was the seat of discretion. It alone could determine policy, could choose between alternatives. It could not delegate this power. This was the notion of a will as something arbitrary, capricious, unaccountable, irresponsible, and the restraints on the legislative will were provided in a system of "balances," including the system of representation, the independence of the executive and judiciary and the necessity of obtaining the joint consent of senate, house and executive in enacting a law. Eventually the Supreme Court also asserted its power of veto on the legislature.

Thus the legislative will passes through the judge and the executive on the way to the citizen. Each official, down to the last policeman, has a certain field of power and immunity limited by disability and responsibility, in exercising the powers of the collective will. Within that field it is his own purposes, definitions, investigations, classifications and valuations that are final. There he is the sovereign. His will is the state-in-action. He is the state.

Following the Eighteenth Century psychology courts and lawyers deny that discretion resides anywhere except in the legislature or people. But the will of the state is not a far-off will expressed at a certain time in the past, and the state is not an entity residing now somewhere, nowhere. The will of the state is the will-in-action. It is discretion, and discretion resides wherever there is power (Freedom) and immunity. What we have noted with respect to the policeman on the street is true all the way up to the highest authority. His field of discretion is the field where his will is the collective will. An administrative board or commission listens to the testimony and arguments of employers, laborers, "the public," and then fixes a minimum wage. Within the limits of reversal by the court its will is the will of the people. It is the state.

So it is up the line until we reach the Supreme Court, the place where pure reason is supposed to lodge. It, too, has its field of power and immunity. There the habits, ideals, definitions, classifications, valuations of its members are the will of the people-in-action. We have seen how, in its field of Freedom and immunity the court has legislated by definition. It changed the meaning of due process of law and thus amended the federal and every state constitution. It changed the meaning of property and liberty as used in the Fourteenth Amendment, and thus took over from the states the final determination of what was due process of law in the regulation of property and business. On the other hand, by changing the meaning of due process of law as applied to life and personal liberty, the court left to the states the power to deprive workingmen and others without property of their common law and federal rights of indictment by grand jury, trial by a petit jury of twelve, the right to be confronted by witnesses, the right to exemption from self-incrimination, the right to be present throughout the trial, and the right to have the federal courts determine whether a state court has been terrified by a mob. In 1890 Congress had prohibited all contracts in restraint of trade in interstate commerce. The court, in 1896, defined literally the term "restraint of trade," and thereupon dissolved the Trans-Missouri and Joint Traffic Associations of Railways.[1] Afterwards the court reduced the definition of restraint of trade by reading into it a definition of "rea-

[1] U. S. v. Trans-Missouri Freight Association, 166 U. S. 290 (1897).

sonableness," and "rule of reason," thereupon, while dissolving the
Standard Oil Company, permitted it to retain certain contracts in restraint of trade which were deemed reasonable since they were necessary in order to maintain the existing value of the going business.[1]

These and many other changes in definitions have the twofold
effect of permitting the legislatures to legislate and permitting the
court to legislate. The change in definition of due process, particularly, has opened up a large field for the state legislature in criminal
cases; the change in definitions of property, liberty and restraint of
trade has opened up a large field for the federal court to legislate in
property cases. In each field of power and immunity thus redistrib-
uted by definition, the particular legislature, executive or judge has
his field of discretion, where his will with its habits, definitions, investigations, classifications, valuations and ideals, is the will of the
state.

These shifts in definitions are of course not arbitrary. They spring
from new conditions. Yet they are discretionary. The collective
will takes on a different aspect from that as understood in the Eighteenth Century. It is no longer a merely capricious unaccountable
will of a personal sovereign, but it is a will that proceeds by deliberative process of law. It is no longer a separation of human faculties
into compartments, but it is an apportionment to individuals, whether
citizens or officials, of a share in formulating and executing the working rules of society. A new definition is a new valuation of facts, a
new valuation is a new classification, a new classification is a new
proportioning of inducements in the national economy, a new proportioning is legislation, and legislation is a change in the working rules
of the concern. Legislation resides wherever discretion resides, and
the collective will is not the will of the legislature alone, but is the
habits, ideals, definitions, investigations, classifications, valuations,
discretion and behavior of judges and executives who have official
power and immunity in formulating the working rules.

These shifts in the meaning of both discretion and due process are
illustrated in the modern procedure of creating administrative bodies
and clothing them with certain powers and immunities necessary
to deal with the new aspects of property. Such are the public utility
and interstate commerce commissions, the industrial and minimum
wage commissions, the fair trade or market commissions. Legis-

[1] Standard Oil Co. v. U. S., 221 U. S. 1 (1910).

latures found the subject-matter entrusted to these boards too complicated for direct action, while courts possessed only the negative
powers of protection against extortion or confiscation, and not the
powers of positive regulation. Yet with the courts remains the two-
fold question of determining whether these boards exercise unconstitutional delegation of legislative power, and whether in exercising it they deprive persons of property and liberty without due process of law.

The following case arose.[1] A statute required railroad companies to furnish reasonably adequate service and authorized a commission to ascertain, in particular cases, what that service should be
and then to issue an order binding the company to furnish it. The
commission issued an order requiring a company to furnish a slight
additional service to some fifty farmers in a locality not hitherto supplied. Two theories developed in the Supreme Court of the state,
which may be exhibited in the accompanying table:

Extortion....................40c.
Unreasonable................35c.   Reasonable $\begin{cases} 34\text{c.} \\ 26\text{c.} \end{cases}$
Unreasonable................25c.
Confiscation................20c.

If the rate, say 40c. charged by a company, yields 10% on the
value of the property it may be deemed to be extortionate, and if a
rate fixed by the commission at 20c. yields 5% on the property it may
be deemed confiscatory, that is, non-compensatory. The courts,
by virtue of the common law on petition of private parties, and without express legislative authority, are competent to prohibit the extortionate rate, and, by the constitutional restraints of due process
are competent to prohibit the confiscatory rate if imposed by the
legislature.

They are also, independently of statute, competent to prohibit
the unreasonable rate, say 35c. which, however, does not reach the
level of extortion, and are competent, if authorized by the statute,
though not independently of statute, to prohibit the unreasonable
rate, 25c. which does not reach the level of confiscation. But between
the outside limits of unreasonableness is the indefinite field of reasonableness. Here the court divided. The dissenting opinion held that,
for a commission to be authorized to select any point within these

[1] M., St. P. & S. S. R. R. Co. v. R. R. Com., 136 Wis. 146 (1908).

limits of reasonableness was a delegation of legislative discretion. The legislature itself has such power. It may arbitrarily select any point down to the level even of confiscation, since its selection is made in view of policy and expediency, which is the field of discretion. But, for an administrative body to select such a point, even within the field of reasonableness, is the exercise of legislative discretion. Similarly, for the court to review the evidence and then to select that point would also be legislative discretion usurped by the court.

On the other hand, the prevailing opinion of the court held that the selection of the point, under the statute in question, was not an exercise of discretion but the investigation and ascertainment of a fact. The legislature may declare a general rule, namely, that rates and services shall be reasonable. It may then declare that the law shall go into effect upon a certain contingency, and the contingency in this case is the ascertainment of the fact by the commission as to what is the reasonable rate of service. The law assumes that there is *only one* such rate; that it is discoverable by investigation but is undisclosed until that investigation is completed and the order issued. The discovery of a fact is not peculiar to the legislature. It is a mental process involving no discretion; it is a process practiced also by judges and executives. The power to ascertain facts is therefore a power that may be delegated. Yet even the ascertainment of a fact is a process such that reasonable men may differ regarding the location of the fact, and if the commission acted as reasonable men within the domain of reason the court should not investigate the facts anew and substitute its valuation for theirs.

Thus we have two theories of reasonableness and unreasonableness, each of them seeking to avoid the quality of discretion in the ascertainment of value. According to the dissenting theory, reasonableness is not a fixed objective point, but is any one of several points, and an executive or commission, in choosing one instead of others, is exercising discretion. But, according to this theory, unreasonableness, extortion and confiscation *are* fixed objective points, and hence the court is not exercising discretion when it chooses one instead of another, but is merely following the intellectual process of disclosing a fixed point.

But, according to the majority opinion, *all* of the points are fixed objective points, and neither is the executive exercising discretion when it ascertains the point of reasonableness within that domain, nor is the court exercising discretion when it ascertains the point of extortion, unreasonableness or confiscation, beyond which it prohibits the legislature or executive from going. In other words, according to the majority opinion, neither the court nor the executive exercises discretion in investigating and ascertaining a fact, while according to the minority opinion, it is discretion for the executive, but not for the court, to ascertain a fact.

Probably these metaphysical and mechanistic conclusions are required in order to conform to the Eighteenth Century attempt both to separate government into legislative, judicial and executive branches and to separate the human will into will, intellect and action. They tend to preserve the primitive notions of a complete dualism of the objective and subjective world. The objective world is the world of facts, the subjective is the world of feelings, emotions, caprice. Thus the metaphysical and mechanical theory of government and the will "deludes itself with the illusion," in the words of Henderson, "that there is a fact which can be discovered if we are only persistent enough in our search for it, and which, once it is found, will provide a mathematical solution of all rate-making problems."[1]

But, in reality, facts are facts as our habits, investigations and purposes deem them to be facts. In this case the facts were fifty farmers who wanted additional railway service and the corporation that did not wish to give it. Which was more important in the public interest?

V. Economic Theory of Going Concerns

Back of the process of thinking are those fundamental assumptions springing from that sense of fitness and unfitness, or common sense and habit, which evolves with life itself and which is but a sense of the fit proportions in which factors should be combined in order to attain the purposes deemed important. Whether it be named emotions, feelings, habits, intuitions, bias, prejudice, sense of value, sense of justice, it all has its biological root in that adaptation of life to limited resources through proportioning the factors and choosing between alternative degrees of power in contemplation of what is wanted for the future. In the unfolding history of the race and the individual it differs mainly in the expanding range of factors

[1] Henderson, G. C., "Railway Valuation and the Courts," 33 *Harv. Law Rev.* 912 (1920).

that are taken into account and the enlarging power of the individual to induce others to execute his will. Springing biologically from the unconscious reflex actions and reactions of life, then instinctively from acting and reacting with pleasure and pain, then intuitively without thinking, then hesitatingly as the factors are being investigated and weighed, it becomes that process of purposeful thinking which we distinguish as the double process of capitalization and personification, consisting in the inseparable ideals, definitions, investigations, classifications, valuations and choices that accompany dealings with things and persons. Advanced out of the field of thinking about the useful qualities of things to that of thinking about the virtues of persons, it advances into that right or wrong process of thinking and acting under the combined impulse of sympathy and duty which we distinguish as the process of personification, or that process of determining the fit and proper relations that should exist between persons, which is the reasonable working rules that constitute due process of law.

Exalted as this philosophy has become through the Anglo-American process of subjecting officials of government to the jurisdiction of the same courts as private citizens themselves, America has at last attained the ideal of Plato, two thousand years ago, of a government by philosophers. But, whereas Plato would have the nation governed by pure ideas abstracted from feelings, we are governed by a theory of value. Not, of course, by that hedonistic theory of pleasure and pain of Bentham and the economists, in which each pleasure or pain and each person counted as one, but by a theory of personification in which individuals and classes of individuals count according to what is felt to be their relative importance for public purposes. According to this appreciation of relative importance they get the assistance of officials in the form of rights and liberties, and the restraint or neglect of officials in the form of duties and exposures. So that instead of an "organic" theory of the state based on duty, or a "contract" theory of the state based on liberty, we reach what may be distinguished as an economic theory of going concerns based on the authoritative proportioning of inducements in a world of limited resources.

We may distinguish these as the duty-theory, the liberty-theory and the economy-theory of going concerns. The duty-theory, in its various aspects of divine right, royal prerogative, biological analogies, Leviathans, socialisms and dictatorships of the proletariate, ends in the obedience of the individual through fear of a superior earthly power. The liberty-theory in its various aspects of freedom of contract, equality, individualism, anarchism, self-interest, greatest number of equal units of pleasure for the greatest number of equal units of persons, ends in an aggregate of atoms like a basket of marbles held together by a metaphysical entity "the state" or the "general will," or Kant's "kingdom of ends," or by equally metaphysical analogies to physical forces like the attraction of gravitation or the biological organism, or the Leviathan or social labor power. But the economy-theory of the state is the theory of a going concern with its going business, having its roots in the past, its behavior in the present, held together by the hopes of peace, wealth, virtue and the fears of violence, poverty and vice, through the control of which collective action proportions the inducements to individuals to participate in the burdens and benefits of collective power. In short, the economic theory of the state is the theory of proportioning inducements to willing and unwilling persons in a world of scarcity.

The economic theory has its foundation in the suggestion of David Hume,[1] where, when elaborated, ethics and justice are resolved into the *sharing* of limited resources, and utility is resolved into the public purpose of *enlarging* those resources by proportioning the inducements to share in the burdens and benefits. Ethics and economics are thus inseparable, for each proceeds from the principle of scarcity. Economics is the proportioning of factors, and ethics is the proportioning of *human* factors in order to obtain the largest desired result from all. The ecomomic theory is one, not of *addition* of units, whether they be pleasures or persons or atoms of wealth, in order to constitute a sum total of "happiness," or "people," or "commonwealth," but is a theory of multiplication of complementary by limiting factors, through which the services of one class, if properly proportioned, *multiply* the services of other classes, and thus enlarge the total happiness, personality, and commonwealth by merely proportioning the factors to the best advantage.

It is a theory which has both its objective and subjective sides of behavior. On the objective side it is, in one and the same process of thinking, a theory of duty, liberty and economy; of duty, for it is grounded on compulsion addressed to unwilling persons; of liberty,

---

[1] HUME, DAVID, *Principles of Morals*, sec. 3, "Of justice" (1777).

for it removes restraints from the will; of economy for it is the collective power apportioning duty and liberty in a world of limited resources. And, on the subjective side of behavior, it is a theory of utility, sympathy and duty; of utility, the wish to subordinate things and persons to self; of sympathy, the willing subordination of self to other persons; of duty, the unwilling subordination to the will of others.

In this way the economic theory of a going concern is a theory both of capitalization and personification; of capitalization, for it is wealth and welfare—wealth, the valuation of instruments; welfare, the purposes for which they are valued. It is a theory, too, of personification, for it is a valuation of the virtues and vices of self and others for whose purposes wealth and welfare should or should not exist.

Properly interpreted, this was the ruling principle of Adam Smith, and it was only by picking out and abstracting that part of his theory which exalted individual initiative and criticised governments for suppressing initiative, that his successors of the classical economists distorted his notion of the wealth of nations. Adam Smith started with a view of the forest but his followers lost themselves in the woods. For Smith addressed his inquiry to the statesman or legislator, as proposing "two distinct objects: first, to provide a plentiful revenue or subsistence for the people, or more properly to enable them to provide such a revenue or subsistence for themselves; and secondly, to supply the state or commonwealth with a revenue sufficient for the public services. It proposes to enrich both the people and the sovereign." [1] And Smith changed the point of view, as Cannan points out, from "the older British economist's ordinary practice of regarding the wealth of a nation as an accumulated fund," to that of the *annual* labor of the nation, which is the true "fund" that "supplies it with all the necessaries and conveniences of life." [2] Further, the *per capita* production, which is the true measure of whether the nation is "better or worse," depends on the "skill, dexterity and judgment with which its labor is generally applied," and on the "proportion between the number of those who are employed in useful labor and those who are not so employed." But, finally, while the "natural progress of opulence," depends on the proper proportioning of commerce, manufactures and agriculture, yet this proportioning has been ingeniously interfered with by conquest, slavery, landed estates, the discourage-

[1] *Wealth of Nations*, 1:395, Cannan's ed.　　　　[2] *Ibid.*, at p. 1.

ment of agriculture, bands of useless retainers, expensive vanity of great proprietors, and the false teaching that nations are enriched by "beggaring all their neighbors." [1] A return to the true spirit of Adam Smith is a return to a political economy that teaches the best proportioning of inducements by the state to useful and useless persons.

Adam Smith had, indeed, suggested an entirely different mechanical theory which was the one picked out by his successors, based on the several principles of individualism, self-interest, liberty, division of labor, no associations or governments, and divine providence, but this theory was set forth in order to indicate the best policy that governments should pursue in proportioning inducements and restraints to individuals. On the basis of this theory he would have the governments break up the great estates into individual ownership and the gilds and corporations into individual units. [2] He could not, of course, see the necessity and economy of the mass production brought about afterwards by steam, electricity, chemistry and physics, nor the way in which courts and legislatures have recognized and endowed with power and immunity the industrial governments which organize, marshal, and manage armies of producers for mass production. They, however, also are collective wills animated by a collective purpose, and proportioning also by their working rules, like the state, inducements to willing and unwilling persons to participate in their collective power. Thus in descending circles of proportioning and reproportioning, the collective power of the nation is delegated to subordinate collective powers, and they in turn to individuals, held together by thinking alike.

It is this thinking alike that constitutes collective purpose. We have seen the exact correlation that exists between collective powers and individual rights. [3] There is no right without its corresponding duty, no effective or actual right-and-duty of individuals without both a correlative power and responsibility of officials to come to the aid of the right by enforcing the duty. Every right has two corresponding duties, the duty of the opposite person and the duty of officials to exercise the collective power upon that person. For, not only is there no right if there is no remedy but there is no remedy if there is

[1] SMITH, ADAM, *Wealth of Nations*, Books III and IV.
[2] *Ibid.*, 1:130, 131.
[3] Above, Chap. IV.

no power to hold officials responsible. The violation of a positive right brings into existence at once, by "operation of law," a remedial "right of action" which is none else than the official duty of courts and executives to enforce the right.

On the other hand, the metaphysical notion that there exists somewhere an objective world of rights and duties superior to the actual rights and duties, goes along with the metaphysical notion that there is somewhere an entity "the state" apart from the officials who determine and execute the will of that state. These metaphysical notions have, indeed, a powerful influence on men's minds, simply because man lives in the future but acts in the present. Thus constituted, he projects outward into a world of ideas his hopes and fears, and gives to his expectations a local habitation and a name.

Yet these ideas are but ideals—they exist, but they exist in the mind. They exist because man craves security for his expectations, and could not act at all as a rational being without the feeling of security. Let anarchy surround him, where there are no officials to bring a collective power to his aid, and he reverts at once to animal fears that crowd out reason with its entire scheme of rights and duties. When his rational expectations are gone the savage in him takes possession. No wonder he fills the sky with deities and entities—they are his hopes.

But the real world of rights and duties about him is the collective will expressed in working rules necessitated by the scarcity of resources. His "freedom" is his power to command the officials according to those rules, who are both the instruments of that will and the actors who determine what that will shall be when it acts. They, too, like him, move toward their habits and ideals, and respond, according to those habits and ideals, to his call for help, if needed. To that extent he enjoys "freedom" as well as liberty, for he has the aid of collective power to give effect to his will.

At this point, however, where this power ends his "disability" begins, for there the collective power ceases to come to his aid. And there also his right ends and his exposure to the liberty of others begins.

So also with his reciprocal duties and liberties. Not only is every right limited by some exposure, if opposite parties are not reduced to the unlimited duty of slaves who have no recognized will of their own, but every right, with its limiting exposure, is further limited by reciprocal duties with their limiting liberty, and this, in turn, corresponds to the extent that opposite parties have power to hold officials responsible. His duties are but the responsibilities of officials to opposite parties, and his liberties are but the immunities of officials which limit those responsibilities.

Thus within this moving framework of power, disability, liability and immunity, determined, as it goes along within the limits of the working rules and necessitated by the scarcity of resources, the will of the individual is the collective will in action. His private purposes are public purposes to the extent that "the public" through the determining powers of its instruments, the officials who exercise that power, both bring the collective power to his aid and protect his immunity from the exercise of that power. His private purposes are contrary to public purposes to the extent that the same actors hold him liable to the will of others, and are indifferent to public purposes to the extent that they expose him to the immunity of others. He is both a public utility and a public disutility—a public utility to the extent that the public powers are granted to his own choices in the form of rights and liberties through freedom and immunity in dealings with officials; a public disutility to the extent that they limit the exercise of his faculties by duties and exposures, through responsibilities and disabilities of officials.

Thus every choice of every official in every authoritative transaction, within his field of power and immunity, is the exercise of a public purpose directed towards proportioning the inducements which collective power creates. It is his behavior accompanying his mental habits, his ideals, definitions, investigations, classifications, valuations and purposes which throw the weight of the concern on one side or the other in determining the part which individuals and classes shall play in the collective economy.

The difference between the executive, such as the policeman, and the legislative or judicial official, consists in the greater deliberation of the latter in making up his mind. This deliberation of the latter is required by that due procedure of law which consists in getting all of the facts and weighing them according to their relative importance before deciding. The executive is closer to the private parties. His sympathies and antipathies towards individuals are more likely to prevail. The legislator must get a majority vote, and his individual will is checked. So with the Supreme Court. Due procedure of law has hit upon the majority vote as a device for compelling individuals in authority to weigh the considerations on which they shall determine the direction given to the collective power. The supreme courts are placed most remote from the individuals whose interests are at stake, where they can review the general principles, and consequently their majority and minority opinions expound at length the grounds on which their conclusions rest. Seldom do their differences of opinion turn on the enumeration of facts—the facts are before them ascertained by lower courts and insisted on by attorneys. Their differences turn on what they deem to be the importance of the facts. By the process of inclusion and exclusion the important facts are included, the unimportant excluded, and the included facts are valued and chosen according to their relative importance. We have noted this process in the historic changes that have occurred in definitions and classifications. In all cases we have seen the process guided by what we distinguish as the sense of fitness and unfitness arising out of habit and custom, which is but the sense of the proper and improper proportioning of limiting and complementary factors needed to bring about what is deemed to be the best proportioning of all. A satisfied sense of fitness is that feeling of harmony and unity attained by fitting the immediate transactions under discussion to the whole scheme of life as perceived and habitually accepted. It is that sense of justice which, springing from the experience of superior power over the individual, is the most satisfying of all human emotions, just as the sense of injustice is the most destructive.

Yet this sense of fitness and justice differs as widely as human character, for it is nothing less than the whole person, with his own internal proportioning of habits and intensities of feelings, in contact with a world which he feels to be fitted or unfitted to it. It differs with age, time, place, and all that goes to make up the heredity and experience of the individual. It is to these differences that we may trace the differences of opinion in the majority and minority opinions of courts and the evolution of definitions and classifications. There is a struggle and survival of mental habits and the sense of fitness such that those whose habits and sense of fitness or justice more nearly fit the predominant forces of society tend to survive and predominate.

The habit of breaking up the will into compartments is reflected in the separation of the collective will into the state and voluntary associations. The state is set apart as an entity having a separate existence and providing preëminently the service of security. But the state, in reality, is the officials in action; their action is the organization of violence according to due process of law; and due process of law is the working rules of officials. Security is not something abstract and separate, a kind of outside force ready to come in when property or liberty is violated, but security is, at the same time, a choosing in advance by officials of the direction in which they will afford security. Property, liberty and voluntary associations exist only to the extent that they are secure, and they are secure only to the extent and in the direction that officials give indication that they will choose to make them secure. This is the direction and extent determined by their ideals, definitions, investigations, classifications, valuations and choices. As the direction and scope of security change by changes in definitions and values, so does the content of property, liberty or association change.

A somewhat similar abstract separation is found in the customary classification of economic theory which separates the factors into land, labor, capital and the entrepreneur, and the corresponding incomes into rent, wages, interest and profit. The classification is made from the standpoint of competition of individuals and concerns. Competition works similarly within each of the factors of land, labor, capital and entrepreneur, and sets limits beyond which the incomes from each may not rise or fall.

But both the individual and the concern belong, at one and the same time, to more than one of the factors. We have here the familiar distinction between *functional* distribution and *personal* distribution. The competitive factors are functional—they operate similarly within each factor. The *combination* of these factors is personal—it determines the prosperity or poverty of the individual. The same may be true of their combination in a going concern. It is an instrument through which personal distribution is effected.

To distinguish just where the entrepreneur function begins and ends is impossible. All of the factors share the risks, and there is a gradation of risks all along from bondholders to stockholders and employees, according to the scheme of organization. Nor can the managerial function of the entrepreneur, which goes along with taking risks, be separated. In some concerns the bankers or absentee stockholders are the real chiefs, in others a strong personality in the executive chair, in others the associated managerial force, in others even the wage-earners, organized or unorganized, have a compelling voice in determining the direction and extent of management.

Likewise with the capitalist function. Even the wage-earners and managers are investors in the business, to the extent of their accrued unpaid wages and salaries and their expectations of continuing jobs, and the formal investor is merely one who agrees to prolong his period of waiting beyond that of the wage-earners and managers. Likewise with land—it is only the location and standing room needed for the combined operation of machinery, improvements, fertility, laborers, managers, or markets, while the income from land ownership is governed by economic laws similar to those which govern incomes from goodwill, patents, franchises and other differential market opportunities. In short, a going concern rises to a third principle of classification, for it includes not only the competitive classification of land, labor, capital and entrepreneur, and the personal combination of these factors in the jobs and positions of individuals, but also that authoritative proportioning of factors through inducements to persons, which constitute political, industrial and moral government.

We have, therefore, instead of the traditional classification, distinguished the division of social relations as positions and concerns. Each occupation is a position or job in a going concern, whether it be the state, the business, or the cultural concern. And the position has two aspects, functional and personal. From the functional standpoint it presents a double function, that of giving and that of taking. It gives service to others through the medium of the concern and takes services from others through the medium of the concern. From the personal standpoint, each person has as many occupations, or positions, as the concerns of which he is a member. He is more or less a citizen or official of the state; a participant in a going business and in the family, church and social organizations. Each of his several occupational activities, proportioned according to his character and circumstance, constitutes both his personality in action and the total of his property interests—in short, his faculties and opportunities.

Finally, from the authoritative standpoint, he is subject to the customs, rules, or laws, that is, the working rules of behavior which have grown up and are enforced by aid of the sanctions, as the case may be, of violence, poverty or opinion, characteristic of the concern where his membership lies. Each concern is made up of positions into which individuals come and go, but the concern goes on. Each individual comes and goes, into and out of positions, and his giving and taking goes on from birth to death. Thus each position is both a function of a concern and a function of a person.

And the giving and taking of each individual is also subdivided into functions. His giving to others is threefold, working, waiting and risking. His working is the operation of his manual, mental and managerial faculties; his waiting is the permission he gives to others to make use of his services before he makes use of theirs. His risking is his planning to overcome chance and get advantage of luck and management. And his taking from others is threefold: compensation for working, waiting and risking, depending upon his power, opportunity and will to induce others to make compensation.

Thus land, labor, capital, and the entrepreneur, are but a classification of proprietary relations of giving and taking. Each is twofold. Ownership of land, labor, capital, and business faculties are the instrumentalities through which he gives the service of working, waiting and risking; and they are also the instruments through which he induces others to make compensation through refusing to work, wait, or risk. In the one aspect they are instruments of use-value or real value, through increase of service, in the other they are instruments of nominal value or price, through power to withhold use-values. In the first aspect they are instruments of "producing power," in, the second aspect they are instruments of "bargaining power." In the one aspect they are instrumental to enlarging the commonwealth, in the other to getting a share of it.

The functional, or rather competitive, classification of land, labor, capital and the entrepreneur, was developed, in economic theory upon the assumption of what we have distinguished as the liberty-theory of the state—a theory which excluded both the prerogative of the King and the monopolistic power of individuals or associations derived from the patents, or special privileges, granted out of that prerogative. The concept of property thus remaining after the elimination of superior political power was that concept of the common law which consisted in the exclusive holding of physical things for one's own use. And the concept of liberty remaining was the absence of compulsion, restraint, or duty in matters of buying and selling imposed by the superior power of the sovereign or of those who derived their authority from him. Property and liberty thus were powerless. They were but the voluntary behavior of individuals who had no power over each other. Abolish special privilege, which is but the power of government, and there remains in the property and liberty of individuals no power of coercion.

This concept fitted in with the liberty-theory of the state in that the latter was a mechanical theory of addition of atoms of physical property and of individuals as separate atoms, the total constituting a mathematical sum of accumlated wealth and population. It led to a theory of production of physical use-values by which each individual added his quantity of physical wealth to the total regardless of the quantity he added, rather than a theory of diminishing value by which each individual both multiplies the efficiency of others and withholds too much addition in order to maintain the prices or bargaining power for himself.

And it led to a theory of population and the pressure of mere numbers on the means of subsistence, rather than a theory of due proportioning of the population among positions by means of which the national wealth is increased faster than the increase of population. It was a theory of accumulated wealth of individuals rather than a proportioning of welfare for all, and a theory of population rather than a theory of government proportioning inducements.

But the volitional classification includes both liberty and power, for a position has the double aspect of production and distribution, with its twofold function of giving and taking. The occupation is a job or position in a going concern and is governed by the customs, rules or laws of that concern, which determine the limits of liberty and power. The individual both gives to the concern and takes from it, according to its organization and his own abilities and importance within the concern. His position is his faculties in action, and the customs and laws of the concern are the limits within which he acts.

We have noted that each individual is a member of several concerns, involving a subdivision of his whole personality in parts. In the case of the highest concern, the state, the official puts into action certain collective powers entrusted to him in his official capacity. He has a double personality, public and private. *Outside* his public powers he, like any other citizen, is subject to authorized transactions governing private concerns and measured off by rights, exposures, duties and liberties. *Within* his sovereign powers he is also limited. His limited power is the same thing as the limited liability of the private person to be compelled to perform, avoid or forbear, as the case may be. The official disability is the exposure not only of the official, but also of the collective power, to the behavior of the citizen, who, to that extent enjoys immunity, or absence of liability. Reciprocally, the official is bound to carry out the will of the citizen, within limits, and the extent of this official liability is exactly equal to, indeed is the same thing as, the power of the citizen to have the collective power of the state exercised in his behalf. But this responsibility is limited by the immunity of the official from discipline on account of his use or disuse of the collective power, and this immunity is the same thing as the disability, or inability, of the citizen to have the collective power do his bidding. Within this immunity he exercises discretion. Thus the official is the state-in-action, and the state-in-action is the authoritative transactions of officials and citizens measured off by the juristic dimensions of reciprocal power, disability, responsibility and immunity.

These observations seem called for on account of certain ontological mysteries which attend notions of a collective will, springing from that twofold weakness of the human mind which creates abstract images endowed with souls and identifies what *ought* to be with what *is*. This weakness operated in the mind of Immanuel Kant, whose Kingdom of Ends was what he thought ought to be, and whose disembodied human beings nevertheless had souls. So it is with notions of sovereignty and the corporate will, carried over from the period when Kant flourished. Sovereignty seems to be the Will of God or the Will of the People, residing somewhere unknown, and, while the corporation has no soul, yet it has a mysterious will somewhere that acts like a soul.

Generally, it will be found that what is intended is that sovereignty *ought* to be the Will of God or the Will of the People, and this idea is expressed as an entity living apart from the actual state which evidently does not meet that ideal; or that the corporate will *ought* to be a human soul but is a bloodless entity different from the human beings who act in its name.

Certain variations, of course, occur in these ontological mysteries, depending on differences among individuals, who, naturally have widely different notions of what *ought* to be or ought *not* to be, arising largely from differences in their habits and wishes. But the mystery is so far removed from the actual that it can accommodate all kinds of wishes without being discovered.   In this way these mysteries have a certain pragmatic value, for, in the name of God, or the People, or the Corporate will, the particular official or agent can do many things which he would not do in his own name. He can always say that he has no discretion in the matter, and that, while as an individual he would do differently, yet, etc., etc.

His statement undoubtedly has a degree of accuracy, for, both in contemplation of law and in obedience to the concern, he has as many personalities as there are concerns of which he is a member. But it is accurate only within limits. These limits are the margins of immunity, and these, being matters of degree, or quantity, can be changed. The principal method of changing them is, as we have seen, a change in the law, or a change in the officials of the concern, usually brought about internally by collective action or externally by the collective power of a superior concern, the state. Within the margins of immunity thus changed, all of the other juristic dimensions of behavior, the power, disability and liability are changed.

These changes actually do occur, when the ontological mystery is partly dissolved, and it is seen that the will of the concern is what the concern does, and what the concern does is what its functionaries do.

There is still another, but related, pragmatic value in these ontological mysteries. By picturing to themselves a superior will, the subordinate executives, legislators, judges, or other agents, can epitomize that will and can apply its commands to any particular case as it arises, without injecting their individual opinions into the merits of the case. The difficulty, however, here arises that each case presents a new variety of facts but the ontological will has been fixed and predetermined for all time. The predicament is theoretically difficult, but it is usually met in the simple way of changing the definitions of the terms which that will had originally employed in expressing its commands. We have seen how this simple method was resorted to in changing the definitions of property and liberty, the definitions of restraint of trade, of due process of law, and so on, wherever the new facts seemed to call for a change. What happened, of course, at these interesting points, was that the court enjoyed a degree of immunity, and there was no superior authority that could prevent the change in definitions, or give to that change a different slant. A change in definitions is such a simple and natural way of changing the constitution from what it is to what it ought to be, and the method is so universal and usually so gradual in all walks of life, that the will of God, or the will of the People, or the Corporate will, scarcely realizes what has happened. The method is, indeed, that common-sense device whereby man can go on believing in unchanging entities, and yet be practical.

And the method is well provided for in the varying degrees of power and immunity within which functionaries act. The limits are not fixed and definite, though they may tend to become more so where the procedure of due process of law is introduced. It is this tightening of procedure which gradually converted the prerogative of the King into the sovereignty of the citizen, and so smoothly has it worked, especially since the Act of Settlement, and so inveterate is that weakness of intellect which identifies an entity that ought to be with behavior that actually is, that, when legal and economic writers in the 18th and 19th centuries began to think about it they identified the sovereignty of the citizen as one of the natural rights of man. This power of man to require officials to do his bidding in conformity to the working rules of the concern became even one of the "faculties" of the human will, a capacity or ability of the individual to act, like the ability to plough, or eat, or think. The actual state, with its actual officials, seemed to be unnatural, a merely coercive power interfering with and overriding the natural liberty of man to use his faculties as he pleased, rather than the collective power by which man's will is made effective. The best that the state could do was to let man alone. Yet these collective powers, exercised on behalf of individuals through the responsibility of officials to them, in accordance with the accepted rules guiding their actions, are the main instruments of modern industry, for they are the source of those encumbrances and opportunities which constitute the incorporeal and intangible capital by means of which feudalism was displaced by capitalism and slavery by liberty.

Economic theory, as we have noted, started with commodities, then shifted to feelings, in order to explain transactions. In the latter field of transactions, a strictly behavioristic theory starts and ends with the transactions themselves. But this is not enough to explain human behavior. Back of behavior is the will. We have described, behavioristically, the judicial process of thinking, which is a process of human behavior, but we have found that it was impossible for the courts to decide disputes without making the distinction between purpose and procedure, the procedure being the regulated behavior, but the "substance" of that regulation being the purpose to be subserved by it.

It is this that we distinguish as the difference between a "behavioristic" and a "volitional" theory of value. A behavioristic theory takes account of *all* the factors of a moving mechanism on the principle of multiple hypotheses, and endeavors to ascertain the part played by each factor in producing the total behavior observed, without regard to any purpose or force that may be supposed to guide the behavior towards any given direction. A behavioristic theory, in other words, is physical science. It reaches its terminus when all the moving factors of a mechanism can be stated in terms of numbers and equations. If the equations turn out, on experiment, to fit the facts, that is the end of it.

An illustration may be found in that science which has most nearly reached the mathematical form, astronomy.[1] Sir Isaac Newton assumed a divine will operating through space and keeping the stars and planets in order according to the principles of the Euclidean geometry and his own differential calculus invented for the occasion. Clerk Maxwell eliminated the divine will by substituting a cosmic ether as the communicating substance through which to explain "action at a distance." Each assumed, however, that the scientist himself was located at a fixed point in the universe, and Einstein, then, by noticing that the scientist himself is moving through space, introduced the doctrine of relativity of motion, but retained the ghost, as it were, of the cosmic ether in the hypothesis of its waves. The final stage is reached when neither divine will, cosmic ether nor the ghost of ether is retained, and the mathematician states, in terms of mere numbers, equations, correlations and lags what actually happens. He gives a "description" and not an "explanation." If, then, by testing his equations in the laboratory, he finds that they fit the facts, he has reached the end of the matter, for he has reduced

[1] Cp. VEBLEN, *The Place of Science*, 15.

to as simple a numerical description as possible the ultimate motions of the universe and the electron. Thus the goal of science is a simple mathematical statement of all complementary factors in a moving mechanism without any of the volitional or metaphysical notions of cause and effect, purpose and instrument, required by a finite mind to explain how it happens that one thing can cause another to move at a distance without the aid of an intervening medium of communication.

This mathematical agnosticism is evidently the goal set up for themselves by the so-called behavioristic schools of psychology and sociology. Applied to economics, it is the statistical or mathematical representation of all the complementary factors that conjoin in a statement of correlations, lags and forecasts of prices. The procedure reduces, very properly, economic phenomena to mathematical formula of prices, and if by proper tests it is found that the formula fit the actual movement of prices, then the explanation is deemed complete. Economics becomes, like astronomy and physics, a set of numbers and equations which we call the movement of prices, found valid by the test of experiment, and all science is reduced to numerical terms without assumptions of cause and effect, purpose and instrument, medium of communication, or other volitional, metaphysical, or ghostly concepts.

On the other hand, a volitional theory goes a step further. After eliminating divine will, cosmic ether and all metaphysics, there remains still the human will which acts mysteriously at a distance, simply because it does not pay attention to *all* the complementary factors but selects out that limiting factor which can be controlled and whose control can thereby be employed to guide the other factors at a distance in space and time. The possibility of control arises from the fact that the limiting factor is a part of a mechanism and that the extent of human control over the entire mechanism depends on the proportions with which it is supplied relative to the other parts. In other words, it depends on principles of mechanism and principles of scarcity.

All of the phenomena of the human will are, in this sense, "artificial," in contrast with phenomena which may be distinguished as "natural." That which is "artificial" is not thereby unnatural, but is the highly "natural" process of the human will, picking out the limiting factors of nature and human nature in order to guide certain

complementary factors into the direction desired by human purpose.
All of the mechanisms with which it deals are themselves artificial,
and, from the standpoint of evolution, they exhibit the effects of
"artificial selection" distinguished from "natural selection." Their
history is the evolution of the automobile or the thoroughbred horse,
not the evolution of the universe or the tiger; the evolution of governments, business organizations, the banking system, the family contract, not the evolution of colonies of bees or herds of animals. In
short, the mechanisms of the human will have evolved in the two
directions which we name "a going plant" and "a going business,"
the one being a purposeful control over physical nature, the other a
purposeful control over human nature, and each according to shop
rules or working rules changed from time to time, but always intended
to control the actions and transactions of the participants.

Economic theory, since the time of the Physiocrats, has endeavored
to get rid of the human will and to explain economic phenomena in
terms of physical and hedonic forces. The human will had been the
main reliance of the Mercantilists and of the economic theory of the
Church fathers. But the will was arbitrary, capricious and contrary
to natural laws. There were two stages of these physical theories
which attempted to get away from the will:—the natural rights and
physical equilibrium stage of foreordained evolution of Quesnay,
Adam Smith and Karl Marx, and the natural selection stage of blind
evolution that followed Darwin, whose distinguished exponent in
economics is Veblen.[1] The theorists of each stage attempted to get
rid of the human will and to explain economic phenomena as the
working out of natural forces, either foreordained or blind. It was
a concept of society as the natural growth of a mechanistic equilibrium.

But a volitional theory takes exactly the opposite point of view.
Economic phenomena, as we know them, are the result of artificial
selection and not of natural selection. Their evolution is like that of
a steam engine or a breed of cattle, rather than like that of a conti-
nent, monkey or tiger. If you watch how the steam engine evolved
from John Watt in 1776 to the Mogul locomotive in 1923 you will see
how economic institutions evolved. The steam engine evolved by
studying the mechanisms of nature, experimenting with the parts,
and then rearranging them, so that steam would act in two directions

[1] VEBLEN, THORSTEIN, *The Place of Science in Modern Civilization*, (1919).

instead of one direction, as nature intended. So with the evolution of that process of behavior which we name political economy. The subject-matter is the habits, customs and ways of thinking of producers, consumers, buyers, sellers, borrowers, lenders and all who engage in what we name economic transactions. The method has been the adoption of common rules applying to the similar transactions of all who come within the same concern. If you watch the development of the credit system out of the customs of business men in buying and selling, borrowing and lending, and out of the customs of courts in deciding disputes, according to the changing common rules, you will see how political economy evolved. The desirable customs were selected gradually by the courts, the undesirable customs were progressively eliminated as bad practices, and out of the whole came the existing economic process, a going concern, symbolized by a flux of prices, and operating to build up an artificial mechanism of rules of conduct, creating incorporeal and intangible property quite different from the unguided processes of nature.

Thus a volitional or economic theory starts with the *purpose* for which the artificial mechanism in question was designed, fashioned and remodeled; and inquires, first, whether that purpose is useful or useless, legitimate or illegitimate, ethical or unethical, right or wrong. Then it inquires whether the artificial mechanism in question accomplishes that purpose in an efficient or economical way, and, if not, what is the limiting factor, out of the thousands of coöperating factors, that obstructs the operation, and to what extent that limiting factor can be, and requires to be, controlled in order to facilitate the mechanism and accomplish its purpose. Then it adopts or changes the shop rules, working rules, common law or statute law that regulate the actions and transactions of participants. It is a theory, indeed, a science, of an artificial and not a natural mechanism. What is the theory of my Ford automobile? That mechanism was designed to move across the country under my guidance carrying a load, and thereby accomplish a purpose deemed useful by me. Suddenly it stops without being directed by me to do so. It gets out of control. I then get out and seek the limiting factor, perhaps a little wire crossing another wire. I change somewhat that limiting factor and resume control of the mechanism. From the standpoint of a behavioristic theory that little wire is one out of several thousand coördinated factors, and it plays but a *fraction of one per cent* in the accomplishment of the total result. But from the standpoint of a volitional theory that little wire was the limiting factor at the moment and under the circumstances, and the control of it at that point of time performed *one hundred per cent* of the total result.

So it is with every operation of the human will. It is always directing itself to investigating, explaining and controlling the limiting factors that obstruct its purposes at the moment and under the circumstances. It is always injecting an "artificial" element into the forces of nature, and that artificial element is its own ultimate purpose accompanied by an intermediate or immediate instrumental purpose of obtaining control of the limiting factor, through control of the mechanism.

Thus it is, also, with all of the phenomena of political economy. They are the present outcome of rights of property and powers of government which have been fashioned and refashioned in the past by courts, legislatures and excutives through control of human behavior by means of working rules, directed towards purposes deemed useful or just by the law-givers and law interpreters. From a behavioristic standpoint many thousands, even millions of factors, must be taken into account in order to explain the phenomena of political economy, all the way from stars to atoms. But from the volitional standpoint, at any particular moment or circumstance, the economist, and indeed also the psychologist, deals with what for him is the set of limiting factors in accomplishing the further purpose which he deems worth while.

This limiting factor is not the same at all times and under all circumstances. At one time it pertains to mechanism, at another to scarcity. At one time it is a crossed wire, at another a supply of gasoline. At one time it is a certain fact in physical nature, at another it is a certain fact in human nature. At one time it is the rate of bank discount, at another it is the World War, at another it is flood or drought. What the economist does, if possible, is to uncover that limiting factor and to point out, if possible, the extent, degree and point of time at which it should be modified or counteracted, in order to control all of the other factors for the further purpose deemed important.

As soon as the economist endeavors to find out the limiting factors in any particular juncture, he is both scientist and business man or politician. And it is difficult to decide at what point he passes from "science" to "art." He is scientist, perhaps, in that he weighs without bias or purpose the relation of cause and effect. He is business man or politician in that when, as scientist, he has discovered the limiting factor, he must decide, as business man or politician, upon the point of time, the degree of emphasis and the extent of operation by which he must control it by recodifying the working rules of the concern in order to modify all the other factors in the direction ultimately desired. The difference, then, between the science and the art of business economy or political economy is the difference between knowing in his laboratory or library *what* to do, and being in a position of power and responsibility where he must know *what, when, how much* and *how far* to do it at a particular time and place in the flow of events. This we designate the principle of timeliness. But there are also two other volitional principles inseparable from the principle of timeliness, which may be designated the principle of anticipation and the principle of caution.

Economic theory, in directing its attention to commodities and feelings, overlooked the significance of property and liberty as those concepts were developed by the courts. Consequently, its definitions of value and cost were fashioned in terms of commodities, or pains and pleasures, instead of terms of persuasion, coercion, command and obedience. The latter are the psychological equivalent, not of commodities, but of habits and customs operating within their legal limits of rights, duties, liberties and exposures. Fashioning our terms, therefore, to suit these proprietary concepts, value, from the social standpoint, is the principle of inducement[1] in human relations and cost is the principle of resistance to inducement. Or, looking at it from the individual standpoint, value is the principle of anticipation and cost is the principle of caution. Each arises from the principle of relative scarcity of resources, which is both the principle of limiting and complementary factors and the principle of controlling the supply and mechanism of the limiting factors. While from the technological standpoint of the physical economists, value was an income, and cost an outgo of commodities; and while, from the hedonic standpoint value was a pleasure, and cost a pain, yet from the proprietary, or volitional, standpoint value and cost are the reciprocal principles of inducement or anticipation, and resistance to

---

[1] Cp. ANDERSON, BENJAMIN, *Social Value* (1911), where, however, the proprietary is not distinguished from the physical.

inducement or caution, that is, the principle of offering and with-holding supply. The "cost," resistance, or caution, may, indeed, be sought to be explained and justified by reference to pain, sacrifice, loss of happiness, but these are merely ethical appeals put forth to justify what is the real behavioristic phenomena, the sheer determi-nation to withhold products or services for any reason or no reason. The cost principle is simply the volitional, proprietary principle of refusing to work or wait, or take risks, to sell or buy, to lend or bor-row, to hire or hire out, until the terms offered are deemed satisfac-tory, or merely because "he don't want to."

It is this proprietary concept that may rightly be named *psycholog-ical cost* and *psychological value*. It includes all the concepts of rea-sonable price, as well as the hedonic concepts in so far as they are de-fined as expected pleasure and pain. Psychological value and cost, signifying the motives back of all valuation and choices, which, from the social standpoint are inducement and resistance to inducement, from the individual standpoint are anticipation and caution, from the behavioristic standpoint are timeliness, are also, from the compre-hensive standpoint, including inducement, anticipation, resistance, caution and timeliness, the volitional concept of purpose.

Thus it is the three principles of anticipation or inducement, cau-tion or resistance to inducement, and timeliness that distinguish a volitional theory from a mechanical theory. Each looks to the fu-ture but describes action in the present. Anticipation and induce-ment are the expectation of gain that induces action in the present; caution or resistance is the withholding of action until the time seems propitious; and timeliness is prompt action of the right kind at the right moment and to the right degree and extent that sagacious an-ticipation and caution seem to dictate.

But cost and value have also an objective physical meaning in terms of concrete commodities and services, in the sense used by the physical economists. Here, cost is the outgo or alienation of goods or services, and value is the income or acquisition of goods or services. And, while the physical economists did not connect up this physical outgo and income with the accompanying feelings yet the connec-tion is so close and the accompanying feelings so intimate that this physical concept of cost and value may properly be named *real cost* and *real value*.

Finally, cost and value have a behavioristic or merely nominal and phenomenal meaning in terms of the actual prices agreed upon in a transaction, on the basis of which commodities or services are transferred. These prices are a scale of measurement,[1] since they are stated in terms of money, and money intervenes between the actual transfer of goods. On this account the term price, which is a mere symbol or number referring to either a unit or the total quantity of commodity or service, may properly be named *nominal cost* and *nominal value*.

It is the union of these three meanings of cost and value that is necessary to construct a volitional theory of value. The essential attribute of a volitional theory is the concept of an ultimate purpose or goal and of the intermediate and immediate instruments made use of to attain that goal. The ultimate goal is psychological in the sense that it is always in the future, whether remote or proximate, and includes the hopes, happiness and virtues of self and others included in such general terms as welfare, social welfare, public good, commonweal, commonwealth, comprehended under the principle of anticipation or purpose. This ultimate goal, is of course vague and indefinite and affords no certain guidance in particular cases. Yet it is in this field that the moving principles of anticipation and caution are found without which human activity would not occur.

The intermediate goal is more concrete, for it is the progressive increase of the control over nature, the "maximum of production" which, while it is a "fog picture," according to Cassel,[2] is yet most substantial, and it constituted, indeed, the whole of the theories of the physical economists. So important is it in the practice and theory of political economy, that we have designated it the field of *real value* and *real cost*.

Finally, the immediate goal is a system of reasonable prices, by which is indicated such a price system as may bring about what is deemed to be a progressive equivalence of both psychological value and psychological cost, or real value and real cost. And since prices in themselves are purely behavioristic social phenomena having no significance except as bearing on the psychological and physical forces and purposes behind them, the system of prices we have designated the field of *nominal value* and *nominal cost*. A reasonable system of

---

[1] CASSEL, G., *Nature and Necessity of Interest*, 69 (1903).

[2] *Ibid.*, "*Der Ausgangspunkt der Theoretischen Oekonomie*, 58 Zeitschr. für Staatsw. 688 (1902).

prices can be judged to be such only as it conforms in some way to the psychological or ultimate goal of welfare and the physical or intermediate goal of production of wealth.

But the means by which these goals are reached consist in the adoption of certain lines of action which are conveniently named "principles." The value principle, looked upon, not as a quality intrinsic in commodities nor in the relation of man to nature, but as a social principle of inducement and an individual principle of anticipation, is none other than that expected power of persuasion or coercion over others which induces performance on the economic side, and gives rise to the claims of rights and liberties on the property side. On the other hand the cost principle, looked upon as a social principle of resistance and an individual principle of caution, is that subservience to others or service to others, which on the economic side is the resistance to performance and on the property side is a duty or exposure corresponding to the right or liberty of others. From this standpoint, both the value principle and the cost principle are eminently psychological, for they refer to the persuasions, coercions, commands and obedience, the anticipation and caution through which expected performance, avoidance, and forbearance are induced or resisted. The immediate instrument of inducement is the price-system, the intermediate instrument is the commodity system, but these are effective only as they influence and are influenced by the unseen psychological system of purposes.

We thus arrive at a theory of going concerns similar to that which Dean Pound sets forth as an "engineering interpretation of legal history." He distinguishes his "engineering interpretation" from the "economic interpretation," but this distinction turns out to be the same as that between the principle of scarcity and the principle of mechanism which characterizes the schools of economic thought. Thus he has identified "economic interpretation" with those economists who have based their theories on principles of mechanism whereas his "engineering interpretation" is based mainly on the principle of scarcity. He finds the "economic interpretation" to be that of Karl Marx [1] and Brooks Adams.[2] Each of these based his theory on the physical or technological facts of the modes of production and exchange of wealth, with its familiar evolution of industrial society

---

[1] MARX, *Zur Kritik der politischen Oekonomie* (1859).
[2] ADAMS, BROOKS, in *Centralization and the Law* (1906).

through the stages of hunting and fishing, pasturage, trade and commerce, and machinery. The accompanying concept of property is that of holding physical things for one's exclusive use, while the concept of sovereignty is that of the aggregate of property-owners. It follows that the concept of the individual is that of an isolated individual, and of society is that of an aggregate of individuals. With these mechanical concepts it is concluded by Marx and Adams that the propertied classes always control the government since it is they who own the tools, cattle and machinery, and their ownership is safeguarded only by control of government. This outcome of physical concepts in the hands of Marx and Adams is readily traceable from the mechanical assumptions of Adam Smith based on his principles of individualism, self-interest, division of labor, liberty, divine providence or harmony, absence of associations and of governments except as protector of the peace and of property, and it is these assumptions that have unfortunately fixed upon economic theory the doctrines which Pound accepts as the economic interpretation.

But his own "engineering interpretation" starts with the scarcity principle as stated by William James, although it was first suggested by David Hume.[1] "In seeking for a universal principle," says William James, "we inevitably are carried onward to the most inclusive principle—that the essence of good is simple to satisfy demand. . . . Must not the guiding principle for ethical philosophy (since all demands conjointly cannot be satisfied in this poor world) be simply to satisfy at all times as many demands as we can." [2] "This," says Pound, "seems to me a statement of the problem of the legal order. The task is one of satisfying human demands, of securing interests or satisfying claims or demands with the least of friction and the least of waste, whereby the means of satisfaction may be made to go as far as possible." Having summarized all of the other mechanical, ethical, biological, economic and metaphysical interpretations of the legal order he finds them all comprehended in this more inclusive interpretation of "social engineering," where the judge as well as legislator, is endeavoring to adjust and harmonize human relations in a world of limited resources.

It will be seen, therefore, that this "engineering interpretation" is quite the same as our "economic interpretation," and points to

---

[1] POUND, *Interpretations of Legal History*, 157.
[2] JAMES, WM., *The Will to Believe*, 195–206.

the fact that both economic theory and ethical theory have also a line of theorists, beginning with Robert Malthus and David Hume, who have made the principle of scarcity predominant and the principle of mechanism subordinate. The two principles are not exclusive—they are interdependent—but when the scarcity principle is given preëminence it brings out another aspect of the individual, of property, of liberty and of opportunity and sovereignty. Property now becomes the power to withhold from others as well as to hold exclusively for self, as was first introduced into the concept in the case of Munn v. Illinois. The individual becomes a member of that concern, the state, which then proceeds to regulate by common rules his power to withhold, since he has chosen to devote his property to a use which is exceptionally limited in supply and upon which others therefore depend for the use of their property. Sovereignty now becomes the collective power of the concern laying down its working rules in the form of the common law, statutory law, equity and administrative orders, for the purpose of better adjustment of men's transactions in a world of relative scarcity of resources.

And it is this principle of the common rule or working rules, which we find to be the universal and ultimate principle of all going concerns. The statement and enforcement of a working rule is accomplished in no other way than by imposing duties on some individuals through the process of restricting their liberties, and it is this process that creates automatically the correlative rights and exposures of other individuals. When the collective concern imposes these ethical duties, it does so through those working rules which guide its officials, foremen, superintendents, judges and legislatures, and which in law, are known as powers, liabilities, immunities and disabilities.

Hence it is that we find the three ultimate principles on which economics, ethics, law, and psychology are based, and applicable to the state, the business concern and the cultural concern, to be the principle of mechanism, the principle of scarcity, and the principle of the working rule.[1] The secondary principles, emerging from these ultimate principles are those of anticipation or inducement, caution or resistance to inducement, and timeliness or acting upon the limit-

---

[1] The eminent Swedish economist, G. CASSEL, has proposed certain of the fundamental concepts here suggested. Cp. CASSEL, *Der Ausgangspunkt der theoretischen Oekonomie*, 58 *Zeitsch. für Staatsw.* 668 (1902) and *Theoretische Socialoekonomie* (2d ed. 1921).

ing factors at the time, to the degree and to the extent that they are deemed to be effective in accomplishing the purposes intended. This action implies the principle of mechanism in that it signifies getting control of the *strategic part* of the mechanism, and it implies the principle of scarcity in that it signifies a due proportioning of the *quantities* of the several factors contributing to the mechanism.

But it implies, above all, the principle of purpose, looking toward the future, of which anticipation, caution and timeliness are its behavioristic and measurable dimensions, but of which the ethical and economic consequences foreseen are its driving force. It is the latter which constitutes the "substance" of the working rules, as we have seen when the Supreme Court changed the definition of "due process of law" from due procedure to due purpose of law. The "substance" of law, as it is the "substance" of the will, is purpose, the difference being that law is *"due purpose"* and the will is *any* purpose.

Economic theory, like legal theory, started with Liberty rather than Purpose. Liberty is the individual's absence of physical coercion. But public purpose is that of giving to the individual by means of common rules binding on all under similar circumstances, a power of calling on government to give effect to his will. So smoothly has this purpose worked, especially in England after the Act of Settlement, that the rights which it afforded came to be looked upon as a natural right of man, in the sense, not of an ideal that man ought to have by the aid of government, but in the sense of something which he previously had by nature and was deprived of by government.

This anarchistic notion of man's will was inseparable from the accompanying anarchistic notion of property. For property was also evidently a natural right, since man could not live without exclusive possession and holding of the physical things which he consumes, or with which he works. And governments deprived individuals of both property and liberty, in two ways, by restrictive or protective legislation, and by grants of franchises to corporations. These concepts of liberty and sovereignty culminated in the French Revolution which established individual property and prohibited all associations.[1]

Adam Smith, influenced by these ideas, as we have noted above, would also abolish all corporations and associations, because they

[1] *Le Loi Chapelier*, 1791.

restricted the liberty of the individual by majority vote, and would reduce government to the lowest terms of maintaining security. There would then ensue a "natural" economy, instead of an "artificial" political economy, which would operate through nature's laws of free competition, demand and supply. This nature-economy is indeed fundamental, and cannot be escaped. It springs from the fact that some of nature's resources are limited, and the limiting factors must be attended to if the complementary factors are to be of any use whatever. But it has greatly been interfered with by collective power exercised through working rules by those who controlled the mechanism and the supply. Instead of abolishing associations as desired by Adam Smith, the weakness of the individual has driven him into corporations and unions, while governments have yielded and have granted to these associations sovereign powers and immunities from sovereign power, until they are far more powerful than those condemned by Adam Smith and the French Revolution. Nations, too, have interfered with the natural economy of demand and supply, by the war-power, the taxing power, the police power, the legal tender power, involved in the creation of those intangible and incorporeal properties, almost unknown to Adam Smith, which reach to the ends of the earth and command obedience wherever the sovereign power penetrates.

These sovereign powers have brought about a very different proportioning of factors from that which might have occurred under the 18th century notions of property and liberty. For the limiting factors are not merely nature's resources, they are the rights of property in those resources, as determined by the accepted working rules of society. And these rights of property are but the purposes of the human will, individual and collective, placed in control of those resources and given power and immunity by law to control the mechanisms by which to withhold from other persons what they need, except on terms to be agreed upon.

The area over which this bargaining activity of individuals extends depends on the expansion of the state. By conquest or purchase, the state expands its territory and thereby expands its market area. By international treaties it opens up opportunities and enforces the bargains of its citizens in all parts of the world. By military preparedness and defense it perpetuates these conquests, purchases and penetrations. This work of government, consisting in the sovereign's transactions with other sovereigns, we have defined as the state's power of expansion, or briefly *Political Expansion*.

But the state also proportions the factors over which it has control. It opens up certain areas, localities or resources, instead of others. It does this, not directly as individuals do, but indirectly through working rules which guide the transactions of individuals. It encourages or protects certain businesses or classes of business, certain occupations or jobs, rather than others. It restrains certain activities deemed detrimental to the whole. Its proportioning of factors is the proportioning of inducements to individuals and associations of individuals to act in one direction rather than other directions. This proportioning of inducements, by means of working rules, to individuals and associations is *Political Economy*.

Thus, while political expansion consists of transactions with officials of other sovereigns by which opportunities are enlarged for citizens, political economy consists of transactions between officials of the same sovereign by which opportunities are proportioned among citizens. The two together constitute a World Economy.

Economic theory, in avoiding ethical notions of purpose, has usually assumed that it is the business of those working rules which we name "the law," to eliminate the unethical attributes of transactions, such as fraud, violence, coercion, deception, and has then operated with the abstract notions of utility and exchange. This is typical of the physical sciences which have been the models for economic science. Yet in a science of human transactions there is no clear dividing line between utility, sympathy and duty, between economics, ethics and law. The law, or working rules of society, take over, as best they can, the inducements of violence and thereby eliminate, as best they can, other unethical inducements. But ethical and unethical elements remain, simply because exchanges are transactions between persons, official and private. Hence a behavioristic definition of political economy as the subject-matter jointly of the sciences of law, ethics and economics, would not be limited to the traditional mechanics of "production, exchange, distribution and consumption of wealth" which are relations of man to nature, but would include them as secondary, and would be defined as primarily a set of relations of man to man, both national and international, which might be formulated somewhat as follows: Political Economy and Political Expansion are the proportioning, by means of the working rules of going concerns, of persuasive, coercive, corrupt, misleading, deceptive and violent inducements and their opposites, to willing, unwilling and indifferent persons, in a world of scarcity and mechanical forces, for purposes which the public and private participants deem to be, at the time, probably conducive to private, public or world benefit.

INDEX